History of Bell County

GEORGE W. TYLER
A photograph taken in 1922

History of Bell County Texas

GEORGE W. TYLER

Edited by Charles W. Ramsdell

COMMONWEALTH BOOK COMPANY

Originally published in 1936.
This edition copyright © 2023 by Commonwealth Book Company, Inc.

All rights reserved. No part of this book may be reproduced in any form or by any means without the prior written consent of the publisher, excepting brief quotes used in reviews.
Printed in the United States of America.

ISBN: 978-1-948986-59-5

Commonwealth Book Company, Inc.
www.commonwealthbookcompany.com

COVER IMAGE: Circa 1940 postcard view of Bell County Courthouse, Belton, Texas.

*To the memory of
My Father and Mother—
Texas Pioneers*

GEORGE W. TYLER

George W. Tyler, the son of Orville T. and Caroline Childers Tyler, was born near Fort Gates, now Gatesville, in the present Coryell County, Texas, on October 31, 1851. His parents had been among the first settlers on Little River in 1834. His childhood was spent at Fort Gates and in school in Belton. In 1864 his parents moved to Salado, Bell County, where they built a spacious and substantial home which is still standing. Young George continued his schooling there and entered Salado College where he graduated in 1871. The next year he attended the University of Virginia and later entered Lebanon Law School, in Tennessee, from which he graduated in 1874. He then settled in Belton and began the practice of law. In 1878 he married Miss Sue Wallace, the daughter of Dr. D. R. Wallace of Waco.

His energy, ability and integrity soon brought him an extensive practice; and his keen interest in the progress of his community kept him in touch with public affairs. He was one of a group of business men who built the first telegraph line into Belton; he was active in the promotion of railroads into Bell County; and he was also largely instrumental in the erection of the first telephone system that served the towns of his county. One of his major interests throughout his life was the promotion of education. For many years he served as president of the board of trustees of the Belton public schools; and his zeal and judgement contributed much to the building of the excellent school system which the town now enjoys. In appreciation of his work one of the ward schools has been named for him. But his educational activities were not confined to his own town. He was influential in the establishment and development of the fine Masonic Home and School of Texas in Fort Worth. In January, 1925, he was appointed by Governor Miriam Ferguson to the Board of Regents of the University of Texas and served with credit on that body until ill-health forced him to resign in January, 1927.

Although he cared little about holding public office, Judge Tyler took an active interest in politics. He was a conservative Democrat and a strict party man. Over a long period he was chosen regularly as a delegate to the State Democratic convention; he was a presidential elector in 1884; and from 1888 to 1892 he was State senator. He was the author of the Texas "Arbor Day" law, and was one of the minority in the Senate who advocated permitting a defendant, in a criminal case, to testify. This has since become a part of the law in Texas.

One of Judge Taylor's major interests, throughout his mature life, was Masonry. He was made a Mason in Salado Lodge No. 296, A. F. & A .M., in 1873 and was Master of that Lodge in 1878. In 1899 he became affiliated with Belton Lodge No. 166 and served as Master in 1902. He received the degrees of Royal Arch Masonry in Belton Chapter No. 76 in 1876 and served as High Priest in 1883. He became Grand Commander of the Knights Templar in Texas in 1914. He also belonged to the Scottish Rite bodies in Dallas. But it was in the Grand Lodge of Texas that he rendered his most distinguished service to Masonry. He was made Grand Master in 1890. While holding this office he went to Mexico and brought about a compact which resulted in the recognition for the first time of a Grand Lodge in Mexico. He later served the Order in many capacities, among which was his membership on the Jurisprudence Committee of the Grand Lodge from 1892 until his death.

During our war with Germany Judge Tyler was county chairman of the Council for National Defense, a member of the legal advisory board under the Selective Draft Act, and, until his other duties became too heavy, the county food administrator. He gave his entire time to this work and carried it forward with great efficiency.

Born of pioneers and acquainted throughout his life with scores of the early settlers and their descendants, he became interested as a youth in the story of his community. This interest ripened with the years and he began gathering materials for a history of Bell County. In 1898 he helped to form the Old Settlers' Association of Bell County, and during the six years of its existence he was the mainspring of its activities. The papers which were read at the meetings he gathered and printed at his own expense. In addition, he interviewed and corresponded indefatigably with the survivors of the early days, and spent much time and money in searching out all available records that could add anything of interest to the story. He was meticulous in striving for accuracy and, although without formal instruction in historical methods, his training as a lawyer and his strong common sense enabled him to apply to the evidence the best canons of historical criticism. He retired from the active practice of law in 1912 in order to devote more time to his history; but he was always so eager to seek out more information that he could never bring himself to finish the task. At his death the writing was incomplete and some was in the form of rough notes. It was left to the editor of this volume to revise and condense the manuscript and, in a few instances, to fill out the narrative.

Judge Tyler was rich in friends who loved him for his integrity, his warm human sympathies and his kindly humor; and his death, at his home in Belton, on October 11, 1927, was widely mourned. This book, which he hoped to finish and leave as a tribute to the men and women who had made Bell County, is now published by his family in the belief that it will be a fitting memorial to him as well as to those for whom he designed it.

AUTHOR'S PREFACE

To dissect the records and traditions of the days long passed; to call out the facts of vital interest to a new generation; to exhibit truly and fairly the characteristics, the successes, the failures of a former generation in the pioneering of a new community; to follow their faint but plodding footprints as they walked through the dark and devious ways of the wilderness to a brighter and better day; to portray something of their way of life; and to bring forward the unrecorded folk-lore of a people of yesterday—these are difficult and embarrassing tasks for the chronicler of those ninety years and more.

Within the restricted limits of these pages we shall do our best to record the progress of Bell County from the days of the first pioneers, before the county was formed, to a period when the memory of our own generation can supply the place of written history.

The writer can claim an intimate acquaintance with the development of Bell County almost from its organization. From the time when he was a small boy, in the late fifties, he has travelled much over this and other central Texas counties and has a fairly clear idea of the growth of the section not only from his own personal observations but from the statements and traditions of many of the people who resided here when it was a young pioneer community. He has himself lived in Bell County continuously since February, 1864—and prior to that date in Coryell County, only a few miles from the Bell County line. His parents were among the first actual settlers, in 1834, in that portion of Robertson's colony now constituting Bell County; and their constant social and business intercourse with a large number of other pioneers, during the writer's boyhood and youth, gave him exceptional opportunity for obtaining correct information about early conditions. But he has not relied exclusively upon recollections and traditions. He has made extensive examination of all written records available and with the most scrupulous care has checked and rechecked every statement. It is impossible to be absolutely free of error, and in this book some errors may be found; but it is given to the public in the belief that is as nearly accurate as it can ever be made, and with the hope that it may be useful to those who wish to know more of the history of this community.

1. *The Gifts of Nature*

Bell County, which contains 1083 square miles, lies in the east-central part of Texas, within the Black Prairie and Grand Prairie regions. The Black Prairie division, which comprises slightly less than half of the eastern half of the county, is mainly gently rolling, with some hilly areas near the larger streams. The western or Grand Prairie division consists of rolling uplands, deeply cut by stream valleys which in many places have stony slopes and steep, rugged bluffs. In some places where erosion has reduced the greater part of the highland, small mesas stand from fifty to two hundred feet above the surface and are known locally as "mountains" or "knobs." In elevation above sea level the county ranges from about 450 feet in the southeastern part to about 1200 feet in the extreme western portion, but the greater part of the county lies between 500 and 800 feet above the sea.[1]

The upland soils are residual, and are derived from various hard and soft calcareous strata, such as clays and marls, soft and hard chalks and hard limestones. These formations have weathered into a variey of clayey soils, some of which, as the Houston black clay, are very fertile. This last covers the greater portion of the Black Prairie in the eastern half of the county. Along the streams are strips of alluvial deposits.

Practically all of Bell County is drained by Little River and its tributaries. This stream—known in Spanish and Mexican times as *Rio San Andres*—is formed at a point about six miles southeast of Belton by the junction of the Leon, the Lampasas, and the Salado. It passes out of Bell into Milam County and flows into the Brazos on the lower east line of the latter county, just above the site of the old town of Nashville. The junction which forms Little River is known as "Three Forks" and has been a conspicuous landmark in all

---

[1] This description of the topography, soil and climate of Bell County in this and the following paragraphs is taken from "A Soil Survey of Bell County, Texas," by William T. Carter, Jr., H. G. Lewis, H. W. Hawker and Hugh H. Bennett, **Report, Bureaus of Soils, of the U. S. Department of Agriculture, 1918.** See also Robert T. Hill, "The Geography and Geology of the Black and Grand Prairies of Texas" in **Twenty-First Annual Report of the U. S. Geological Survey, 1899-1900,** Part VII, pp. 520-523.

Author's Preface

of this section as far back as we have any records or traditions. All early land surveys in this vicinity and for more than a hundred miles above—in the present counties formed out of old Milam County—are based upon this land mark and their field notes usually begin something like this: "In Milam County (or Milam Land District) 45 miles North, 60 degrees West from the Three Forks of Little River," etc. The channel of Little River is deep but only about one hundred feet in width. It has a fall of about seventy-five feet within the fifteen miles of its course in Bell County; and in times of heavy floods it sometimes overflows its broad fertile valley. Besides the three streams which form it, Little River also receives, within the county, the waters of Knob, Boggy, Runnells, Cathey, Darr, Donahoe, and Indian Creeks, and in Milam County the San Gabriel unites with it, after receiving the waters of Brushy, Willis, Berry, and other streams.

The names of the Leon, the Lampasas and the Salado are also obviously of Spanish origin. The Leon, a very swift and crooked stream, with a rapid fall of one hundred and fifty feet in its course of twenty miles within the county, makes a loud roaring sound when swollen, and thus from its roaring like the lion (*léon*) takes its name. Within the county it is fed by the Stampede, Cedar, Owl, Cow House, Nolan, Peppers, Bird and Friar Creeks and their tributaries. The Lampasas and the Salado are likewise reinforced by many small tributaries.[2] The Lampasas falls about three hundred feet in a direct course of twenty-eight miles within the county. These three streams lie in the northern, central and southern parts of the county respectively. The extreme northeastern surface of the county is drained by the Big and Little Elm, the Cottonwood and other small creeks whose waters reach Little River in Milam County.

These streams, in extreme drought, get very low and most of them occasionally stand in pools; but when heavy rains fall they become raging rivers which spread out over the adjacent valleys and carry violent destruction in their wake. The Salado, fed by numerous bold perennial mountain springs, is the most uniform of them all in its constant

---

[2] Salado Creek is still called by the Spanish pronunciation, "Sä-lä'-o," or "Salow"; while the name of the town situated on it has been anglicized.

water supply and never ceases to run from a few miles above the town of Salado to the Three Forks.

There are many wonderful springs in Bell County. The Willow Spring, on Little River, was an early day landmark. On the Salado Creek are the great springs at the village of Salado, besides the Elm Springs, the Willingham and the Rumsey Branch Springs and many others, higher up the stream. On the Lampasas are the Childers Mill Spring (now known as the Brookshire Spring), the Proctor Spring, the Spicewood Spring, the Shaw or Blue Spring, and others. On the Nolan are the Nolan Springs (in Belton), the Shelton Spring, the Russell Jones Spring and the Keel Spring on North Nolan, and the Crawford Spring on South Nolan. On the Leon are the Miller Spring, the Henderson Spring, the Dunn Canyon Spring, the Tanyard Spring, the Aiken Spring, the Moffatt Spring, the Kell Spring, besides those on Bear Creek and Bull Branch. On Cedar Creek is the Kattenhorn Spring. These are only some of the noted springs. There are many others deserving of notice.

All of the springs mentioned are perennial and most of them are little affected by local rainfall. Their waters apparently come from reservoirs deep down in the earth, supplied from far distant watersheds, and they rise to the surface here with a pressure akin to the artesian flow. Some geologists have claimed that they are forced up through fissures in the broken crust of the earth, caused by the Balcones Fault, which crosses Bell County in a course that embraces most of these springs and continues southwest to the sites of the famous springs at Austin, San Marcos, New Braunfels, and San Antonio.

There are also a number of sulphur springs and wells in the county—the old and famous Sulphur Spring on the Salado Creek, the Leonolan Spring at the mouth of Nolan, the mineral well at Salado, the Elliott well on the Leon near Belton, and others.

Bell County has a mild, healthful climate, with a comparatively long growing season and adequate rainfall for agriculture. The mean annual temperature is 65.6 degrees Farenheit. The average date of the last killing frost is March 14, and that of the first in the fall is November 15. The mean annual rainfall is 33.36 inches, and in most years it is well distributed throughout the growing season.

Author's Preface

The country in its primeval state was covered with a high waving grass, called "sedge grass," which grew as thick and as high as wheat in a field ready for harvest. The vast prairies were coated with this luxuriant grass for miles and miles—as far as one could see. And it appeared in all the open spaces in the higher timbered lands. Along the streams, in open bottoms, a species of wild rye likewise grew in the winter and furnished good range for stock. The sedge grass flourished during spring and summer and until the frost fell in the autumn, when it would die and fall down in tangled masses upon the ground. Then under this matted grass grew a winter grass, green, succulent, low-growing but nourishing, upon which animal life subsisted. In the late winter or early spring the Indians used to burn off the dead grass on the prairies and thus bring on an earlier crop of the sedge grass; and as the buffalo, deer, antelope and other grazing animals came in great numbers to this new grass, they were more easily found by the Indian hunters.

Mingled in this grass and lending a charming variety to the landscape were the most beautiful wild flowers of every kind—the lupin or blue bonnet, the verbena, wild lilies, Indian plumes, Indian paint brushes, daisies, trumpet flowers, sunflowers, horsemint, wild phlox, foxgloves, and innumerable other varieties, which splashed the vast areas with brilliant colors and presented a most gorgeous and inspiring picture. No description or painting can ever reproduce those magic scenes which expanded in beauty and loveliness upon the green carpets of the central Texas prairies and plateaus and which brought unbounded admiration and exclamations of joy from the immigrants and visitors to those great expanses of "nature unadorned."

"It is impossible," wrote Mary Austin Holy, "to imagine the beauty of a Texas prairie when, in the vernal season, its rich and luxuriant herbiage, adorned with many thousand flowers of every size and hue, seems to realize the vision of a terrestial paradise. The delicate, gay, and gaudy, are intermingled in delightful confusion, and these fanciful bouquets of fairy nature borrow tenfold charms when associated with the verdant carpet of grass which modestly mantles around."[3]

---

[3] Mary Austin Holly, **History of Texas**, quoted in Baker's **Texas Scrap Book**, p. 330.

"The whole face of the country is changed from what it was in former days. Could you have stood on some elevated point in Bell County in 1833, a most lovely and novel scene would have met your eyes. You would have seen Bell County in her natural beauty, just as she came from the handy workmanship of nature, with her forests undisturbed and her soil unbroken, her broad prairies, luxuriant grass and beautiful flowers of every tint and hue, her clear and rippling streams, the Leon, Lampasas, Salado, Cowhouse, Elm Creek and other streams, slowly winding their way through prairie and forest to the Gulf of Mexico. Again, you might have seen herds of buffalo, antelope, wild deer, and wild horses quietly feeding on the grass or resting in the shade of some live oak grove."[4]

Another old settler bears witness to the same effect: "In the settling of this country I thought it was the grandest scenery I had ever looked upon in all my life. Up to that time it was one vast open prairie country, covered with green grass and decorated with beautiful flowers, and to add to the benefit of the early settlers it was full of game of all kinds, buffalo, deer, bear, turkeys, and antelope. The streams were full of fish of all kinds. The first deer I killed was three miles south of where Belton now is."[5]

In a country so well watered and fertile, animal and insect life was abundant and not all of it was beneficial. Among the birds were wild turkeys, prairie chickens, doves, partridges, mocking birds, orioles, field larks, sparrows, road runners, red birds, humming birds, jays, crows, owls, and buzzards, as well as migratory geese, cranes, brandts, ducks, robins, black birds, and martins. The wild animals found here were buffaloes, deer, antelopes, wild horses, wild cattle, javelinas, bears, cougers, panthers, catamounts, bob-cats, wolves, civit cats, foxes, squirrels, flying squirrels, jackrabbits, swamp rabbits, coons, opossums, beaver, armadillos, and skunks. Varieties of reptiles included rattlesnakes, moccasins, copperheads, chicken snakes, house snakes, coachwhip snakes, lizards, horned frogs, toads, bullfrogs. The streams

---

[4]. Captain H. E. Bradford, "Locating Land in Old Milam Land District" in **Proceedings of the Old Settlers Association of Bell County for 1902, p. 26.**

[5] F. M. Cross, "Early Days in Central Texas." (Mr. Cross, then about fourteen years old, came with his father's family to the Childers' Mill on the Lampasas river in the fall of 1848.)

abounded in fish—mud cat, blue cat, channel cat, gaspergoo, suckers, buffalo, bass, trout, perch, turtles, eels and gars. And the despicable vermin were represented by the various species of flies, fleas, mosquitos, gnats, chiggers, ticks, spiders, granddaddies, cockroaches, crickets, tarantulas, centipedes, stinging lizards, wasps, hornets, mud-daubers, yellow jackets, bats, and a number of others. Among the insects were honey bees, bumble bees, grass hoppers, butterflies (in many gorgeously hued varieties), beetles, devil-horses, and others too numerous to mention.

These classifications and terminologies are palpably unscientific, being simply those of a layman and in the everyday jargon of the people of that early era. We knew nothing of *"flora* and *fauna"* in those days.

A few words may be devoted to the wild horses and wild cattle found here and elsewhere in the southwest by the first comers. There is a plausible theory—if not a tradition—that these animals are the descendants of horses and cattle that escaped from or were abandoned by the Spanish expeditions which entered Texas from Mexico in the eighteenth century. The horses, generally called Indian ponies, sometimes "mustangs," were small but well formed, active, wild and as fleet as deer, but in captivity became docile and tractable and could endure a lot of hard usage. They were dark bay, brown or black, but usually of solid color, with black mane and tail. The wild cattle were generally dark brown or black. They were well formed and fast runners. Generally they herded in considerable numbers. A bunch of about one hundred head was located upon the Cow House Creek, a few miles from Belton, when the county organized. The overhanging rock cliffs along the mountain borders of the valley were supposed to have been resorted to by these wild cattle in storms and stress of weather and this tradition gave the name to the stream. They had "glossy skins, long horns, were very ferocious, stayed in the cedar brake all day and fed at night. They were a great nuisance if they got into a settlement, as they would break all the fences down and mix with the domestic cattle until driven away."[6]

The first settlers who came into this beautiful country had to fight for it. Various tribes of wild Indians claimed it

[6] Memorandum of interview of Isaac Williams with Dr. Alex Dienst.

for their hunting grounds and strove to keep out the inevitable white man. From the east had come the Caddoes, remnant of a once powerful people in Louisiana, driven westward across the Sabine and the Trinity. On the north were the Tehuacana, the Wacoes, and other small tribes. On the south and southwest were the Tonkaways and the Lipan Apaches; and though these tribes were generally friendly they were not to be trusted when either horses or scalps were within tempting reach. West and north were the most dreaded of all, the powerful and warlike Comanche, who dominated all that vast western plains region from the Rio Grande to the present state of Kansas and penetrated as far east in Texas as the Black Land prairies. Though these Indians frequently fought among themselves, they had a common grievance against the whites who were despoiling them of their cherished hunting grounds. The chiefs of different tribes now and then made treaties with the whites, but their young warriors could not be restrained from stealing horses and attacking isolated pioneer families. The story of Indian warfare in Bell County will be recounted in subsequent chapters.

CONTENTS

A Memoir of George W. Tyler, by James B. Hubbard   vii
Author's Preface   xi
The Gifts of Nature   xii

Part I. ROBERTSON'S COLONY AND EARLY MILAM COUNTY, 1827-1850

  I. The Nashville or Robertson Colony, 1827-1836 .   1
      1. The Colonial Grants
      2. Settlements in Robertson's Colony, 1830-1836—Nashville
 II. The First Settlements along Little River . . .   12
III. The Texas Revolution and Indian Troubles, 1836-1837   26
      1. The Revolution and the "Runaway Scrape"
      2. A Few Settlers return to Little River and Leon
      3. Robertson's Ranger Company
      4. The Second "Runaway"; Crouch and Davidson killed
      5. A Few Settlers again return to Little River
      6. The Indian Attack on the Taylor Family
      7. Indians attack Colonel Sparks and the Rileys
      8. Frontier Battalion of Rangers at Fort Milam
      9. Little River Fort built by George B. Erath
     10. The Elm Creek Fight
     11. The Post Oak Massacre; Little River Fort abandoned
 IV. Troubles with Indians on Little River and in Upper Milam County, 1837-1843 . . .   56
      1. Renewal of Hostilities under President Lamar
      2. Capture and Release of Norris Party by Jose Maria, 1838
      3. Indian Attacks on Morgan and Marlin Families; Indian Victory at Morgan's Point, 1839
      4. The Bird's Creek Fight, May 26, 1839
      5. Indian Raid at Tenoxtitlan, 1841; Fort Bryant
      6. Fight between Captain Ross and "Big Foot," 1842
  V. The Advance of the Milam County Frontier, 1843-1850   76
      1. Pioneer Settlers return to Upper Little River
      2. Annexation of Texas to the United States and War with Mexico

3. Cameron, the New County Seat; Better Protection from Indians
4. The New Settlements
5. The First Schools
6. Indians again

VI. Residents of Bell County in 1850 94

Part II. THE FRONTIER COUNTY

VII. The Creation and Organization of Bell County, 1850 107
1. The Organic Act
2. "The Charter Oak" Election
3. The County surveyed; County Seat located and named Nolanville
4. The Beginnings of Nolanville (Belton), 1850
5. County Officers elected and Organization completed

VIII. The Early County Records 121
1. The Deed Records
2. First Marriage Record
3. The First Session of the Commissioners' Court
4. The Probate Court
5. The District Court

IX. Ten Years of Growth, 1850-1860 131
1. How the New Settlers came and how they lived
2. Belton in the Fifties
3. The Official Business of the County
4. The Early District Court
5. New Communities and Settlers in the Fifties
6. The Early Schools
7. Farming, Stockraising and Transportation

X. Indians, Frontier Rangers and Gold Hunters, 1850-1860 174
1. Indian Raids
2. Bell County Volunteer Rangers, 1859-1860
3. The Gold Hunters from Bell County, 1858-1859

XI. Bell County in the Civil War 194
1. Ante-bellum Politics and Secession
2. The Bell County Volunteer Companies
3. Official and Private Aid to Soldiers and their Families
4. Civic Activities during the War

XII. Reconstruction, 1865-1874 244
1. The Fall of the Confederacy

Contents

    2. The First Period of Military Rule, 1865-1866
    3. Disturbances in Bell County: Early-Hasley Feud; Murder of Duncan and Dawes
    4. A Brief Return to Local Self-Government, 1866-1867
    5. The Return to Military Rule, 1867
    6. The Old Ku Klux Klan in Bell County, 1867-1870
    7. The Constitutional Convention of 1868-1869
    8. The Regime of E. J. Davis, 1870-1874
    9. The Honey Incident, 1873
   10. The Last Indian Raids

Part III. MATURITY AND MATERIAL PROGRESS

XIII. The Old Order Changes, 1874-1890 . . . 281
    1. The Return to Self-Government
    2. The Founding and early History of Salado
    3. Cattle Drives and the Old Trail through Bell County
    4. Spread of Farming; Barbed Wire and Windmills
    5. The Grange
    6. The Break-up of an Outlaw Gang
    7. Problems of the County Government
    8. New Enterprises
    9. The Coming of the Railroads
   10. The Rise of Temple
   11. Politics in the Eighties

XIV. Twenty-five Years of Growth, 1890-1915 . . 327
    1. "Hard Times" and Agitation for Relief
    2. Public and Private Improvements in the 1890's
    3. The War with Spain, 1898
    4. The Return of Better Times
    5. Population Trends in the County, 1890-1910
    6. Improvements in the Public Schools
    7. The Agricultural Experiment Station and its Work
    8. Good Roads Movement and Advent of the Automobile

XV. Private Educational Institutions of Bell County . 349
    1. Salado College
    2. Baylor College for Women
    3. The Belton Academy
    4. The Thomas Arnold High School

XVI. In the World War—and After 368
    1. The First Effects of the World War
    2. The Selective Draft and its Local Administration
    3. Local Civic Organizations in Support of the War
    4. The Armistice and the Return of the Soldiers
    5. Material Conditions during and after the War

XVII. Some Institutions in Bell County 381
    1. Freemasonry in Bell County
    2. The First Odd Fellows Lodge
    3. Banks in Bell County
    4. Fairs in the County
    5. The Sanctificationists of Belton
    6. The Temple Stag Party
    7. The Old Settlers Association of Bell County, 1898-1904

Index 405

LIST OF ILLUSTRATIONS

	Page
George W. Tyler	Frontispiece
Mrs. Lewis M. H. Washington Judge O. T. Tyler Colonel Hermon Aiken Colonel E. Sterling Robertson	32
The Martin Luther Houston home, near Little River The William Reed home, on Little River	64
The Thomas Duncan home, near Three Forks The former Sam Hasley home, at Little River Fort	96
Bell County's "Charter Oak"	112
Dr. B. D. McKie D. D. Rosborough Judge D. T. Chamberlin	128
Shady Villa Hotel, Salado Old Stage Barn, Shady Villa Hotel, Salado	160
Old rock house, Salado The Robert Cox home, near Belton	192
The W. T. H. Hartrick home near Belton The Shanklin home, on the Lampasas	224
The Robertson home, near Salado	256
The O. T. Tyler home, Salado	272
Salado in the early Seventies	288
Stinnett's Mill, on the Salado Summer's Dam, on the Salado	298
Belton: north side of square	320
Dr. S. J. Jones Faculty of Salado College, about 1873	352
Hardy Hall, Baylor College for Women, Belton Presser Hall, Baylor College	384
Marker in front of Judge Tyler's home, and the George W. Tyler Park Marker	404

LIST OF MAPS

	Preceding
Robertson's Colony and Bell County	1
Bell County about 1885	281

xxiii

PART I
ROBERTSON'S COLONY AND EARLY MILAM COUNTY, 1827-1850

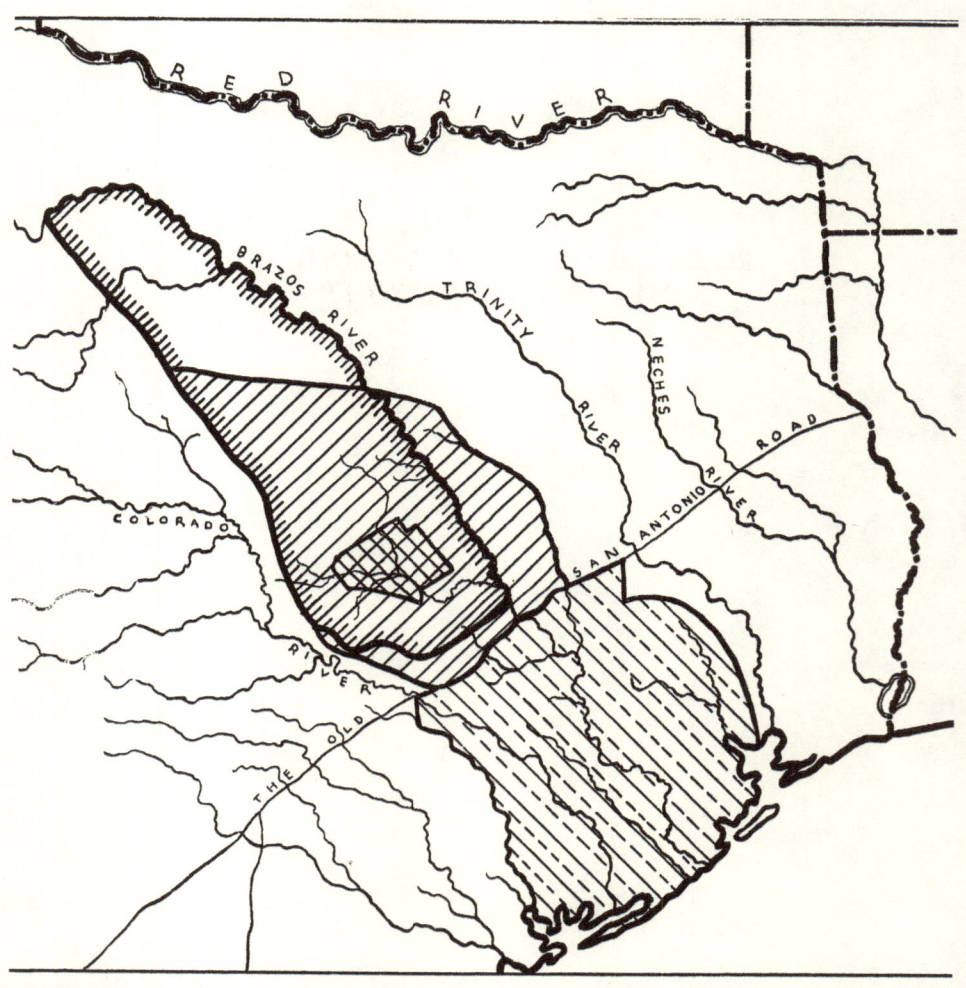

CHAPTER I.

THE NASHVILLE OR ROBERTSON COLONY, 1827-1836

1. *The Colonial Grants*

During the century and a quarter of Spanish rule in Texas the region now included in Bell County lay outside the influence of the few scattered towns and missions established in the province and was barely touched, if traversed at all, by the recorded explorations of Spanish officials. Since the Spaniards left no local impress upon the county, we shall not be concerned with them here. The history of the Bell County area as the home of civilized man began with the coming of a little band of settlers in 1834 as immigrants from the United States to the Nashville or Robertson Colony in the Mexican province of Texas. It will be necessary, therefore, to recount briefly the troubled history of the founding of that colony.

Stephen F. Austin, as successor to his father, Moses Austin, in 1821 led the first authorized Anglo-American immigrants into Texas and located them, two years later, on the lower Brazos. The news of the Austin enterprise aroused great interest in the United States especially in the western states of Tennessee, Kentucky, and Missouri, where numbers of people who had been ruined by the great panic of 1819 were looking about for new homes. Men of means became interested in the liberal terms which the Mexican government allowed contractors who would introduce immigrants; while poorer men learned that in Texas they could obtain large amounts of land at a merely nominal price.

Land grants in Texas to contractors, or "empresarios," were governed by the Mexican federal law of August 18, 1824, and the state law of Coahuila-Texas of March 24, 1825. The federal law provided that foreigners must not, without the approval of the federal executive, settle within twenty leagues of the international boundary nor within ten leagues of the coast; that not more than eleven leagues of land could be held by one person; and that no titles to land should be granted to nonresidents of the Republic of Mexico.[1] The state law allowed to the contractor or em-

[1] Gammel, **Laws of Texas,** I, 97-98.

presario who had obtained a grant for the purpose a premium of five leagues and five *labores* of land (23,025 acres) for every one hundred families introduced by him; but forbade the introduction of more than eight hundred families on any single grant. If he received in excess of eleven leagues (48,706 acres) he must alienate the excess within twelve years. If he failed to introduce as many as one hundred families within six years from the date of his contract, it became void. Every family brought in was entitled, normally, to one *labor* (177 acres) of farming land and twenty-four *labores* of grazing land, making a total of one league, or 4,428 acres. An unmarried man could receive only one-fourth as much as a married man; but if he should later marry he was to receive enough more to make a full league. If he married a Mexican woman he was to receive one-fourth more than otherwise. The immigrant must pay the state in three installments—four, five, and six years from the date of the grant—$30 for each league, $3.50 for each irrigable *labor,* and $2.50 for each non-irrigable *labor*. A native or naturalized Mexican could obtain as much as eleven leagues at the price of $100 a league for grazing land, $150 for tillable but non-irrigable land, and $200 for irrigable land. The colonist must "improve" or "occupy" his land within six years; but these terms were not well defined. If he should leave the republic he lost title to the land. Both the federal and the state law guaranteed the contracts between the empresario and the families which he introduced.

Early in 1822—and, therefore, before these laws were passed—a group of citizens of Davidson County, Tennessee, stimulated probably by the news of the large grant to Austin, formed a "Texas Association" for the purpose of obtaining a similar grant. The agent whom they sent to Mexico, Robert Leftwich, with the assistance of Stephen F. Austin, received a contract from the legislature of Coahuila-Texas on April 15, 1825, for settling eight hundred families within six years in a large tract lying above the old San Antonio-Nacogdoches road. The boundaries of the grant ran from the crossing on the Navasota River along the San Antonio road across the Brazos to the watershed between the Brazos and the Colorado rivers, thence along that divide northwestward to the "Comanche trace" (at a point now probably in Eastland County), thence along the said trace east and southeast to where it crossed the Navasota, and down that river to the point of beginning. The contract, however, was made with Leftwich himself as empresario instead of the company. This caused great dissatisfaction on the part of the latter and delayed further action. Finally on October 15, 1827, a new contract was made with the company itself; but although men were sent to explore the region no actual settlers were introduced. This seems to have been due to the desire of the majority of the Tennessee stockholders to get large tracts for themselves as absentees and for speculative purposes —which indicates that they were ignorant of the provisions of the colonization law.

Sometime in 1830 a sub-company was formed and on October 1 of the same year Sterling C. Robertson, one of the original stockholders, became the agent or empresario of the Nashville Company. He had been in Texas as early as 1825 or 1826 and had become the most active member in pushing the colonization project. In the meantime, however, the Mexican government, alarmed at the evident desire of many persons in the United States for the acquisition of Texas, had passed the law of April 6, 1830, which virtually prohibited further immigration from the United States and suspended all contracts which had not been fulfilled. Robertson, who had come into Texas with some settlers for his colony was notified that his contract was suspended. After fruitless appeals to the Mexican officials, he put the matter into the hands of Austin who was just setting out for Saltillo to take his seat in the legislature. Austin failed to obtain recognition of Robertson's claims and found that a French company was about to get a contract for the lands in question. As he was anxious to get the region settled as a protection to his own colony which lay just below it, and as he believed the French company would not be able to settle it, he forestalled the French scheme by getting the contract for himself and Samuel M. Williams. At least this is the explanation which he afterwards gave for his action. Robertson was bitterly disappointed and declared that Austin had betrayed him. A long drawn-out controversy ensued.

In December, 1831, Robertson presented a petition to the alcalde's court of Austin's colony to the effect that he had introduced more than one hundred families before the expiration of his contract and that, the Mexican officials being in ignorance of this fact, the suspension of his contract had been illegal. Many witnesses were examined, but Austin and Williams were not represented. The hearings dragged on. In February, 1834, the ayuntamiento (local council) at San Felipe gave the opinion that Robertson had not forfeited his contract. Robertson then went to Saltillo and in May, 1834, while Austin was a political prisoner in Mexico, obtained an order from the governor that the colony be restored to him. Williams now appealed to the legislature of Coahuila-Texas which declared that the governor had no authority to decide which contract was valid, that the question should be left to the judiciary, and that pending such decision the colony should be restored to Austin and Williams. By the time the decree to this effect reached Robertson the Texas Revolution had begun. Nothing was done, and Robertson remained in possession.

It does not appear that Austin and Williams settled very many families in the Robertson Colony while it was in their hands (1831-1834); but in 1833, while Austin was in Mexico, Williams sold permits for the location of a number of large claims within the grant, ranging from three to eleven leagues each. They fronted on the Brazos and Little rivers, in the present counties of Robertson, McLennan, Falls, Milam and Bell, and embraced much of the most desirable lands. While these grants were in the names of Mexican citizens—"Coahuiltexanos"—as required by the colonization law, yet in reality they were made to American land speculators. The speculator would obtain a power of attorney from some Mexican (usually an ignorant peon) which authorized the agent to apply for the concession, to have the land surveyed, to pay the government price thereon, to comply with the other requirements of the colonization law, to apply for and receive from the State government of Coahuila and Texas the *testimonio* or final title, and to take possession of and to sell the land at his discretion. These documents were intended to serve as deeds to the land and they have been so construed and sustained by our supreme court. Of course they constituted a palpable evasion of the law which restricted such grants to native Mexican citizens. Unfortunately, Robertson and those who were associated with him, after he recovered control of the colony in 1834, regarded these grants as illegal and encouraged colonists to settle upon the lands. This led to much trouble and litigation later on, as we shall see.

As soon as Robertson recovered possession he began actively to introduce settlers into the colony. In the summer of 1834 he visited Louisiana, Mississippi, Tennessee, and Kentucky to advertise his colony and bring in immigrants. A thin but steady stream trickled in along the Brazos, the Navasota, and the Little River. In November, 1835, the Texas revolutionary provisional government ordered the land offices closed; but other immigrants continued to come although they could not get titles until the land offices were re-opened after the Revolution. Robertson's claims were later recognized by the Republic of Texas; but dispute arose over the number of families he had introduced and the amount of premium lands to which he was entitled. The state supreme court in 1847 sustained his claim to 100 families brought in before the renewal of his contract in May, 1834, and to 171 families and 108 single men between that date and the closing of the land offices in November, 1835. Apparently 221 families were brought in after that date; but he was allowed no premium lands for them.

2. *Settlements in Robertson's Colony, 1830-1836—Nashville*

The immigrants to the various colonies in Texas came by a variety of routes and by many different modes of travel. Those from the Atlantic and Gulf states and from Europe usually came by water to the mouth of the Brazos and thence dispersed into the interior. Those from the valley of the Mississippi generally came down the great river to New Orleans and thence by the Gulf route. But a great many traveled overland in wagons drawn by oxen or horses and camped out at night under the broad canopy of nature. Most of these came by one of two routes: by boat up the Red River to Natchitoches and thence through San Augustine and Nacogdoches along the old San Antonio road; or through Arkansas to the Fulton Crossing on Red River and south through Eastern Texas to the San Antonio road. Usually these overland journeys were made in companies or caravans of people—families or single men—who kept together for mutual assistance and protection. Few records were kept of these long and toilsome migrations and their stories are now lost except where family tradition has preserved them.

One such caravan was that in which the writer's own people, Captain Goldsby Childers and family, made their adventure in 1833 from the comfortable home-life in the "old States" to the wilderness of a Mexican colony in the primeval forests and on the uninhabited prairies of Texas. This party was made up in the vicinity of Quincy, Illinois, to which state all or nearly all of them had but a few years previously immigrated from Kentucky, Tennessee and other southern states. Nearly all of them were descendants of Virginia and Carolina ancestors who had crossed the Appalachian mountains in the tide of the great westward movement which began after the Revolution and sought homes in the rich valleys of the eastern tributaries of the Mississippi.

From the best information available[1] this company consisted of the following personnel: Captain Goldsby Childers, wife and nine children; Reverend Isaac Crouch (Baptist), wife and several children; Dr. Robert Davidson, wife and four children;——— McCandless, wife and several children; Elder John Parker (Baptist) and wife; James W. Parker, wife and four children; Elder Daniel Parker, wife and several children; and a number of single men, Heman Chapman, Geo. W. Chapman, Joseph G. Ferguson, "Old Man" Rhodes, Ezekiel Robinson, and Empson Thompson. There were possibly a few others, so that the company comprised some forty or fifty people.

Each family had a wagon drawn either by horses or by several yoke of oxen; some had two wagons. There were two or three carryalls drawn by horses—evidently it was a party of fairly well-to-do immigrants. The men and some of the older girls rode on horseback. At night the camp was pitched at some suitable place, well provided with wood and water. Each family had one or more good tents which were set up at the camps.

Their route was from Quincy down the east side of the Mississippi, across the river by ferry at St. Louis, thence through Missouri and Arkansas. They crossed White River near Batesville, the Arkansas River at Little Rock, the Red River at Fulton and turned westward to Clarksville in Tex-

---

[1] Statements of the writer's mother, Mrs. Caroline (Childers) Tyler and of Captain Wilson T. Davidson, both of whom as children were members of the party; reminiscences of the Parker families and others; sundry historical data furnished in many published biographies, sketches, etc.

as. Following the Caddo Trail southwards to the San Antonio Road, they crossed the Trinity at Midway and the Brazos at Tenoxtitlan, and thence moved down to the Devers Settlement in Austin's Colony (now in Washington County), not far above old San Felipe. This was the route then used by many of the overland immigrants. About three months were consumed in making the journey. A most wonderful phenomenon occurred while they were encamped on the banks of the White River, September 13, 1833. That was the night on which "the stars fell," a night from which for many years time was reckoned by thousands of people.

With the reopening of Robertson's Colony in the summer of 1834 the men of these families visited the upper country and selected locations for the lands to which they would be entitled on becoming members of the colony. Nearly all of them joined that colony but they selected their lands in various localities. Elder John Parker and James W. Parker, later joined by a number of other relatives and friends from the "States," located on the Navasota River, near the present town of Groesbeck in what is now Limestone County, where, for protection against the Indians, they built a block house and stockade known in Texas history as Parker's Fort. Here occurred the bloody tragedy of May 19, 1836, when part of the little band were massacred by the Indians and the rest driven away. Elder Daniel Parker settled in the Burnet colony in eastern Texas. The families of Goldsby Childers and Dr. Robert Davidson, as we shall see in the next chapter, made their location on Little River in the present county of Bell, whither they were still accompanied by several single men of the caravan.

The first village established within the limits of the Robertson Colony was Tenoxtitlan on the Brazos just above the crossing of the old San Antonio road. It was established not by the colonists, however, but by a small garrison of Mexican soldiers under Colonel Francisco Ruiz in July, 1830. Near the garrison a small village grew up which, even after the departure of the soldiers, was for many years a regular stopping place for immigrants, prospectors and travelers. With the growth of other towns near by, Tenoxtitlan gradually dwindled and disappeared.

More important in the history of the upper country was the old frontier town of Nashville. It was situated on the west bank of the Brazos about two miles below the mouth of Little River, in the present county of Milam, just where the I. & G. N., or Missouri Pacific, railroad crosses the river. It was on a beautiful, slightly undulating plateau, and on a small prairie which extended a mile or so down the river. Several springs of clear water gushed from under the bluff. It is uncertain when the first house was built there; but it was probably in 1834, soon after Robertson recovered control of the colony and began directing immigrants up the river. The town was regularly laid out in 1835 and was named for Nashville, Tennessee, where the promoters of the colony and many of the early immigrants had formerly lived. For awhile it was a sort of colonial capital where empresario Robertson maintained his office and transacted his colonial business. It became the rendezvous for those who made their way into the colony to locate their lands and set up their new homes. It was the *entrepot*—the Jamestown—of all this upper country. Here the newly arrived settlers rested after their long journeys from the old states. Here they procured their outfits and supplies when they set out to found their homes, and thither, as a rallying ground, they fled for protection when driven back by the Indians.

The village, in its early days, consisted of a cluster of small log and board houses erected near the river bluff. Some were built of red cedar or oak logs, hewn or unhewn. A few were framed and weatherboarded with whip-sawed siding. A fort or block-house was built of cedar logs, in which the people of the village collected when attacked or threatened by the Indians. It was constructed in the usual way of frontier forts, with port or gun-holes through which the besieged could defend themselves against the enemy's approach.[2]

The population of Nashville was unstable, for it consisted mostly of colonists on their way to the country above, and perhaps did not comprise more than twenty or thirty families at any one time. In a general way it may be stated that nearly all the first settlers of the Bell County territory sojourned at some time at Nashville. Among

---

[2] Some of the logs from the foundation of this historic fort were salvaged in recent years by the people of Cameron, and from these timbers, felled nearly a century ago, interesting souvenirs have been made. The writer possesses one—a beautiful gavel—through the kindness of Miss Katherine Henderson of Cameron.

the residents of the village during the middle thirties were: Lige Bailey, *James Bell,* Gid Bowen, *Calvin Bowles,* John Dull Brown, *Geo. W. Chapman, Heman Chapman, Goldsby Childers, Isaac Crouch, Robert Davidson,* Robert Fleury, Jacob M. Harrell, Jack Hopson, *James Howlett,* Neil McLennan, John McLennan, Laughlin McLennan, Sterling C. Robertson, James Shaw, Alexander Thomson, William D. Thomson, Thos. C. Thomson, and others. Among those who were at Nashville, more or less, during the same period were: Captain Thomas H. Barron, *Captain John Bird, Ben Bryant,* ——— Campbell, John Chalmers, Albert Chalmers, *David Clark,* John Cockrell, Robert M. Coleman, John H. Connell, *Mrs. Matilda F. Connell,* James Coryell, *John R. Craddock,* Moses Cummings, *Aaron Cullins, Daniel Cullins,* Francis T. Duffau, *George B. Erath,* Wm. M. Eastland, Masilion Farley, Moses Farley, *Stephen Frazier,* Jas. A. Graves, George Green, *Moses Griffin,* Jacob Groos, Caleb M. Hubby, Henry Ickleberger, Frank W. Johnson, *Henry Kottenhorn,* Wm. B. King, Wm. H. King, *Daniel McKay,* Lewis More, Morris Moore, William Moore, Daniel Parker, Isaac Parker, John Pool, Nat C. Raymond, Thomas Roberts, William Roberts, *E. S. C. Robertson, James Robinett,* Joseph Rowland, *E. Lawrence Stickney,* Ethan Stroud, Gus Sullivan, Jas. G. Swisher, John Taylor, *Orville T. Tyler,* Lewis M. H. Washington, W. S. Wilson, and many others.

The names italicised in the above lists are those of persons who have been identified in some way with the territory now forming Bell County. Some of them gave their blood, others even their lives, to wrest it from the savage Indian. The others, though more fortunate in that respect, spent their lives here in toil and hardships, cut off from relatives and friends, deprived not merely of the luxuries but even many of the comforts of life, struggling to gain a foothold in this virgin land and to provide homes and win happiness for themselves and their posterity.

Nashville became the county seat of Milam County under the Republic and so remained until Cameron was laid out in 1846, excepting for a short period in 1842 when Caldwell was the county seat. The village was incorporated, along with a number of other leading towns by an act of the First Congress of the Republic of Texas which was approved June 5, 1837.[3] With the removal of the county

---

[3] Gammel, **Laws of Texas,** II, 1299.

seat to Cameron in 1846 and the successful establishment of the settlements in the upper country, Nashville gradually dwindled away until it was a mere country post office at the beginning of the Civil War. It was entirely abandoned when the Houston and Texas Central Railway reached Hearne, only five miles away, in 1867 or 1868.[4] A few old gravestones are all that is now left to mark the spot which was once the center of life of this great upper Brazos country.

In order, probably, to place his land office more nearly in the center of his colony, Robertson established the village of Sarahville de Viesca further up the river on the western heights overlooking the great falls of the Brazos a few miles south of the present town of Marlin. The village was laid out some time in the summer of 1834 and the land office was placed there about October 1 in the same year. Here resided the land commissioner, William H. Steele, who issued titles to the settlers, and Moses Cummings, the "principal and scientific surveyor," who ran out the land selected by the colonists. Here, too, were kept the maps, field notes, proofs of immigration, and records which, collectively, were denominated the "archives" of the colony. Although an important place, officially, Viesca must have been a very small one, for when Morrell arrived there in December, 1835, he found only one family residing there and forty prospectors from Tennessee looking for lands.[5] The place was abandoned in 1836 because of the disturbances during the Revolution and the massacre at Parker's Fort. During the days of the Republic a frontier ranger station was established there under the name of Fort Milam; but in time this, too, was abandoned and the name Viesca disappeared from the map of the country as did the other two colonial towns, Tenoxtitlan and Nashville.

The name, Viesca, was probably given in honor of the first governor of Coahuila and Texas, José Maria Viesca

---

[4] Most of the facts concerning old Nashville were obtained from a paper of Frank Brown, "Nashville," in the **Proceedings of the Old Settlers Association of Bell County, 1903**, pp. 49-51. Other information has been obtained from Wm. T. Davidson, J. Mac Thomson, from the writer's father, O. T. Tyler, and his mother, all of whom resided at or visited Nashville in the thirties.

[5] Z. N. Morrell, **Fruits and Flowers**, 41.

(1827-1831), and was first applied to the district or municipality of Viesca. There seems to be no published record of the creation or the boundaries of this district; but it was represented in the Convention of 1832 at San Felipe de Austin, and as a municipality in the General Consultation and the General Council of 1835.[6] On December 26, 1835, the General Council upon motion of Alexander Thomson, of the municipality of Viesca, changed the name of both the municipality and the town to Milam in honor of Ben Milam, the hero who had fallen on December 7 in the Texan attack on San Antonio.

[6] Gammel, **Laws of Texas,** I, 479, 508, 551.

CHAPTER II

THE FIRST SETTLEMENTS ALONG LITTLE RIVER

One who tries to tell the story of the first actual settlement of any portion of the great frontier of Texas is faced with serious difficulties. There is no ample record from which he may draw the facts. The pioneers themselves were too busy to write down their experiences even if they had thought it desirable. In fact, for this Bell County area the only contemporaneous records are the archives of Robertson's Colony, now in the General Land Office at Austin. But these do not contain a word about the *actual settlements* of the colony. They relate solely to the distribution of lands. The applications to the Empresario, Sterling C. Robertson, his acceptance of the colonists, the field notes of the land surveys made by the Colony Surveyor, Moses Cummings, and the granting of the final titles by William H. Steele, the Commissioner on behalf of the "Supreme Government of the State of Coahuila and Texas"—these documents, in the Spanish language, very meager in their recitals, are all that are now available in the "colony archives." They were written unpretentious record books constituting the *protocol,* and a copy of the final title (the *testimonio*) was made and delivered to the colonist. This was his deed to his land. Here the record ended. Whether the colonist settled upon the exposed land thus acquired, as he was therein "notified" to do, or whether he returned to the safer precincts of the older communities and villages, is not disclosed by the colony records.[1]

---

[1] To prove how little information these records contain, though of quaint and curious interest themselves, a translation of one of those titles or **testimonios** is here inserted. It was issued in Spanish to the writer's grand-father, Captain Goldsby Childers, more than ninety-two years ago and is still well preserved.

"The citizen William H. Steele, Commissioner appointed by the Supreme Government of this State for the partition and possession of lands and issuance of titles to the new colonists in the enterprise of colonization of the Nashville Company.

Whereas Goldsby Childers has been received as a colonist in the enterprise of colonization contracted with the Government of the State of Coahuila and Texas by Robert Leftwick on the 15th of April, 1825, and after-

The few fragmentary allusions to Robertson's Colony found in histories, Court proceedings, magazines, newspapers and other publications relate only to the general features of the colonization contract, its construction and execution, the difficulties and reverses met with in the introduction of immigrants, the forfeiture of the colony in 1830, the grant to Austin and Williams in 1831, the resultant bitter controversy between the rival claimants of the territory and the restoration of the colony to Robertson in 1834. There is no authentic detailed account anywhere, known to the writer, of the personal history of the colonists, nor of their experiences and progress. With the issuance of the final titles to their lands they disappear forever from the records of the frontier.

No system of recording deeds, sales, or transfers between the colonists then existed, but was first provided for by law after the independence of Texas, when the Congress of the Republic of Texas replaced the Mexican colonization procedure, under the empresarios, with the American system of county records. There were, there-

wards conceded to the Nashville Company on the 15th of October, 1827, and the said Goldsby Childers having proved that he has a family and finding in his person the requirements provided in the law of colonization of the State of the 24th of March, 1825, in conformity with said law and the provisions in said contract which authorizes the settlements of families within the limits of the proper enterprise on any part of the vacant lands which the same Company had contracted for; and of the instructions which govern me, dated the 4th of September, 1827, and additional article dated the 25th of April 1830, and in the name of the State, I concede, confer and put in possession, real and personal, of one league of land to the aforesaid Goldsby Childers which land has been surveyed by the surveyors Moses Cummings and Thos. A. Graves previously appointed for the purpose under the situation and following boundaries (here follow the field notes which, for brevity, are omitted) and comprehending one league of land in superfices. The said land belongs to the temporal class in four twenty-fifth parts, which serves as a classification for the price which he is bound to pay the State for it, according to the 22nd Article of said law, and under the penalties therein established, being notified that within one year he is bound to establish permanent land marks in each angle of the land and that he is bound to settle it and cultivate in conformity with the provisions of the law.

fore, no records of deeds for this territory until after the colonial period, when Milam County was organized, in 1836, under the laws of the Republic of Texas. Unfortunately, all of the old county records of Milam County were destroyed when the court house at Cameron was burned in 1874, and the only trace of them is found in a very meager and unsatisfactory "Abstract," made by a Mr. Joseph H. Traynham, just before the fire. Some of the old deeds and other documents have been re-recorded in the respective counties now embracing the lands involved in such instruments—counties formerly included in old Milam of the period of the Republic.

The only remaining sources are the declarations of the colonists themselves, the well authenticated traditions passed along by their immediate descendants and the reliable folk-lore of the country. In these respects the opportunities of this writer have been exceptionably favorable for obtaining the correct details of that unique and basic period in Bell County history.

The writer's father, Judge Orville T. Tyler, was one of the first colonists in the Bell County area. So was his mother, Mrs. Caroline (Childers) Tyler, daughter of Captain Goldsby Childers, another of the first colonists. His two

> Therefore using of the powers that have been conceded to me by the proper law and following instructions I issue the present instrument and order that a copy be taken of it and delivered to the party interested, that he may possess and enjoy the land, him, his heirs and successors or whom of him or of them may have cause or right.
>
> Given in the Village of Viesca on the 10th of September, 1835.
>
> (Signed) Guillermo H. Steele
>
> Witness
> Manuel Ma Valdez
>
> Witness
> Elijah S. C. Robertson
>
> Identical with the original title which is in the archives, from which this is copied for the party interested this day by the undersigned in the form prescribed by law.
>
> Given in the Village of Viesca the 10th day of September, 1833.
>
> (Signed) Guillermo H. Steele
>
> Witness
> Elijah S. C. Robertson
>
> Witness
> Niles F. Smith."

uncles, Robert Childers and Prior Childers, and his two aunts, Mrs. Catherine (Childers) Stickney and Mrs. Amanda (Childers) Craddock, were also children of Captain Goldsby Childers and all of them were present with him in his colonial settlement. All of these people lived to ripe old age and long after the writer came to manhood, and his association with them was frequent and intimate. He was personally acquainted with the widow and all of the children of Dr. Robert Davidson, one of the first group of colonists. He was long and very intimately associated with one of those children, the Hon. Wilson T. Davidson, who wrote and published, in several papers, reminiscences of the colonial days. The writer also personally knew William Reed and Jefferson Reed, who resided with their father, Michael Reed on Little River in the colonial period, and he often consulted with them about these matters. About 1877 or 1878, he met Mrs. Catherine (Frazier) Chapman, wife of Geo. W. Chapman, daughter of Mrs. William H. Taylor by her first marriage. She was a member of the Taylor family in Taylor's valley, on the Leon, and Geo. W. Chapman then resided with Captain Goldsby Childers, all in the Bell County colonial settlement. The events of that period were freely discussed by Mrs. Chapman on that occasion and several interviews with her, given to others, have been published and are in the writer's files. He is acquainted with Mrs. Cornelia Rich, daughter of Moses Griffin, another colonist, and with whom he has discussed some phases of the colonial period of Bell County, though her information was mostly derived from her parents, since she was too young to remember that far back. To the above list could be added many persons who were colonists in other sections of Robertson's colony or of other adjacent colonies and who were acquainted with some or all of the Bell County colonists or knew otherwise of their settlements, and also many of the descendants of such non-resident contemporaries. Their names are too numerous to catalogue here.

Reared in the very atmosphere of these traditions, with a lifetime of intimate association with many of the actors in those tragic episodes of our local history and having spent long years in earnest research in all sources available to him, the writer modestly claims to be qualified, at least in some degree, to speak on these matters. Admitting always the possibility of error, as we must in all human endeavors, yet he is further sustained by the fact that he has traced and accounted for the movements of practically all of the contemporary colonial grantees of land in this area and thus, by elimination as well as by positive tradition, he is able to call the roll of the first company of men who "felled the trees and broke the glebe" in the uninhabited domain later erected into the County of Bell.

Based upon the sources of information already explained the writer states that there were *eight and only eight* actual settlements within the present limits of Bell County during the colonial period which extended up to the declaration of Texas Independence, March 2nd, 1836. These in alphabetical order and with dates of survey, title and settlement and quantity of land, were as follows:

Colonist	Date of Survey	Date of Title	Settlement	Quantity
Goldsby Childers	Aug. 25, 1835	Sept. 10, 1834	1834	League
Robert Davidson	Dec. 30, 1834	Dec. 30, 1834	1835	League
John Fulcher	Oct. 16, 1834	Sep. 12, 1835	1834	League
Moses Griffin	Feb. 1835	July 27, 1835	1834	League
John Needham	Oct. 27, 1834	Dec. 30, 1834	1834	¼ League
Michael Reed	Oct. 26, 1834	Dec. 29, 1834	1835	League and Labor
William H. Taylor			1834	League
Orville T. Tyler	Dec. 10, 1834	Feb. 27, 1835	1835	League

Neither the date of the survey nor of the title evidence the date of the settlement upon the land. Some moved upon their lands before, some after these acts. Nor can it be stated who was the *very first to come*. But it is certain that all of the above named colonists were actually living upon their lands not later than the fall of 1835. Most of them came in 1834.

Five single men—colonists—had also selected their colonial lands—one fourth league each—within the Bell County area and were actually residing therein during the colonial period (1834-35) but not upon their own lands nor had they begun improving them. Their names, with some particulars, follow:

Colonist	Date of Survey	Date of Title	Arrival
Thomas Childers	Feb. 20, 1836		1834
Robert Childers	Feb. 20, 1836		1834
James Franklin Childers	Feb. 20, 1836		1834
Jefferson Reed	Oct. 28, 1834	Nov. 3, 1834	1834
William Reed	Oct. 17, 1834	Dec. 25, 1834	1834

The First Settlements Along Little River

Besides those already named there were seven other single men who, though they had selected their colony lands in other sections of Robertson's enterprise, had come into the Bell County territory in 1834 and resided therein during the colonial period. Their names were: Heman Chapman, Geo. W. Chapman, William Frazier, Stephen Frazier, ———— Rhodes, Ezekiel Robinson, and Josiah Taylor.

Thus the colony comprised a total of twenty men, most of whom, however, were young men, unmarried, who made their homes with the other members of the colony, as is shown incidentally in the subsequent recitals.

Passing up the stream, the way they came, these colonists were geographically distributed, on each side of the river, in the order given below. All of their grants fronted on the river, in the order given below. On the north bank of Little River, Captain Goldsby Childer's league was the lowest down stream, at the present county line—some four miles southwest of the present town of Rogers. The change in the county line of 1860 cut off a part of his league into Milam County, but by the first county line of 1850 it was all included in Bell County. In 1834 his family consisted of his wife, Mrs. Elizabeth (Thomas) Childers, and nine children: Thomas (21), Robert (19), James Franklin (16), Catherine (14), Prior (12)), Amanda (10), Caroline (8), Elizabeth (3) and Mary Jane (1). He came with his family to his colonial league in the Bell County territory in the fall of 1834. He had selected the land in the summer of 1834, and it was surveyed sometime prior to August 25, 1835.

It was here at the home of Captain Goldsby Childers that what was undoubtedly the first sermon in Bell County was preached by the Rev. Z. N. Morrell. With five friends from Tennessee (his former home) he arrived at the Falls of the Brazos, on horseback from Mississippi on December 27th, 1835. Here they found but one family. But close by was the camp of about forty Tennesseeans, who were all out on Little River hunting lands. After a short rest they also set out for the Three Forks of Little River about thirty-five miles southwest. There were no roads except small trails through the wilderness, difficult to follow. They came to a cabin on Little River.

"Mr. Childress (Childers), whose wife was a Baptist, was the occupant and owner of that little lone cabin in this wilderness and the family and land-hunters decided that they must have a sermon after supper; and accordingly I preached my first sermon in Texas, in camp, on the thirtieth of December, 1835."[2]

Three of Captain Childers's sons—Thomas, Robert and James Franklin—being also entitled to *one-fourth of a league* (1107 acres) of land each under the colonization law, made their selections adjoining their father's, above and below, which were surveyed February 20, 1836, only eleven days before the Declaration of Independence ended the colony operations, and hence they never obtained their final titles. They had not yet made any settlement or improvements on their land but were living at the time as members of their father's family. With Captain Childers was living also Heman Chapman and his brother, Geo. W. Chapman, Ezekiel Robinson and "Old Man" Rhodes, all single men.

Next above Childers, and some two miles distant, was the one-fourth league on which John Needham, a single man, settled. About four and one-half miles above Needham was the league selected by Dr. Robert Davidson, including the site of the present villages of Little River and Wilson Valley. Dr. Davidson moved on the land about September, 1835, with his family which consisted of his wife, Mrs. Rebecca (Landis) Davidson, and four young children: Wilson T., Eliza, Mary and Justus. Dr. Davidson was killed by Indians June 4, 1836, on Walker's Creek, Milam County. The particulars of this tragedy are narrated elsewhere.

Next above, and adjoining Davidson's, was the league selected by Moses Griffin. The upper line strikes the stream about opposite the Three Forks and here in the bottom, near the upper corner of his league, he built his first cabins, which have been mistaken by some people in later times as the site of "Fort Little River or Fort Griffin." His family then consisted of his wife, Mrs. Barzilla (Curry) Griffin, and some eight children: Williamson, Mary Ann, Aora Van, Martha Jane, Seabell, Caroline, Joseph W. and Avery. Other children—James E., David C., Cornelia and two others, whose names are unknown to the writer—were born later.

About one and three-eighths miles above Griffin's was the league selected by William H. Taylor. It embraced the Taylor's Valley of the present day, which was named for him. Here, in the valley, he settled. The records of the

[2] Rev. Z. N. Morrell, **Flowers and Fruits of 46 Years in Texas**, 41-44.

colony do not contain the field notes nor other evidence that the league was surveyed, except that the field notes of an adjoining tract (the Redding Roberts league) call for a "corner of the William H. Taylor survey." He had not obtained his final title when Independence came and his colonial location seems to have been abandoned, probably owing to his death not long afterward. Anyway, the location was later broken up into smaller surveys and taken up by his widow (under her former name) and her sons and others. Thus the names of Margaret Frazier, William Frazier, Stephen Frazier and others appear on the county map in place of the William H. Taylor league. His family then included his wife, Mrs. Margaret (Frazier) Taylor; his son by a former marriage; Josiah Taylor; Mrs. Taylor's three children by her former marriage with Frazier, William, Stephen, and Catherine Frazier; and their two younger children, Seymour Brown Taylor and J. Wilson Taylor. It was while living in this cabin that the Taylor family were attacked by Indians, November 12, 1836, and made their heroic defense, as related in another place.

Beginning on the south bank of Little River and again passing upstream, the first settlement was that of Michael Reed on his *labor* tract (177 acres), opposite his league which was located on the north bank, at Reed's Lake. With him resided his two sons, William Reed and Jefferson Reed, single men, each of whom had selected a one-fourth league, the former on the south bank of Little River adjoining the Michael Reed labor on the lower line, the latter on the north bank of the river adjoining John Needham's survey on the lower line. Next above and adjoining the Reed settlement was the league of John Fulcher. His family then consisted of his wife, Mrs. Mary Josephine Fulcher and probably three small children, Willis, Emiline and Martha. Nearly eight miles above Fulcher's was the league selected and occupied by Orville T. Tyler, embracing the confluence of Nolan Creek with the Leon River and extending around by the Shallow Ford and nearly to the military crossing subsequently (1848) made by the United States troops and now the site of the dam. It adjoins the league on which Belton stands.

This league was surveyd by Moses Cummings, Colony Surveyor, for Gustavus E. Edwards. Tyler came to Empresario Robertson's headquarters, at Viesca, early in 1835, looking for a location for his colony league. Here he met Edwards, who, having become dissatisfied with the country, offered to sell his location for the expenses (about $40.00) that he had incurred for surveying, etc. Tyler visited and inspected the league, in company with the Surveyor, Moses Cummings, and, returning to Viesca, accepted the offer of Edwards and took over the selection as his own, and the final title was issued to him.

These eight colonists built the old time frontier pioneer log houses, consisting of a single log room, or of two rooms with a passage way between, all roofed with boards held in place by weight poles. The floors, if any, were split logs, flat side up, and were known as "puncheon floors." The chimneys were usually built of sticks laid crib-fashion. The open spaces or cracks between the logs in the house walls and between the sticks in the chimney were daubed with mud or clay—"chinked"—to keep out the cold and the rain. These houses were provided with small square openings which served the double purpose of ventilation and as port or gun holes for defense against the attacks of Indians. Buffalo robes, bear robes, and the pelts of other fur-bearing wild animals were utilized as floor coverings and for some articles of winter clothing.

A family usually brought with them an ox-wagon and a team of one or two yokes of steers, a few saddle horses, a few head of cattle and hogs, crude farm implements and kitchen utensils, household goods, bedding, clothing, some supplies of sugar, coffee, salt, flour (when obtainable), molasses, bacon, tobacco, etc. Such things were obtainable at Nashville, some forty miles below, or at Tenoxtitlan and Washington, lower down on the Brazos River. Nearly every family brought with them to the country an "English steel mill," which, when set up and fastened with bolts to a post or tree and operated by a hand crank, ground the family supply of corn meal. The country abounded in wild game—bear, deer, turkeys and small game. In winter the buffalo came down from the northwest country in great herds. The streams afforded good fishing. And the woods were full of wild honey, grapes, plums, haw berries, pecans and walnuts. For fresh meat, and for self-defense, they relied upon the old flint-lock rifle, the powder horn and the leaden bullet, moulded at home. Conditions would not have been

The First Settlements Along Little River

bad, if only the settlers could have been free from the menace of Indians.

In order to complete and perfect the titles to their lands under the Mexican colonization laws they were required to put in cultivation a certain amount of land within two years—four acres to the league and small grants in proportion. In compliance with this requirement, and to provide for their future bread supply, these colonists began at once to clear, fence and break small bottom fields or patches; and when the revolutionary troubles began, these improvements had made good progress in a small way. All of their improvements—cabins, fields, etc.—were located in the bottoms near the streams, for convenience of water, fuel, building and fencing material, and for better protection against Indians, who preferred the open country for their operations.

The country was full of friendly Indians, traveling to and from their villages and hunting buffalo, deer, and other game. It was not uncommon for them to camp near the cabins of the settlers and exchange neighborly visits.

A large party of friendly Lipan Indians came into the valley of Little River, in the summer of 1835, and set up their tepees—quite a number of them—near the home of Captain Goldsby Childers. As was the custom, the Childers family invited them to spend the day and to share a good dinner at the cabin, and the Indians shortly afterward had the Childers family to return the visit and share a feast with them at their tepees. The writer's mother, a daughter of Captain Goldsby Childers and then a mere child, well remembered this incident and told him that the dirt floors of the Indian homes were covered with rugs made of the skins of bear, buffalo and deer, nicely dressed, and that the Indians were hospitable and well behaved and served a really good dinner of corn bread, venison, honey and coffee.

With the friendly tribes the settlers never had any trouble unless some reckless or ill-disposed white people mistreated them. Then they became enraged and sought revenge upon even the innocent whites. But the savage tribes were quite different. They were generally on the war path, either against the whites or against some other Indian tribe, or, most frequently, against both.

In the fall of 1835, the writer's father, O. T. Tyler, purchased at Nashville a pony, packed on him some plow tools, camp bedding and supplies and driving this pony ahead of him, walked from Nashville to his colonial land on the Leon at the mouth of Nolan. There he boarded the following winter with the Taylor family in Taylor's Valley, just across the river from his land, while he cleared four acres of heavy bottom timber in the northeast corner of his league; made rails, *carried them on his shoulder* and built a fence around the patch; caught up his pony, which meantime had grown fat on the wild bottom rye, broke the land, planted it in corn and had it growing when he and other settlers were compelled to abandon the country. He was within a day's travel of Houston's army, hastening to join it, when he met returning home men who had partcipated in the battle of San Jacinto.

Besides those already listed as actual residents in what is now Bell County, a number of other persons applied to and were accepted as colonists in this region by the empresario and commissioner of Robertson's colony. A few of these really visited their lands and looked over the country but, deeming the menace of Indians and other conditions too hazardous for immediate settlement, preferred to wait and so remained with their families in the lower country about Nashville, Tenoxtitlan, Wheelock, and other places. These were:

Grantees	Date of Survey	Date of Title	Quantity
Wiley Carter		Jan. 17, 1835	¼ League
Charles Curtis	Dec. 15, 1834	Jan. 12, 1835	¼ League
George Dougherty	Mar. 3, 1835		League
David Mumford		Mar. 20, 1835	League
Jesse Mumford		Feb. 25, 1835	League
Wm. C. Sparks	Oct. 19, 1834	Oct. 20, 1934	League

Wiley Carter died at Wheelock, Robertson County, about 1848. His widow and children, as did all of the others above named, came to their Bell County lands and made permanent homes there. Their descendants are still numbered with the population of the county.

The larger number of colonial grantees, whose lands were located within the Bell County area, had never visited the Little River country at the time of their grants, nor for many years afterward and many of them not at all. They were accepted as colonists and lands were titled in their names without their personal presence upon the lands or selection thereof, though some of them doubtless came to the colony land office at Viesca and there obtained their land papers. The colony promoters, being anxious to enroll the required number of colonists during the time limit of the contract, were apparently disposed to grant lands to all who came and they did not make a very strict application of the requirements of actual settlement upon the land, though some of the colonists doubtless intended to occupy their lands at some time in the near future. The following, and possibly a few others, thus acquired colony titles or claims to land within the Bell County area, during the colonial period of 1834-35:

Grantees	Date of Survey	Date of Title	Quantity
David Anderson		Feb. 12, 1835	2/3 League
Daniel H. Campbell		July 14, 1835	League
Juan Cardon		Dec. 27, 1834	League
Nancy Chance		Aug. 13, 1835	League
Willis Collins			6 Labors
Matilda F. Connell	Dec. 11, 1834	Feb. 3, 1835	League
Alexander Duggin	Nov. 3, 1834	Dec. 9, 1834	League
Joseph L. Hood	Nov. 28, 1834	Dec. 23, 1834	League
Samuel Humm	Nov. 4, 1834	Dec. 9, 1834	League
Warren Lyman	Sep. 17, 1835	Aug. 20, 1835	League
Thomas Polk			League
Henry Purdom	Sep. 13, 1835	Sep. 17, 1835	League
Redding Roberts			League
Baldwin Robertson		Dec. 23, 1834	League
Abner Smith	Oct. 28, 1834	Dec. 9, 1834	Labor
Thornton Stone			League
John Waugh	1834	Dec. 27, 1834	¼ League
Wm. Woodford	Nov. 29, 1834	Dec. 23, 1834	League

Reference has been made to the location of Mexican eleven-league surveys during the period of 1831-1834, when Austin and Williams had control of the Robertson Colony territory. These grants extended along Little River as far up as Three Forks and a number of the colonists, on the restoration of Robertson's control, located their headrights in conflict with them, being advised by Robertson that the Mexican grants were illegal and void.

The headrights of Warren Lyman, Willis Collins, Thomas Childers, Robert Childers, Prior Childers and Henry Purdom (in part) conflicted with the six league grant to José David Sanches. The remainder of the Purdom headright conflicted with the eleven-league grant to José Antonio de Peña, now in Milam County. Those of Goldsby Childers, Jas. F. Childers, Abner Smith and Jefferson Reed, conflicted with the four-league grant to José Nepomucena Arocha. Those of John Needham, Michael Reed, David Anderson, Robert Davidson, Moses Griffin, Sam Humm, and Alex Duggin (in part) conflicted with the eleven-league grant to Maximo Moreno. Those of David R. Mumford, Jesse Mumford, and George Dougherty conflicted with the eleven-league grant to Miguel Davila. Those of William Reed, John Fulcher and Wm. C. Sparks conflicted with the Antonio Manchaca six-league grant; but the grant was abandoned or obliterated and the colony surveys held.

Thus it appears that twenty-three (over one-half)) of these colony headrights were jeopardized by the senior locations of the "eleven-league" claims which were later held by the courts to be valid.[3] A number of the colonists finally lost these lands and relocated an equivalent amount in other parts of the State. Others made compromise settlements and held their lands, acquiring the superior title of the "eleven leaguers." There was much litigation in later years over these latter claims, but the controversies generally were on questions of boundaries and not of title.

The Taylor-Frazier family, on the north bank of the Leon, and the Tyler settlement on the south bank, both at the mouth of Nolan, were the highest upstream of all the colony settlements. They were the extreme outposts—the very frontier. Beyond them there was not one white man.

These people—the Chapmans, Childers, Davidsons, Fraziers, Fulchers, Griffins, Needham, Reeds, Robinson, Rhodes, Taylors and Tyler—the first settlers in Bell County territory—and numbering about fifty people in all, were residing here when the conflicts between the Texans and the Mexican government plunged the country into the throes of the revolution of 1835-36 which, for a time, wiped out the small but auspicious beginnings of our colonial development in Bell county territory.

We leave them here in their lonely cabins in the pathless jungles and bottoms of Little River and the Leon,

[3] Martin vs. Parker, **26 Texas Reports,** 254-262.

face to face with the wild Indian tribes of the plains. The winter of 1835-36 passed over them there. Our story will return to them in the spring of 1836, when lowering clouds of revolution overshadowed Texas and war's shrill note echoed through the land.

CHAPTER III

THE TEXAS REVOLUTION AND INDIAN TROUBLES

1. *The Revolution and the "Runaway Scrape," March-April, 1836*

Late in March, 1836, the quietude of the settlers of Little River and the Leon—the Bell County territory—was suddenly broken by the startling news that General Santa Anna had invaded Texas with a large and well-equipped army; that the Alamo had fallen with the sacrifice of all the defending garrison; that General Sam Houston, in command of the little Texas army, was in full retreat eastward from Gonzales; that Santa Anna was in pursuit with greatly superior forces; that the people of west, south, and central Texas were fleeing for safety toward the Sabine; that, added to all this, the hostile Indians, incited by the Mexican Government, were about to descend in great hordes from the northwest to attack the settlers on all frontiers; and, indeed, that all Texas was in a panic!

There was nothing for these settlers to do but abandon their newly made homes and join in the general flight or be ground to pieces between the oncoming Mexicans and the Indians. With much haste and confusion they gathered up the most necessary of their belongings, secreted or buried the remainder, and took up the line of retreat eastward with the general hegira, the "Runaway Scrape." Everybody went away from the Bell County territory, not a soul stayed behind. However, as they got rather a late start, they did not travel as far eastward as some others. Most of them went via Nashville, expecting to strike the old San Antonio road below there, cross the Brazos, and thence proceed to Nacogdoches and the Sabine.

Captain Goldsby Childers, with his family, however, proceeded by way of Milam (formerly Viesca) at the Falls of the Brazos, to Parker's Fort on the Navasota. The Parker and Childers families had come to Texas together, in 1833, by the overland route and were old friends. While encamped at the Falls young Thomas Childers, eldest son of Captain Childers, accidently shot himself, inflicting wounds from which he died the next day a few miles east of the Brazos, and he was buried there. Some other families also gathered at Parker's Fort, including John Berry and family, the step-mother of General Ed Burleson (then in Houston's army) with her five children and one of the Burleson children, the Harris family, Dr. McKinney's family—all from Bastrop (Mina)—the Addison family and others. The old men prepared to make their stand at the Fort, which consisted of a strongly built block-house, surrounded by a stockade, about which the refugees were encamped.

All of the young men of the Bell County colony, after assisting in escorting the families to the settlements at Nashville and Parker's Fort, assembled at Tenoxtitlan, where they enlisted with many others in the Texas army and thence set out at once to join General Houston. Among these were Heman Chapman, Geo. W. Chapman, Robert Childers, William Frazier, Stephen Frazier, John Needham, William Reed, Jefferson Reed, Josiah Taylor, and Orville T. Tyler. But they did not reach the army in time to participate in the victory of San Jacinto. When they had arrived within a days travel of the battle ground they met soldiers who were in the fight and who were then returning to see after their fleeing families. The struggle being over it was, of course, useless to proceed and most of the party turned back toward Nashville.

2. *A Few Settlers Return to Little River and Leon; Working Out the Corn Crops*

As the war was ended and Texas was now free and independent, all hearts were turned toward the abandoned homes of the settlers. But the menace of the Indians was still hanging over the Little River and Leon country and the families who had fled to Nashville did not regard it as safe to return, but several of the men did return.

The Childers family at Parker's Fort, supposing that the other families would do likewise, came back at once to the Little River home and, being the only family in the country, their home became the headquarters for all the men, while they diligently worked out and laid by the small crops of corn they had planted just before the "runaway." These men, for mutual protection against the Indians, kept together and worked out all the crops up and down the river whether the owners were present or not. The purpose was to provide subsistence for all the families, who were expected to return later on, and thus they hoped to be able to maintain the crude settlements which they had begun.

3. *Robertson's Ranger Company,* 1836

It was a part of the Mexican plan for the invasion and subjugation of the Texas colonists to incite the hostile Indians of the west to rise up against the white settlements and make a war of extermination against them. The Consultation had authorized the raising of ranger companies to guard the frontier. Such a company was enlisted for three months service in Milam County soon after independence was declared, and was composed of men from all parts of the county, with headquarters in Milam (formerly Viesca) at the Falls of the Brazos. It never got into action, however, as the great "Runaway Scrape" had dispersed the people and the battle of San Jacinto had been fought and won before it was equipped and ready for service, and thereafter its organization (merely nominal) fell to pieces. It is probable that the full company never met at all. Here is the muster roll of the company:

Captain—Sterling C. Robertson

Lieutenants—Jno. A. T. Graves, M. B. Shackelford

Sergeants—Thos. H. Barron, Walker Phillip, Warren Lyman, Calvin Bowles

Corporals—James Hudson, Enoch M. Jones, Moses Griffin, G. W. Morgan

Privates—Samuel T. Allen, Paton Byrne, David W. Campbell, Nathan Campbell, Michael Castleman, Eli Chandler, Robert Childers, Francis M. Childress, James R. Childress, Willis Collins, Patrick Connell, Augustus W. Cook, Henry Cook, James Coryell, John R. Craddock, Britton Dawson, David Dawson, James Dunn, Stephen Eaton, Robert Ferguson, Benjamin F. Fitch, John Fulcher, Henry Fullerton, Thomas A. Graves, John Marlin, Jeremiah McDonald, Hardin McGrew, John McLennan, Edward McMillan, James McMillan, Robert Moffitt, William Moffitt, Daniel Monroe, Andrew J. Morgan, John C. Morgan, Stephen Morgan, William J. Morgan,

Jesse Mumford, John Needham, Elijah Reed, Joseph Reed, Thos. J. Reed, Elijah S. C. Robertson, Thomas Ross, Jno. D. Smith, Wm. C. Sparks, Levi Taylor, Richard Teal, Jasper N. M. Thompson, Jno. Walker, Ezra Webb, Jno. B. Webb, Thomas R. Webb, A. Wilkinson, Jno. Wilkinson.

It will be noted that several members of this company were settlers on Little River: Moses Griffin, Robert Childers, Jno. Fulcher and Jno. Needham. At least one member of the company, Jno. R. Craddock, participated in the battle of San Jacinto as a private in Captain Wm. W. Hill's company, Colonel Ed. Burleson's Regiment, being company H, 1st Regiment, Texas Volunteers.

4. *The Second "Runaway"—Crouch and Davidson Killed by Indians*[2]

The returned settlers in the Bell County territory had about completed their work of plowing out and laying by the corn patches, and were gathered at Captain Childer's for the time, when, about the first week in June, 1836, two messengers came in haste from Nashville with the announcement that they had been sent up to warn these people on Little River and the Leon of an immediate invasion by Indians from the northwest and to urge them to hasten back to Nashville for protection. The messenger also brought the first news of the fall of Parker's Fort, which had occured on May 19, only a few days after the Childers family had parted with their friends there. A number of the Parker family had been killed and others captured, including Cynthia Ann Parker (then a child) whose sad history is familiar to all old Texans.

The Little River settlers gathered up such of their belongings as they could carry in a wagon, drawn by a yoke

---

[1] N. C. Duncan in **The Central Texan** (Franklin, Texas) of September 17, 1915.

[2] MS. account by O. T. Tyler and statement of Mrs. O. T. Tyler and Robert Childers, all of whom were participants; John Henry Brown, **Indian Wars of Texas**, 43-44; Wilson T. Davidson, **Old Settlers of Bell County, Proceedings of, 1901;** Jas. T. DeShields, **Border Wars** of **Texas**, 165-166, 200-203. A fuller account of this episode, the "Second Runaway," prepared by this writer, appears in Dr. James M. Carroll's **The History of Texas Baptists,** 96.

of oxen, and with a few loose cattle, started for Nashville. They camped the first night at the Walker Spring, some six or eight miles east of where Cameron now stands. Here lived Henry Walker, Daniel Monroe and William ("Camel-back") Smith, who were also preparing to retreat to Nashville but, not being ready, told the Childers party to go ahead, as they would go by a different route anyway.

The Childers party consisted of Captain Goldsby Childers and wife, Mrs. Elizabeth (Thomas) Childers, their four daughters, Catherine, Amanda, Caroline and Elizabeth, their three sons, Robert Franklin, and Prior (a boy), Orville T. Tyler, Rev. Isaac Crouch. Dr. Robert Davidson, Mr. Shackelford, Mr. Rhodes, Ezekiel Robinson, and the two messengers—five women and girls, one boy and eleven men—seventeen in all.

Leaving Walker Spring, they had gone only a few miles when those who were driving the cattle a short distance in the rear of the wagon, gave the alarm by calling out, "Indians! Indians!" and ran at once to the wagon. Captain Childers was walking about a hundred yards ahead of the wagon. On hearing the alarm he hurried to the wagon, at the same time repeating the alarm to Messrs. Crouch and Davidson, who were riding on horse-back a quarter of a mile ahead. In fact, they had left the party, intending to push on ahead and join their families that night at Nashville, not realizing that there was any immediate danger. They at once turned back to join the others at the wagon. But the Indians—supposed to be about two hundred in number, and well mounted—observed them and, suddenly dividing into two columns, passed on each side of the wagon, about one hundred yards distant and, speeding ahead, cut off the retreat of Crouch and Davidson. They fired a large volley at the people in the wagon as they passed, but did no damage. Captain Childers, an old Indian fighter in Kentucky, who had commanded a company of volunteers in the Black Hawk War in 1832, took command and ordered all to use the horses as breastworks, but to fire no shots at the Indians until he should give the word—thus reserving for close quarters their fire, which the Indians sought to draw as they passed. Finding they could not reach the wagon, Crouch and Davidson again turned and fled in the opposite direction and were overtaken by the Indians some half mile away and were cruelly killed in full view of their friends, who could render them no assistance. During this time, and while the Indians were parleying over the disposition of the spoils of their victims—their horses, saddles and clothing—the Childers party turned aside to a grove, a few hundred yards away, there unhitched the oxen from the wagons, tied them to the wheels, and prepared to make the best defense possible. But the Indians, for some reason, did not attack them—they seemed to fear to approach the wagon—and finally withdrew. The Childers party then beat a hasty retreat in close order toward Little River, some mounted, some on foot, as there were not mounts for all. They expected every moment to be attacked but reached the river bottom in safety, crossed over on a natural raft made of drift wood. swimming the horses above, traveled on until night and pitched camp. They reached Nashville in the afternoon of the next day—their escape being regarded as almost miraculous.

The two messengers, while the party was expecting an attack at the grove, deserted them most ingloriously, and when the Childers party arrived at Nashville, they soon learned that one of the deserters had arrived ahead of them and had spread the report that he had fought the Indians desperately, had killed several of them, and had seen the last of the Childers party killed, he being the only one to escape alive. The names of the messengers are omitted here because they left honorable descendants in our country who are respected by all.

After leaving the Childers party, the Indians appeared at the cabins of Walker, Monroe and Smith and kept up an attack upon them nearly all day. The three families there got together in one cabin and defended themselves by firing through port holes. No Indians were killed but some were wounded and toward night they retired. The Walker, Monroe and Smith party, well mounted, made their way safely to Nashville, arriving soon after the Childers party.

Incidental to this true story it may here be mentioned that Mr. O. T. Tyler, of the Childers party, was suffering with a seriously crippled foot and was made to ride on horseback in the retreat. He carried behind him little Caroline Childers, then only nine years old. The first marriage license that was ever issued in Bell County contained their names and they were married at old Fort

Gates, December 26, 1850. They were the revered parents of this writer. And thus tragedy and romance were blended all along on the bloody frontiers of Texas.

5. *A Few Settlers Return to Little River*

So far as is known, this second runaway left not a single white person within the territory now constituting Bell County. All were gone, leaving their cabins, household goods and little crops for the Indians to destroy at their pleasure.

Following the achievement of Texas independence at San Jacinto, April 21, 1836, the *ad interim* government of the new Republic of Texas, being without resources except contributions and loans from friends in New Orleans and elsewhere, was unable to maintain an army after the battle and most of the soldiers of Houston's army were discharged during the month of June, 1836. With no armed protection whatever against the Indians, the perils of the upper country were real. It had become a *terra prohibita*—a forbidden ground. To risk its dangers and hardships again seemed foolhardy. And, so, most of the Bell County colonists took up their abodes temporarily in the lower country, about Nashville, Tenoxtitlan, Washington, and San Felipe, there to obtain the means of subsistence by farming and stockraising, while awaiting the coming of a brighter day on the frontier. Nevertheless there was not wanting a few brave spirits with the hardihood to try again to occupy their up-country homes.

It is certain that Captain Goldsby Childers and his family returned to their Little River home in the summer or early fall of 1836. It is believed by this writer that William H. Taylor and family came back to their home on the Leon about the same time. And possibly a few others came during this period, looking for locations; but accurate information concerning them is not available, and if they came, they hurriedly went away. The Taylors remained until the attack on their cabins by Indians, described in the succeeding pages, when they abandoned the country for ten or fifteen years.

It is also certain that the only family of the Bell County colonists who remained in the neighborhood during the winter of 1836-37 was that of Captain Goldsby Childers.

Top, from left to right: Judge O. T. Tyler. Photograph of a painting. Mrs. Lewis M. H. Washington. She and her first husband, Dr. Robert Davidson, were in the first group of settlers on Little River in 1834. Dr. Davidson was killed by Indians near the present site of Cameron in June, 1836. Photograph in possession of Miss Myrtle Cloud, Austin.

Bottom, from left to right: Colonel Hermon Aiken, founder of the old town of Aiken and one of the first settlers of Salado. Colonel E. Sterling C. Robertson, son of the empresario Sterling C. Robertson. He donated the land for Salado College on which the town of Salado was built. From a painting.

They did not deem it safe to remain in the cabin home on Little River but, finding that they were too much exposed to danger from the Indians, especially after the Taylor experiences, they accepted the invitation of Lieutenant George B. Erath to go to the Little River Fort where they resided during the remainder of the winter in comfortable cabins built for them. The family of Daniel Cullins, one of the rangers, also resided in the Fort at the same time, and these were the only families that remained in the Bell County territory during that winter of 1836-37.[3]

6. *Indian Attack on the Taylor Family, November* 12, 1836

As already stated, Mr. William H. Taylor and family in 1834 or 1835 had settled in the pretty little valley, now long known in their honor as the "Taylor Valley," on the north bank of the Leon River, just opposite the mouth of Nolan Creek, about two miles southeast of where Belton was subsequently located. The site of their cabin is now in a farm and is several hundred yards from the Belton and Taylor Valley road (*via* mouth of Nolan). The members of this family have already been named.[4] Their cabin was built near the bank of Leon River, accessible to a spring which flowed out of the bluff bank of the stream. It was the usual double log cabin of the frontiersman, consisting of two cribs of rooms, with an open passage way between, all covered with one roof of rived boards, held down by roof poles laid across the boards and these were fastened down by wooden pins. This family, after taking part in the "Runaway" of April, 1836, had returned to their cabin in the summer or fall of 1836. It later came to light that the Waco Indians and the Tonkawas were at war and that the Wacos claimed that the Taylor family had harbored or were friendly to the Tonkawas, the fact probably being that the Taylors, like all of the settlers, had tried to keep on friendly terms with all of the tribes without discrimination.

[3] "Memoirs of Geo. B. Erath," **Southwestern Historical Quarterly,** XXVI, 274-275. Also, statement to writer by his mother, Mrs. Caroline Childers Tyler.
[4] See page 19.

On the bright moonlight night of November 12, 1836, their yard dog aroused the Taylor family, who had retired for the night. They at once discovered that a party of eleven Indian men were in the yard and set about their preparations for defense. The dog was killed promptly by an arrow. An Indian then attempted to break down the door leading to the passage between the room occupied by Mr. and Mrs. Taylor and that of the boys, at the same time asking how many men were in the house, demanding a supply of tobacco and the surrender of the party. Mrs. Taylor promptly replied, "No tobacco, no surrender." Mr. Taylor told them there were ten men in the house. The Indian denied Taylor's statement and Taylor shoving a board through a space between the logs gave him a painful punch in the stomach, which sent him reeling back toward his companions. Just then Mrs. Taylor opened the door and called to the older boys, who were sleeping in the other end of the cabin. They hurried across the passage and joined the rest of the family. They then placed a table across the door to bar it and placed the younger Frazier boy, about twelve years old, on the table with a good rifle and told him to shoot the first Indian who entered the passage. This door, made of boards, had an open space of a few inches at the top, through which the boy could plainly see. In a moment an Indian who had brought an axe from the woodpile approached the door, through the passage, and young Frazier with a well aimed shot killed him instantly. Another Indian approached, intending apparently to remove the dead Indian, when Mr. Taylor fired at him through a crack and tumbled him, mortally wounded, on top of the other. Fearing to make further advances upon the house, the Indians then resorted to one of their favorite methods, that of burning them out. They set fire to the unoccupied part of the cabin and soon had it roaring in flames and practically consumed. The fire, spreading along the dry roof boards across the passage, rapidly approached the room occupied by the Taylors. It happened that besides a supply of water, there was a barrel of home-made vinegar and a large quantity of buttermilk in the room. When despair seemed to overwhelm Mr. Taylor and he proposed surrender to the superior force, stating that while the Indians would doubtless kill him and the boys, Mrs. Taylor and the girl would be taken captives and their lives spared, Mrs.

Taylor, with dauntless courage, refused to consider the question of surrendering, declaring that she would rather be burned alive. She leaped upon the table and loosening the roof boards between her room and the burning roof of the passage threw them aside and thus checked the course of the flames and with the liquids mentioned, handed up to her by the children, she put out all of the fire which threatened their part of the cabin. During this time Mr. Taylor and the older Frazier boy each wounded an Indian out in the yard. Finding that the bullets were running short, Mrs. Taylor and the girl got down by the fire and moulded more bullets, while Mr. Taylor and the boys were guarding the house through spaces between the logs. While she was thus engaged she saw an Indian's face, through a hole burned out between the fire jam and the wall of the house. He was either trying to get a shot at them or to start a fire at that part of the house. Grabbing a wooden shovel she threw a shovel-full of coals and hot embers right into the Indian's face, eyes and breast, exclaiming, "Take that, you yellow scoundrel." He howled vociferously and fled, with unbearable pain, to the main body of the Indians. The attacking party now held a hasty council, and, with one brave dead, another mortally wounded and two others wounded and one seriously burned, they evidently decided that they could not rout the Taylor people from their cabin and that they, themselves, had had enough of the fray. They at once withdrew and were seen no more.

Hanging to the logs over the passage way was a large lot of fat bear meat and when the heat of the flames reached this and the hot grease dripped in large quantities down on the wounded Indian lying there, he sent up most excruciating and pitiful yells, but Mrs. Taylor answered back to him, through the spaces between the logs: "Howl, you yellow brute! Your meat is not fit for hogs, but we'll roast you for the wolves!"

The Taylor family, later on during the night, fearing the return of the Indians with increased numbers, abandoned their cabin and took to the river bottom for protection and escape. They arrived early next morning, with such of their house-hold belongings as they could bring on horseback, at the cabin of Captain Goldsby Childers, some fifteen miles below on Little River. A party of young men, composed of Geo. W. Chapman, Robert Childers and others repaired to the Taylor cabin and found everything just as when the Taylors left. There were the burned portion of the cabin, the two dead Indians, roasted and well "basted" with the bear grease, and the dead dog.

Another account is that Geo. W. Chapman and his party were out ranging and came to the Taylor cabin the next day after the attack and finding the situation as above, feared the Taylors had been captured, carried away and probably killed. Chapman was engaged to the Frazier girl and was, of course, greatly excited until the family were found safely housed at the Childers cabin. Whatever the fact was about Chapman's party, the romance was not lost, as he subsequently married Miss Catherine Frazier and they lived in Bell County in the later forties and early fifties.

The writer once met Mrs. Chapman (nee Frazier) and by request she gave a full narrative of the foregoing attack and their escape, in substantial agreement with the account here given. His notes of this interview were unfortunately lost in a fire, which burned his law office in Belton, August 1, 1881.[5]

[5] Accounts of this episode have been given by several writers. Among them are: John Henry Brown, **Indian Wars and Pioneers of Texas,** 38, Letter in **Belton Journal,** February 11, 1886; James T. DeShields, **Wilbarger's Indian Depredations in Texas,** 298; **Border Wars of Texas,** 136; Captain Shapleigh P. Ross, Letter in **Belton Journal,** 1886, Letter in **Dallas News,** February, 1893; Captain Wilson T. Davidson, Letter in **Belton Journal,** January 28, 1886; Colonel John S. Ford, Letter in **Dallas News** February, 1893; Joseph Cater, Articles in Temple **Mirror** April 24 and May 1, 1897, and December 25, 1899; Statements to writer by his father Judge O. T. Tyler, and by his mother, Mrs. Caroline Childers Tyler. From these and from other sources this writer has compiled the account above given.

All of the writers relate about the same facts in the main but differ in some details. The most material questions raised by these differences are (1) Did this attack occur in 1835 or in 1836? (2) Did the Taylors, after abandoning their cabin, take refuge in Little River Fort or at the home of Captain Goldsby Childers, or elsewhere? These questions will necessarily have to be considered together.

Most of the writers—Brown, DeShields, Ross and Cater—place the event in 1835. Davidson says 1836, as does John Henry Brown in his letter to the **Belton Journal.** None of the writers state any reason for the dates they assign or as to the place of refuge. Those details were treated by all as mere passing incidents of their stories. Cater had the advantage of a personal interview with Mrs. Taylor and her daughter, Mrs. Chapman. Ford had talked with Mrs. Chapman. Probably Brown also interviewed the Taylor boys, Brown and Wilson, but they were little tots at the time of the attack and could

7. Indians Attack Colonel Sparks and the Rileys, 1836

In the same month of November, 1836, Colonel William C. Sparks, Michael Reed, and Jack, a negro belonging to Colonel Sparks, set out from Tenoxtitlan, on the Brazos to establish their homes upon their colonial headrights, located on the south side of Little River some ten or fifteen miles below the present site of Belton. Mr. Reed had previously settled upon his land but had abandoned it in the "Runaway." Arriving there they pitched camp at a place not far from the present little station of Sparks on the M. K. & T. railroad. On the same day they constructed a pen for their corn, a wagon load of which, drawn by oxen, Mr. Reed had brought with him. Late in the afternoon Mr. Reed crossed over the river to spend the night with Mr. John Welch, a newly arrived immigrant. With the exception of the Childers and Taylor families, elsewhere mentioned, the country was unoccupied. During the night Indians attacked Colonel Sparks and Jack. Many shots were fired, which were heard by Reed and Welch on the opposite side of the river. Colonel Sparks and the negro, in the dark, sought refuge in a thicket. The Indians, seemingly afraid to continue the attack on the camp, finally retired and in the morning

know only the family tradition. The ohers wrote from second hand information. The first account was written by Brown and appeared in his paper **The Belton Democrat** in 1860, over twenty years subsequent to the event, and all the others came forth some fifty years after the attack, so that one cannot feel absolutely certain as to the historical accuracy of these details.

In the fall of 1835 Davidson, then about five years old, resided with his parents about six miles from the scene of the Taylor tragedy and would naturally have had some personal knowledge or recollection of it, yet he claimed none and relied entirely upon the information of others.

During the fall and winter of 1835, the writer's father, the late Judge O. T. Tyler, boarded at Taylor's house while clearing and putting in cultivation land on his own colonial grant immediately opposite the Taylors, on the south bank of Leon. He often talked with the writer about his sojourn with the Taylors and he was conversant with this incident, but never spoke of it as having occurred prior to his residence there nor as having been related to him by the Taylors nor did he mention the fact of the cabin of the Taylors having been burned by Indians previous to that time. His information about the attack was derived from others—not from the Taylors, as it would have been had it occurred in 1835.

Sparks and Jack struck out for Tenoxtitlan. Reed and Welch, soon visited the camp and finding no one there also returned to the settlements below on the Brazos. Near the mouth of Brushy Creek on the San Gabriel, Colonel Sparks and Jack met *en route* two brothers named Riley, with their wives, children, another young man, two wagons and their effects, going to the Little River country. Sparks, advising them of his recent experience, urged them to return but they would not, and moved on. Inside of a mile the Indians appeared, professed friendship for the Rileys and claimed that they were only following Sparks and Jack. The Riley party then decided to return to the lower country and were about to re-enter the Brushy Creek bottom when the Indians appeared on each side of the wagons and thus accompanied them to the creek. As the wagons reached the creek, an Indian jumped on the lead horse, cut loose his harness and was about to whirl in an offensive attitude when one of the Rileys shot him dead. The fight then started. The young man of the party, with the women and children, fled to the brush and, keeping on afoot reached the settlements on the Brazos in about two days. One of the Rileys was mortally wounded but killed two Indians before he expired. The other Riley brother killed two of the red-skins—making

There is no evidence that the Taylors rebuilt their house or ever returned there to reside until about 1848 or 1850, when Mrs. Taylor, a widow, came back to the Taylor Valley from old Nashville.

In November, 1835, there were several settlers on Little River who were nearer to Taylor's cabin than Captain Childers. They were Moses Griffin, Dr. Robert Davidson, John Fulcher, Michael Reed and John Needham. The Taylors certainly would not have passed by all of these settlements and gone on down to Captain Childer's home, if this event had occurred in 1835. But in November 1836, Captain Goldsby Childers was the nearest settler to the Taylor cabin and the only settler then residing on Little River, within the present limits of Bell County, and there was nowhere else for the Taylors to go.

Brown and Davidson say the family took refuge in Little River Fort. Ford names Captain Childer's home. DeShields says the Fort in the Wilbarger book but says Captain Childers' home in his "Border Wars." Ross and Cater mention neither, but Ross, in the **Belton Journal,** says they went to the nearest neighbors and that they were found in the bottom, and, in the **Dallas News,** that they went to Nashville; while Cater says they went down the country to a place of safety. All very clear!

The writer's mother, Mrs. Caroline Childers Tyler, was, in 1836, ten years old and was residing with her father, Captain Goldsby Childers, on Little River and she repeatedly stated to the writer that five in all. The Indians then fled and the surviving Riley laid his brother's body on a mattress and covered him with sheets and quilts, mounted one of the horses and arrived next day at Yellow Prairie, in the present county of Burleson. He returned with a party and buried his brother.

8. *Frontier Battalion of Rangers at Fort Milam, 1836-1837; Death of James Coryell*

The citizen soldiers of the Republic of Texas, organized for the Revolution, were generally disbanded by or during the month of June, 1836. The people of the upper frontier country had cause to apprehend attacks by Indians; and, although there were no means of paying soldiers, companies for the protection of the frontier were at once formed. The men were promised a certain amount of pay, but they had to serve on credit, except that they were to receive lands in addition—320 acres for three months service, 640 acres for six months, etc.—the lands to be located at their own expense. Those living up the country joined the frontier service, but this comprised merely a few scattered ranger squads, poorly organized and scantily equipped, and they were unable to give full protection

the Taylors came to her father's home on Little River the morning after the attack and remained there some time; that she well remembered the fact; that while in the bottom before coming in sight, they greeted the Childers family with loud shouts, recognized as made by the Taylors as there were no other people up the river; that their clothing was torn into shreds and that they were tired and hungry. She further stated that the claim of some writers that they fled to Little River Fort was a mistake—that there was no Little River Fort at the time of the attack.

Lieutenant Erath built Little River Fort in the latter part of November and in December, 1836, (See **Southwestern Historical Quarterly, XXVI,** 274-275), which verifies the statement of the writer's mother. There was no fort for the Taylors to go to.

That this episode occurred in 1836 and that the Taylors fled to Captain Goldsby Childer's home fit all of the conditions then existing while the contrary statements are irreconcilable with the contemporary facts.

I will venture to add that this attack on the Taylor family, following upon the almost total abandonment of the settlements upon the upper Little River and the Leon, probably was the immediate and potent cause for the establishment of the Little River Fort at Three Forks a month later.

to the settlers and almost none to those on the extreme borders—on Little River and the Leon.[6]

When the first congress of the Republic of Texas met in October, 1836, steps were taken to provide some sort of defense of the country against Mexicans and Indians, although the government was still without funds, with no resources readily convertible into money and, as yet, with no system of taxation or revenue. It was forced to rely upon the patriotism of citizen volunteers, already impoverished by the sacrifices and dislocations of the revolution against Mexico.

The Act of December 5, 1836,[7] "To protect the Frontier of Texas," required the president of the Republic to raise immediately a battalion of mounted riflemen, to consist of two hundred and eighty men, for a term of twelve months or upward, each man to furnish himself with a horse, rifle and a brace of pistols (if procurable), subject to inspection by the inspector general of the army. The corps was to be officered and paid the same as the other corps of the army, with an addition of fifteen dollars per month for furnishing horses and arms. The president was authorized to increase this force, if necessary, to one regiment of five hundred and sixty men, rank and file. He was also required to have erected such block houses, forts and trading houses as were needed to check Indian depredations.

It was doubtless this battalion that was referred to by Major Erath in the following quotation:

"In the fall of 1836 a battalion of rangers for the defense of the frontier was raised of which I became a member. We were promised twenty-five dollars a month and 1280 acres of land for every twelve months service, the government furnishing ammunition and rations, but we furnished our own horses and arms—and we lived for the most part on game out of the woods. I have known more than one man, enlisting, to give his whole claim for land and money in advance for a horse, saddle and bridle, with which to serve for it. Ammunition was the only thing furnished us and some beef now and then."[8]

[6] "Memoirs of Geo. B. Erath," **Southwestern Historical Quarterly, XXVI,** 273.
[7] Gammel, **Laws of Texas,** I, 1113.
[8] "Memoirs of George B. Erath," **Southwestern Historical Quarterly, XXVI,** 273.

The Texas Revolution and Indian Troubles

It seems, although the records are not quite clear, that Major Robert M. Coleman was first placed in command of the frontier battalions, but was succeeded in January, 1837, by Major William Smith.

The old village of Milam (formerly Viesca) at the Falls of the Brazos, was the headquarters of a small company of the battalion, commanded by Captain Thomas H. Barron. There was a crude block-house of logs and a stockade and it was then designated as Fort Milam.[9] Here is a muster roll[10] (possibly incomplete) of the company:

Captain—Thomas H. Barron

Lieutenants—Charles Curtis, David W. Campbell, Geo. B. Erath.

Sergeants—Hardin Nevill, William Neale, Lee R. Davis, James McLochlan.

Privates—Jesse Bailey, Silas Bates, John Barron, David Clark, James Coryell, William R. Cox, Aaron Cullins, Daniel Cullins, Anson Darnell, Charles Duncan, Green B. Duncan, Alfred Eaton, Thos. H. Eaton, Bradley Emmons, David M. Farmer, Robert Ferguson, Benjamin Fitch, John Folks, Stephen Frazier, Jacob Gross, Jack Hopson, Thomas James, Sam Johnson, Ben Long, R. H. Matthews, Thomas Matthews, William Matthews, Green McCoy, Jerry McDonald, Lewis Moore, Morris Moore, Claiborne Neal, ——— Parsons, Joseph Proctor, Sterrett Smith, Empson Thompson, John Tucker.

While serving in this ranger company at Fort Milam in the fall of 1836, Mr. James Coryell, together with Sam Barton, Mr. Berry, Michael Castleman, Ezra Webb, and one other (name forgotten) went out one morning about half a mile from the Fort, on the road to Perry Springs, to cut a bee tree. Having cut the tree they were sitting around eating honey and talking. Mr. Coryell told the others that he had been sick and was unable to run, if Indians came—the Indians were then very troublesome, so much so that all families on that section of the Brazos had gone into Viesca for protection. In a short time the men heard a noise as of sticks breaking and looking

---

[9] **Ibid,** 274.
[10] Newton C. Duncan: Letter printed in **The Central Texan** of September 17, 1915.

up saw twelve Caddo Indians near them, too near for them to try to get away. Coryell had the only gun that was ready—another was empty, still another failed to fire. Coryell rose to his feet and simultaneously three Indians fired at him and he at them. He fell mortally wounded and was scalped by the foe. The other men of the party being without arms, ran and escaped; but Berry, an old friend of Coryell, at first stood his ground and snapped his gun until he was compelled to make a hasty retreat.[11]

Mr. Newton C. Duncan, upon whose authority the above account is based, was a boy living in Viesca at the time and had seen and talked with Coryell on the very morning of his death.

There is another story that Coryell was killed while surveying on Coryell Creek, but that is a mistake. The James Coryell one-fourth league on Coryell Creek was surveyed by Luther T. Parchin in May, 1835, and was titled June 22, 1835.[12] James Coryell was present at the survey, but this occurred more than a year previous to his death at Viesca. Because of this survey Coryell Creek and Coryell County were named for Mr. James Coryell, the victim of the above tragedy.

9. *Little River Fort Built by Lieutenant Geo. B. Erath*

Geo. B. Erath says: "On the first of October (1836) I enlisted in a corps of rangers then commanded by Colonel Coleman, and served as lieutenant under Captain (Thomas H.) Barron, who was stationed at the Falls of the Brazos (Fort Milam).

"In the early part of November, 1836, I, with two sergeants, Lee R. Davis and (James) McLochlan, was placed in command of a few over twenty men taken out of Captain Barron's Company and sent to establish the fort on Little River, about a mile from what is known as Three Forks, near the banks of the Leon. Colonel Coleman with a few men went with us to the point designated, and after we had travelled, marked, cut out, and measured a road

---

[11] Newton C. Duncan, in **Old Settlers Association of Bell County, Proceedings for 1903**, pp. 18-19.
[12] Records of General Land Office: Robertson's Colony, 771-775.

from the Falls to the spot, he left me, continuing on measuring a road to his fort[13] on Walnut Creek about six miles east of where Austin now stands, and six or eight miles above Hornsby's, then the highest settlement on the Colorado."

"An attempt to settle the country had been made the winter before, and here and there unfenced patches of corn, planted in the spring, had reached maturity in the unusually favorable season, and had not been eaten up by buffalo or other wild stock. By going or sending out I could procure a few bags of nubbins, and I issued my men an ear of corn apiece a day for bread, which they ground on a steel mill. Our meat was wild game, which was plentiful. Honey had to be kept in rawhide or deerskin sacks with the hair outside, and at Christmas we had several hundred pounds about the Fort. A very little coffee was brought up with us, and used with great economy. Coleman left me three or four axes and some other tools, a wagon and two yoke of steers, and the steel mill already mentioned. Pots and other cooking utensils and useful household things were found around the evacuated country in or near deserted cabins where the settlers had hidden them in thickets or other favorable spots before running away.

"My memory for details on almost all subjects is good, but I am at a loss to account for the amount of work done that winter by my men who had to guard, hunt, cook, dress deerskin, and make clothes of it, particularly moccasins, and in all ways provide everything, and yet in six weeks time, by Christmas, I had up seven or eight houses with wooded chimneys, well covered, and with buffalo hide carpets down. I can say, however, that I had the honor to command a set of men unexcelled in capacity and industry, all of whom became good citizens of Texas. I know of but one now alive, Lewis Moore, living about six miles above Waco. Robert Childers, living in Bell County, is another who was with us, but not enlisted. One of the soldiers, (Daniel) Cullins, had his family with him, and occupied a cabin to himself as did also Mr. Goldsby Childers, who with his family and another grown son besides the one

[13] "Coleman's Fort."

I have already mentioned, was with us."[14]

The following is believed to be a correct roll of the seventeen rangers composing Lieutenant Erath's squad at Little River Fort: Lieutenant George B. Erath, commander; sergeants, Lee R. Davis and James McLochlan; privates, Jesse Bailey, David Clark, Aaron Cullins, Daniel Cullins, David M. Farmer, John Fokes, Jacob Gross, Jack Hopson, Green McCoy, Lewis Moore, Morris Moore, Claiborne Neal, Sterrett Smith, Empson Thompson. There were a few more whose names are unavailable to the writer.

Corporal William P. Bird, son of Captain John Bird, and a participant in the Bird's Creek Fight May 26, 1839, was at this fort just before and after that fight. He describes Little River Fort thus:

"Captain John Bird" (with the company of rangers) "camped on Little River near a deserted Fort (did not learn the name) which was 150 or 175 yards from the river. It consisted of a row of log cabins on the northwest side and postoak pickets eight or ten feet high on the other three sides, with another cabin in the center."[15]

Geo. Wilkins Kendall, the historian of the famous Santa Fe Expedition, in 1842, alludes even more briefly to this fort:

"In the afternoon we reached Little River, where we camped for the night. * * * * The place where we encamped on Little River was the site of an old picket fort, garrisoned some years previous by a detachment of Texan soldiers, who were stationed there to keep a lookout for Indians. The location is one of exceeding loveliness, healthy and combining every advantage for a flourishing settlement."[16]

A more detailed description is that of Captain Wilson T. Davidson who probably never saw the Fort itself. His family had left the country before it was built, and did not return to Bell County until after 1850; and the remains of the structures had been removed by Mr. Moses Griffin on his return to the place in the 1840's. But the general features of the Fort were known to the settlers of the late

---

[14] "Memoirs of Major Geo. B. Erath," **Southwestern Historical Quarterly, XXVI,** 274-275.
[15] Letter of William P. Bird, published in the **Belton Journal** for May 15, 1890. (More than fifty years after Bird's visit.)
[16] Geo. W. Kendall, **Narrative of the Texan Santa Fe Expedition,** Vol. I, p. 87.

forties and Captain Davidson, following the early traditions current on his return, gives the following general description of the Fort and of its location:

"Geo. B. Erath, first sergeant (Lieutenant) in Captain Barron's company, was placed in command of a squad of twenty odd rangers in the early part of November, 1836, and stationed at a place about one mile north of the Three Forks, three or four hundred yards east of the Leon river on the high ground about one and one-half miles west from the present railway station of Little River on the M. K. & T. Railway. During the months of November and December, 1836, Sergeant (Lieutenant) Erath and his men built there a fort consisting of a block-house, a stockade and seven or eight log cabins inside the stockade. This fort was first known as Little River Fort, sometimes as Smith's Fort and the Block House, but was afterward known as Fort Griffin, as it was situated upon the headright league of Moses Griffin, one of the early pioneers of Bell County. The old fort stood some forty or fifty yards immediately south, and in front of, the log cabin subsequently erected by Moses Griffin, which later was replaced with the residence building which still stands upon the spot, and said building and surrounding lands, including that upon which the fort stood, are now (1902) the property of Mrs. Sam Hasley, a daughter of Moses Griffin. The block-house was about sixteen feet square, the four walls built of logs to the height of about eight or ten feet and the gable ran up with a continuation of the logs and the roof was made of bur oak boards held down by weight poles in the usual mode of construction the pioneer's cabin. The block-house and cabins were protected by a stockade or picket fence surrounding it and enclosing about half an acre of land. There were portholes cut through the logs of the block-house through which to shoot the enemy in case of attack or siege. A spring just outside of the fort and about one hundred yards away furnished water. Captain Goldsby Childers and his sons, Robert and Frank, assisted the rangers in building the fort and the families of Captain Childers and Daniel Cullins resided quite a while in two of the cabins inside the fort, for protection from the Indians."[17]

[17] Wilson T. Davidson in "The History of Old Fort Griffin," **Old Settlers Association of Bell County, Proceedings for 1902,** pp. 7, 8.

The stockade was constructed of split logs set upright in the ground, close together, edge to edge, making a solid wall some seven or eight feet high and provided with port holes.

The ground on which the Fort stood is now (1924) owned by Mr. Lewis Merritt, a great grandson of Moses Griffin. The gravel road from Belton to Little River station, after crossing the Leon, ascends the hill and then turns at a right angle toward the north. From the point of the turn the site of the Fort is straight ahead to the eastward, some thirty to fifty yards.[18] The spring is at the head of a gulch to the left of the turn in the road and northwestward from the Fort site, while the Moses Griffin residence stood some fifty of seventy-five yards, northward between the two large old live oak trees.

This old land mark of the Republic of Texas is not to be confounded with another Fort Griffin on the Clear Fork of the Brazos, in Shackelford County not far from Albany, a garrison and outpost established by the United States troops soon after the Civil War.

As we shall see presently, around Little River Fort occurred several thrilling episodes in the annals of the county. It was probably never occupied continuously or for any great length of time after its evacuation in the late spring of 1837, but, nevertheless, during the long absence of the settlers, it served in the late thirties and in the early forties as a headquarters or meeting place for rangers and other frontier troops and for citizen companies who patrolled the upper country in later years and for travelers, surveyors, hunters, and adventurers, until the settlers came back to make their permanent homes in the country.

10. *The Elm Creek Fight, January 7, 1837*

Late in December, 1836, Lieutenant Charles Curtis had arrived at Little River Fort with orders to take over command. On January 4, 1837, Sergeant James McLochlan came in from Fort Milam with special orders for Lieutenant Erath to proceed to Fort Coleman on Walnut Creek about

---

[18] Oral statement to writer by Mrs. Cornelia Rich, daughter of Moses Griffin, whose childhood (from about 1846) was spent there.

six miles east of the present city of Austin with dispatches for Colonel Coleman. He also reported "that about twelve miles away on the waters of Elm Creek he had seen the tracks of some dozen Indians on foot going down the country." It was "determined that these Indians should not be allowed to go down the country to do mischief," but there was some delay, due to the shortage of horses and a rain, in getting into action. On the morning of the 6th, Lieutenant Erath was dispatched by Lieutenant Charles Curtis in pursuit of the Indians. His squad, consisting of fourteen men and boys, was as follows: Lieutenant Geo. B. Erath, in command; sergeants, James McLochlan, Lee R. Davis; rangers, David Clark, John Fokes, Jacob Gross, Jack Hopson, Green McCoy, Lewis Moore, Morris Moore, Empson Thompson; volunteers, Robert Childers, Frank Childers, ——— Lishley. Setting out from Little River Fort the squad travelled until late in the afternoon, when they struck the Indian trail in the Elm Creek bottom, some five miles north of the present station of Ad Hall on the Santa Fe railroad. After nearly sixty years Major Erath thus recorded the engagement:

"And behold! instead of a dozen the signs showed nearer a hundred, all on foot and going down the country toward the nearest settlements. We followed, and came to where they had camped the whole day before during the rain. Their fires were still there; they had erected eight or ten shelters out of sticks and grass; each could shelter eight or ten men. The trail made a plain road; it was no trouble to follow. An Indian, or an old hunter, could have told by the cut of the moccasin soles to what tribe they belonged; but we did not have the art, and were perplexed on the subject. It was agreed that if they were wild Indians we could manage them; but if Caddos, or the like, we might find our hands full.

"At nightfall, about twenty-three miles from the fort and about eight from where Cameron now stands, we lost the trail, but soon heard the Indians call to each other in the bottom not half a mile away. I fell back half a mile, and sent McLochlan and Robert Childers on again to reconnoitre. They returned before midnight, reporting that they could not find the camp. About four o'clock in the morning we saddled our horses and tied them to trees, and went on foot to where we had lost the trail, and at dawn found it again, going down into a ravine. We followed the ravine which ran parallel with a creek several hundred yards to another ravine at right angles, and here the Indians had turned square down to the creek. Following toward the creek, we heard the Indians coughing, and going up a bank across a bend came in full view of them less than a hundred yards away, all dressed, a number of them with hats on, and busy breaking brush and gathering wood to make fires. We dodged back to the low ground, but advanced toward them, it not yet being broad daylight. Our sight of them revealed the fact that we had to deal with the formidable kind, about a hundred strong. There was not time to retire or consult. Everybody had been quite willing to acquiesce in my actions and orders up to this time. To apprehensions expressed I had answered that we were employed by the government to protect the citizens, and let the result of our attempt be what it might, the Indians would at least be interfered with and delayed from going farther down the country toward the settlements.

"They were camped in a small horseshoe bend. We took position at a point under the bank of the creek. It was not light enough for all to see the sights of their guns. Our distance from them we thought at the time to be fifty yards, but it proved to be not more than twenty-five. While waiting there for it to grow lighter, altogether undiscovered by the Indians, a large spotted dog came from them to us, without creating any disturbance whatever, and went quietly back again.

"When we fired some of them fell about the fires, but most of them stooped to grab their guns, and then took posts behind trees, raised a yell, returned the fire, and flanked out from both sides to get into the creek where they could see our strength. Half of us had jumped upon the bank. Had we all had pistols, or the six-shooters of the present day, we could have charged them and kept them running. But as it was, we had to keep our positions to reload our guns. They opened a heavy fire with their rifles. Their powder out-cracked ours; if a shotgun was heard, it was but once or twice out of five or six hundred shots. No bows and arrows were seen.

"After a few minutes Clark and Frank Childers on my right flank were mortally wounded from the fire up the creek. Telling the wounded ones to go back as far as they could, I ordered my men to fall back in two squads, to the other side of the creek, to gain the top of the bank, and to post themselves behind trees, which they did, while I stood in my old position under the bank, loading my gun and watching the Indians approach. As the men got posted, the Indians commenced charging with a terrific yell. I retreated to the other side of the channel of the creek, but found myself under a steep bank five or six feet high. The Indians came on, and jumped down the bank on their side where I had been. One had his gun within a few feet of me, fired, but missed me. I couldn't miss him, and he fell right before me. This shot and the fire of my men from their new position caused them to dart back again a few feet behind trees. I made an effort to get up the bank with my back to it and my face to the enemy; holding by a root with one hand, I swung partially up, but fell back. My men called to know if I was hurt; I said 'No, help me up the bank!' Lewis Moore and Thompson lay down on the ground, reached their hands down and pulled me up with my gun.

"Rallying them now, I had Davis fall back fifty or sixty feet with one squad and take a new position; I with the rest covered his movement. Then we fell back about the same distance beyond them; they covered our retreat; and so we continued, standing and retreating alternately, till we got several hundred yards to an open bottom. The trees were elm, about six inches in diameter, and the balls of the Indians kept striking them. My left reached the bank of the gully into which we had first descended. There was a big thicket on the opposite side. The Indians now charged us with great fury and yells, and we could not be blamed for seeking shelter. Seeing Indians dashing toward us on the right, McLochlan and I took to a big tree, and McLochlan presented his gun to shoot, but could not. I had mine loaded, took good aim at a bunch of Indians close by, but had no time to note the effect of my shot. McLochlan and I ran to another thicket, while the Indians, who still kept up their terrific yelling, got between us and the other men. Fifteen or twenty steps more and we reached the ravine that went square up from the creek, and here we found the wounded Clark who said something to us about fighting to the last or we would all be killed. McLochlan said he had nothing to fight with, as his gun was broken.

Clark told him to take his, but he did not, but went on up the gulley and found the other men. I stayed a little longer with Clark, who was then sinking, but went on when I saw a half dozen Indians coming. I reached a different prong of the gulley. After going two or three hundred yards more I got to open ground, reloaded my gun, and, seeing some of my men on ahead among the elm trees, called to them, and they waited for me.

"The Indians no longer advanced; they went back. Some of them found Clark around whom they yelled and whom they butchered up. But they did not find Frank Childers, who had set down by a tree, leaned his gun upright against it, and died there within twenty-five steps of the thickest fighting. I collected my men, found one missing, who we rightly supposed got out of the way uninjured. We heard the Indians turn their noise from a yell to a howl. I thought then that they would not stay long in the place, and that we might remain around and later in the day go back to look after our dead men, but I cannot blame my men for rejecting my proposition to do so. Several of them informed me that they would never have gone into the affair except for the possibility of being impeached for cowardice or disobedience to authority.

There were several narrow escapes during the fight; a ball broke McLochlan's ramrod, another his gun lock, and still another went through his powder horn and let the powder out. One went through a handkerchief on his head and cut his hair, and another went through his coat.

"We arrived at the Fort that night, Saturday, the 7th of January, 1837. I started the next morning with four men for Colorado Fort to carry out the orders I had received, and have never been back to the battle ground since.

"Next day Lieutenant Curtis sent McLochlan there with about fifteen men to bury the dead. He arrived after nightfall and from various signs concluded the Indians were still there. He sent one of his men on to the Falls of the Brazos by a roundabout way to inform Major Smith; and himself returned with the rest to Little River Fort. The messenger sent disseminated the news along the way, and it got down to Nashville and to the few settlers below clear to Washington County, creating considerable fear of Indians. On the night of the 9th of January, just after I arrived at the Colorado Fort with the news, and about the time McLochlan got back to Little River Fort with the supposition that the Indians were still around, a big snow storm came up and sleet and ice delayed all movements.

"I got back to Little River Fort on the 16th, and learned from Curtis that a dozen men from the Fort had gone down to meet some more from the Falls and that, with what volunteers they could muster from the settlements, a big battle was to be given the Indians. That same evening of the 16th of January, the men who had gone from it, and Major Smith with his men from the Falls, arrived at Little River Fort. They had found Childers untouched where he had died at the battle on Elm Creek. The Indians apparently remained only long enough to gather up their dead, which according to their own statement later was ten."[19]

While the rangers were forced, by superior numbers, to fall back and abandon the fight, yet the attack had the effect of turning the Indians back and probably saved several families—those of Neil McLennan and others—living only a few miles below, from attack and possible massacre. The result, however, was dearly bought by the death of two men in a land where men were scarce.

So much for the military features of the Elm Creek fight. From the morning of the attack, January 7 to the night of the 16th, when Major Smith and his men arrived at Little River Fort from the battle ground, not a word reached the Fort as to the fate of David Clark and Frank Childers, who had been left wounded on the field. Did the Indians find them and brutally murder them? Did they linger long in death agonies from their wounds? What had been their fate? The parents, sisters and brothers of Frank Childers, all of them were compelled to endure this awful suspense—worse than death to his old heart-broken mother —for nine horrible days and nights, to be told at last that he was "found sitting against a tree, stone dead!" He may have lived hours, possibly days and nights after receiving his mortal wound, before death relieved him of his suffering.

With such tragedies, with such heavy sacrifices, with tears and agony, did the pioneer fathers and mothers of our Bell County territory and of all Texas purchase for us this goodly land.

---

[19] "Memoirs of Geo. B. Erath," **Southwestern Historical Quarterly, XXVI**, 276-280. Another account of this fight is given in John Henry Brown, **Indian Wars and Pioneers of Texas**, 46-47.

11. *The Post Oak Massacre; Little River Fort Abandoned, June, 1837*

Lieutenant Charles Curtis was, in the spring of 1837, succeeded in the command of Little River Fort by Captain Daniel Monroe. Time passed at the Fort without incident until about May or June, 1837, when Captain Monroe and his squad of rangers were ordered back to Fort Milam on account of Indian depredations in that section.

At that time the families of Captain Goldsby Childers and of Daniel Cullins, one of the rangers, were still residing in the Fort and certainly that there were none in the Little River country outside the Fort. These families, in their varied experiences on the frontier, running away from their cabin homes and returning thereto, over the rough and unmarked trails of the wilderness had worn out and broken up their wagons—the same old wagons in which they had emigrated from the "States" several years before—and their teams had been stolen by the Indians. It was deemed unsafe for them to remain in the up country after the departure of the rangers from Little River Fort. In these circumstances Captain Monroe dispatched five of his men to Nashville to procure wagons and teams with which to transport these families and their household belongings to that place. Jesse Bailey, Aaron Cullins, David M. Farmer, Claiborne Neal and Sterrett Smith composed the detail. They went to Nashville, obtained the wagons and teams and were returning to Little River Fort. As they approached a small isolated grove of post oaks in the prairie they were surprised from ambush by a band of Comanche Indians and all were killed. Since they failed to come in, Captain Monroe sent out from the Fort a scout party, who, following the usual route, came upon the horrible scene. There were evidences of a desperate struggle and that the rangers were outnumbered. The bodies of Aaron Cullins and Sterrett Smith were found in one of the wagons, and those of the others, Jesse Bailey, David M. Farmer and Claiborne Neal, were found scattered on the prairie between the wagons and the motte of timber. The Indians took away all of the teams, guns, and pistols. As there was no survivor the particulars of this tragedy will never be known. It occurred at a place in Milam County then known as the Post Oak Springs, which later became the residence of

The Texas Revolution and Indian Troubles

Ad Hall, for whom a small station of the G. C. S. F. Railway was named. It is only four or five miles from the scene of Erath's Elm Creek Fight of January 7, preceding.[20]

Soon afterward the rangers evacuated Little River Fort and departed for Fort Milam. Little River Fort was never again occupied as a military garrison, though visited now and then by troops and parties passing through the country. As Daniel Cullins was a ranger, it is supposed he took his family back with him to Fort Milam.

Captain Goldsby Childers and family returned to their cabin home on Little River, some twelve miles below. Although the Indians were very threatening and it was unsafe to remain there, the family had no transportation to take them away.

Later on a Mr. Franks and his wife, who travelled and traded with the friendly Indians, happened along with their peddling wagon and stopped a few days with the Childers family. While there, some friendly Indians, of whom as well as of hostile tribes, there were several bands in the country, gave warning one day of an intended attack that night by the hostile Indians upon the Childers home. All preparations were made. Powder horns were filled, bullets were moulded, guns cleaned, loaded and primed, the doors were barred with Frank's goods boxes piled against them, and thus they calmly awaited all night for the attack. But for some reason the Indians did not show up. Captain Childers then decided to abandon his home and lands and go back to the settlements until conditions were better and life became safer in the up country. Accordingly, on invitation of Mr. Franks, the Childers family went with him to his farm in Mound Prairie, near Groce's Retreat, in Montgomery county. There they engaged in farming and made a fine crop for the year 1838; but on account of sickness were compelled to leave. Captain Childers then, 1838, moved to Burleson county (which was organized about that time) bought land about eight miles below Caldwell,

[20] Newton C. Duncan in **Old Settlers Association of Bell County, Proceedings for 1903;** depositions of Mrs. Susan C. Kincaid and Thomas S. McCandless of Tennessee, as to death of their kinsman, David McCandless Farmer, in cause No. 4775, Kincaid vs. Garrison, District Court of Bell County, (1898-1900); Jas. T. DeShields: **Border Wars of Texas,** 237-238.

built a good double log cabin and lived there several years until death deprived him of his faithful and devoted wife and a young daughter, Elizabeth, and broke up his family circle. Selling his Burleson county home, he again set face toward the frontier and returned, about 1840, to his cabin on Little River.

After his departure from Little River in June or July 1837, and until the time or near the time of his return there in 1840, it is almost certain that not a single white person resided in the present territory of Bell County. The deadly menace of the Indians made such a thing impossible until sufficient numbers came to afford complete defense against the hostile hordes.

In fact, only a few people were left lower down on Little River. Major Erath, speaking of Milam County in the fall of 1839, says: "The settlement of the county was retarded so that in the fall of 1839 only about twenty-five families, in four settlements, including the town of Nashville, remained in the Southeast corner of the county. Counting a number of young men, there were only fifty voters at the fall election in the whole county."[21] During these years he alternated between serving as captain of rangers and leading land surveying expeditions, and found it difficult to hire men to go surveying on account of the danger of Indians.

The family of Neil McLennan and one or two others were living at Walker's Spring, some eight miles east of where Cameron now stands; Captain Shapleigh P. Ross and family were on Pond Creek, near its mouth; two or three families were at Fort Milam, at the Falls of the Brazos; all others were at or about Nashville. These were the four settlements above alluded to by Major Erath. In the country above them were no people at all on the Brazos, Little River or the Leon.

And thus our county—the Bell County territory—was "abandoned to solitude" and the Indian.

Such occasional movements as occurred in this territory or on its immediate borders, indicative of conditions prevailing here, will be noted briefly in the pages to follow. They constituted the only interruptions of those weird years

[21] "Memoirs of Geo. B. Erath," **Southwestern Historical Quarterly, XXVII**, 30.

when the cabins of the colonists stood vacant and deserted and their chimneys smokeless, when the buffalo grazed on the prairies and cut out his trails on the hill sides, when the painted and feathered knight of the tomahawk, wild monarch of the plains, sported in triumph over the sad ruins of our attempted civilization. But their days even then were numbered, for the time of their final departure was near at hand.

CHAPTER IV

TROUBLES WITH INDIANS IN THE LITTLE RIVER AND UPPER MILAM COUNTY AREA, 1837-1843

1. *Renewal of Hostilities under President Lamar*

During the six years following the abandonment of Little River Fort the present Bell County remained unoccupied by the white man, save for occasional hunters, traders, ranging companies, land prospectors or surveying parties. The upper line of settlements had receded into lower Milam County. The Indians regarded the whole region as their traditional hunting grounds and resented the approach of the white men whose permanent settlements meant the destruction of the game upon which the red men subsisted. Moreover, the smaller tribes who dwelt along the Brazos and its tributaries—such as the Caddoes, Anadarkoes, Ionies, Keechies, Tonkaways, Lipans, and Wacoes—were pressed back upon the settlements by the fierce and powerful Comanches and Kiowas of the west and north and had no place to go if dispossessed by the whites. The Indians, however, had no conception of private property in land, nor did the authorities of the Republic of Texas admit that the Indians held any title to the soil. The Republic could pay its debts only with grants of land; and numbers of Texans who held land certificates wished to locate their lands in this beautiful upper country. Conflict was inevitable. During 1837 and 1838 Mexican officials on the Rio Grande were intriguing with all the Indian tribes along the upper frontier with the purpose of bringing about a general war against the Texans and were promising them assistance in driving the whites from the country. The plot was probably the primary cause of the sudden outbreak of Indian troubles at this time.

Mirabeau B. Lamar became President of the Republic of Texas in December, 1838. He believed that the Indians must be dealt with sternly, for he had no confidence in the pacific policy which his predecessor, General Houston, had pursued. Because of evidence that the Cherokees in eastern Texas had been in correspondence with the Mexican officials, he sent a force against them in July, 1839, which drove them out of Texas. In March, 1840, occurred the Council

House fight in San Antonio, in which a group of Comanche chiefs were killed when they resisted being held as hostages for white prisoners in the hands of their tribe. In August of that year the Comanches went on a great raid to the coast about Victoria, killing a large number of whites and driving away a great many horses, only to be followed and defeated on Plum Creek a little north of the present town of Lockhart. In October, 1840, Colonel J. H. Moore led a force of rangers into the Comanche territory and inflicted a severe defeat upon one of their villages, killing about one hundred and thirty of their warriors, near the present Colorado City. The Indians learned that war with the Texans was unprofitable; but Lamar's aggressive policy was expensive and before the end of his administration, December, 1841, the Republic was heavily in debt and its currency worthless. Nor had all his efforts given absolute protection to the frontier. The ranging companies raised under the authority of the Congress were called out for only short periods of two or three months, and could not cover all points of the scattered frontier settlements. The Indians slipped into the settlements to drive off horses and attack such small parties of whites as they could catch at a disadvantage. The incidents which are related in the following pages do not tell the whole story of the upper Brazos frontier, but they may serve to illustrate the constant dangers to which the Texas pioneers of this period were subjected.

Rev. Z. N. Morrell says that once in 1837 while he was preaching in a little log cabin with a dirt floor, in Nashville, "Just about the time the services closed on Sunday the Indians dashed upon us and killed two men in sight of the congregation." As preachers and people carried guns with them to church, the men immediately mounted and gave pursuit, but the Indians escaped up Little River.[1]

Once in 1838 when Stephen Frazier was bringing the mail on horse-back from Independence (then known as Coles Settlement) on the Yegua to Nashville, some Indians chased him right into town. One big stalwart fellow came right up by the side of Frazier and tried to grapple his bridle reins. Frazier, so closely pursued that up to this time he had been unable to use his rifle, struck the Indian over the head and knocked him to the ground and thus

[1] Morrell, **Flowers and Fruits,** etc., 69.

made his escape, receiving only a slight wound at the hands of his pursuers.[2]

The Indians made frequent raids to Nashville and twenty-five or thirty miles below. They came right into town at night and stole horses, taking two from one stable one night in the thickest settled part of town. Old Mr. Neal went out one morning to drive up his calves and was murdered by Indians so near by that his screams were heard by women in the town while he was being scalped! Later on his son was killed by Indians three or four miles above the town. One day news reached the school being taught by Mr. Hughes that the Indians were right in the edge of town, when the children made a break for the door. Here the teacher planted himself and began to call out, "Go back! Go back," but they all ran around and between his legs, leaving the teacher alone, and with bare heads and disheveled hair, they flew to their homes, each one believing that a Comanche was right on his heels.[3]

In October, 1838, a party of twenty-three men, who were surveying lands in the southwest part of the present county of Navarro, about one mile west of the present town of Dawson, but then in Milam (or Robertson) county, were attacked by about three hundred Indians, chiefly Kickapoos. After a desperate struggle lasting all day and into the night, six only of the party escaped, leaving seventeen of their comrades dead on the field. Among the dead was Euclid M. Cox. Wm. F. Henderson, who was long afterward an honored citizen of Corsicana, Walter P. Lane, a veteran of the Texas Revolution and afterward a distinguished Brigadier General in the Confederate Army, and William ("Camel-back") Smith (mentioned before in our account of the "Second Runaway") were among the six who escaped. W. P. Lane, William Smith, Violet and another man of the survivors were severely wounded. The Indian death loss was said to have doubled that of the Texans.[4] The affair occurred on a little creek which from

[2] Captain Wilson T. Davidson: MS. of Address to old Settlers Association of Bell County, 1901.
[3] **Ibid.**
[4] Brown: **Indian Wars and Pioneers of Texas,** 47-50. The Kickapoos were northern Indians, famous as hunters and warriors, and were as well armed as the whites. They were more than a match, at equal numbers, even for the Comanches.

this circumstance bears the name of "Battle Creek," and where, in 1885, John P. Cox and Rev. J. Fred Cox, sons of Euclid M. Cox, erected a befitting monument, on which the names of the participants are engraved. A fence was built to enclose the monument and a lone tree, behind which Cox had stood and killed several Indians before receiving his death wound.

2. *Capture and Release of Colonel Norris' Surveying Party by Chief José Maria—A Masonic Incident*—1838

Colonel James M. Norris, a Mr. Taylor and three others were surveying land three or four miles northeast of the present site of Belton, sometime in the late thirties. Buffalo were numerous on the prairie. The party were working toward a hill and suddenly found themselves surrounded and made prisoners by a large body of Anadarko Indians who were hunting buffaloes. The principal chief of the Indians was José Maria[5]—the name of the other or second chief is not recalled. The latter insisted on killing the entire Norris party and ordered his men to string their bows, which they did with alacrity and evident eagerness to execute the order. José Maria expostulated with the other chief and they had quite a heated conversation on the question. At this moment Mr. Taylor made a Masonic sign that was readily understood by José Maria and the latter immediately stepped between Mr. Taylor and the other chief. José Maria could speak English and he talked in that language a few moments with Mr. Taylor, but the other Indians did not understand what was said. José Maria then turned to the other chief and they had a spirited colloquy in Indian language as to what should be done, José Maria evidently insisting, in opposition to the other chief, upon saving the lives of the prisoners. He made such an impression upon the Indians under the control of the other chief that they quietly, one by one, unstrung their bows. Mr. Taylor who was a Master Mason, afterward asked José Maria where he had received the degrees of Masonry and

---

[5] Brown refers to "José Maria, the noted chief of the Anadarkoes, who had been so severely wounded in his victorious fight with the whites in Bryant's defeat near Marlin, in January, 1839." Brown, **Indian Wars and Pioneers of Texas**, 96.

he replied that he was made a Master Mason in a French Lodge in Canada and that he was of the family of the great Tecumseh, who was killed at the battle of the Thames.⁶ The Indians then moved away, leaving the whites unharmed and free to resume their surveying.

The location of this occurrence was doubtless on Peppers Creek, not far from Midway—about where the late Mr. Joe Miller subsequently long resided. Colonel Norris, a lawyer then residing at Caldwell, was interested in the Nancy Chance League in this locality and was there about that time, as is evidenced by our land records.

3. *Indian Attacks on the Morgan and Marlin Families near Fort Milam; Indian Victory over Whites at Morgan's Point,* 1839

Somewhere not far from the Falls of the Brazos (Fort Milam) was a place called Morgan's Point. Near this place resided, unprotected, the families of George Morgan and John Marlin, who apparently were defying fate or rather the Indians. On January 1, 1839, a little after dark, the house of George Morgan was broken into by Indians and in a few minutes two men and three women were tomahawked and scalped. One young girl, wounded, feigned death. She and three small children, who hid themselves in the yard, escaped.

⁶ This incident was related by Colonel Norris to the late Captain James Boyd of Belton, who, by request, embodied the facts in a letter to the writer, September 29, 1914. The late Don A. Chamberlin, of Belton, once told the writer of the same incident as having been related to him by Colonel Norris. The writer was well acquainted with Colonel Norris who was a man of unquestionable integrity and veracity. But it seems probable that even if the Colonel's memory of José Maria's statement was accurate, the old chieftain must have embroidered his tale with considerable romance. His tribe, the Anadarkoes, a division of the Caddo confederacy, had lived along the Trinity and Brazos Rivers for some three hundred years. They had never lived in Canada; they were in no way related to the tribe of Tecumseh; nor did Tecumseh's wide-spread conspiracy of 1811 reach as far west as the Caddo confederacy. The Caddoes and Anadarkoes had long been in contact with the French and Spanish in Louisiana and eastern Texas and José Maria's Spanish name strongly indicates some personal relations with Spanish or Mexicans. It is therefore possible that he had been initiated into some Masonic lodge in Texas or Louisiana.

Troubles with Indians, 1837-1843

On January 10th following some seventy Indians attacked the house of John Marlin, but met with such a warm reception from Marlin and three other men that they hastily withdrew with a loss of seven Indians killed and others wounded. A negro took fright during the attack at Marlin's house, escaped to the settlment twenty-five miles below and reported these occurrences there.

A party of forty-eight men was organized, with Major Benjamin Bryant chosen to command them, and repaired to the scene. They discovered the Indians, José Maria, chief of the Anadarkoes, at the head, in a post oak woods and began an attack. The Indians fell back to a branch, which action was mistaken for a retreat and the whites became careless, losing their formation. Then the Indians turned upon the attacking party unexpectedly and put them on the run and won a decided victory. The attacking party lost ten men killed and had five wounded, including among the latter Major Bryant, who was succeded in the command by Ethan Allen. Among the participants who either before or after this event, were connected with the history of our Bell County territory were Major Benjamin Bryant, Wiley Carter, Thomas Duncan, Andrew McMillan, Wilson Reed, Ethan Stroud.[7]

Their success in this engagement greatly encouraged the Indians and their boldness increased. Their frequent excursions aroused the fears of the lower settlements. But their "haughtiness was hastening them on to a fall," as we shall presently see.

4. *The Bird's Creek Fight, May* 26, 1839

The Third Congress of the Republic of Texas, at its first session (1838-39), passed several laws providing for the enlistment for three months service of mounted volunteer rangers to protect the frontiers. Each company was to consist of a captain, first and second lieutenants, three sergeants and fifty-three privates.

The ranger forces which engaged in the desperate battle with Indians known as the Bird's Creek Fight were organized under the provisions of these laws.

---

[7] Major John Henry Brown in **Texas Almanac for 1868,** 49, 51.

Captain John Bird, in command of the rangers, was killed in the battle and was succeeded in command by Lieutenant Nathan Brookshire, whose official report of the affair, published in the annual report of General Albert Sidney Johnston, Secretary of War of the Republic of Texas, in November, 1839, is as follows:[8]

"REPORT OF THE BATTLE FOUGHT ON LITTLE RIVER BY N. BROOKSHIRE, CAPTAIN COMMANDING."

Camp Nashville, May 31st, 1839

SIR—On Monday the 20th inst., Capt. Bird left Fort Milam with a command of fifty men, for fort Smith,[9] on Little River. On Friday morning we reached that point; on Sunday morning, following, Lieut. Ervin was despatched with a guard of twelve men, to Col. Burleson, with five men who had deserted. Shortly after Lieut. Ervin's departure, three Indians came within sight of the encampment, in pursuit of buffalo. A spy was soon despatched in pursuit of them, who gave chase to them, but without any effect. The spies returned and reported a small body of Indians. At one o'clock, P. M. Capt. Bird marched against them with a command of 35, rank and file; after advancing about five miles in the prairie, came in sight of 27 in number; we pursued them three miles further, when we came within 175 yards of them arrayed in battle order. A charge was then ordered, but to no effect, owing to the speed of their horses, though this charge was kept up for three miles. Finding the pursuit in vain, a retreat was ordered; after retreating about one half mile, we found ourselves surrounded by about forty Indians, hurling their arrows upon us from every direction; we discovered in our front, about 600 yards, a ravine; between our lines and the ravine, were the main body of the Indians, who made a desperate effort to keep us out, but in vain; we routed them and gained a favorable position. The Indians then retired to

[8] Report Sec'y of War, 1839, pp. 45-46. Dr. Alex Dienst of Temple has one of the original printed pamphlet copies of the report of General Albert Sidney Johnston, while Secretary of War of the Republic of Texas, as above mentioned, and to his courtesy the writer is indebted for the opportunity to use Lieutenant Brookshire's report of the Bird's Creek Fight. This pamphlet is very scarce and almost unobtainable. The writer has never seen Lieutenant Brookshire's report of the battle printed in any other publication.
[9] Little River Fort.

the top of the hill, three hundred yards off. In about a half hour a reinforcement of about two hundred Indians came up in full view, making about two hundred and forty or fifty strong. After drawing up their lines, the warwhoop from one end of their line to the other was heard, which shrieked in the ears of our gallant little band, which was followed by a desperate charge from every point; but our boys gave them such a warm reception they were handsomely repulsed, though the charge continued one-half hour. After which time they returned to the top of the hill, carrying off a great many dead and wounded, together with a considerable number of horses,—they rallied again, and made a more desperate effort than ever to rout us from our position; but the Anglo Saxons then being buoyed up with a spirit of victory, gave them a warmer reception than ever, and repulsed them again. After fighting upwards of one hour, with a heavy loss of men and horses, they then drew off their men to their rallying point, where they remained until dark,—we snugly kept our places. The Indians then separated into two bodies and marched off, throwing up in the air a composition of something that had the appearance of lightning, which we supposed to be a signal for retreat. About nine o'clock we secreted our dead in the ravine, as well as possible, and took up the line of march down the ravine, in order to gain the timber, a distance of three miles, carrying off our wounded with us.[10] This body of Indians was composed of Caddoes, Kickapoos and Comanches; the Kickapoos and Caddoes we supposed to be with them from the great quantity of guns they fought with; several of them also spoke the English language to

---

[10] William P. Bird, son of Captain John Bird, was corporal of his father's company and participated in the battle. In a letter written to the **Belton Journal** and published in that paper May 15, 1890, he says:

"After the Indians left, which was about dark, the company carrying Hall and Allen (and Hansell) returned to the Fort. In about a week a burying party went back, but found the bodies in such condition they could do nothing with them. One of Gray's arms was cut off and hung in a little pinoak opposite the mouth of a little ravine. Bird and Weaver were tied together and laid at the mouth of a little ravine. All were scalped. The party went back after another week and buried the bones on the field. The Indians also buried their dead at the same place. The whites dug "Buffalo Horns" up, stuck the horns on the skull and stuck his skull on a pole and left it standing."

us while fighting. About two o'clock A. M. we reached Fort Smith,—on Monday evening we took up the line of march for this place (Nashville), for the purpose of recruiting our horses, and getting medical aid for the wounded. We will leave this place to-morrow morning, together with a hundred of the citizens, for the battle-ground, to inter the dead and see what other discoveries we can make,—from all appearances the Indians are in general commotion. I regret much to report that we sustained a loss of seven men out of our little band, killed and wounded. Killed, Capt. John Bird, Serg't Weaver, of Lieut. Evan's command, Jesse E. Nash, H. M. C. Hall and Thomas Gay; wounded, Lieut. Wm. R. Allen and G. Hansel, both slightly. The enemy's loss was about thirty to forty killed on the ground, and about the same number wounded: an immense number of horses were killed dead on the ground. It being in the night, and the small force, prudence did not dictate the examination of the battle-ground. I herewith, in conclusion, transmit to you a list of those who participated in the action: Capt, John Bird, Lieut. Wm. R. Allen, Serg't. B. Vickory, Serg't. M. P. Shark, Serg't. J. Slack, Serg't. Wm. Weaver, Corp'l. Wm. Bird; privates, James Brookshire, Wm. Ayres, Wm. Badgett, Joseph S. Marsh, T. Fort, J. H. Hughs, G. W. Grimes, Jas. Stephenson, Louis Kleberg, A. J. Ivey, G. W. Hansel, M. Hastings, Hall, Kuyzer, Wm. Peters, Blanc, J. and T. Robinett, Rowan, Gavins, Hannum, Gay, Menifee, Powers, Winkler, Mills, J. E. Nash, all of which is respectfully submitted."

 (SIGNED)   "NATHAN BROOKSHIRE,
            Capt. Commanding."

Lieutenant Brookshire's brief account of the military movements and casualties are thus given in his own words, written five days after the battle, and this must be ever regarded as the basic authentic history of the event.

A number of accounts of this battle have been written and printed in the course of years and there are many

> Some have claimed that the rangers carried Captain Bird and the others killed in the battle to Little River Fort and buried them there. Lieutenant Brookshire and Corporal Wm. P. Bird both verify the claim of most writers that the dead were left on the field and buried there subsequently. Hall was carried with the two other wounded men to the Fort, died the next day and was doubtless buried there.

Top: The Martin Luther Houston home, near Little River. Built in the 1840's. The original portion, in the center, is built of logs which are now boarded over. Courtesy of Mrs. W. S. Reed.

Bottom: The original William Reed home on Little River. Built in 1850 of bur oak logs. Photographed in 1936. Courtesy of Mrs. W. S. Reed.

traditions among our people of incidents connected with it, the authenticity of which can not be adjudged by those now living. All of the actors in that struggle and all of its historians are now departed. Since this fight occurred within the present Bell County the writer yields to the temptation to transfer to these pages a more detailed and colorful account than appears in the military report of Lieutenant Brookshire, even though it involves the repetition of some of the facts. It was written by Major John Henry Brown about 1859 and printed in the first number of his newspaper *The Belton Democrat,* issued March 10, 1860. It was again printed in *Texas Farm and Ranch* in the eighties and finally in the bound volume of his Indian histories published after his death.[11] From this, principally, are the statements following made up and most of the wording is his own. His sources were personal statements of men who participated in the battle and visitation to the scene of conflict while a citizen of Belton from about 1858 to 1863. He may also have seen Lieutenant Brookshire's report. The writer knows of no earlier and certainly of no more reliable unofficial description of the Bird's Creek Fight.

On April 3rd, 1839, Lieutenant William G. Evans arrived at Fort Milam[12] with a fraction of a company, comprising thirty-four men, from Houston. On May 6th following Captain John Bird arrived there with a full company of men from Austin and Fort Bend counties. As senior officer, Captain Bird took command of both companies.

A mutiny occurred in camp requiring that seven men be escorted by a guard to Colonel Ed Burleson, at Bastrop, for court martial. The provisions had given out and the men had to subsist on wild meat alone—that occasioned the mutiny. A guard of twelve men from Captain Bird's company were detailed to escort the prisoners to Bastrop, under command of Lieutenant James Irvine.

Captain Bird, deciding to accompany the guards and prisoners in force a part of the way, they arrived at Little River Fort (then deserted) on the night of May 25, 1839,

---

[11] **Indian Wars and Pioneers of Texas,** 70-73.
[12] Not the old Fort Milam at the Falls heretofore mentioned, but another built by Capt. Joseph Daniels of the Milam Guards, from Houston, and located about two miles from the present town of Marlin.

and camped. Next morning Captain Bird and Nathan Brookshire accompanied the guard and prisoners a few miles, leaving Lieutenant William R. Allen in charge of the force at Little River Fort. On returning to the Fort, Bird and Brookshire "came upon three Indians skinning a buffalo, routed them and captured a horse loaded with meat." During their absence a small party of Indians had chased "a gang of buffaloes very near the Fort," but, discovering the Americans, had "retreated North over the rolling prairie."

After inspection of arms and ammunition and detailing two men to remain on guard at the Fort, Captain Bird, with his force of forty-four men, set out in pursuit of the Indians. "In about for miles they came in view of about fifteen or twenty Indians and chased them without over-hauling them. The enemy were well mounted and could easily elude them, but seemed only to avoid gunshot distance, and continued at a moderate speed on the same course, through the broken prairie. Now and then, a single Indian would dart off in advance of his comrades and disappear, and after pursuing them some four or five miles, small parties of well mounted Indians would frequently appear and join the first body; but still the retreat and pursuit continued."

"After traveling some eight or ten miles in this way, through the prairie, the Indian force had been materially augmented, and they halted and formed on the summit of a high ridge. Bird immediately ordered a charge, which was firmly met by the enemy and they came into close quarters and hot work. As they mingled with the Indians on the elevated ridge, one of Bird's men, pointing to the next ridge beyond, sang out, 'Look yonder, boys! What a crowd of Indians!' and the little band of forty-five men beheld several hundred mounted warriors advancing at full speed. They immediately surrounded our men and poured a heavy fire upon them. The intrepid Weaver directed Captain Bird's attention to a ravine two hundred yards distant and at the base of a hill, as an advantageous position. Bird, preserving the utmost composure amid the shower of bullets and arrows, ordered his men to dismount, and, leading their horses in solid column, to cut their way down to the position named.

"Cutting their way as best they could, they reached the head of the little ravine, and made a lodgment for both men and horses, but a man named H. M. C. Hall, who had persisted in remaining on his horse, was mortally wounded in dismounting on the bank. The ravine was in an open prairie with a ridge gradually ascending from its head and on either side, reaching the principal elevation at from two hundred and fifty to three hundred yards. For about eighty yards the ravine had washed out into a channel and then expanded into a flat surface. Such localities are common in the rolling prairies of Texas. The party, having thus secured this, the only defensible point within their reach, the enemy collected to the number of about six hundred on the ridge, stripped for battle and hoisted a beautiful flag of blue and red, perhaps the trophy of some previous victory. Sounding a whistle they mounted and at gentle and beautifully regular gallop in single file, they commenced circling Bird and his little band, using their shields with great dexterity. Passing around the head of the ravine, then turning in front of the Texan line, at about thirty yards—a trial always the most critical to men attacked by superior numbers, an one, too, that created among Bird's men a death-like silence and doubtless tested every nerve—the leading chief saluted them with: 'How do you do?' repeated by a number of his followers. 'At that moment,' says one of the party, 'my heart rose to my throat and I felt like I could outrun a race-horse and I thought all the rest felt just as I did. But just as the chief had repeated the salutation the third time, William Winkler, a Dutchman, presented his rifle with as much self-composure as if he had been shooting a beef, at the same time responding: 'I dosh tolerably well; how dosh you do, God tam you!' He fired and as the chief fell, he continued: 'Now, how dosh you do, you tam red rascal!' Not another word had been uttered up to that moment, but the daredevil impromptu of the iron-nerved Winkler operated as an electric battery, and our men opened on the enemy with loud and defiant hurrahs—the spell was broken, and not a man among them but felt himself a hero. Their first fire, however, from the intensity of the ordeal, did little execution, and in the charge, Thomas Gay fell dead in the ditch, from a rifle ball.

"Recoiling under the fire, the Indians again formed on the hill and remained about twenty minutes, when a second charge was made in the same order, but in which they made a complete circuit around the Texans, dealing a heavy fire among them. But the nerves of the inspirited defenders had now become steady and their aim was unerring—they brought a goodly number of their assailants to the ground. They paid bitterly for it, however, in the loss of the fearless Weaver, who received a death ball in the head, and of Jesse E. Nash, who was killed by an arrow, while Lieutenant Allen and George W. Hensell were severely wounded and disabled: and as the enemy fell back a second time, Captain Bird jumped on to the bank to encourage his men, but only to close his career on earth. He was shot through the heart by an arrow by an Indian at the extraordinary distance of two hundred yards—the best arrow shot known in the annals of Indian warfare, and one that would seem incredible to those who are not familiar with their skill in shooting by elevation.

"They were now left without an officer. Nathan Brookshire, who had served in the Creek war under Jackson, was the oldest man in the company, and at the suggestion of Samuel A. Blaine, was unanimously called upon to assume command. He assented, and requited the confidence reposed in a most gallant manner.

"For the third time, after a brief delay on the ridge, the enemy came down in full force, with terrific yells, and an apparent determination to triumph or sacrifice themselves. They advanced with impetuosity to the very brink of the ditch, and, recoiling under the most telling fire from our brave boys, they would rally again and again with great firmness. Dozens of them fell within twenty or thirty feet of our rifles—and almost every shot killed or wounded an Indian. Brookshire's stentorian voice was heard through the lines in words of inspiring counsel. The stand made by the enemy was truly desperate; but the death dealing havoc of the white man, fighting for victory or death, was too galling for the red man, battling for his ancient hunting grounds, and after a prolonged contest, they withdrew with sullen stubborness to the same position on the ridge, leaving many of their comrades on the field It was now drawing towards night, and our men, wearied with the hard days work, and not wishing to provoke a feeling of desperation among the discomfited foe, concluded it would be unwise to hurrah any more, as they had done, unless in resisting a charge.

"The Indians drew up into a compact mass on the ridge and were vehemently addressed by their principal chief,[13] mounted on a beautiful horse and wearing on his head a buffalo skin cap, with the horns attached. It was manifest from his manner and gesticulations, that he was urging his braves to another and last desperate struggle for victory—but it would not do. The crowd was defeated. But not so with their heroic chief. Failing to nerve the mass, he resolved to lead the few who might follow him. With not exceeding twelve warriors, as the forlorn hope, and proudly waving defiance at his people, he made one of the most daring assaults in our history, charging within a few paces of our lines, fired and wheeling his horse, threw his shield over his shoulders, leaving his head and neck only exposed. At this moment, the chivalrous young James W. Robinett sent a ball through his neck, causing instant death, exclaiming, as the chief fell, 'Shout boys! I struck him where his neck and shoulders join!' A tremendous hurrah was the response. The Indians on the hill-side, spectators of the scene, seeing their great war chief fall within thirty feet of the Americans, seemed instantly possessed by a reckless frenzy to recover his body; and, with headlong impetuosity, rushed down and surrounded the dead chief, apparently heedless of their own danger, while our elated heroes poured among them awful havoc, every ball telling upon some one of the huge and compact mass. The struggle was short but deadly. They bore away the martyred chief, but paid a dear reckoning for the privilege.

"It was now sunset. The enemy had counted our men— they knew their own force—and so confident were they of perfect victory, that they were careful not to kill our horses, only one of which fell. But they were sadly mistaken—they were defeated with a great loss, and as the sun was closing the day, they slowly and sullenly moved off, uttering that peculiar gutteral howl—that solemn, Indian wail—which all old Indian fighters understand.

"Brookshire, having no provisions and his heroic men being exhausted from the intense labors of the day, thought it prudent to fall back upon the Fort the same night. Hall, Allen and Hansell were carried in, the former dying soon after reaching there. The next day Brookshire sent a run-

---

[13] Most accounts of this affair call this chief by the name of "Buffalo Hump," others "Buffalo Horns."

ner to Nashville, fifty miles. On the second day his provisions exhausted, he moved the company also to Nashville. Mr. Thompson received them with open arms and feasted them with the best he had. Brookshire made a brief report of the battle to the Government, and was retained in command until their three months of service expired, without any other important incident.

" 'Bird's Victory', as this battle has been termed, spread a gloom among the Indians, the first serious repulse the wild tribes had received for some time, and its effect was long felt."

The creek on which Captain Bird and his comrades fell is known to this day as "Bird's Creek."

"Mrs. Nancy Ferguson, in the fifties, located her preemption survey at the head of Bird's Creek, including most of the ground on which the battle was fought. The late Mr. John Ferguson, her son, stated that when they moved there many evidences of the struggle were still visible, such as bones, Indian arrow heads and bullet marks on trees."[14]

It is not known how many Indians were engaged nor their loss in killed and wounded, but estimates of the former at three to six hundred, and of the latter at ten to one hundred have been given by the different writers on the subject. The Indians thus suffered quite a setback in their bold raids upon the settlers below and were never more quite so troublesome as they had been for the years 1836 to 1839.

The Bird's Creek battle ground is located about one and one half miles northwest of the present city of Temple in Bell County just beyond the "Santa Fe Dairy," on the north of the Temple and Moffatt public road.

Major Brown says that he had before him "copies of the (official) muster rolls of both Bird's and Evan's Companies, in which are designated those who were in the battle, excepting one person. The list does not show who composed the prisoners or guard. Lieutenant Irvine and L. M. H. Washington, however, were two of the guards." The original muster rolls, he says, were "burned in the Adjutant

[14] Miss Mable Pendleton, **History of Bell County,** (Prize Essay), p. 5.

General's office." His rolls of the two companies here follow.[15]

Captain Bird's Company

Men in battle: Captain John Bird, commanding; Second Lieutenant William R. Allen; Second Sergeant William P. Sharp; First Corporal William P. Bird; Privates William Baggett, Milton Bradford, Thomas Bradford, Daniel Bradley, James Brookshire, Nathan Brookshire, (chosen to command after Bird was killed), Eli Foreman, Timan C. Fort, H. M. C. Hall, Warren Hastings, Geo. W. Hensell, James Hensley, William Hensley, J. H. Hughes. A. J. Ivey, Edward Jocelyn, Lewis Kleberg, Benjamin P. Kyger, T. W. Lightfoot, Green E. Lynch, Jesse E. Nash, A. G. Parker, G. W. Pentecost, Jonathan Peters, William Peters, E. Rector, Joseph H. Stack, John D. Thompson, one unknown.

Men left in charge of Little River Fort: Joseph S. Marsh, F. G. Woodward.

Men not in battle, including the guard, prisoners, and those left at Fort Milam: First Lieutenant James Irvine; Second Corporal George Allen; Privates John Atkinson, William Ayers, Joseph H. Barnard, C. Beisner, Joshua O. Blair, William Blair, Jackson E. Burdick, Stephen Goodman, M. J. Hannan, W. Hickson, Wm. J. Hodge, Lewis L. Hunter, J. D. Marshall, James Martin, Joseph McGuines, Neil McCrarey, James M. Moreton, J. W. Stoddard, Henry Verm, Bela Vickery, Charles Waller, L. M. H. Washington.

Lieutenant Evan's Company

Men in the battle: First Sergeant William H. Weaver; Second Corporal Samuel A. Blain; Privates Thomas Gay, Charles M. Gevin, W. W. Hannan, Thomas S. Menefee, Robert Mills, H. A. Powers, James W. Robinett, Thomas Robinett, John Roman, William Winkler.

Men not in the battle, left at Fort Milam: First Lieutenant William G. Evans; Second Sergeant J. O. Butler; First Corporal Thomas Brown; Musician A. Bettinger; Privates Charles Ball, Grafton H. Boatler, Littleton Brown,

---

[15] A comparison of the two rolls discloses that of the thirty-five men named in Lieutenant Brookshire's report, seven are not in Major Brown's list; and that of the forty-five men named in Major Brown's roll seventeen are not included in Lieutenant Brookshire's report.

D. W. Collins, Joseph Flippen, Abner Frost, James Hickey, Hezekiah Joiner, John Kirk, Jarrett Menefee, Saban Menefee, Thomas A. Menefee, Thomas J. Miller, Frederick Pool, Jarrett Ridgeway, Washington Rhodes, John St. Clair, John Weston.

Casualties

Killed in battle and left on field: Captain John Bird, Sergeant William H. Weaver, Thomas Gay,[16] (or Gray), Jesse E. Nash.

Mortally wounded in battle and died at Little River Fort: H. M. C. Hall.

Wounded in battle and recovered: Second Lieutenant William R. Allen, Private George W. Hensell.

Some weeks later a squad of rangers from Nashville came to the scene of the Bird's Creek fight for the purpose of burying Captain Bird and the other dead. Having attended to this duty, they proceeded up the east side of Leon River in pursuit of Indians and while encamped for the night on the banks of a small creek, their horses stampeded during the night and all ran away. From this incident the creek took its name and is to this day known as "Stampede Creek."

5. *Indian Raid at Tenoxtitlan,* 1841; *Fort Bryant,* 1841(?)

In May, 1841, Indians came into the village of Tenoxtitlan, killed a Mr. Campbell, who was sleeping on a bed on a porch in front of Mr. Joseph Rowland's house, stole the horses of Mr. Rowland that were tied to the posts of the porch and other horses in the village and in the neighborhood and got away, though hotly pursued next morning by posses of the citizens. Judge Rufus Y. King, late of Belton, then a boy, was spending the night at Mr. Rowland's and was sleeping in the same bed (next to the wall of the house) in which Mr. Campbell was killed, but he was not molested. An arrow was shot clear through Mr.

---

[16] William P. Bird gives the name of this man as **Gray.** Letter to **Belton Journal,** cited **ante.** But it is given as **Gay** in Lieutenant Brookshire's report, and that name appears in Brown's list of Evan's company engaged in the battle, while Gray does not appear on either roll.

Campbell's body and he made one lunge from the bed and fell dead. This, of course, aroused young King from his deep sleep and he gave the alarm.[17]

A place of some importance in those days was on Little River, near the present line of Milam and Bell Counties, and known as Bryant's Fort. Colonel Ben Bryant and his brother, Lafayette Bryant, moved from Tenoxtitlan with their families and settled there between 1840 and 1842, and, probably, two or three other families, for mutual protection, gathered around them. They built a blockhouse and prepared for defensive operations against attacks by Indians. Mr. John C. Reid, our first County Clerk, had, in connection with Mr. Wm. G. Bayne of Wheelock, a store at Fort Bryant in 1847.[18] In later years (the seventies) a village or trading place was established not far from the old fort, under the name of Bryant's Station, with a store or two, post office, blacksmith shop, Masonic Lodge, etc. It disappeared with the coming of the railroad to Rogers in 1880.

6. *Fight between Captain Ross and "Big Foot,"* 1842

In 1842, Captain Shapleigh P. Ross, then living near the present site of Cameron, headed a small party of settlers in pursuit of a band of Comanches who had stolen some horses there the night before. They pursued the Indians to "The Knobs," in the lower part of the present Bell County, near Reed's Lake, where they suddenly came upon the Indians skinning a buffalo. Both sides had been in a rain and the powder in their flint lock guns and holster pistols was wet. A fierce struggle ensued, in which an Indian was killed by Mr. Bryant. Ross saw "Big Foot," the Comanche Chief, coming toward him full speed on horseback. He threw one of his holster pistols, striking "Big Foot" on the shoulder and was about to strike him with the butt of his rifle, when another Indian rushed up behind Ross and was in the act of cleaving Ross's head off when young Shapleigh Woolfork (Ross's nephew) quickly came to his rescue

[17] Judge Rufus Y. King in **"Old Settlers Association of Bell County"** for 1902, p. 5.
[18] Mrs. Hanna Smithwick Donaldson in **"Old Settlers Association of Bell County"** for 1904, p. 25.

and knocked the Indian off his horse, at the same time falling from his own horse. The Indian mounted behind Big Foot, and both dashed off, attempting escape, hotly pursued by Ross and Woolfork on their horses. Suddenly the Indians came to the steep bluff of a ravine, went over it head-long and were soon floundering in the mire and water. Woolfork came next and over the bluff he went too. Ross managed to halt his horse at the brink, dismounted, jumped down the bluff and into the mêlée, to prevent the Indians from double-teaming on Woolfork. Ross and Big Foot looked death into each other's faces. They drew their hunters knives. Big Foot, bedecked in war paint, his long plaited hair hanging down his back, lunged at Ross, but his foot slipped, he missed Ross and fell. Before he could rise, Ross seized him by the hair with his left hand and drove his knife to the heart with his right. Thus ended Big Foot. Woolfork, meanwhile, had dispatched the other Indian and the contest was over.

When General Sam Houston became President of the Republic for the second time, December, 1841, he reversed the Indian policy of Lamar in favor of pacific measures. But it was more than a year, on March 31, 1843, before his agents were able to get together the chiefs of the Caddoes, Ionies, Anadarkoes, Keechi, Wacoes, Tawakanoes and a few other small tribes on Tawakano (or Tehuacana) Creek, east of the present site of Waco, and conclude a treaty of peace with them. Later in the spring of that year Houston sent Joseph C. Eldredge, Superintendent of Indian Affairs, at the head of a commission to visit the other wild tribes on the upper Trinity and Red River, especially the Comanches, and to induce them to meet at Bird's Fort on the West Fork of the Trinity, near the present city of Fort Worth, there to negotiate a general peace. The Comanches and Wichitas did not come in; but the other tribes attended and a general treaty was agreed upon, September 29, 1843. One important feature of this treaty was a provision that trading houses should be located above the settlements and a line established just below the trading houses, running generally from northeast to southwest to divide the country of the Indians from that of the whites. No whites were to go above the line nor any Indians below, except with the permission of the President. This treaty was approved by the Texas senate on January 31, 1844.

During 1844 President Houston continued his efforts to make peace with the Comanches. Finally, they came in to a great council on Tawakano (Tehuacana) Creek, where, on October 9, 1844, another treaty, similar to the one of the previous year, was agreed to by all the tribes. President Houston himself attended this council. In the fall of 1845 two other councils were held with the tribes of the northern frontier at "Trading Post No. 2," some ten or twelve miles east of where Waco now stands and north of the Brazos, and the treaties of 1843 and 1844 were reaffirmed.[19]

[19] For a more detailed accout of these treaties, see Anna Muckleroy, "The Indian Policy of the Republic of Texas," in **Southwestern Historical Quarterly**, XXVI, 184-205.

CHAPTER V

THE ADVANCE OF THE MILAM COUNTY FRONTIER, 1843-1850

1. *Pioneer Settlers Return to Upper Little River*

It must not be assumed that the peace treaties with the Indians removed danger from the frontier or made the way safe for settlements. The situation was greatly improved, since the tribes no longer raided in large bodies below the lines of posts; but small groups of young warriors whom the chiefs could not control sometimes slipped down into the edge of settlements to hunt a scalp when the opportunity presented itself. Major Erath tells of four Indians coming down to the Monroe settlement, just below the present town of Cameron, in the fall of 1844 and stealing some horses. They were overtaken by the whites and killed.[1] Such things continued to occur all along the frontier for many years.

The general situation was ameliorated very much by the increase of settlements in the lower part of Milam County and in the newly created county of Robertson east of the Brazos, especially those about Wheelock and old Franklin (not the Franklin of today). There were some families about the Falls of the Brazos and at the new Fort Milam, near the present town of Marlin. On lower Little River the settlements were increasing, and on Walker's Creek and the lower portion of Pond Creek a few families were maintaining themselves.

Thus the way was gradually opening for the colonists who had been in the present Bell County in 1834 and 1835— the real first settlers, the pioneers of Bell County, who had been forced out twice in 1836 and again finally in 1837—to return to their abandoned cabins. And one by one, a few of these families drifted back. Some, however, had become firmly established in the lower country; others had sold out their colonial claims; others still had been called by death; and, so, several of them never returned. But later on many of their descendants came to join the citizenship of the county.

[1] "Memoirs of Major George B. Erath" in **Southwestern Historical Quarterly**, XXVII, 34.

It is very difficult, in the absence of documentary records, to follow the returning footsteps of these people and to fix the approximate dates of their arrival or of the coming of the new adventurers. The principal sources are family traditions and the memories of old settlers who were honest to the core but, unfortunately, not very accurate in the matter of names and dates. If there be any errors in the account which follows, the writer must beg the indulgence of the reader; in the cause of accuracy he has exhausted every source known to him, and he has endeavored to record only such facts as seem well authenticated.

Probably the first of the upper Little River settlers to return was Captain Goldsby Childers. As we have previously seen, he had settled temporarily in Burleson County in 1837, but on August 11, 1840, he wrote from old Nashville to President Mirabeau B. Lamar,

"I have made a crop of corn on little river this year and am now ready to move my family on my land 12 miles below Little River Fort but hearing that station is now evacuated I am at a loss to Know what to do. I can't possibly settle there without some assurance of protection and there are at least twenty families in the same situation (that is) they haven't made corn but they fully intend to settle their lands this fall if there was any protection given them by the Government.

Your obt. sevt.

G. Childers.

P. S. I hope your Excellency will let me know as quick as possible what I am to depend on."[2]

No reply from Lamar has been found, but it seems quite unlikely that, in view of the turbulent state of the frontier for the next two or three years, Childers would have taken his family back to this exposed position. Nor is there any evidence that any of the "twenty families" he mentioned ventured into the same section during that period. If family tradition is correct, it was not until 1843 that Goldsby Childers, with his sons Robert, Prior, and William P., a mere boy, returned to permanent possession of their old deserted cabin. In 1844 Robert Childers brought thither his young wife, Adaline Moore Childers.[3] In 1844 or 1845 Moses Griffin and his family, including his grown son, Williamson Griffin, returned to their old home at the Three Forks; and

[2] **The Papers of Mirabeau Buonaparte Lamar,** III 430-431.
[3] Statement dictated to Geo. W. Tyler by Mrs. Adaline Moore Childers, widow of Robert Childers.

in 1845 Michael Reed and his sons Jefferson, William, John B. and Jake, came back to their abandoned home on Little River. These, with the family of Benjamin Bryant, already mentioned as living a little further down on Little River, seem to have constituted the entire white population of the present Bell County when the Republic of Texas was admitted into the great American Union as a state, December 29, 1845.

2. *Annexation of Texas to the United States and the War with Mexico*

Ever since the Revolution from Mexico most Texans had desired the annexation of their country to the United States. The majority of them were natives of that country and were proud of it, and they felt that under the Stars and Stripes they would be safer from Mexico and the Indians, while increased immigration would insure the more rapid development of the new country. The question of annexation had been a political issue in the United States for years, and in 1844 it became the dominant one, with the Whigs opposing and the Democrats favoring it. The Democrats won, electing James K. Polk to the presidency over Henry Clay; and on March 1, 1845, a joint resolution of the United States Congress providing for the annexation of Texas was approved by the retiring President, John Tyler. Acceptance or rejection rested with the people of Texas. Thereupon President Anson Jones, of Texas, on May 5, 1845, issued two proclamations: one, calling the Congress of the Republic into session to approve the terms of the joint resolution of the Congress of the United States; and the other, calling a general election for delegates to a constitutional convention to assemble at Austin on July 4 to vote on annexation and to draft a constitution for the contemplated State of Texas. Both bodies met and accepted the terms offered by the United States, and the convention soon presented a new state constitution which was ratified by popular vote in October, 1845. The Congress of the United States accepted this constitution on December 29, 1845, which day the Supreme Court of the United States has declared to be the true date of the annexation of Texas. On February 16, 1846, the First Legislature of Texas assembled at Austin, the new Governor, James Pinckney Henderson, was inaugurated, and the Republic of Texas passed out of existence.

The area claimed by Texas at this time extended from the Sabine on the east to the Rio Grande on the southwest and west to the source of that river, and from the Gulf on the southeast to the Red River and west of the 100th meridian of longitude, to the Arkansas River on the north. It included portions of the present states of New Mexico, Colorado, Kansas and Oklahoma. But Mexico disputed the claims of Texas to the region south and west of the Nueces and Medina Rivers and prepared to hold it More than that, Mexico had never given up her claims to the whole of Texas and had declared that annexation to the United States meant war.

Anticipating trouble, President Polk sent General Zachary Taylor with a small army to Corpus Christi in the fall of 1845. Early in 1846 he ordered him to the Rio Grande. When he arrived near the present town of Brownsville he was met by a Mexican army and the war was on. The story of the War with Mexico lies outside the scope of this work, and it is necessary only to say that the volunteers from Texas gave a good account of themselves under both Generals Taylor and Scott. When peace came with the treaty of Guadalupe-Hidalgo in February, 1848, Mexico not only conceded the boundary of the Rio Grande but gave up a large portion of her northern territory.

3. Cameron, the New County Seat; Better Protection from the Indians

As already stated, the population of early Milam County was concentrated in the lower limits, about Nashville and Tenoxtitlan, for protection against the Indians. With the exception of a brief period at Caldwell in 1840, and that seemingly without clear authority of law, the county seat had been at Nashville ever since the organization of the county under the laws of the Republic. But immigrants had begun pouring into the section above Nashville as soon as the peace treaties were made with the Indians, 1844-1845, and with the shift in the center of the county's population there was a demand for the relocation of the county seat. An act of the First Legislature, approved April 4, 1846, provided for such a relocation and appointed seven commissioners—Wm. D. Thompson, Isaac Standifer, Winfred Bayley, J. Turnham, Daniel Munroe, Benjamin Bryant, and Augustus Sullivan—to select the location, purchase land for the town, name it and survey and sell the lots. They selected a place which they named Cameron, in honor of Captain Ewen Cameron, a Mier prisoner who had been shot in Mexico in 1843 by order of Santa Anna. The records of Milam County were removed to Cameron as soon as the necessary county buildings could be erected. The new town attracted a number of people, among whom were many who later became residents of Bell County.

The Congress of the Republic of Texas, by the Registration Act of December 20, 1836, had authorized the clerks of the county courts to record in their offices all deeds and other instruments relating to lands situated within their respective counties. Therefore, prior to the organization of Bell County and the opening of its recording office in August, 1850, all such instruments affecting lands situated within the present county of Bell were recorded at Cameron. There, also, all suits concerning the same were brought and the final judgments entered in the court records. After the organization of Bell County, and before a fire in the spring of 1874 destroyed the court house of Milam County and all its old records, many of these papers relating to Bell County were re-recorded in Belton.

The founding of Cameron was a proof of confidence in the development of this frontier region. Annexation to the United States and, even more, the victorious termination of the war with Mexico, not only drew more attention to Texas but gave prospective immigrants greater confidence in the future of the country. The lure of cheap and fertile lands in this attractive new West was felt throughout the older states, and particularly in the South. A new and steady wave of immigration set in to the country of the Brazos; and settlers boldly brought their families up the Little River and its western tributaries.

Although trouble with the Indians had not ceased, the situation was becoming less dangerous. The smaller tribes along the Brazos, decimated by war and disease, found themselves no longer able to cope with the ever-increasing numbers of the white man. The Lipans and Tonkaways, reduced to a feeble remnant of their former strength, became allies of the whites. The Caddoes and their associated tribes sought peace as they were crowded into new lands further up the Brazos. The Wacoes professed friendship. A company of Texas rangers was stationed near the Waco village on the Brazos. In the spring of 1846 the United States Government had sent into Texas two commissioners, P. M. Butler and M. G. Lewis, to treat with the Indians. They succeeded in making a treaty with a number of tribes, including some of the Comanches and Kiowas, at a great council held on the upper Brazos near Comanche Peak and thus removed some of the danger to which the frontier was subjected while the ranger companies were drawn to Mexico during the next two years. Although the wild tribes on the western plains, that is, the western Comanches, did not always keep the peace, those nearer the settlements were less disposed to give trouble than formerly. Indian agents, appointed by the United States, went out among the tribes to make friends with them. Fortunately for the settlers, the Comanches found ample diversion in plundering the border states of Mexico and did not often come down into the Cross Timbers except in the winters. In 1849, after the War with Mexico had ended, the United States army took over the task of giving protection to the frontier and established a chain of posts from the Red River to the Rio Grande along the line of Ft. Worth, Ft. Graham on the Brazos, Ft. Gates on the upper Leon, Ft. Grogan on the Colorado, and Ft. Martin Scott at Fredericksburg. Although these army posts proved inadequate to check the occasional swift forays of the Comanches into the settlements, they instilled a measure of confidence into the land-seeking newcomers who continually pushed their way up the streams which flowed into the Brazos from the west. In 1849 the new town of Waco was laid out by George B. Erath at the site of an old Indian village on land belonging to Jacob de Cordova. In the future Bell County little groups of settlers had moved up above the Three Forks on the Salado, the Lampasas, the Nolan and the Leon. Far up on the latter stream a small settlement had begun to grow up around Ft. Gates, later to become Gatesville.

4. *The New Settlements*

In 1846 Captain Goldsby Childers, and his son Prior Childers, principally on the account of the poor health of the latter, left their old home on Little River and went up among the rough hills of the Lampasas River. They pitched their camp at a bold spring flowing into a ravine emptying into the Lampasas on the south bank and they called the place "Spicewood Spring." It is about one-half mile above the present bridge on the Austin road. Thither they brought up from their home below a stock of cattle and hogs and turned them loose on the unlimited and unoccupied range, where the grass and the mast were fine. They threw up a log cabin and "batched it" for quite a while. At this time there was not a settlement above Three Forks.

From 1847 to 1849 several more of the original colonists of Little River returned to their former homes in that community. Among these were: John Fulcher and family (1847 or 1848); Mrs. Catherine (Goldsby) Stickney and husband, E. Lawrence Stickney, with her sister, Caroline Childers (1847); Jesse Mumford, David Mumford, and George Dougherty and their families (1848); Orville Tyler (1848); John R. Craddock and his wife, Amanda (Childers) Craddock (1848); and Mrs. Margaret Taylor, again a widow, with her children, Stephen and William Frazier, Seymour and J. Wilson Taylor, Caroline (Frazier) Chapman and her husband, George Chapman, and Mrs. Taylor's stepson, Josiah Taylor.[4]

Around the Fulcher home were grouped several newly arrived families — those of William Stephens, Nathaniel Shields, Mitchell Garrison and others—so that the community was known as "Fulcher's Colony." On the Salado Creek were James K. Blair, C. B. Robert, E. N. Goode, Mr. Kuykendall, Frank Morrill, Reese Morrill, Samuel Wheat, and Archibald Willingham, at the Salado Springs. At Childers Mill on the Lampasas were Joel D. Blair, Goldsby Childers, Robert Childers, James M. Cross, T. J. Neighbors, James Shaw (at old "Shaw Crossing" just below the bridge on the present Austin road), E. Lawrence Stickney, Orville T. Tyler and others. Dred R. Hill and W. F. Hill, about this time, settled on the Leon, and Joseph Bishop, Josiah Hart and others in the Cedar Creek section. John B. Willis and William Connell were on Darr's Creek. Many others came into our territory during 1848 and 1849, as will appear in

[4] Statement to George W. Tyler by his mother, Mrs. Caroline (Childers) Tyler.

the roll of citizens to be given presently, but one can not say just when each of them arrived.

The situation of the settlers of this new community is quaintly described by the late Mr. Wm. E. Blair, from whom we quote: "Now these people had to have bread to eat * * * and it was forty miles to Cameron, the nearest place for breadstuff for sale, and corn meal couldn't be had at any price and flour was twelve pounds to the dollar, * * * but just in the nick of time, old Johny Pennington moved in from Illinois and settled at the Sulphur Spring on the "Salou" (Salado Creek, the Spanish pronunciation, Sal-ä'-o, having been retained) who had a steel mill to grind corn with and bade everybody to come and grind. We boys used to take our sacks of corn on our shoulders and wade in the creek all the way except where it was too deep to wade. This was on account of snakes and ticks, there being no roads running up and down the streams at that time—all of the buffalo trails ran cross-wise."[5]

Sometime in 1848 Robert Childers and his brother-in-law, Thomas W. Walden, damned up a bold spring branch on the south side of the Lampasas and built a little corn mill operated by an over-shot water wheel—a tub mill affair —but which was sufficient for the requirements of the sparse settlement about it. Mr. Blair says that on the day the water was turned on and the mill started all the neighborhood came and spread a picnic on the ground and made quite an affair of it. As this crude enterprise in the wilds of this upper country became the nucleus of a considerable, though temporary, settlement of people for those times, the humorous account prepared by M. H. Shanklin, whose father, Mr. Gordon W. Shanklin, subsequently acquired the site and rebuilt and modernized the mill, is here given

"The first settlement on the Lampasas River in Bell County, so far as our information goes, was a cabin built by Captain Goldsby Childers and his son, Prior, in 1846 at a spring on the south side of the river between the present bridge and the present Shanklin Mill. Shortly after this, Robert Childers and Tom Waldon put up a little tub-mill where the Shanklin Mill now stands. They built a temporary dam and race and used the water to run their mill, which consisted of a hopper, one pair of burrs and two

[5] W. B. Blair, "Reminiscences." (MS.)

large barrels or hogshead, all on an open wood frame, and a buffalo hide over the hopper, and one over each barrel, (to keep the wild turkeys from eating up the corn and meal in their absence) constituted the only roof or covering for this outfit. The only dependence for the pioneers at that time for bread was the old steel mill run by hand * * * and this water mill was a great boon to the settlement. By running day and night it is said to have ground eight bushels of corn in twenty-four hours. The neighbors (and this included those living as far as twenty-five or thirty miles down the river) would bring shelled corn and exchange it for meal. Life was too short to wait for the grinding. It is said that Bob Childers (afterward so well known as "Uncle Bob") knew so well the speed and capacity of this mill that he was in the habit of filling up the hopper with corn and going home or hunting or fishing and then returning at the right time to refill it—whether day or night—and the legend further goes that he even went as far as Cameron on business. David Moore, son of our uncle Lovick Moore, was miller at one time and when the dam broke and the outfit got to working badly, a Mormon (whose name was Tony) was employed to repair it and run it.* * * The set of burrs were cut out by Gus Kerr from stone obtained in Washington County, Texas, where they were first operated a while by Kerr, who afterward gave them to Tom Walden and Bob Childers. The latter sold the place * * * about 1849, but these burrs, it seems, did not go with the mill site, and after being set up at old Fort Gates in 1850 and at Bob Childers' place on Elm Creek in 1854, they finally fell into the hands of old man Copeland, at Gena, in Falls County, who ran them until he died and the old burrs are said to be now lying at the bottom of a tank where the Mill fell into decay:"[6] The little contraption was known at first as "Childers Mill."

Mr. James M. Cross later took Walden's place in the mill, which then took the name of "Cross and Childers Mill." Since its acquisition by Mr. Gordon W. Shanklin,

[6] M. H. Shanklin: "Early Days on the Lampasas," **Old Settlers Association of Bell County for 1902,** p. 18. Mr. W. B. Blair, in his "Reminiscences," says that these burrs were set up and operated by Robert Childers at the old Childers home on Little River before he moved to the site on the Lampasas.

in 1856, it has been known as the Shanklin Mill, though it ceased operation more than thirty years ago.

The mill site comprised twenty-three acres of land purchased by Robert Childers from E. S. C. Robertson, fronted on the south bank of the Lampasas and lay astride the small stream which, fed by several large springs, furnished the motive power. The land and the water have in recent years been utilized for an irrigated garden, for which the place is well adapted.

The little mill made a center around which this small community—then the extreme frontier settlement in central Texas—gathered for mutual protection against the Indians. Hither came all travelers and prospectors, either to locate here or to obtain information and protection, while investigating the adjacent country in which they were seeking to establish their new homes. Mr. James M. Cross sold the place he had settled (later known as the Brookshire place) to Mr. Joel D. Blair and improved another (known as the "Bois d'arcs") in the present Elm Grove neighborhood. Mr. T. A. Supple put up a little store, which he later sold to Mr. John M. Payne. The latter moved the goods to Nolanville when that village was located and was the first merchant of the new county seat of Bell County.

6 The First Schools

Recurring to the settlements on the lower Salado Creek and at Three Forks, the people there, about 1849, employed Mr. E. N. Goode to teach a school in the residence lately occupied by Mr. Kuykendall, who had moved away. It was situated on the bank of the creek opposite where Mr. J. Morton Smith erected a water mill and gin in the seventies. On the retirement of Mr. Goode, a Mr. Edrington taught the little school. The roll of patrons and pupils is worthy, it seems to us, of preservation. Three or four of them are still living; the others have passed away. But many of their descendants are among our present citizenship; others are scattered over the country. Here is the nearly complete roll:[7] Children of James K. Blair—William B., Joel D. Jr.,

---

[7] From statements dictated to the author by John M. Roberts and the late C. Bent Roberts and "Reminiscences" (MS.) of the late Mr. Wm. B. Blair.

John; Children of James M. Cross—William B., Francis Marion, Seluda (Mrs. Wm. Wills); children of Moses Griffin —Joseph, Avery, James, David C., Jane (Mrs. Tom Duncan), Caroline (Mrs. Sam L. Hasley), Belle (Mrs. William Perkins), Cornelia (Mrs. Eugene Rich), and Mary Williams, niece of Mrs. Griffin; children of Reese Morrill—DeKalb, Green, Evaline; children of Cornelius B. Roberts—William, Nathan T., David, John M., Mary (Mrs. Wm. B. Blair), C. Bent Jr., James T.; children of Samuel Wheat—George, Susie; children of Granger McDaniel—Stacy, and Moncie.

The people about the Childers Mill neighborhood on the Lampasas induced Mr. E. Lawrence Stickney (a lawyer from Mobile, Alabama, who had, as a youth in 1836, cast his fortunes with the colonists of Texas) to teach a school at this place. This was also about 1849. They had erected a small clap-board building on the bluff, overlooking the mill and the river, which was used for all public purposes. Here Stickney also taught a writing school both for the children and the grown-ups. Mr. Henry B. Elliott taught a singing school, "the four-note system," in this building. Here was taught the first Sunday School in Bell County territory. And here Rev. Henry C. Cook (Methodist) preached and Rev. James E. Ferguson, our first Methodist Circuit Rider, warned the people "to flee from their sins and from the wrath to come." Here is a partial roll of the patrons and pupils of this little school:[8] Children of C. B. Roberts—Mary (Mrs. Wm. B. Blair); children of John Bowles—Doke, Pete, David C., a girl (Mrs. John McDowell); children of Goldsby Childers—Caroline (Mrs. O. T. Tyler), William P.; child of A. T. McCorcle—Henry T., child of T. J. Neighbors—T. J. Jr.; children of E. Lawrence Stickney— Richard, Mary (Mrs. John P. Key).

Mr. W. B. Blair speaks of another school of later date at the Childers Mill, taught by a Mr. Allen, of Williamson County, who was employed by James K. Blair and John Bowles to teach it at $20.00 per month, they to collect the tuition from the other patrons.[9] He also claimed that Goode's school, on the Salado, was the first, but the evidence of himself and others, taken all together, indicates that this school and the one taught by Stickney at Childers Mill were

---

[8] From statement dictated to the author by the late C. Bent Roberts and other sources.
[9] W. B. Blair, "Reminiscences."

The Advance of the Milam County Frontier

about contemporaneous and that they were opened either in 1848 or 1849, most probably in the latter year.

As has been stated, Fort Gates had been established on the upper Leon by the U. S. Army in 1849. At that time the site was in Milam County, later (1850) in Bell County and lastly (1854) in Coryell County. The first garrison consisted of one hundred cavalrymen under command of Captain James G. Snelling. Among the officers was Lieutenant Horace Haldeman, who later became a prominent citizen of Bell County and a gallant artillery officer in the Confederate Army.[10]

At the solicitation of the supply department, Orville T. Tyler, Colonel Wm. C. Dalrymple and Henry McKay took the contract to furnish corn and hay for the Post, and Robert Childers that of supplying them with beef on foot.

The family of Captain Goldsby Childers, Richard G. Grant, Job Friley, and some others, whose names are not available, removed to Fort Gates. The military authorities there built good comfortable houses for all and, as some new immigrants also came, the fort became somewhat of a civilian settlement, as well as a military garrison, and they were all living there when Bell County was organized. These houses were built of hewn logs, barked, the spaces neatly filled with lime mortar, and they looked very nice. The officers' houses and soldiers' barracks were built the same way. Being of perishable material, however, they have long since decayed and disappeared and the site is now in cultivation as a farm.

In 1853 the line of posts was moved farther west and Fort Graham, Fort Gates and the others were superseded by Fort Belknap, Fort Phantom Hill, Fort Chadbourne, Fort McKavitt and others, several of which were occupied until the beginning of the War between the States.

In complying with their contract, Tyler, Dalrymple and McKay installed a large train of wagons, drawn by oxen, and they bought corn down on Little River and on the Brazos and hauled it to the Fort. Their route became known as "the Old Corn Road" and was visible for many years.[11]

When the garrisons were moved these gentlemen con-

[10] J. H. Chrisman, "Early History of Coryell County," in **Proceedings of Old Settler's Association of Bell County, 1903,** pp. 38-39.
[11] **Ibid,** p. 42.

tinued to furnish corn to the troops at Forts Phantom Hill and Chadbourne, their route beyond Fort Gates being equally well known for a long time as "the Old Phantom Hill Road."[12]

When the War Department of the United States Government established the line of forts already mentioned, a military road was laid out from Austin *via* Georgetown, Salado Springs, the Childers Mill on Lampasas, the present site of Belton, crossing Leon at the present dam and thence on the high ridge to a point in the neighborhood of the present town of Moody, where it forked, one road going to Fort Graham and the other to Fort Gates. Along this road the soldiers marched to take their stations at these garrisons and all of their supplies except corn and hay, were hauled in large military wagons drawn by mules. It was for many years known to the old timers as the "Military Road."

Later a short cut-off was laid out by the military authorities from Fort Gates to Georgetown by way of Sugar Loaf Mountain, on Cow House, and Comanche Gap, on Lampasas.

At this time there was practically no farming in the Bell County territory, except on some small fields on Little River. The people engaged principally in stockraising—cattle, horses and hogs, which ran loose upon the range and cost the owners nothing. The best unimproved land brought only fifty cents per acre.

The country was full of deer, bear, antelope, turkey and other wild game, and the streams abounded in fish. The prairies were covered with green grass ("old sedge") four or five feet high, waving like a wheat field, and the whole country was profusely and gorgeously decorated with variegated wild flowers—the lupin (blue bonnet), verbena, Indian plume, sunflower, lilies of all colors, violets, plum blossoms, haw blossoms—and it was beautiful.

6. *Indians Again*

During the period from 1844 to 1850 Indians, friendly and hostile, made frequent visits into and near the settlements in the Bell County territory. The friendly tribes

---

[12] F. M. Cross, **Early Days in Central Texas,** pp. 14-18.

The Advance of the Milam County Frontier

were petty thieves and beggars, who pitched their camps in or about the settlements and depredated upon the white people. The hostile bands made periodical raids into the settlements and along the route of travel, stealing horses and occasionally committing murder. Our traditions mention many of these events of which authentic accounts are not available.

During the last years of the forties—say about 1849—a band of about sixty friendly Tonkaway Indians camped at the Salado Springs. They frequently visited the homes of settlers residing down the Salado Creek and stole small articles of food, clothing and household effects and greatly frightened the women and children. Finally a committee of citizens politely but firmly requested them to leave and they promptly did so.[13]

One of the last important raids made by the Indians in this territory, prior to the organization of Bell County, is related by the late Mr. Wm. B. Blair. In 1849 the horses of Mr. John Williams were stolen by Indians at the Falls of the Brazos while he was moving on his way west from Arkansas. A man known as "Cow House" Taylor and young John Potter, while encamped on the Cow House Creek near the mouth of Taylor's Branch, saw a squad of Indians driving a large herd of horses up the valley. Potter was sent to notify the settlers below and a posse of men and youths were soon on the trail, consisting of William Armstrong (District Surveyor), Joel D. Blair, Jas. K. Blair, Wm. B. Blair, Fayette Bryant, Jas. M. Cross, Riley Cross, Thos. J. Neighbors, John Potter, Jack Shaw, Wm. ("Camel-Back") Smith, Wm. Smith, Jr., and Orville T. Tyler. The trail was struck and followed to the headwaters of the Leon River, where the posse was met by Lieutenant Geo. E. Pickett and a squad of United States troops, with pack-mules and Mexicans to drive them, sent out from Fort Gates. Lieutenant Pickett reported that he had found the Indians encamped in a bottom on a branch and charged them with his full force, Mexicans excepted, and recovered all the horses except nine head on which the Indians made their escape while the charging party were breaking their way through a dense thicket. The Indians were making saddles out of sedge grass and ornamenting the tails and

---

[13] Reminiscences of Mr. John M. Roberts, MS. (His date for this was 1851.)

foretops of the horses with some very rare and beautiful feathers. The meeting of the two pursuing parties came very near being a tragedy. The citizen posses were down in a valley, following the Indian trail and discovered Lieutenant Pickett's squad up on a shinoak mountain, and mistaking them for the Indians looking for a place to descend the mountain, charged them at first sight and fired several shots, but the two parties recognized each other before anyone was hurt. When the soldiers looked about for their Mexicans they found that the latter had deserted their packs and hidden themselves in a deep ravine. The two parties returned together to Fort Gates, where the recaptured horses were left and they were later delivered to Mr. Williams at Georgetown.[14]

Illustrative of conditions about this period some experiences in 1846 related by Colonel Hermon Aiken are here introduced.

Major Ben Bryant, at Bryant's Fort on Little River, J. Mercer on the San Gabriel and Captain Merrill on Brushy Creek, held the outposts of the settlements, at that date. All "had their houses strongly picketed in." Colonel Aiken journeyed from the Brazos toward Austin by way of Mercer's and Merrill's. "After a hard day's ride," he says, "occasionally secreting myself from Indians seen in the distance hunting buffalo, which blackened the face of the prairies, about one hour after night I arrived at the tall picket fence of Captain N. Merrill. All was silent and dark. I hailed. After some time the Captain asked who was there. Finding that I belonged to the white tribe he came out and opened his gate and admitted me. Had my horse put in a strong picket stable, cared for and locked in. * * * He told me that I was fortunate as the Comanches were watching about dark for him." The next morning Colonel Aiken went on, crossed Walnut Creek, and there took violently sick with a chill, followed by a very high fever. He got down, stripped and staked his horse, and there remained until early dawn the next morning and then proceeded toward Austin. Within two hundred yards of where he had thus lain ill and asleep from drowsiness a fresh trail was encountered, made by Indians driving a large bunch of horses. Later on he saw a posse of white men on the trail and at once knew that

[14] Reminiscences of the late Mr. Wm. B. Blair, MS.; also MS. Reminiscences of Mr. John M. Roberts, whose date for this episode was 1851.

they were in pursuit of the Indians. On arriving at Austin he learned this was true and that the Indians had stolen thirty head of horses ten miles below Austin. The posse "lost the trail and returned without the horses." Colonel Aiken considered it providential that the Indians, in passing so near, did not discover him and that his presence was not betrayed by his horse.[15]

He describes another episode thus: "In December 1846, being in Austin and desirous of examining the country in a northeast direction, the San Gabriel, Salado, etc., and down Little River, I supplied myself with some provisions and set out. Nothing of particular note occurred until I was warned by a cold norther to turn my back to it and make for Bryant's Station. When within about eight miles in the Post Oak woods on the south side of Little River, a bleak cold cloudy day, I suddenly came upon a large encampment of Comanche Indians.

"I felt that my life depended upon my coolness and sagacity. I was immediately ordered to 'vamoose.' I felt that my trusty derringers could do me no good with such numbers and to leave so suddenly would almost ensure a ball in my back and I would try a little stratagem. And having several land patents just issued from the Land Office upon parchment, a seal attached by a blue ribbon which looked very official, myself and horse tolerably well apparelled, I pulled out one of the patents. opened it, told the men around me as best I could that I wanted to see the chief, mentioning over the names of Sam Houston, Burleson and others that I supposed they were familiar with. They pointed out his tent. As I rode up to his tent he came out and ordered me to 'vamoose.' I did not heed him but rode up and handed him the open parchment, pointing out the name of Sam Houston and the great seal of the land office. A crowd of minor chiefs gathered around as they could not talk English and I but little Spanish. I could not make them understand my important mission. After some consultation they handed me the patent and again ordered me to 'vamose.' I put away my patent, buttoned up my coat, and started off as careless as possible. When I had got some timber between us I put spurs to my horse and did some very responsible riding and soon made the river. It was saddle

[15] Colonel Hermon Aiken, "Fireside Tales," in MS.

skirt deep, a swift current and I had to cross quartering up-stream. I did not consult the chances of my horse going down stream or any other danger. When about half way across I heard a yell in the bottom behind me. My horse took the fright, made the bank and another mile I was safe at Bryant's Station."[16]

Colonel Hermon Aiken relates that, in 1848, he and others (all residing presumably at Caldwell) planned a land prospecting tour to the head waters of the Cow House and the Leon, but the others for various reasons failed to get off and he made the trip alone, starting on horseback, with twenty days provisions in a wallet and a forty foot rope with which to "stake" his horse. Proceeding by slow and cautious rides, skirting the timber on the north side of the Leon, sometimes venturing to take the prairie from one point of timber to another, sometimes secreting himself in a ravine as a squad of hunters passed by, sleeping without fires, climbing hills, descending into valleys, selecting lands, with water, timber and all that was desirable, when he had the whole to choose from, at the end of twenty-five days he found himself one hundred forty miles from home and out of provisions. Filling his wallet with mineral specimens, he turned homeward, subsisting upon sweet grapes, plums etc. On the second morning of the return journey, he discovered, about two miles off, two Indians who appeared to be flanking him on the timber side. About noon he got into a deep dry branch, Stampede Creek, raked his wallet for a few crumbs, examined his fire arms and put them in first class order. He had twenty four rounds without reloading and did not fear a small force except from ambush. He had proceeded about one mile to a point of timber (the Alonzo Beeman place of later days) "when an athletic warrior, nearly naked, richly painted, his head decorated with feathers, his rifle cocked across his horse, charged out from behind a thicket," about fifty yards away. Colonel Aiken drew both holsters, wheeled his horse and had a sight upon the Indian in less than a minute, by which time the latter had approached within fifteen steps. Seeing that it would be fatal to raise his rifle the Indian began pleading for his life. In response to questions he said that he "was a Tonkawa, that his name was Lewis and that he was a

[16] Colonel Hermon Aiken, "Fireside Tales," MS.

big captain." Aiken replied that he "was Captain Aiken, a big little captain," and, though having him in his power, "would spare him if he would never molest a white man again." This was readily agreed to and their mutual faith was pledged by a division of Colonel Aiken's tobacco. The latter told Lewis "that he must go and not turn around" or he would be shot and thus the Indian took his departure. But Colonel Aiken realized his precarious situation as he was compelled to pass very near Indian villages or camps on Cedar Creek, Peppers Creek, and Bird's Creek, as he was not acquainted with the river bottoms and the meanderings of the streams and must take as direct a route as possible. Safely crossing Cedar Creek and attaining the highest ground to the south, (where he later resided when he wrote this sketch, 1851-1857), he could see various squads of Indians back in the prairie. Shaping his course to Pepper's Creek, he there saw a squad of Indians proceeding toward the war crossing of the Leon, the "Shallow Ford," where the Mexican war soldiers had crossed in 1846. He concealed himself in a ravine until they passed out of sight. Starting again he says he saw the largest droves of lobos (wolves) that he ever beheld, apparently over fifty, on the trail of the Indians and again he halted, as he feared so large a number. He crossed Bird's Creek between the Cater place and the Experimental Farm station, following a dim buffalo trail, camped for the night in a small opening in the dense thickets, hungry, thirsty, fatigued and sick. At daylight he resumed his journey and arrived at the home of Moses Griffin, who had recently returned to his colonial settlement near Three Forks. After a good breakfast for himself and his faithful steed, he proceeded to Cameron during that night and on the next day to his home to the astonishment of all, for he had been reported killed by the Tonkawas. He thus describes his appearance on arrival at home. "My dress was in ribbons, my pants torn off above the knees, each leg tied up in a pocket handkerchief, hat 'all a-come down' and beard of four weeks. It was difficult to know to what tribe I belonged."[17]

[17] Colonel Hermon Aiken, "Fireside Tales," MS.

CHAPTER VI

RESIDENTS OF BELL COUNTY IN 1850

Before describing the formal organization of Bell County under an Act of the Legislature, we shall attempt a difficult and somewhat delicate task; namely, to enumerate the people who constituted the citizenship of the county at the time of its organization in 1850. It should be interesting, not only to their descendants but to others of the present generation as well, to know the names, ages, and nativities of all the people who lived in the county when its corporate existence began.

There are no records from which this information can be completely and accurately obtained. The writer, through the courtesy of Mr. E. W. Winkler, of the University of Texas Library, has a complete copy of the United States Census of 1850[1] for Milam County, in which the people of Bell County are enumerated as citizens of Milam County. But their geographical locations are not shown on this census, and the problem is how to identify and segregate those who then resided *in the Bell County section* of Milam. The writer has bestowed much time and labor upon this problem and has exhausted every source of information available to him. His personal acquaintance with a large number of these people and his traditional knowledge of many more, acquired from his parents and others who were among that citizenship, have greatly aided him in making up the roll of the original Bell County population. A few people not shown on the Census of 1850 rolls, but known to him to have been here at the time, have been added. He also has, through Mr. Winkler's kindness, obtained a complete copy of the original census rolls of Bell County for 1860, which has aided him in many particulars.

The Census is followed as to the names, ages and nativities of those who were enumerated therein; but similar information concerning those whose names have been added has been derived from other sources. The geographical distribution of all these people is based upon what is believed to be authentic information, carefully checked and verified.

[1] Photostatic copies of the original rolls of 1850 and 1860 in the Census Bureau at Washington, D. C. were obtained for the Library of the University of Texas by Mr. E. W. Winkler and were loaned to the writer.

Residents of Bell County in 1850

Unless otherwise stated, the occupation of the head of each family, as well as of the unmarried man, was farming and stockraising. The number of slaves owned by each family or individual is added in parenthesis.

In the following enumeration, the groups under "I" include those who are known to have been living within Bell County at the date of its organization, August 5, 1850. Under "II" are grouped those whose presence within the county at that date is uncertain. If not present then, however, they came very soon afterwards.

At Childers' Mill (Now Shanklin's Mill) on the Lampasas

I

Joel D. Blair, 42, Tenn.; Fereba H., 26, Ky.; James S., 1, Texas; Marzie Riggs, 15, Tenn.

Dr. William D. Eastland, 24, Physician, Ala.

Archibald T. McCorcle, 37, Ga.; Caroline E. M. C., 23, La.; James A., 8, Texas; Levina R., 6, Texas; Whipple W., 1, Texas.

Thomas J. Neighbors, 33, S. C.; Lucy J., 28, Va.; Mary A., 6, Miss.; Frances, 4, Miss.; Joel, 3, Texas.

John M. Payne, 24, merchant, Tenn.

James Shaw, 45, S. C.; Mary, 40, Ky.; James J. 18, Ill.; Wickliff K., 13, Mo.; Mary E., 12, Ark.; America A., 10, Ark.; William W., 6, Ark.; Thomas J., 4, Texas; John A., 1, Texas.

William ("Camel-back") Smith, 47, N. C.; Milam, 17, Miss.; Ramson, 11, Texas.

E. Lawrence Stickney, 32, lawyer, Md.; Catherine M., 30, Ky.; Mary E., 11, Texas; William H., 10, Texas; Lydia, 8, Texas; Emma C., 6, Texas; James Francis, 2, Texas; Elizabeth Wood, 1, Texas.

Thomas A. Supple, 23, merchant, N. Y.

Thomas W. Walden, 45, Ga.; Matilda, 42, S. C.; Aaron, 17, Ala.; Ellen, 15 Ala.; Adaline 11, Texas; Francanna, 9, Texas.

Thomas A. Walden, 21, Ala.

Total, 44 whites.

II

John Bowles, 48, Miss.; Milly C., 42, Tenn.; Hiram R., 23, Ala.; James Frank, 21, Ala.; John B., 18, Ala.; Caroline, 15, Miss.; William, 13, Ala.; Greenville P., 12, Miss.; Emeine, 11, Miss.; David C., 10, Miss.; Maria, 8, Miss.

Joseph E. Townsend, 20, grocer, Tenn.; Mary, 17, Ala.

Total, 13 whites.

On the Salado Creek

William Bailey, 85, Va.

Ira E. Chalk, 24, N. C.; Phebe, 16, Ga.

Whitfield Chalk, 39, millwright, N. C.; Mary M., 17, Ga.; William T., 1, Texas; John W., 5 mos., Texas.

James M. Cross, 39, Tenn.; Lucy, 38, Va.; Riley, 21, Tenn.; William B., 18, Tenn.; Francis Marion 16, Miss.; Saluda, 13, Mo.; James M., Jr., 11, Mo.; Virgil A., 9, Mo.; Joshua, 7, Mo.; Ewing, 4, Texas.

Henry B. Elliott, 37, surveyor and farmer, Tenn.; Matilda, 28, Miss.; Sarah M., 2, Texas; Mary E., 1, Texas.

Edward N. Goode, 27, Va.

James Hash, 30, Ill.

William K. Karnes, 48, Tenn; Rebecca, 48, Tenn; Ellen M., 18, Ark; Narcissa H., 16, Ark.; Penelope, 13, Ark.; Annis O., 11, Ark.; William E., 8, Ark.; Alparitta, 3, Ark.

Cornelius B. Roberts, 43, Tenn.; Rhoda, 41, Ga.; William J., 20, Ala.; Nathan T., 19, Ala.; David P., 17, Ala.; John M., 15, Miss.; Mary A., 14, Miss.; Cornelius B., Jr., 12, Miss.; James T., 11, Miss.; Emily C., 9, Miss.; Abram M., 7, Miss.; Jeremiah J., 2, Texas; Jesse R., 4 mos., Texas.

Samuel Wheat, 62, Va.; Cynthia, 35, Ky.; James, 20, Ark.; John, 18, Ark.; Susanna, 15, Ark.; Samuel, 12, Ark.; George, 10, Ark.

Archibald Willingham, 61, Ga.; Eleanor, 55, Ga.; Marion, 36, Ga.; Alfred, 25, Ga.; Wilson, 20, Ga.; Sterling S., 16, Ga.

Total, 57 whites.

In Wilkerson Valley on the Lampasas

I

James K. Blair, 46, Tenn.; Elizabeth R., 47, Va.; Solomon, 22, Tenn.; William B., 16, Tenn.; Joel, 14, Ark.; John, 12, Ark.; Alfred, 10, Ark.; Albert, 10, Ark.; Martha J., 8, Ark.; George E., 5, Ark.; Zachariah T., 4 mos., Texas.

James Green, 26, Mo.

P. Levy, 31, Tenn.

William Alexander White, 16, Tenn.

Melville Wilkerson, 32, Tenn.; Eveline, 28, Tenn.; Nancy E., 6, Texas; Sarah M., 4, Texas; Ruth, 2, Texas. (5 slaves)

Total, 19 whites, 5 slaves.

II

Willis H. Bruce, peddler and farmer, 38, Tenn.; Elizabeth, 40, Tenn.; Mary, 11, Tenn.; William E., 8, Ark.; Adaline, 5, Ark; John, 1, Texas; Emily J. Harris, 16, Tenn.; Isabella Harris, 14, Ark.

Ira Stroud 24, Iowa; Rebecca C., 23, Ala.; Isaac B., 4 mos., Texas; Hiram C. McDaniel, 3, Texas.

Total, 12 whites.

On or Near Little River, South Side

I

John Anderson, 32, N. C.,; Elizabeth E., 20, Texas; Lewis W., 1, Texas; Amanda Warren, 11, Tenn.

William Birdeshaw, 21, S. C.

Mrs. Harriet Carter, 30, Ala.; William J., 12, Texas; Samuel H.,

Top: The home of Thomas Duncan, son-in-law of Moses Griffin, built near the Three Forks in 1847. Duncan came to Texas with David Crockett from Tennessee, and stopped first in Robertson County, then later became one of the first pioneers of Bell County. He was killed just after the Civil War by a party of "bushwhackers" who lured him from his home one night on pretense of wanting to buy a fine horse he had. The same group of desperados were later lynched in the old jail at Belton.

Bottom: The center part of this building was the two story home of Mrs. Sam Hasley, daughter of Moses Griffin. It was built in the late 1850's and stood just across the road from old Fort Little River. This building still stands, and is located about a quarter of a mile above the place where Leon and Lampasas rivers join to form Little River.

Residents of Bell County in 1850

10, Texas; John C., 7, Texas; Jesse Frank, 3, Texas; Wiley S., 1 ,Texas.
Jacob Carr, 21, Tenn.
William Connell, 32, Tenn.; Louisa, 27, Mo.; D., 5, Texas; James, 4, Texas; William, infant, Texas.
Milton W. Damron, 26, Tenn.; Sarah, 18, Mo.; Sarah, 11 mos., Tex.
John Danley, 30, blacksmith, Tenn.; Mary, 29, Ky.; Charles Wesley, 9, Mo.; Nathan B., 6, Mo.; Sarah, 5, Mo.; W. Campbell, 3, Texas; Andrew, 1, Texas.
John Fulcher, 52, Tenn.; Mary, 43, La.; Willis, 18, Texas; Henry C., 15, Texas; Martha A., 12, Texas; Francis F., 10, Texas; Nathaniel, 7, Texas; John E., 3, Texas; Mary A., 1, Texas. (3 slaves).
Mitchell Garrison, merchant, ———; E., 31, N.C.; William M., 6, Texas; John T., 4, Texas; Elleanor, 2, Texas; Emiy, infant, Texas.
——— Jarnigan, ———.
Daniel McKay, 33, N. J.; Jane E., 18, Ga.; John P., 2, Texas.
David R. Mumford, 41, Ga.; Sarah, 37, Ky.; Mary, 15, Texas; Nancy A., 13, Texas; Richard, 11, Texas; Thomas, 9, Texas; Julia, 5, Texas; Catherine, 1, Texas. (3 slaves).
Michael Reed, 62, Tenn.; Martha, 64 (?), Va.; Michael Jr., 12, Miss. (6 slaves)
William Reed, 34, Ala.; Emeline, 24, Ala.; James M., 9, Texas; Martha, 6 ,Texas; Sarah A., 3, Texas; Wilson, 6 mos., Texas. (3 slaves)
Nicholas Shields, 28, La.; Samantha, 20, Tenn.; Catherine, 2, Texas; Jesse Williams, 11, Texas.
William Stephens, 52, Ky.; Agnes, 44, Tenn.; Job 21, Ark.; John, 19, Ark.; Nancy, 14, Mo.; Mahala, 12, Mo.; Peter 10, Mo.; Mary, 8, Texas; William, 6, Texas; Amanda, 3, Texas.
Charles W. Stone 33, Md.
Joseph Wheat, 35, Ala.; Melita, 36, Tenn.; Drewery N., 13, Ark.; Samuel D., 11, Ark.; William J., 9, Ark.; Adaline, 6 Ark.; Peter, 2, Texas; Isabel C., 5 mos., Texas.
James B. Wills, 55, Va.; Annie, 42, Tenn.; Wm. R., 24, Mo.; Archibald, 11, Mo.; Alexander, 9, Texas.
Total, 91 whites, 15 slaves.

II

Daniel Alexander, stone mason, 50, Me.
John M. Cathey, 22, Tenn.; Hannah, 17, Ill.; William J., 2, Ark.
Granger McDaniel, 50, Va.; Mary, 36, Tenn.; Abner, 21, Tenn.; Elizabeth, 18, Tenn.; Stacey, 17, Tenn.; David, 15, Tenn.; Sarah, 12, Texas; Mary A., 10, Texas; Mahala, 8, Texas; Matilda, 7, Texas; Lewis, 4, Texas; Jeanette, 2, Texas; John, 6 mos., Texas.
Reese Morrell.
Joseph Reville, 23, Ind.; Arva Z., 27, Ill.; John T., 5, Texas; Leroy, 3, Texas; Mary J., 1, Texas; Simeon, 5 mos., Texas.
Gabriel Smith, 38, Penn.; Lucinda, 22, Texas; David, 4, Texas; Sarah E., 2, Texas; Mary S., 6 mos., Texas. (1 slave).
Benjamin F. Worley.
Total, 30 whites, 1 slave.

On or near Little River, North Side

James Anderson, 50, N. C.; Elizabeth, 44, N.C.; Eliza M., 18,

N.C.; John C., 16, N. C.; Catherine, 14, Mo.; Martha, 11, Mo.; Louise, 9, Mo.; William, 7, Mo.; Susan, 5, Mo.; Job B., 4,Texas; Ampudia, 1, Texas.

Peter Banta, 39, Ky.; Susan, 38, Vt.; Sarah, 11, Ohio; Juliet, 7, Mo.; Isaac, 3, Texas; Miranda, 1, Texas.

Nehemiah Beardsley, 41, physician, N. Y.; Alvira, 25, N. C.; Susanna, 16, Ohio; John C., 13, Ohio; David G., 11, Ind.; James B., 7, Mo.; Obed H., 5, Texas; Ephraim P., 2, Texas; William R., 1, Texas.

Geo. W. Chapman, 35, Ohio; Caroline, 26, La.; Sarah, 10, Texas; Nancy A., 7, Texas; Catherine, 5, Texas; John, 3, Texas; Thomas, 4 mos., Texas.

John R. Craddock, 38, Va.; Amanda, 26, Ky.; Ann, 14, Texas; Virginia, 13, Texas; Margaret, 12, Texas; Emily, 10, Texas.

William Dudley 24, Ky.

James Fletcher, 27, Ark.

Moses Griffin, 56, Ga.; Barzilla, 46, Ga.; Joseph W., 21, Ala.; Avery V., 19, Ala.; James E., 17, Ala.; David D., 15, Texas; Martha J., 12, Texas; Francis C., 10, Texas; Sibel, 8, Texas; Cornelia, 6, Texas; Mary A. Williams, 17, Miss. (2 slaves).

Williamson Griffin, 26, Ala.; Louisiana, 21, Ill.; Caldora, 1 mo., Texas.

Mrs. Sarah Lawler, 41, Tenn.; Levi, 24, Ala.; John J., 22, Ala.; Newton, 16, Ala.; Tabitha J., 14, Ala.

Jefferson Reed, 32, Ala.; Patsy, 27, Ala.; Amanda H., 10, Texas; David S., 7, Texas; Etna, 4, Texas; John W., 2, Texas. (5 slaves).

John B. Reed, 41, Ala.; Emeline, 24, Ala.; James M., 9, Texas; Martha, 6, Texas; Sarah A., 3, Texas; Wilson, 6 mos., Texas; (3 slaves).

John C. Reid, 36, Tenn.; Mary, 24, Tenn.; James C., 9, Texas; Ann R., 2, Texas; Louisa, 1 mo, Texas.

Abram Shelley, 53, Va.; Jane, 29, Mo.; Thomas, 9, Mo.; Amanda, 7, Texas.

John Staepel, 28, Germany.

Total, 82 whites, 10 slaves.

II

Richard Beardsley.

John Dunlap, 36, Mo.; Mary A., 22, Miss.; James, 11, Texas; Mary E., 9, Texas; Ann J., 4, Texas; Calvin, 3, Texas; Mary Cherry, 45, Ga. (1 slave).

Thomas J. Eubank, 32, Ga.; Caroline, 24, N. C.; Eliza, 3, Texas; Louisa, 1, Texas.

Calvary Giddings, 29, Ky; Mary, 32, Tenn.; John W., 11, Mo.; Absolem M., 9, Texas; William E., 7, Texas; Rebecca A., 4, Texas; James N., 2, Texas.

John Marshall, 42, Ill.; Elizabeth, 46, Tenn.; William, 17, Ark.; Martha J., 15, Ark.; Robert Pleas, 13, Ark.; Sarah E., 10, Ark; James C., 9, Ark.

Lewis Marshall, 26, Ill.; Hannah, 22, Ark.; James, 6, Ark.; Mary J., 3, Texas; Ivis, 2 mos., Texas.

Robert Marshall, 75, S. C.; Elizabeth, 66, Tenn.; Margaret, 44,

Ill.; Elizabeth, 34, Ill.
Total, 35 whites, 1 slave.

Taylor's Valley on the Leon, Including Friar's Creek

I

Henry C. Cook, 39, N. C.; Mary, 31, Miss.; Jeremiah Caddel, 28, Ala.; Sarah McAnulty, 52, Ga. (3 slaves).
Joseph Dennis, 39, Tenn; Ice, 32, Tenn.; Disa, 12, Tenn.; Joseph S., 11, Ark.; Cleopatra, 8, Ark.; Margaret, 7, Ark.; William N., 5, Ark.; Sarah T., 3, Ark.; Lawson, 2 mos., Texas. (1 slave).
Mrs. Margaret Taylor, 53, Ky.; Seymoore Brown, 16, Texas; J. Wilson, 13, Texas.
Total, 16 whites, 4 slaves.

II

James Ashley, 35, Ky.; Ann S., 24, Tenn.; Mary H., 1, Texas.
William Ashley, 25, Ky.; Mary A., 18, Ky.; James A., 1, Texas.
Isham Cook.
James Cox, physician, N. C. (2 slaves).
Neal M. Dennis, 47, Ky.; Charity, 46, Ky.; John I., 22, Tenn.; Audley H., 20, Tenn.; Joseph, 19, Tenn.; George, 17, Tenn.; Maria, 13, Tenn.; Mary C., 12, Tenn.; Amanda, 10, Tenn.; Mildred, 8, Ark.; Livonia, 7, Ark.; Semphronia, 7, Ark.; Neal, 4, Ark.; Winnie Hall, 60, Ky.
John Early, 35, Mo.; Martha, 22, Ill.; Thos. P., 12, Texas; Nancy O., 10, Texas; Sarah C., 8, Texas; William M., 7, Texas; Benjamin T., 6 mos., Texas. (2 slaves).
William P. Roberts, 20, Texas.
Total, 30 whites, 4 slaves.

Military Crossing on the Leon (at the Present Dam)

I

Dred R. Hill, 35, Ga.
William F. Hill, 33, Ga.; Martha, 30, Ga.; Maria, 12, Ga.; Mary, 8, Ga.; Thomas, 6, Ga.; Sarah, 3, Texas. (6 slaves).
Total, 7 whites, 6 slaves.

Nolan (or Havens) Valley on Nolan Creek, and the Cowhouse Section

I

Benjamin Adams, 21, Ky.
Daniel Havens, 31, Ala.; Delila J., 26, Ky.; Mary, 11, Mo.; Harvey, 9, Texas; James, 7, Texas; Delila J., 5, Texas; Nancy, 3, Texas; David, 2, Texas; Elizabeth, 1 mo., Texas.
Silas M. Havens, 27, Ala.; Jenanna, 19, Mo.; Julia A., 2, Texas; Thomas J. A., 1, Texas; Nathan Shuffield, 13, Ala.
Thomas D. Havens, 28, Ala.; Louisa, 25, Ark.; Sarah M., 4, Texas

Marshall G., 3, Texas; John R., 1, Texas.
Thomas Havens, 57, Tenn.; Abigail, 56, N. C.; Asa A., 20, Mo.; Alvin B., 17, Mo.; Sarah, 14, Mo.; Hannah E. Purdon, 21, Ala.
Richard H. Potter, 51, S. C.; Nancy, 51, N. C.; Richard M., 18, S. C.; Lucinda, 16, S. C.; Drury D., 15, S. C.; Martin, 10, Ga.
Benjamin L. Stewart, 28, carpenter, Tenn.; Sarah, 20, Ill.; James I., 4 mos., Texas.
John Taylor, 38, Ky.; Eleanor, 35, Ohio; Alma, 15, Mo.; Teancum, 13, Mo.; Joseph M., 11, Mo.; Sarah E., 9, Ill.; Mary, 7, Ill.; John, 5, Texas; Hiram, 3, Texas.
Isaac Williams, 21, Ala; Louisa, 18, Ark.
Total, 46 whites.

II

Joel Casey, 45, Va.; Charlotte, 35, Tenn.; John H., 15, Ark.; Preston, 13, Ark.; William, 9, Texas; Margaret J., 8, Texas; Elijah, 6, Ark.; Flora, 5, Ark.; Taylor, 3, Texas.
Total, 9 whites.

On Pepper's Creek

I

William Pepper, 33, Tenn.; Eveline, 27, Ala.; Mary J., 9, Ark.
Total, 3 whites.

The Cedar Creek Section

Joseph Bishop, 55, Ala.; Nicy, 34, Mo.; Samuel W., 18, Ark.; Joseph, 12, Ark.; Nancy, 10, Ark.; Tennessee, 7, Texas; James, 3, Texas; Miles, 4 mos., Texas.
Josiah Hart, 55, Ky.; Milly, 42, Ky.; Aaron, 18, Ark.; Moses, 15, Ark.; Isaac, 13, Ark.; Martin, 11, Ark.; Joseph, 6, Texas; Meredith, 4, Texas; Emily T Burks, 14, Ark.; Oliver Burks, 11, Ark.
James Kell, 60, S. C.; Elizabeth, 58, Ky.; Archibald, 32, Ind.; Matthew, 22, Ind.; Abraham, 21, Ind.; Francis M., 17, Ind.; Scott McD., 15, Ind. (4 slaves).
John Miller, 48, Tenn.
Total, 26 whites, 4 slaves.

II

Hermon Aiken, 40, surveyor and farmer, N. H.; Margaret E., 26, Germany; Joseph 12, Texas; John W., 3, Texas; James H., 1, Texas; Mary Boyd, 20, Germany; Margaret Boyd, 2, La.
Total, 7 whites.

Fort Gates (Now in Coryell County)

I

Captain Goldsby Childers, 60, Va.; Caroline, 24, Ky.; William P., 14, Texas.

Residents of Bell County in 1850

Robert Childers, 35, Ky.; Adaline, 24, Ala.; Thomas P., 3, Texas. (3 slaves).
Prior Childers, 28, Ky.; Julia, 20, Texas; Thomas F, 3 mos.; Texas.
Lieutenant Horace Haldeman, 29, Officer in the U. S. Army, Pa.; Anne B., 26, Pa.; Henry, 5, Pa.; Anne, 1, Pa.; Mary Ehler, 30, Pa. (U. S. Garrison).
David Smith, 50, Tenn.
Orville T. Tyler, 40, Mass. (2 slaves).
Total, 16 whites, 5 slaves.

II

Thomas Deaton, 22, N. C.; Harriet, 21, Ark.; Frankin C., 3, Texas; James M., 1, Texas.
Sol Friley, merchant.
Henry McKay.
Total, 6 whites.

Location Not Known

I

J. F. Clark
John W. Coleman, physician.
Thomas G. Crawford, 25, school teacher, Ala.
Matthew Given, 20, Ky.
Stephen Goodman.
John C. Henry, grocer, 24, Tenn.
James Riley Sutton, 18, Ark.
John Taylor, 33, Conn.; Sarah J., 26, England; John, 20, Ohio; Edwin, 16, Texas; Esther A., 13, Texas; Melvina, 1, Texas; Sarah F., 2 mos., Texas; Mary A. McKany, 8, Texas; Henry McKany, 6, Texas.
Thomas Trimmier, 60, S. C.; Martha, 58, Ga.; Mary, 16, Ala.; Obediah, 15, Ala.; Sarah, 13, Ala.; Thomas J., 11, Ala; Valones J. Lemons, 11, Ala. (4 slaves).
William H. Tichenal, peddler.
James E. Williams, 32, Ill.; Nancy, 45, Ky.; Nancy A Beck, 2, Texas. (1 slave).
Total, 27 whites, 5 slaves.

II

John C. Burris, 40, Ala.; Elizabeth, 28, Ala.; William, 2, Texas; Minerva, 6 mos., Texas.
John C. Caddel, 29, Ala.
Moses Cornelison, 37, Ky.; Nancy, 47, N. C.; Elihu, 17, Ill.; Margaret, 13, Mo.; Elizabeth A., 10, Mo.; Nancy J., 8, Mo.
Charles Curtis (?).
John Hughes, 35, blacksmith, Ky.; Emily A., 31, S. C.; William F., 9, Texas; Martha P., 5, Texas; Ruth E., 3, Texas; John, 1, Texas.
James A Tharp.
Total, 19 whites.

When tabulated, the above enumeration yields the following totals:

	Families	Members	Single Men	Total Whites	Slave Owners	Slaves
Group I:	67	403	31	434	16	54
Group II:	23	149	12	161	4	6
	90	552	43	595	20	60

Roster of the U. S. Garrison at Fort Gates

While at Fort Gates the census taker enumerated the soldiers stationed there in 1850. The officers were:

NAME	AGE	RANK	NATIVITY
James G. Snelling	27	Captain	Minnesota Territory
Horace Haldeman	29	Lieutenant	Pennsylvania
George E. Pickett	25	Lieutenant	Virginia
George L. Willard	22	Lieutenant	New York
Charles B. Alvord	24	Lieutenant	New York
Edward W. Johns	23	Surgeon	Maryland

In addition there were ninety-four soldiers, including sergeants, corporals musicians, etc. Their nativities were thus set down: America 23; England 7; Ireland 45; Germany 11; Canada 2; Scotland 2; Mexico 3; Italy 1.

Lieutenant Horace Haldeman was born in Lancaster County, Pennsylvania, August 14, 1820. He served as lieutenant in the 11th U. S. Infantry throughout the Mexican War and was stationed at Fort Gates in 1849. He served later at other frontier posts. He surveyed the Military Road from Austin to Fort Gates via Belton. He resigned from the army in 1858 and settled on Elm Creek in Bell County, at Old Troy, where he engaged in breeding fine horses. At the beginning of the war he was invited to return to the North and accept a commission in the United States Army with promise of rapid promotion, but he chose to cast his lot with his adopted state and with the South. He entered the Confederate Service as commander of Haldeman's Battery in Walker's Division with the rank of Major. When General Lee surrendered, he brought his entire command back to his ranch in Bell County, having sunk the guns in Red River, and giving each man a written discharge, disbanded them there. After the war he resided for a time in Belton, and later moved to Calvert where he died in 1883.

Lieutenant George E. Pickett was later the famous Major General of the Confederate Army who led, at Gettysburg, one of the bloodiest charges in history. Replying to an inquiry, the Adjutant General of the United States, in a letter to the writer, dated July 12, 1926, says:

"The records of my office show that George Edward Pickett, who in 1850 was serving as 2nd Lieutenant, 8th United States Infantry, and who was stationed at Fort Gates, resigned from United States service June 25, 1861; later became Major General in the Confederate States service and led the famous Pickett's Charge at the battle of Gettysburg on July 3, 1863. He died July 30, 1875."

Coincident with and following upon the organization of the new county there was a steady immigration and within a year the population more than doubled. This is clearly shown by the first official "Jury List" made up by the Commissioners' Court on February 18, 1851, six months after the organization, on which appear the following additional names of men who had moved in during the latter part of 1850 or early in 1851:

Moses Allen, Roswell Barnes, John Beck, H. Benge, M. A. Brittain, Allen Bryant, Barney Bryant, Jesse Bryant Walter Burch, ——— Buzby, H. Caldwell, Wm. Caldwell, John Cates, Thomas Caufield, Norman Chatfield, G. T. Chisholm, James C. Clark, Sr., James C. Clark, Jr., J. R. Clary, John S. Clary, J. E. Collins, A. H. Colter, Nathan Cox, Ziba Cox, Joel Coxey, Daniel C. Crawford, John Cullis, Wm. Cullis, John Cuthrew, Joseph Depew, M. Donaldson, James Drake, Robert L. Elliott, Alex. Glenn, James M. Glenn, Jno. B. Goodman, G. Berry Harris, Henry Harris, H. F. Hoover, W. A. Hunt, C. G. Karnes, Jacob Karr, Thos. Kenzie, Milton H. Langford, Frank M. Lewis, Samuel Lewis, Thos. Magness, John Mills, Wm. Mills, William Minear, A. G. Moore, Horatio M. Morrison, M. Morrison, James McCrea, Thos. McKenzie, Dr. Louis A. Ogle, Simon Odell, John Pennington, Theophilus Petty, John Potter, Elisha Puett, Warren Puett, James Richards, ——— Saxton, Horatio Shelton, John Shelton, Jas. T. Sherrod, Geo. F. Shipp, Sr., Geo. F. Shipp, Jr., Daniel Sinclair, Evan Singletary, John Smith, Wm. Smith, Jr., Irving Stewart, Isaac N. Stubblefield, R. Lock Stubblefield, Lorenzo Vancleeve, G. Vaughan, M. Ward, A. J. Whitney, ——— Whitney, Matthew Wilkins, David Williams, Isaac W. Williams, Sr., John Williams, J. Williams, Jr., John B. Woodward, Jordan Wyatt, Absolem Yarbrough.

PART II

THE FRONTIER COUNTY, 1850-1374

CHAPTER VII

THE CREATION AND ORGANIZATION OF BELL COUNTY, 1850

1. *The Organic Act*

These settlements had now become large enough to justify a local government of their own. As the pioneers pushed farther up-country they found it increasingly irksome to have to go all the way down to Cameron, the county seat of Milam, to transact their legal business. Moreover, it was the policy of the State to lay out new counties along the frontier as rapidly as the spread of settlements would justify it. As early as January, 1848, the settlers south of Little River and the Salado sent a petition to the Legislature praying for the erection of a new county, to be called "Clear Water."[1] This petition was not acted upon; but when the Legislature met again, late in 1849, petitions were laid before it for three new counties on the upper Brazos and Little River. These were to the counties of Falls, McLennan and Bell. The last petition, introduced on December 10, 1849, by the Hon. George E. Burney of Cameron, then representing Milam County in the Legislature, was reported favorably on December 15, and became a law on January 22, 1850.[2] The new county was named Bell in honor of Peter Hansborough Bell who had just assumed the office of Governor. The act took effect immediately. Its provisions were as follows:

"AN ACT TO CREATE THE COUNTY OF BELL"

"Section 1. Be it enacted by the Legislature of the State of Texas, that all the territory comprised within the following described limits, to wit: Beginning in the north-east boundary of Williamson County, at a point bearing south sixty degrees west from the northeast corner of league No. eight, on the west bank of the Brazos River, in the name of S. Frost; thence north sixty degrees east to a point bearing south thirty degrees east from the south corner of McLennan County; thence north thirty degrees west to, and with the southwest boundary of McLennan county thirty-two miles; thence south, sixty degrees west to a point from which a line runs south thirty

---

[1] Memorial No. 241 in "Memorials and Petitions"; Office of the Secretary of State, Austin, Texas.
[2] **House Journal** 3rd Legis., 244, 280, 297, 617. Gammel, **Laws of Texas,** III, 501.

degrees east to Williamson county, and with the latter to the place of beginning, will enclose within this county nine hundred and fifty square miles, and shall be called the county of Bell.

Sec. 2. Be it further enacted, That the following desribed territory shall be attached to, and form a territorial part of said county of Bell, to wit: Beginning at the north-west corner of the above described county, and run north thirty degrees west with the south boundary of McLennan county to the dividing ridge between the waters of the Brazos and Colorado rivers; thence with said dividing ridge to the west corner of Williamson county; thence with the north boundary of Williamson county to the south-east corner of said Bell county.

Sec. 3. Be it further enacted, That the Chief Justice of Milam county shall organize said county of Bell in acordance with law, and shall within three months after the passage of this Act, order an election for five Commissioners, all of which shall reside within the limits of said new county, and shall cause said election to be advertised at three public places in said county, at least ten days previous to said election, and when said election shall have been had, due return thereof shall be made to the said Chief Justice of Milam county within ten days thereafter; who shall open and compare the same, and shall certify under the seal of his office, the result of said election.

Sec. 4. Be it further enacted, That it shall be the duty of the Commissioners so elected, or a majority of them, to proceed to locate the county seat for said county of Bell, and shall locate the same as near the center of said county, as land, timber, and water will admit, and may, if they think proper, employ a surveyor, at the expense of said county, and may make, or cause such surveys as may be necessary for the purpose of ascertaining the centre of said county as will ensure the permanent location of said county seat; and said Commissioners shall have power to purchase for the use, and at the expense of said county, not more than three hundred and twenty acres of land, or may receive the same as a donation, and shall lay off the same, or a part thereof into convenient squares and lots as may be necessary for a court house, jail, clerks offices, churches, and school houses as the Commissioners may think proper, and shall offer the remainder for sale at public auction, on such time and terms as they may deem most conducive to the interest of said county, and shall apply the proceeds of such sales to the erection of necessary public buildings for the use of said county.

Sec. 5. Be it further enacted, That so soon as the County Court of said county shall be properly organized, it shall be the duty of the Chief Justice to notify the Commissioners thus elected or their successors, to come forward and make a fair exhibit of all their official acts as such Commissioners, at which time their functions shall cease unless the Chief Justice shall think it necessary to extend their term of service.

Sec. 6. Be it further enacted, That it shall be the duty of the Chief Justice of Milam county, so soon as the county seat of said Bell county shall have been located, to order an election for all county officers of the said new county; and the votes polled in such election shall be returned to said Chief Justice of Milam county, in accordance with law, who shall issue certificates of election to the officers elected in the same manner as he is required to issue certificates of election to the officers of Milam county and that the said new county shall belong to the third Judicial District of the State of Texas.

Sec. 7. Be it further enacted, That the Commissioners elected and acting, shall be allowed and paid out of the county treasury of said county, the sum of one dollar per day each, for every day they may be necessarily employed in the discharge of duties herein assigned them; and that this act take effect and be in force from and after its passage.

Approved, January 22nd, 1850."

The boundaries of the attached territory are not very definite, but they evidently included a vast area lying between the upper Brazos and Colorado rivers and now embraced wholly or partly in the counties of Coryell, Lampasas, Mills, Brown, Hamilton, Comanche, Eastland, Erath, and Burnet.[3] The area of the county as now existing is 1083 square miles or 693,120 acres.

2. The "Charter Oak" Election

Hon. Isaac Standefer, then Chief Justice of Milam County, proceeding under the provisions of the Act of the legislature recited above, ordered a special election in the Bell County territory for five commissioners to *organize the county*. In order to distinguish them from the regular commissioners who later constituted the Commissioners Court (styled also the County Court) they will be designated herein as Special Commissioners. Their tenure was temporary and their functions specific.

So far as known, no election had ever before been held nor had any voting place ever been established in the Bell County territory—in fact most of the settlers had arrived there contemporaneously with or subsequent to the last preceding general election in Milam County, which occurred on the first Monday in August, 1848.[4]

---

[3] Fulmore, Z. T., **History and Geography of Texas**, etc., 284.

[4] It seems that Geo. W. Chapman, residing in the vicinity of the Three Forks and the present village of Little River, held the office of Justice of the Peace of Milam County in 1850, but it is almost certain that he had been **appointed** thereto by the Commissioners Court of Milam County and that there had been no **election** for the

109

The place designated by Judge Standefer for holding this special election was on the Leon River, at the crossing of the military road from Austin to Ft. Gates. It was very near the center of the new county and most convenient and accessible to the few scattering voters of that time. On the east bank of the river, just below the crossing, in a group of three or four Live Oak trees, stood the cabin of Mr. Wm. F. Hill, the only house in that vicinity. It has long since crumbled by decay and the trees shading it as well as the land on which they and Mr. Hill's cabin stood have all tumbled into the river with the "caving" of the bank, caused by the swirling waters of the dam maintained there in later years.

About fifty to seventy-five yards east of Mr. Hill's cabin was a large spreading lone live oak tree. It still stands there in all of its majesty. Under this grand old oak the election was held and the five Special Commissioners were chosen. Here was performed the first corporate or charter act by the citizens of the new county and the author of this work has therefore christened the old tree as

BELL COUNTY'S "CHARTER OAK"

an adaptation of the name of the famous historic tree of the American colonial days.

The place of this election was lost history, as there are no records whatever of the event and the memory of it has faded away with the passing years and with the demise or removal of those participating and of their contemporaries. The author's first information of it was acquired, quite by accident, in a conversation with the late Captain Samuel W. Bishop, of Killeen, at a picnic at the Miller Spring, given by Mr. W. P. Denman to about one hundred "old timers" early in August, 1916. On the 23rd of the same month, the author employed a photographer and had two large photographs of this tree made. On November 5, 1917, by previous appointment, Captain Bishop came to Belton and accompanied the writer to this tree and identified it as the one under which the election was held, as above stated, and as the same tree shown in the photographs. We were accompanied on this occasion by County Judge Mallory B. Blair,

office at the last preceding election in 1848, as there were then few if any voters in the Bell County section of Milam County to hold such an election.

now Associate Justice of the Court of Civil Appeals, at Austin, City Marshall Mack McCorcle, the late Mr. P. L. Ellis and Mr. James J. Bishop, son of Captain Samuel W. Bishop. These gentlemen found the circumference of the tree, by actual measurement one foot above the ground, to be fourteen feet, and the height by careful estimate, about fifty feet. On our return to Belton Captain Bishop executed and left with the author a full sworn statement of all the facts remembered by him connected with this election, at which he was personally present but did not vote. He was then a lad about eighteen years old and came to the election with his father, Mr. Joseph Bishop, then living at the spring where the village of Moffett now stands. His recollection was that some thirty or forty men participated in the election, which was held by three men acting as election judges and in which the voting was by oral ballot, or *viva voce*. Of those present he remembered only Joseph Bishop, John Danley, Joseph Dennis, Josiah Hart, Dred R. Hill, Wm. F. Hill, William Reed and Isaac Williams. Captain Bishop knew of no other survivor of those attending this election and it is almost certain that there was none other in 1917, and now he has passed away, having died at Brownsville, Texas, on September 14, 1919. Mr. John M. Roberts and Mr C. Bent Roberts, sons of Mr. C. B. Roberts (who was on of the five Special Commissioners chosen at this election) in separate conversations with the author, confirmed Captain Bishop's account of the event by stating that they were boys at their father's home on the Salado at the time, that they did not go to the election, but that their father, Mr. C. B. Roberts did attend, that they well remembered the event and that the election was held at the military road crossing of the Leon. Both of these men have since passed away.

It is practically certain that but for the testimony of Captain Bishop—a man of good character and of unquestioned veracity and integrity—the *locality* of this incident in our early history, interesting as it is to us now, would have vanished absolutely from our county's annals. True, it is known from the provisions of the Act creating the county and from a few meager allusions to the report of Mr. Joseph Dennis, chairman of the Special Commission, contained in the minutes of the regular commissioners court, months afterward, that an election must have been held *somewhere,* but, these records did not disclose, and no one else knew until Captain Bishop spoke, *where* it was held, nor would the history and identity of "Bell County's Charter Oak" have otherwise been preserved to us and to posterity.

The old tree is about a quarter of a mile from the corporate line of Belton, where this line crosses the Belton and Temple pike (at the Tatum hill), and from there to the high ground east of the river a full view of it can be had by looking to the right hand or down the Leon River. It stands near a tenant house on Judge G. M. Felt's farm, is the only live oak tree about there, and can be reached by a turn-out to the right at the east end of the present highway bridge, leading directly to the Charter Oak, some two hundred yards below.

Our county pride should move us to take suitable action for the preservation of the beautiful old tree and the ground on which it stands.

The *date* on which the Charter Oak election was held is not known to the author. Captain Bishop could only remember that it was in the spring of 1850. The election order was made by Judge Standefer at Cameron and the returns were made to him. Whatever records he made concerning the event, if he made any, were destroyed when the court house of Milam County was burned in 1874. Since the Act of January 22 required Judge Standefer to call the election within three months, or not later than April 22nd, and the election had to be advertised at three public places within the limits of the new county for *at least ten days* previous to the date of same, it may reasonably be inferred that it occurred sometime in April, 1850.[5]

The members of the Special Commission thus chosen were: Joseph Dennis (who became Chairman), John Fulcher, Cornelius B. Roberts, Josiah Hart, Melville Wilkerson. Upon

---

[5] In a law suit filed in the District Court of Bell County in the fifties, the course of action was a promissory note dated "Nolandsville, June 8, 1850," which indicates that the county had been surveyed and the county seat located and **named** prior to June 8, 1850. See final Records, District Court of Bell County, Book A, p. 22. It must have taken some weeks after the election for the Special Commissioners to receive their commission from Chief Justice Standefer, to meet and organize, to survey the county boundaries, ascertain its geographical center, consider rival locations for the county seat, make the final selection, agree upon its name, etc., all apparently done prior to June 8, 1850.

Bell County's "Charter Oak" under which the first commissioners met to organize the County in April, 1850. It is just east of the Leon River, north of the bridge on the Belton-Temple highway.

them devolved the duty, under the Act, of surveying the county boundaries, locating, laying out and naming the county seat, of selling lots and erecting public buildings, etc.[6] All of them have long since passed away, leaving behind them honorable names, and many of their descendants are still residing among us or in the nearby counties. Diligent inquiries among these descendants have failed to turn up any documents, memoranda or other evidence pertaining to this important historical event, and vain searches have been made in the files of old newspapers of 1850 found in the State Library, in the Library of the University of Texas, in the Public Library of Houston and in the Rosenburg Library of Galveston.

3. *The County Surveyed, County Seat Located Laid out and Named Nolanville*

The five Special Commissioners chosen at the Charter Oak election promptly proceeded in the discharge of their duties. Under their direction, William Armstrong, Surveyor of Milam Land District, with Levi T. Lawler and William J. Roberts as chain carriers, ran out and established the boundaries of Bell County proper (exclusive of the territory attached to it, but subsequently segregated and erected into other counties), and he also located the geographical center of the county, said to have been at a point some two miles southwest of the place chosen.

Several places near the geographical center were offered and considered for the county seat—Childers Mill, Nolan Springs (also then called Walnut Springs), Three Forks and perhaps others. According to tradition Messrs. Dennis and Hart favored Nolan Springs, Mr. Wilkerson's choice was Childers Mill, while Messrs. Fulcher and Roberts preferred Three Forks. Mr. Wilkerson finally came over to Nolan Springs and that settled it.

The Nolan Springs were on the Matilca F. Connell League, the extreme western grant on the south bank of the Leon River in the Bell County part of Robertson's

[6] This section is principally rewritten from the author's paper, entitled "Bell County's Charter Oak," printed in **The Belton Journal** of January 3, and in **The Temple Telegram**, of January 5, 1918, accompanied by the same cut of the old tree as shown herein.

colony. Mrs. Connell had become the wife of Thomas J. Allen and they had offered to donate to the county 120 acres of land on the western boundary of the league, lying across the Nolan Creek and including the springs, in consideration of the permanent location of the county seat thereon. This offer was accepted by the Special Commissioners. They located the county seat upon this tract of land and gave it the name of NOLANVILLE. The town was named for the bautiful, clear mountain stream meandering through it, which itself had been named for the famous Philip Nolan, the young Irish adventurer, whose expeditions and tragic death are well known to readers of early Texas history.

Early travelers and surveyors, unknown to each other, and without knowledge of the true location of Nolan's Fort —which is not positively known to this day—had, long before the advent of the settlers, named two little streams for Philip Nolan—the little creek that flows through Belton and another one in Johnson County, on which the town of Blum, on the Santa Fe Railway, is located. In both instances the name was often erroneously spelled Noland instead of Nolan by the early settlers, and our early county records, with few exceptions, followed this erroneous spelling as "Noland's Creek," "Nolandsville," etc. While neither of these streams appears to have been the real site of Nolan's fatal encounter with the Spanish soldiery, yet both of them have retained the name to this day. So much for the name first given to the capital of the new county of Bell.

The Special Commissioners had the town site--Nolanville—or at least a large part of it, laid off into blocks, lots, streets and alleys, with a court house square in the center, making reservations for public purposes as directed by the Act creating the county. Col. Henry B. Elliott was the surveyor and Mr. E. Lawrence Stickney made a plat of the town which was subsequently adopted by the regular commissioner's court as the "official map of Nolanville." It was drawn upon a piece of coarse, unbleached domestic and is still preserved in the office of the County Clerk.

The Special Commissioners, surveyor, chain carriers and others engaged in surveying and laying off the town of Nolanville, camped on the ground and did their own cooking while performing this work, as there were neither houses nor other people here.

The Creation and Organization of Bell County

The valley now comprising the heart of the little City of Belton was, in 1850, in a wild and lovely state of nature, dotted with groves of small live oak, elm, hackberry, cedar and other trees, dense thickets of dogwood, haw and other bush growth, mustang grape vines climbing over the tree tops and hanging in graceful and lovely festoons, while luxurious grass (old sedge), as tall as ripe wheat fields, waved in all the open spaces. There was a beautiful grove of medium-sized live oak trees where the Bell County court house now stands. And all along the creek banks were large trees of walnut, sycamore, willow, pecan, white oak, burr-oak, hackberry, etc. The landscape was beautiful and inspiring.

Tradition says that, in the early forties, hunters from the lower country occasionally camped at Nolan Springs (now in Belton) and gave them the name of "Horse-head Springs," because a horse head had been hung up by some hunter in the fork of a walnut tree that stood near the principal spring and had remained there for many years.

4. *Beginnings of Nolanville (Belton)*, 1850

Before the special commissioners had finished laying out the county seat, people began moving into Nolanville. Nearly all of those then residing at the Childers Mill on the Lampasas came at once. Among them were A. T. McCorcle, John M. Payne, T. A. Supple, E. Lawrence Stickney, Joe Townsend and others. About the same time came John Danley, John C. Henry and others from the "Fulcher Colony," John C. Reid and others from the Reed settlement, all on Little River.

Clap-board shanties, log cabins, brush arbors, tents and other improvised shelters were hastily thrown up for temporary purposes and the thickets, high grass, and other marks of the wilderness began to disappear from the valley and the adjacent hills. Foot-paths and trails to the springs, stores, and other places about the village were soon beaten out. Logs and rived boards, for building purposes, were obtained from the river bottoms nearby and cedar and oak logs from the hills. Mrs. Sarah Lawler built a large shed in which to board the men who were putting up the crude houses. The boards for this shed—the first made for a roof in Nolanville—were rived by W. B. Cross, F. M. Cross and Simeon Odell.

It is difficult to trace the genesis of the settlement of the town and the erection of houses with positive accuracy, as there is no record of these details to guide one and the claims and traditions of the very few surviving "old timers" are conflicting and often irreconcilable. All stories seem to agree, however, that the first two structures erected in the new county capital were John Danley's blacksmith shop and John M. Payne's store, both log cribs, located at intersection of Penelope and East Water streets. Mr. Danley had set up a smithy in the Reed and Fulcher settlement down on Little River, in 1849, and this he moved to Nolanville. Mr. Payne purchased Mr. T. A. Supple's little stock of goods at Childers Mill and with it he opened up as the first merchant of Nolanville.

Other improvements followed soon, but these three structures—Payne's store, Danley's blacksmith shop and Mrs. Lawler's shed—were probably the only houses up when the election for the regular county officers occurred, on August 5, 1850, although there were a number of people camping about, awaiting the sale of town lots before putting up houses for themselves.

The Special Commissioners to organize the county, although authorized by the Legislature not only to sell town lots but also to erect public buildings, did not attempt this latter function, but passed it on to the regular Commissioner's court. As shown by their verbal report and as recited in old deeds to town lots, the Special Commission held the first sale of town lots on Monday, August 26, 1850, the day on which Judge Danley qualified his colleagues in the county government. Whether the sale was public or private we can not say, but it was probably public. This enabled intending settlers to obtain lots and erect buildings on them.

Joe Townsend put up a shanty of some sort and opened a saloon (called a "grocery" in those days) on the south side of the square. A. T. McCorcle opened a small store near the southwest corner of the square on the west side. Later on he built a two story house there, residing in the second story and keeping his store below. Mr. W. H. Tichenal, having no house, sold goods from his wagon on the square. John C. Henry, with a barrel of whiskey and a tin

The Creation and Organization of Bell County

cup, held forth under a tree down under the hill just east of the present main street bridge.

Buildings of more substantial character soon followed. The Belton Hotel, one story, at the southwest corner of the square, was built by Mr. Isaac Miller from Lockhart. It was subsequently owned and operated successively by Mr. John S. Blair and Mr. Oliver H. Bigham, Robert Childers (1861), Sam W. Bigham, Caleb Pendarvis, Isaac Williams, Alfred Evans and perhaps others. It was the first hotel in the village and was continued in operation until destroyed by fire in April, 1892. Mr. E. E. Stewart built a store at the northeast corner of the square, where the Belton National Bank now stands. James D. Roberts, merchant, erected another at the northwest corner of the square, where Ray & Elliott's building now stands. Another store house was built by William Hundley, merchant, at the southeast corner of the square.

These first houses were constructed mostly of materials produced in the country. Weatherboarding and roofing were done with boards rived of burr-oak, Spanish oak, etc. Studding and rafters were usually of round native cedar flattened on one side. The frame work was either of sawed cedar or hardwood and the flooring was generally hardwood. This hardwood lumber, also called "rawhide," was sawed from native woods—elm, hackberry, cottonwood, the different oaks and cedar. Sills, sleepers and joists were of oak, elm, or cedar logs. Hardwood lumber was rip-sawed by hand at first but later by steam saw-mills. The first mill was probably that of Ira Chalk and Whitfield Chalk, begun on the Salado in 1849 and later known as the Ferguson Mill. It was followed by others, notably that operated by Joseph Dennis at a spring on Bird's Creek, near the Midway Gravel Pit of the present day, where a few families lived and, according to a tradition, gave to the place the name of Marietta. James M. Cross and Joseph Dennis opened up a lumber yard at Nolanville for the sale of hardwood lumber and other building materials and also caried a small stock of pine lumber. The latter was hauled on ox wagons from a saw mill operated in Bastrop County on the north bluff of the Colorado River, a few miles below the town of Bastrop. William B. Blair and F. M. Cross were the teamsters on these trips. Yard fences were built of rails and poles, cedar pickets, etc. Everybody in Nolanville obtained drinking water from the Nolan Springs until wells or cisterns were provided at their respective homes.

At first the residences were mostly on the south side of the Nolan, but later the residence section on the north side became more popular. The locations of the earliest homes and by whom built can not be given with much detail for want of reliable data. That of E. Lawrence Stickney appears to have been below the creek bluff, at the upper end of the present "Confederate Park." On this bluff, just above, was the home (in 1853) of Mrs. Wright and her sons, Jack and Thomas C., who came to Nolanville in 1851. Others were on the high ground on the south side, along south Pearl Street, and on the lower levels of the north side. Most of this construction was temporary and, after the owners generally moved to other locations and built more permanent homes, these first log structures soon disappeared.

It is needless to say that we have not accounted for all of the earliest business and residence buildings, but have done the best possible under the circumstances.

5. *County Officers Elected and Organization Completed*

In the meantime the proceedings of the Special Commissioners—the survey of the county boundaries, the location, laying out and naming of the county seat—were officially reported to Hon. Isaac Standefer, who at once ordered an election for county officers of Bell County to be held on the first Monday (5th day) in August, 1850, that being also the day for the general biennial election for county officers throughout the State.

There is no record of the names of the election officers nor of the number of voting places. The writer believes that the polls were opened at Nolanville only and that all of the qualified electors of the county who participated voted there, as the small number of voters did not require the holding of elections elsewhere. And tradition says that the election occurred in John Danley's blacksmith shop. It may have been held there or in the live oak grove in the court house square.

At this election for the first set of officers for Bell County, the following persons were chosen:

John Danley, Chief Justice; John C. Reid, County Clerk;

Stephen Goodman, County Treasurer; William Reed, Sheriff; William Birdeshaw, District Clerk;[7] Wm. F. Hill, Assessor and Collector of Taxes; Peter Banta, Jas. K. Blair, James M. Cross and John Taylor, County Commissioners; James Anderson, Robert Childers and Henry Elliott, Justices of the Peace; and Matthew Givens, Constable.

Returns of the election were made to Hon. Isaac Standefer, Chief Justice of Milam County and he issued the proper certificates of election in due course to those thus chosen.

Hon. John Danley, Chief Justice elect, journeyed down to Cameron and appearing there before Judge Standefer took the oath of office on Saturday, August 24th, 1850. Returning to Nolanville he then, on Monday, August 26th, 1850, administered the official oath to the sheriff, county clerk, treasurer, justices of the peace and constable. The other officers elect were qualified in due time, as well as those elected or appointed later. They were Jas E. Williams, Ira Stroud, Wm. F. Hill, Deputy sheriffs; E. Lawrence Stickney, David T. Chamberlin, Deputy County Clerks; E. Lawrence Stickney, Deputy District Clerk; T. G. Crawford, Nathaniel Shields, James Kell, John W. Coleman, Justices of the Peace; John W. Coleman, E. Lawrence Stickney, Notaries Public.[8]

[7] The records do not show who was elected District Clerk at the election for county officers on August 5, 1850. Messrs. John M. Reed and Frank B. Reed, both reliable gentlemen, stated to the author that the person elected was Mr. William Birdeshaw, also known as "Major" Birdeshaw, a cousin of their mother. Because of his youthful appearance his age was questioned, and he was thought ineligible to hold the office. He said he would go back to Yalobusha County, Mississippi, where his people lived, and obtain proof of his majority. He left on horseback for Mississippi for this purpose but for some reason did not return to claim his office. These facts were obtained by the Messrs. Reed from their father, Mr. John B. Reed, who, while enroute from Mississippi to Texas, met Mr. Birdeshaw on his way; also from the lips of Mr. Birdeshaw himself, who afterward became a Primitive Baptist preacher, visited Bell County and was their guest about 1900, and preached at Little Flock, Rogers and several other places in the county. The U. S. Census of Milam (including Bell) County for 1850 list William Birdeshaw, 21 years old, school teacher, native of South Carolina, as living with Michael Reed, who then resided on Little River.

[8] Record of Official Oaths and Bonds, Bell County, Vol. 1, pp. 1-39. Minutes of Commissioners' Court of Bell County, 1850, 1851, 1852.

The office of District Clerk having become vacant by the departure of William Birdeshaw, R. E. B. Baylor, the District Judge, on December 28, 1850, appointed Dr. Wm. D. Eastland to the position and he qualified on January 7, 1851.[9]

The county officers took up their respective duties and the government of Bell County was soon a going concern.

[9] Record of Official Oaths and Bonds, Bell County, Vol. 1, pp. 1-39. Minutes Commissioners' Court of Bell County, 1850, 1851, 1852.

CHAPTER VIII

THE EARLY COUNTY RECORDS

At last had come local government, records, courts and the law to Bell County—to a people who had hitherto been a "law unto themselves," and to a land which for unnumbered centuries had been the abode of the savage Indians.

The inauguration of the several divisions of the county government will be noted briefly—the Deed Records, the Marriage Records, the Commissioners' Court the Probate Court and the District Court—the crude beginnings of those instrumentalities of organized society, transplanted from the older States and from across the sea, which through the succeeding years have continued, with slight interruptions, to function peacefully in Bell County.

1. The Deed Records

Mr. John C. Reid qualified as County Clerk, on August 26, 1850, and was, under the law, the Recorder of deeds and other instruments pertaining to lands and slaves.

Under date of "Nolanville, August 27, A. D. 1850," written across the top of Book A, pages 1 and 2, of the Deed Records of Bell County, appears the first instrument pertaining to lands ever recorded in the new county. It is a Bond for Title to a tract of land out of the Thomas Childers headright, from Goldsby Childers and Robert Childers to Nehemiah Beardslee, dated January 12, 1850, witnessed by William Armstrong and O. T. Tyler, and authenticated for record on August 27, 1850 by William Armstrong, one of the subscribing witnesses, before John D. Reid, County Clerk of Bell County, and filed for record on the same day. On pages 3 and 4 is the full conveyance of said land (247½ acres) from Goldsby Childers, Robert Childers, Prior Childers and wife, Julia A. Childers, dated August 23, 1850, witnessed by James Anderson and John Dunlap, authenticated before John C. Reid, County Clerk, on August 27, 1850, and filed for record the same day.

On pages 5 and 6 appears a deed from Goldsby Childers to Nehemiah Beardslee for 250 acres of said Goldsby Childers' colonial headright league on Little River, for a consideration of $200.00, with John Dunlap and James Anderson as subscribing witnesses, who authenticated it before John C. Reid, County Clerk, August 27, 1850, and the deed was filed for record on the same day.

In the same Book A, page 7, is the first record of the sale of a lot in Nolanville, to John Dunlap for $31.00, dated August 26, 1850, and signed by Joseph Dennis, Josiah Hart, C. B. Roberts, John Fulcher and Melville Wilkerson, who are correctly described at "Commissioners for the location of the County Seat of Bell County and for the sale of lots."

The next entries record patents from the State of Texas to William Thompson for a tract of more than two labors of land on Cow Creek, now in Coryell County, and to Obadiah B. Smith, assignee of James M. McLaughlin, to 320 acres of land now in Comanche County.

The last two tracts of land were then within the territory attached to Bell County, and were properly recorded in Bell County. There are in our first record books many instruments pertaining to lands now embraced in a number of the counties to the west and northwest of Bell County. All of these records, and very many more, are in the handwriting of E. Lawrence Stickney, who, however, did not formally qualify as Deputy County Clerk until November 20, 1850.

Thus began the "Deed Records" of Bell County, now comprising over three hundred large volumes. Formerly they were written in long hand but latterly everything is typewritten. A patented system of indexing (the Campbell system) enables those familiar with it to search the records with reasonable dispatch, but this work, for many years, has mostly been done by abstract makers. The records are so voluminous that the old time private search of land title records is impracticable and no longer dependable.

2. *The First Marriage Record*

Book A, page 1 of the Marriage Records of Bell County, contains the record of the first marriage license ever issued in the new county. It is dated October, 1850, and authorized the joining in matrimony of Mr. O. T. Tyler and Miss Caroline Childers. The return indorsed thereon recites that the document or writ was "executed" by Hon. John Danley, Chief Justice of Bell County on December 26, 1850. This marriage occured at Fort Gates, then a United States Military garrison, about five miles below the present town of Gatesville, on the Leon River, and then in Bell County but now in Coryell County. There was not, at that time, a minister or other person than Judge Danley, and the Chief Justice of McLennan County, authorized to solemnize the rites of matrimony within perhaps 75 or 100 miles of Fort Gates.

A curious thing about this marriage license, the original of which the writer now has before him, is that our County Clerk then had only *half of a county seal,* and it made an impression upon only *one side* of the paper, with a red wax wafer affixed.

The couple thus united, in the then wilderness of the present county of Coryell, were the parents of this writer.

3. *The First Session of the Commissioners' Court*

The Commissioners' Court, in those days sometimes styled the "County Court," first assembled in a special session on October 8, 1850, under a call issued by the Chief Justice. There was a full attendance: Hon. John Danley, Chief Justice, presiding, Commissioners Peter Banta, Jas. K. Blair, James M. Cross and John Taylor, and John C. Reid, County Clerk and William Reed, Sheriff, attending.

The first legislative act of the court was to divide the county into four Commissioners' and Justices' beats and to define their boundaries. The territorial area of the county, as well as the village of Nolanville, was quartered by the Waco and Austin road, for one line, and the channel of Little River, up the Leon to the mouth of Nolan Creek and up the Nolan to its forks, thence to the divide between North Nolan and Cow House and thence with that divide to the western county boundary, for the other line. The county was thus divided into four beats, all converging in the village.

These divisions were designated also as election precincts. William Stevens, Thomas Trimmier, Josiah Hart and John Marshall were appointed presiding officers of election and their respective residences were designated as polling places. A. T. McCorcle was also named as an additional presiding officer for Nolanville and Robert Childers for Fort Gates.

Elections for Justices and constables in the several beats were ordered to be held on October 21, 1850.

Another election ordered for the same day, October 21, 1850, concerned an event of great interest to Texas. As expressed in the order, it was "to ascertain the voice of the people under the proclamation of the governor upon the compromise with the United States" for the sale of "the Santa Fe region." This was that vast area between the present western boundaries of Texas and the upper Rio Grande, which had been in dispute between the State and the Federal Government since the close of the War with Mexico. Texas had claimed all the land to the Rio Grande under an act of the Congress of the Republic of Texas, December 18, 1836; but after Mexico, by the Treaty of Guadalupe-Hidalgo in February, 1848, had ceded all the territory between Texas and the Pacific to the United States, the latter government ignored the claims of Texas and the dispute became very acrimonious. Finally, by an act of September 5, 1850, the Congress of the United States offered Texas $10,000,000 for the disputed area, and Governor Bell submitted the question of accepting this offer to the voters of the state. The people voted for the sale and the Legislature formally accepted the proposition in an act passed on November 25, 1850. Texas thus parted with her claim to 98,380 square miles, or 62,963,200 acres, of her domain and received in return the means of paying the heavy public debt which had been incurred during the troublesome days of the Revolution and the Republic.

At this same session the first "reviewers" for several roads were appointed:

From Nolanville to Cameron, on the north side of Little River—Neal M. Dennis, Geo. W. Chapman, John Marshall, John Dunlap and Moses Griffin.

From Nolanville to Cameron, on the south side of Little River, via Reed's Ferry—William Stephens, John Fulcher, Granger McDaniel, C. B. Roberts and Joseph Dennis.

From Nolanville to the Waco Village—William F. Hill, Calvary Giddings, Thomas Trimmier, John Bowles, and Thomas J. Neighbors.

From Nolanville to intersect the road from Georgetown to Fort Gates, on the north side of Cow House Creek, at the foot of the mountain—R. H. Porter, Joel Casey, John Taylor, Thomas Havens and B. L. Stewart.

The place of this and several subsequent meetings of the Commissioners' Court, (prior to the completion of the temporary court house, mentioned later) is not definitely known, but the "old timers" have ever claimed that Chief Justice Danley's blacksmith shop on East Water street was the place, and that his anvil served as a table around which the members of the court sat during their deliberations. This seems likely since there was at that time, apparently, no other available meeting place. Why seek another anyway? The blacksmith was an important person in our western frontier democracy and his shop was a common meeting place.

The first regular term of the Commissioners' Court opened on November 18, 1850. Mr. Joseph Dennis appeared on behalf of the special commissioners who had been chosen at the "Charter Oak Election" to organize the county, and reported the actions of that body, of which he was chairman. The report and the accompanying papers were read and ordered to be filed, but they are not now to be found in the archives of the county. The minutes tell us that he reported the survey of the county boundaries, the location and surveying of a part of the county seat—Nolanville—into blocks, lots, squares, streets and alleys with a map of same made by Mr. E. Lawrence Stickney, a schedule of the lots sold therein and of the notes received for same, and other particulars connected with the performance of their duties. Accounts for compensation and expenses incurred in this preliminary organization, amounting to $372.44, were presented at this session (and subsequently) and were audited and approved, but as yet there was no money on hand for their payment. The town lots were sold on credit and at very low prices.

Mr. Dennis also presented to the court a deed from Thos. J. Allen and wife, Matilda F. Allen (formerly Matilda F. Connell) conveying to Bell County the 120 acres of land out of the Matilda F. Connell colonial headright league on which Nolanville, the county seat, had been located. This deed recited that it was given "in consideration of the permanent location of the county seat of Bell County thereon." It was dated July 30, 1850, and is recorded in Book A, page 90, of the Deed Records of Bell County.

The functions of the special commission thus ended and they passed off the stage of action.

Record books, stationery, press, seal, and furniture for the county offices were purchased with funds realized from the conversion of notes received in the sale of town lots. Commissioner James M. Cross was appointed county agent *pro tem* for the sale of the town lots in Nolanville and for the collection of the proceeds thereof. He was ordered to hold a public sale of town lots on the fourth Monday in December (December 23,) 1850, on a credit of six and twelve months with two good sureties as theretofore.

The county agent was ordered to receive, on the day of the lot sale, sealed bids for the erection of a temporary courthouse and clerk's office and to let the contract to the lowest bidder. The building was to be of frame construction, 18 by 30 feet, to be located at the southeast corner of the public square and to be completed in time for the Spring term 1851, of the District Court. (This order was later modified, as we shall see.) The building was to be paid for in town lot notes.

Road precincts were defined and numbered and overseers therefor were appointed, in their numerical order: Dred R. Hill, John Bowles, Archibald Willingham, Abram Shelly, John Marshall, Cornelius B. Roberts, Richard Beardsley, and Jefferson Reed. James M. Cross, Jas. E. Williams, Wm. K. Karnes, Henry B. Elliott and John C. Reid were named as reviewers of "a road from Nolanville to Chalk's Mill, ultimately to lead to Bastrop. A license was granted to Dred R. Hill to maintain a ferry on the Leon River at the crossing of the Military road (where the dam now stands) and the court fixed the schedule of ferry fees to be charged. The county agent was ordered to convey to the Methodists the church lot reserved for them. The session lasted two days, with a full court present.

A special session held on December 14, 1850, modified the former order for erection of a temporary court house. The location was changed to the center of the court house square, and the size of the building was reduced to 16 by 18 feet. A detail of the specifications is set out in the minutes from which it appears that the entire construction was to be of native material, except the shutters, facings and casings of the doors and windows, which were to be of pine lumber. Completion in time for the Spring term of the District Court was again required.

No mention is made in the subsequent minutes of the name of the successful bidder on the temporary court house nor of the amount of his bid, but it is otherwise well known that the contract was let to Mr. Thomas D. Havens and the minutes of May 19, 1851, recite that the county agent was ordered to pay the contractor in full settlement for the building the sum of $199.00. The oft-repeated story that this building cost $90.00 is evidently a mistake.

A six day session was opened on February 17, 1851, at which in addition to routine matters, the first tax levy was made. One-half the State rate for 1851 (7½ cents on the $100.00 assessed valuation and 25 cents poll) and one half of the State rate of occupation taxes were fixed by the court.

It should be noted in passing that up to this time the county had received no revenue whatever and possessed no available resource except the small amounts in cash and notes realized from the sale of town lots in Nolanville. These funds were applied to the organization expenses and the remainder was transferred as a temporary loan to the general fund for the payment of current expenses. And this condition necessarily continued until the taxes for 1851 should be assessed and collected during the latter part of the year. Thus the financial situation of the county was rather straitened. But fortunately the expenses were small and the creditors cheerfully waited for the county's tax-money to come in.

At a brief and unimportant session, held on May 19, 1851, some drastic orders against delinquent lot buyers were entered, to be enforced by the county agent. The temporary court house was received and the county agent was ordered to pay for it out of the town lot funds.

At a two days session in August, 1851, County Treasurer Stephen Goodman reported his receipts to date as $111.60 and his disbursements as $50.27; and the "plan of Nolanville as drawn by E. Lawrence Stickney under the direction of Joseph Dennis" was adopted "as the official map of record and a guide for the issuing of titles to lots in said town."

These are the condensed notes of some of the labors of the Commissioners' Court—our county legislature—during the first year after its inauguration of the machinery of a new county. The records are meager but sufficient to exhibit the very crude and provincial methods of launching a county government in a wilderness one hundred and seventy miles from the nearest port (Houston) and before there was a mile of railroad in the State. These simple records, page by page, volume by volume, unfold the progress, step by step, of the subsequent official annals of Bell County and we here remark that the old fathers did very well under all the circumstances.

During the construction of the little "16x18" court house, and for years afterward, the county officers transacted their official business in the different business houses about the village and these buildings were of a very primitive character. Even after its completion, the accomodations of the court house were so palpably inadequate that these officers, most of whom were engaged in some private business as well, kept their official books and papers and performed their official duties in whatever house they used for their outside employment or in cut-off spaces rented for offices.

Thus the county records traveled around the village from place to place with the changes in the personnel of the officers and with the mutations of their private business occupations.

4. The Probate Court

Another function of the Chief Justice was to serve as judge of the Probate Court of the county. The first term of the Probate Court of Bell County was held on the fourth Monday in November (November 25th), 1850. Tradition says that this also occurred in Judge Danley's blacksmith shop on East Water Street, in Nolanville. One can imagine that the Probate Docket lay spread out upon the anvil. The record is:

"Present—Hon. John Danley, Chief Justice, Jas. E. Williams, Deputy Sheriff, John C. Reid, Clerk.

"No business presenting itself, the Court adjourned."

The first business presented to this court was on June 30, 1851, when the application of Mrs. Margaret Taylor to probate the will of John Waugh, deceased, was continued, no parties appearing. At the same session S. Brown Taylor and J. Wilson Taylor, minors over 14 years old, chose Mr. Nathaniel Shields as guardian of their persons and estates, which was confirmed by the Court. Geo. W. Chapman, whose wife was formerly Miss Caroline Frazier, was a witness as to the age of Wilson Taylor. These people, the Taylors and Fraziers, were participants in the Indian affair known as the "Taylor Fight," which occurred in November,

Left to right: Dr. B. D. McKie, D. D. Rosborough, Judge D. T. Chamberlin

1836, in the valley still bearing the name, some two miles below Belton and fully related in another place.[1]

The machinery of the Probate Court thereafter continued on its dreary course, administering upon the estates of the dead, appointing guardians for the persons and estates of minors, lunatics, etc., and exercising, under the law, a general control over these matters. It seems unnecessary to pursue the chronological routine of the Probate Court beyond its inauguration.

The Constitution of 1869 transferred the probate functions to the District Judge, while that of 1875 vested them in the County Court, which exercises all of the powers of the former Chief Justice. The title "Chief Justice" has disappeared from our county government.

5. The District Court

The first term of the District Court of Bell County was opened in the little "16 x 18" temporary court house, already mentioned. This important event, the first assertion of juridical authority and of the administration of the written law ever witnessed in this part of the then wilderness, occurred on Monday, April 7th, 1851.

The venerable R. E. B. Baylor, of Washington County, Judge of the Third Judicial District of Texas, presided. He was lawyer, judge, statesman and Baptist minister. Dr. William D. Eastland, District Clerk, recorded the minutes and decrees of the Court, while William Reed, our first Sheriff, proclaimed the opening of the first trial court ever held this side of the "Lower Cross Timbers." Josiah F. Crosby, also of Washington County, the District Attorney of the District and a distinguished lawyer, prosecuted the "pleas of the State."

The Grand Jury, the first ever empanelled in the county, was composed of David Havens, foreman, John Anderson, John Bowles, Allen Bryant, Walter Burch, William Caldwell, John M. Cathey, Milton W. Damron, James M. Glenn, Thos. T. Havens, Warren Puett, Horatio Shelton, James T. Sherrod, Benj. L. Stewart and Matthew Wilkins. Matthew Givens was appointed bailiff of the Grand Jury.

The following were empanneled as members of the

[1] Ante, page 33.

petit jury: Benjamin Adams, James Ashley, James F. Bowles, Geo. W. Chapman, Daniel C. Crawford, Joseph Dennis, John Dunlap, John Fulcher, John Havens, William K. Karnes, Jacob Karr, John Pennington, Theophilus Petty, James Richards and Lorenzo Vancleve.

When Court convened there were nine original civil causes pending on the docket and one case appealed from a Justice Court. The first of these original suits was numbered and styled thus:

No. 1.—Jas. A. Graves and wife, Mary A. Graves, Administrators with the Will annexed, of Frederick Neibling Sr., deceased *versus* Christopher Cruise. The petition signed by "Giddings" (J. D. Giddings of Brenham) as attorney for plaintiffs, bears no file mark but this is indicated by the date of the citation which was issued on January 23, 1851. Suits Nos. 2, 3, 4 and 5 were by the same attorney and for the same plaintiffs and against Alex Frazier, C. A. Johnson, James B. Burns and John Lewis, respectively. All of these suits were for "locative interests," fees and expenses incurred by the deceased Neibling in locating lands in Bell County for the respective defendants, prior to the organization of this county. The citations were printed in the "Texas State Gazette," then published at Austin by Cushney & Hampton and a printed copy of the citation is attached to the Sheriff's return subsequently filed in each case, sworn to by Joseph W. Hampton before James M. Long, Notary Public, Travis County, Texas, October 8, 1851. The citations were published four weeks beginning with February 22, 1851. All of the nine cases were continued until next term of court, except one which was settled by compromise.

The appeal case was from the court of Nicholas Shields, Justice of the Peace, and was thus numbered and styled in his Court: No. 1—Daniel Alexander vs. Milton W. Damron.

The Grand Jury returned two indictments for assault and battery and one for larceny, the trials of which were continued to the next term and the Court, after a three days term, adjourned.

CHAPTER IX

TEN YEARS OF GROWTH, 1850-1860

1. *How the New Settlers Came and How They Lived*

The organization of Bell County gave assurance to prospective immigrants of the permanence and stability of this frontier section, while the reports which went back to the older settlements concerning the fertility of its soil and the abundance of wood, water and grass for stock—all of which were of the first importance to the pioneers—lured home-seekers in increasing numbers. This was a period when a heavy tide of immigration was pouring into Texas from the older states and pushing out to the line of the frontier, and Bell County was getting its share.

The settlers came both from the older settled sections of Texas—the lower Brazos and eastern Texas—and directly from other states. If the men came first to prospect the country and select locations, they usually came on horseback in small parties of from two to ten, camping out at night either in the wilds or near the cabin of some earlier settler. If their families came with them, or when the families subsequently came, they traveled in the wagons of the old "prairie-schooner" type, drawn, usually, by two or three yokes of oxen, though sometimes by horses or mules; and where possible, several families traveled together for mutual protection against Indians and to aid each other in crossing the streams. The covered wagon, in which rode the mother and smaller children, carried the scanty household goods and supplies; a few head of cattle, driven by the father or by the older boys and sometimes the girls, all on horseback, followed by the family dog brought up the rear. There were no roads, but mere trails and sometimes nothing but the course of the sun to guide them. In crossing streams where the banks were steep or slippery it was necessary to double the teams and pull up one wagon at a time. Sometimes they had to cut their way through the woods.

After arriving at the location of their future home, they first pitched camp and made it as comfortable as possible until they could build a cabin. Single men usually came on horseback, and either camped out on their location or boarded with some near-by settler, helping in the work of building his home, fencing and breaking his land, or attending his stock. Most men brought with them a few farming implements; some brought a few slaves or drove considerable herds of cattle and horses, and even hogs, from their former homes. Generally, the new arrivals carried such supplies as they could transport, but during their first year in the new country they depended largely upon the prior settlers for corn, bacon and other provisions. Almost every family brought along an "English steel mill" for grinding corn into coarse meal. It was fastened to a post or the wall of the cabin and operated by a hand crank—a slow process but a very necessary one, for there were few water mills in the country and these might be many miles away from the settler's home.

As soon as possible after arriving at his location, the settler built his house. It was usually of logs, notched and fitted at the corners, but was sometimes weatherboarded on cedar studding with boards rived from burr-oak and spanish-oak. The roof, at first, was likely to be made of rough boards which were held in place by weight poles pinned at the end with wooden pegs. Sometimes shingles, rived from spanish oak, were used, but this was rarely the case. Eventually, shingle mills were set up to saw shingles from hard woods, cedar, or even cotton wood or willow. Few houses were ceiled. The cracks or openings between the wall-logs were "chinked" with mud or mortar; the chimneys were made of sticks and mud or of crude stone masonry. The floors, at first, were either dirt or puncheon (split) logs. Later on the houses were built of "rawhide" lumber, sawed from native oak. The nearest pine was in Bastrop County and was rarely used in the early days, and then only for doors, casings, window shutters and flooring. For several years window glass was a rarity. The first brought to the county was placed in the house of Judge D. T. Chamberlin in Belton in 1854.

As soon as possible the settler fenced in a small field to protect his crop from the stock. This was before the days of barbed wire, and making a fence was extremely laborious. Most fences were of oak or cedar rails, eight rails high, of Virginia "worm" construction, "staked and ridered." When the material was close at hand, some settlers built stone fences. Remains of these old rock fences are still to be seen here and there. Yards and cow pens were usually built of rails or poles.

The furnishings of the houses were simple. Tables, chairs and beds were home-made. The cooking was done in the fireplace in iron skillets, frying-pans and pots, the latter usually hung from an iron bar or crane. Neighbors, by turns, killed a beef and distributed it around, in quarters or otherwise, once or twice a week. In Belton someone occasionally operated a butcher shop for a time. Pork, mutton, venison and other game and fish were common in town and country. The merchants of Belton and a few little stores in scattered parts of the county supplied the people with coffee, sugar, salt, pepper, and other provisions, as well as with tobacco, calico, jeans, domestic, gingham, denim, shoes, boots, hose, thread, hats, etc.

The man wore home-made clothing of buckskin, homespun, jeans, or denim, overcoats made from blankets, heavy shoes or boots, wide-brimmed wool hats, or caps made of cloth or coonskin, cotton and wool shirts. The women wore clothing of homespun, calico, gingham or woolens and homemade sunbonnets. In fact nearly all clothing was cut and made at home by the good women. Of course, nearly everyone had a "Sunday" suit or dress for company or for visiting which was bought at the store. Some families recently "from the states" brought with them nice "store made" things—even silk and satins—but unless very carefully preserved these fineries succumbed in due time to the trials of a hard country life. But the young ladies looked just as sweet in their homespun, calicoes, or ginghams as in the finest silks, and they were "in style" in either. As the population increased and prospered, the merchants carried better stocks from which the men could buy ready-made clothing and the women could select their costumes from a better assortment.

Rawhide was the article of most universal use among all the people. Saddle trimmings, harness, shoes belts, lariats, whips, quirts, bell collars, plowlines, floor mats, chair-bottoms, door and window shutters were fabricated from this material and numerous other uses were found for it. It was indeed the "rawhide age," back in the fifties and sixties, for rawhide was plentiful and cheap.

The early settler knew nothing of breech-loading guns, nor of cartridges and cartridge belts. His gun, if not an old flint-lock, was muzzle-loading, the powder and shot, or rifle ball, being forced down with the ram-rod, and the priming was the percussion cap. His ammunition was carried in a rawhide or coonskin pouch, swung over the shoulder by a rawhide strap, and a powder-horn was attached to the pouch. He could buy shot at the stores, but rifle balls were moulded at home. Derringers and holster-pistols soon gave place to the Colt's revolver. For various purposes a large hack-knife or bowie-knife generally formed a part of his outfit and was used for many purposes about the camp or at home—for cutting away brush in hunting or traveling, for "sticking" a beef, a deer, or other large animal, and also for personal defense in close quarters. There was no law against bearing concealed weapons until about 1870, and men usually traveled with six-shooters swung to their belts or saddles, or in their saddle bags. This did not mean that they were desperate or dangerous men but that they felt they must be ready to protect themselves against Indians, wild animals and other perils of an unsettled country.

Prior to the Civil War there were probably not a dozen buggies or carriages, at any one time, in Bell County. People usually traveled on horseback, or if the whole family went along, by wagon. And yet, though people lived far apart, they were good neighbors and visited often—men, women and children on horseback. In those days, of course, the women without exception rode on the old-time side-saddle and in riding skirts. A woman astride was unheard of and would have shocked the whole community.

The publisher of Belton's first newspaper, having no buggy and being unwilling to submit to the slow speed of the ox-wagon, improvised an unique outfit in which he made a trip in the summer of 1858 to Hempstead, the terminus of the H. & T. C. Railway. *The Public Ledger* of Philadelphia published the following account by its Texas correspondent, which was reprinted in the Belton paper:

> Talking about buggy riding!—Yes, friends, they are all the rage, but you seldom see a sulkey. I have seen two, however; one was regular, the other was of the most primitive make-up imaginable. A gentleman, in undress, drove up behind an old black horse. He was seated upon a dry goods box which was plumb down upon the axle, confining a pair of stout farm wagon hind wheels; attached to this was a pair of rough hewed ashen poles for shafts, whilst the horse was breeched with grass rope fixings, and the lines were of white cotton ditto. In his box he had his saddle bags, a sack of wheat, a few oats, hand saw, a hammer and a few nails. My companion soon recognized him and we hail-fellowed all around. Shade of Franklin! It was a printer and editor on his way to Houston to buy paper. He had come 125 miles in that trim to take the cars. We spent a merry

evening with our philosophic friend, listening to anecdote after anecdote from his well stored mind, and after hoping he might arrive safely at home with paper in the sulkey, without being compelled to use saw or hammer, we goodnighted the hand of (Andrew) Marschalk (Sr.) of the "Belton Independent," and wished perpetual sunshine to the heart of the independent Marschalk of Belton.[1]

The people were kind, generous and hospitable as they are in all new settlements. There were no hotels except in larger towns, but in every home there was welcome to the friend and the stranger alike, without money and without price—a home as long as he wanted to remain under the settler's roof. To charge for entertaining a friend, an acquaintance, or even a stranger, was almost unheard of. And the good women rode for miles on horseback to nurse the sick and relieve the distressed. Honesty was almost universal. There were no banks at first and people kept their money in their homes or on their persons with perfect safety. Often large sums were intrusted to others to be carried to a distant place, there to be paid over in some business transaction. Travelers with large sums of money on their persons with which to buy lands could and often did go anywhere they pleased with impunity. Robbery or murder for money was of the rarest occurrence and was pursued and punished by a swift and avenging nemesis that few culprits escaped. As the stock of the settler ran at large in the open range without herders, it required *summary treatment* of the horse-thief and cow-thief to protect them, and that is why the thieves were sometimes disposed of *without expense to the county*.

Although life was hard and laborious in these early communities, the people were not without amusements and pleasures. The men found recreation in hunting the abundant game, such as deer, antelope, bears, turkeys, wild-cats, catamounts, panthers or cougars, wolves, and the smaller quarry like squirrels, o'possums, and coons, or in running down and capturing wild horses and cattle. The streams were well stocked with fish, and the men and boys, often the women and girls, found sport with pole and line or with "set hook."

In the winter time the young people attended balls in town or parties at some settler's home in the country where they threaded the old square dances on the puncheon floors. Music

[1] **The Belton Independent,** August 7, 1858.

was furnished by one or more regular fiddlers, employed for the occasion. At the end, late in the "wee sma'" hours, refreshments of cake, coffee, chicken and other delicacies were served. It was not uncommon to dance all night. Where rigorous church influence prevented dancing, candy pullings and "play-parties" were a favorite form of entertainment. In the summertime, watermelon parties, moonlight picnics, pecan hunting, grape and plum hunting, dewberry parties brought boys and girls together to play, talk and court under proper chaperonage. Barbecues and community picnics brought out young and old—usually on the "Glorious Fourth" or in connection with political campaigns when the candidates for office made addresses on the "glorious principles" of their parties. "First Mondays" and election days were of special interest to the men.

According to tradition, the first observance in Bell County of the Fourth of July was in 1852, when the people assembled in Belton, on the south bank of Nolan Creek, under the shade of a group of oak trees, just below the present Yettie Tobler Park. One of the old trees, a large white oak, is still standing. Nothing is known of the celebration, but it was a campaign year and the election was to be held in August, it is safe to assume that the oratory was furnished mostly by the local candidates.

Horse and pony races were occasions of great interest and zestful rivalry. Betting was lively. Money was scarce; but horses, cattle, guns, and even negroes and lands changed hands and much excitement resulted, emphasized sometimes by a fist fight or even a tragedy. One notable instance of the latter kind occurred about 1859 or 1860, when a largely attended horse race was staged in Taylor's Valley, near Belton, between horses brought from Coryell County by George W. Haley and others and horses owned by Dave Williams and others of Bell. The races were run, the debts paid, and all went well until late in the afternoon when the parties returned to town and indulged in too much bad liquor. A quarrel ensued, guns came into play, and one of the Haleys was killed by one of the Williams party.

About 1859 came the first circus that ever visited this section of the country. It was the famous old John Robinson circus, fresh to this day in the memories of the old timers. The big tent was spread in south Belton, near the present site of the Tarver school building. People came from near and far; and among those who had made the pilgrimage with his parents was this writer, then a small boy residing in Coryell County, some twenty-five miles away. He saw things that day which he has never fogotten—clowns, acrobats, trained ponies, lions, elephants and other animals he did not know really existed, although his mother had often read to him about them in children's books. These marvels, the toy balloons and the red lemonade made a perfect day, a great event; and he and the other boys returned home with the conviction that there was nothing more wonderful to be seen in this world.

2. *Belton in the Fifties*

On October 4, 1850, the Post Office Department at Washington established a post office at Nolanville and on that day appointed Dr. William D. Eastland as its first postmaster. The mail was carried on horseback between the Waco Village and Austin, via Nolanville. Col. Geo. E. Burney and Mr. John S. Blair, both of whom then lived in Waco, were the contractors. This was a link in the long line of mail service from Clarksville, near Red River (thence extending eastward to Memphis and the "old States") to San Antonio and Brownsville, on the Rio Grande. The first mail riders on our section of this route can not be named; but we know that young Swan Bigham was the mail rider in the fall of 1851, that he resigned after three months service and was succeeded by young William S. Riggs, a nephew of Mr. Blair. It required two days to make the trip each way and the rider spent the night at the terminals and at Mr. Joel D. Blair's home, at the Childers Mill on the Lampasas.

In 1852 Messrs. Burney and Blair, the mail contractors, inaugurated a weekly stage line with terminals at Waco and Austin via Belton (formerly Nolanville) and Georgetown. One of the "stage stands," where horses and sometimes drivers were changed, was maintained at Belton in charge of an employee of the company. The stage carried passengers and their personal baggage as well as the mail. Belton was then, and until the railroads came, on the main upper thoroughfare across the State, whether by stage, buggy, wagon, horseback or other mode of conveyance, from north and east Texas to Austin, the State capital, to San

Antonio and other sections of south and southwest Texas and to old Mexico.

The travel was so heavy, indeed, that in 1857 another line of passenger stages, over the same route, was put on by Messrs. Sawyer and Compton.[2] In 1858 they obtained the mail contract and became the sole operators of the stages, which arrived daily from Waco and Austin with stages and hacks alternating.[3] Later it was carried by the stages only which provided a daily mail and passenger service until the building of the Santa Fe Railroad in 1881.

The arrival of the weekly mail stage was a thrilling event in the life of our little village on the Nolan. The late Mr. P. L. Ellis thus graphically described it:

"The great overland stage, with its pompous driver flourishing a whip, its handle ornamented with silver rings, the lash ending in a silken thread, with four beautiful horses bearing heavily upon the rein, the driver with a trumpet to his mouth, notifying the good people of Belton that the United States Mail, *a month old*, was arriving. The post office was a board building on the west side of the square. T. A. Supple, the postmaster, stood in the door, hat off, ready to take charge of the mail. The New Orleans *Picayune*, Brownlow's *Whig*, etc, were quickly opened and a good reader gave the eager crowd the news."[4]

A semi-weekly horseback mail between Belton and Marlin, and a weekly one between Belton and Cameron were inaugurated in 1857;[5] and a similar weekly mail between Belton and Gatesville was put on in 1859.[6]

For reasons not now known, a movement was begun in the fall of 1851 to change the name of Nolanville, the county seat. It has been claimed by some that another post office in Texas—possibly on the other Nolan stream—was so similar to Nolanville as to cause some confusion and delay in the mail service to our village and that the change was desirable in order to avoid this trouble. Tradition tells us that a petition to the Legislature, prepared by Dr. William

---

[2] **The Belton Independent,** June 25, 1857.
[3] **The Belton Independent,** May 22, 1858; June 6, June 28, 1858.
[4] P. L. Ellis: "Belton in the Fifties"—**Proceedings of Old Settlers Association of Bell County for 1902,** p. 32.
[5] **The Belton Independent,** June 25, 1857.
[6] **The Belton Independent,** March 19, 1859.

D. Eastland, the post master, who is also reputed to have selected the new name, was circulated for signatures by Col. Hermon Aiken and others. At any rate, by an act approved December 16, 1851, it was provided:

"That the name of Nolanville, given to the County Seat of Bell County, be, and is hereby changed to that of Belton, and that Belton be hereafter the name of said County Seat."[7]

The Act went into effect immediately and the town has ever since been known by the name of Belton. On April 22, 1852, the Post Office Department at Washington recorded the change of the name of the post office from Nolanville to Belton and reappointed Dr. William D. Eastland as post master. The minutes of the Commissioners Court use the name Belton for the first time, in the date line of a special session held on May 1, 1852.

A numerously signed petition from citizens of Belton and Bell County, dated January 5, 1852, asking that the name be changed back from Belton to Nolanville, was filed with the Legislature and is now in the archives of the Department of State, at Austin. It throws no light, however, upon the question of why the change was made or upon the origin of the new name.

Why the name of Belton was selected—supposedly by Dr. Eastland—has been the subject of several conjectures, the historic value of which, however, are deemed insufficient to justify their recital here.

The most reasonable explanation is, we think, that the word Belton is a contraction for the words Bell and Town and that it was deemed an appropriate name for the county seat of a county named Bell. On this probable explanation being submitted, in 1916, to the late Mrs. Helen M. Eastland (widow of Dr. William Eastland) then residing in Oklahoma City, she replied: "Dr. Eastland told me that he suggested the name of Belton . . . that (the explanation suggested above) was probably the reason the name was adopted. I never heard any other reason than the contraction of Belltown."

Although it is impossible to give exact dates, we may indicate some of the improvements in Belton in the early years of its existence.

[7] Gammel, **Laws of Texas,** III, p. 891.

About 1854 or 1855, James A. Stringfellow erected a two-story concrete building on the south side of the court house square, in which he opened a saddlery and harness business. It was later purchased by Col. E. B. Warren and was occupied by his son, Henry J. Warren for a saloon, and became known as the "Warren building." About the same time Mr. Ellis Stackpole, from Houston, erected a store building and opened up as a merchant. The location is not certain, but it was somewhere on the square.

A two-story frame building was erected by Col. E. B. Warren at the southwest corner of the square (where the Christian Church now stands). He sold it to John C. Henry, and it became known as the "Henry building" and for awhile as the "Henry and Foster building," while Mr. Robert B. Foster was a partner of Mr. Henry. The first story was used for general merchandise, saloon, etc., by Jack Warren and later by Henry and Foster. It was also called the "Exchange." The second story was used a a public hall for all purposes—District Court, religious meetings, lodges, balls, and dancing schools, since it was about the only general assembly hall in the village for a number of years. The *Belton Journal* was first issued there in 1866, and occupied the building for about fifteen years. Mr. Stackpole, about 1856, erected also the St. Charles Hotel on the northeast corner of the square, where Mr. V. Nigro's store now stands. It was a two-story frame and weatherboard building, with porch extending on the whole front of both stories. It was owned and operated, successively, by E. M. Stackpole, John S. Blair, John M. Pope and by Silas A. Kingsbury, who conducted it until his death which occurred soon after the War between the States. His widow leased it to Haymond Brothers, Mrs. Bartlett and others, successively, who operated the hotel until it was destroyed by fire in April, 1875. Another merchant who built a business house and traded therein for several years was Mr. Charles P. Cruger, from Houston.

About 1854 came Mr. Norman Austin, who had a store at the west corner of the north side of the square until about the end of the Civil War, when he moved to California. In the early seventies he returned to Belton and resumed the mercantile business in a two-story stone building erected by him on the east side of the square and which is still standing.

Ten Years of Growth, 1850-1860

The most conspicuous business houses erected in Belton, in the fifties, were those built by Mr. Isaac Jalonick and Dr. William D. Eastland, about the center of the north side of the square in 1855 or 1856. They were two-storied, of stone, adjoined, and had ornamental fronts of sawed native stone. The upper story of each was fitted up as a residence for the owner. These buildings, probably among the first stone buildings put up, were destroyed by fire in 1879 and the present buildings are reconstructions by Miller Brothers and H. C. Denny, then the owners. Jalonick, later associated with Mr. John F. Smith, did a general mercantile business. The store was closed soon after the Civil War began. Dr. Eastland operated a drug and book store, later selling the building to Mr. Robert C. Miller who, with John J. Baker, had carried on a mercantile business up to the Civil War. About 1855, Mr. W. S. Rather came from Houston to Belton and built a two-story frame building on the north side of the square and engaged in merchandising, using the second story as a residence.

Another two-story stone building was erected in the middle fifties on the south side of the square by Mr. E. Mills, who merchandized in the lower story and resided in the second story and so continued until the war in 1861, during the last years having Mr. Charles A. Bigelow as a partner. Mr. A. D. Potts has owned and occupied the building since 1872.

Mr. John H. Powers ("Uncle Jack") and his brother, Tazewell W. Powers, did a small mercantile business in a one-story frame building at the east corner of the north side of the square. A blacksmith shop was opened in the fifties on the west side of Main Street by James Lambert and Jas. P. Coop. From 1857 till 1862 Mr. David Hirsh did a mercantile business in a frame two-story building on the north side of the square, about where the People's National Bank stands. He resided in the second story. Dr. J. A. Ewing, in the late fifties, had a drug store in the Stewart building already mentioned.

A small log house on the west side of North Pearl Street, opposite the west end of Second Avenue of the present day, was used quite a while in the early days for school and church purposes, all denominations worshiping therein. Among the ministers who first preached there were Revs.

John Carpenter, Finis E. Foster, Levi Tenny, J. Fred Cox[a] and others.

Early in 1854 Rev. Finis E. Foster, a Cumberland Presbyterian minister, held a successful revival in the log cabin and, following this, Col. Hermon Aiken, a member of this denomination who then resided on Cedar Creek some six miles north of town, raised a subscription among people of all creeds and erected the Cumberland Presbyterian Church, a one-story frame building situated where the First Methodist Church now stands. Here again all denominations worshiped, by turns, and here schools were taught, in the fifties, by Judge Erasmus Walker, Edward W. Kinnan and others. For about sixteen years this was the only church building in Belton. The war in the early sixties delayed the building of such structures and greatly retarded the expansion of the town in many other ways. After the completion of the second court house in 1860, religious services were often held in the District Court room. But in summer time the shady groves along the Nolan and other streams, under the old-time brush arbors, were the most popular gathering places for camp-meetings, revivals, "July Fourths," and political speakings.

In 1857 Judge David T. Chamberlin and Belton Lodge No. 166, Ancient Free and Accepted Masons, jointly erected a two-story stone building on the west side of Main Street, where the south half of the Harris & Saunders building now stands; but the structure has been twice burned and rebuilt (in 1881 and in 1882). The ground floor was occupied by Chamberlin and Flint as a law office, the second floor as a Masonic lodge room. It was also used by the Odd Fellows Lodge, the Union Sunday School and other bodies. About this time Mr. James P. Reed built a one-story stone residence at the northeast corner of the town plat, on Wall Street—long since demolished and rebuilt with lumber by Mr. Reed himself. Another like structure at the northwest corner of the same block, on Penelope Street, was put up by Judge John Danley. The late Major A. M. Hanna occupied it for many years as a residence. It was last used in connection with a lumber yard and was demolished as late as 1922.

[a] Son of Euclid M. Cox, who was killed by Indians in the Battle Creek fight, see **ante,** p. 58.

Ten Years of Growth, 1850-1860

In the late fifties Mr. Oliver H. Bigham began the erection of a two-story stone building, at the outside southwest corner of the court house square, for a hotel. It was octagonal in form and of rather an elaborate design for a small village of that time. The stone work was completed, when for some reason the work was suspended. The war came on soon afterward and it was never completed as originally designed. The naked, gloomy walls stood there for a decade or more. In the early seventies it passed into the hands of Messrs. Robert H. Turner and John T. Gilbert who remodeled it into the usual rectangular form and completed it as two store rooms, with lofts above in the customary style. Part of it is now owned by the Knights of Pythias Order.

During the late fifties Mr. John C. Henry built a two-story stone residence on the west side of north Main Street. The Federal building—the U. S. post office—row stands on the same lot. One-story frame residences were erected by Judge D. T. Chamberlin, Dr. John W. Embree, Mr. Isaac Jalonick, Mr. E. W. Kinnan, H. E. Bradford, Mrs. A. S. Isbell—all on the west side of north Main Street—and by Marshall McIlhenny on the east side, where the Tyler Grammar School building now stands.

Rev. Finis E. Foster owned and fenced a farm tract extending on Main Street from the town plat (the present Second Avenue) to the present Tyler Grammar School lot and eastward to the old military (or Waco) road, embracing some fifty acres or more. It included the present high school ground and all of the Jno. T. Alexander and Alexander and Hanna additions. His residence stood on the east side of the present Penelope Street, west and a little south of the present Fifth Avenue. Col. Jno. T. Flint's residence stood on the west side of the present north Pearl Street, as now extended, at the intersection of the present Seventh Avenue. He had something like seventy-two acres enclosed and this included all of the present Baylor College grounds and Santa Fe Railway track west of Main Street.

Other large tracts, with residences thereon, were those of Mr. Frank Pendleton (the Pendleton addition); Mr. Norman Austin (now the Trapp place); Neal M. Dennis, a little southeast from Austin's, later owned and occupied by Col. E. B. Warren; Joel D. Blair on the hill east of the compress and south of the Cotton Mill, where his old house—a relic of the past—still stands; Mrs. Venable and Judge Erasmus Walker, southeast of the Cotton Mill; Mr. Moore, Major John Henry Brown (author of "The History of Texas," etc.), and John Wesley Scott, all on the Lampasas road, west of Baylor College. The last two are now owned by Baylor College, the president's residence being on the exact spot where Major Brown's house stood. Dr. William D. Eastland owned from Main Street to Leon Heights, north of an including the Santa Fe right of way; David Williams owned what was later known as the John M. Pope place, on the Military road.

Other residences on the north side of the Nolan were those of Dr. J. A. Ewing (built by H. E. Bradford) on the lot embracing the present Santa Fe depot ground and Santa Fe Park; Col. Silas Hare, on Central Avenue, the present Cameron Lumber yard; Robert B. Foster on the north side of Central Avenue, where the Ice Factory now stands; Jno. M. Payne, on east Water Street; Abram W. Richard; Charles and William Bock, and a number of others.

Residences on the south side of the Nolan were: on Pearl Street, Dr. A. C. Willingham, Geo. B. White, Moses Cornelison, John T. Roberts, William Smith; John H. Lee, and R. D. Kinney (near the cemetery); Mrs. Sarah A. Kelton; Albert Tobler, on the south end of the present Yettie Tobler Park; Sam Kegley, west of the park; Horatio Shelton, at the Shelton Spring; and several others.

Judge Wilson Y. McFarland's old home still remains, on the Killeen road, on the high ground in West Belton—it formerly included all of the present McFarland addition. The ante-bellum home of Judge X. B. Saunders, still standing, was on a large tract of land, now mostly covered with residences, in the southwest part of Belton. Prior to and during the war the south portion of the present Yettie Tobler Park was occupied as a tanyard operated by Mr. Albert Tobler.

Most of the improvements in the town, during the fifties, are thus accounted for, but not, of course, in their chronological order, for that is impossible.

Returning to the business section it may be stated that most of the remaining spaces on the four sides of the court house square were, in the fifties, practically filled in with small one story frame buildings for small merchants, drug stores, offices for lawyers and doctors, saloons, etc., though

Ten Years of Growth, 1850-1860

a few vacant spaces remained. In those days and for many decades afterward the better class of business houses were on the north side, which was built up solidly during the first three decades, and the larger volume of dry goods and general merchandizing was conducted there, while the south side was mostly given over to saloons, billiard halls, bowling alleys, and gambling halls, and enjoyed the classic name of "Smoky Row." In later decades this class of business drifted around to the east side, which for a long time was locally known as "Rat Row."

It is seen that the county seat was enjoying a healthy growth and development, considering the sparse population of the country, when the blight of war fell upon it in 1861 and, as it always does, struck down and paralyzed for a time the efforts of our people to make further civic advance.

3. *The Official Business of the County*

The beginnings of the county government have already been described. It will be recalled that the first public building erected by the county was the little frame court-house, sixteen by eighteen feet, which was built in the spring of 1851. Within a few years the county authorities decided that the community had made sufficient progress in civilization to require the construction of a jail. On February 22, 1854, the commissioners' court adopted specifications for a jail to be built on Lot 4, Block 22, North Pearl Street, Belton, and ordered the sheriff to let the contract to the lowest and best bidder at a public bidding. As the specifications for this "bastile" may now appear strange, though of a standard common in those days, they are here given in condensed form.

It was to be constructed of ten-inch oak logs, squared and resting on a foundation of hard rock five feet thick. There were to be two rooms, one above the other, each twelve feet square on the inside. The walls, as well as the floor, of the lower room consisted of a double thickness of logs with upright iron slats between the inner and outer logs and securely bolted to them. Two small windows, ten inches square, with heavy iron bars, sufficed for light and fresh air. The upper room had walls of a single thickness of ten-inch oak logs, with two windows of the same size as those in the lower room, and likewise barred. The whole was roofed with oak shingles. The entrance to this prison was through a heavy oak door, strapped and barred with iron, in the upper room. Through a trap door in the floor of the upper room the victim of the law was thrust into the dungeon below. The contract was let to Mr. Oliver H. Bigham at $2500, and the building was accepted by the court on May 21, 1855.

After all these well-devised specifications and elaborate precautions for the construction of what must have been one of the best jails in this part of Texas, one would think that it should have evoked the pride of the citizens and the respect of the prisoners. But the old-timers say that both classes of our citizens soon lost all regard for it, and that prisoners seldom if ever spent the night in it unless there were special guards—one notable exception being a man who felt himself safer from his enemies inside than out. When the whole country was open and free and there were so many interesting diversions outside, who would want to stay in a little twelve by twelve log crib that he couldn't even see out of? The writer first saw this building (from the *outside*) when a small boy in 1861 or 1862. It was in service until about 1872 when it was sold at auction and was replaced by another on the same lot.

In the meantime the 18 by 18 frame court house had become totally inadequate—the county had been renting court rooms and offices elsewhere for some time—and on November 21, 1855, this building was ordered to be sold at auction, the purchaser to remove it within thirty days. The county had no money with which to build a better court house, however, until the state came to its aid. On August 21, 1856, the legislature passed an act, over the veto of Governor Pease, providing that the state should relinquish to each county nine-tenths of the state tax collected therein for the years 1856 and 1857 on the condition that said taxes be applied, "first, to the erection of good and substantial public buildings, or to the payment for the same, if already erected and not paid for, and afterwards to such general purposes as may be directed by the commissioners courts of the respective counties." The other one-tenth of the taxes was to be passed to the credit of the Free Common School Fund of the State. The expenses of the state government at this time were very moderate, and it was able to come to the aid of the counties because it was paying its expenses out of the $5,000,000 in United States bonds which it had received a short time before from the federal government in payment for the Santa Fe region. By means of the state taxes thus retained Bell County was able to accumulate some $4,000 as an initial payment on a new court house. But this was not enough; and to provide a county fund to meet further payments, the legislature on February 12, 1858, passed a special act empowering the county courts of Gonzales and Bell Counties to levy a special tax for court house purposes.

At the special term, April 1, 1858, the court decided to build the second court house. Mr. William Bock was employed to prepare plans and specifications and these were adopted on the 10th. They were quite elaborate and are recorded in full in the minutes. They called for a good substantial building, 50 feet north and south 60 feet east and west. Entrances with double doors and transoms on top and sides were provided on the north and south fronts, and a wide main hall extended from the north door to intersect a cross hall extending across the south side of the building, and from the east and west ends of this cross hall, stairways ascended to the second floor, but there were also entrance doors at each end of the cross hallway. Rooms for the county officers opened off each side of the main hall, with stone partition walls between them, and all of the lower or ground floors were laid in sawed native stone flagging or tile. Over each stairway, on the second floor, was a small jury or consultation room. The remainder of the second floor was the court room. The building was covered with drawn oak shingles, hip-roof construction; with proper gutters, down spouts, etc. Fire places below and fire places and stoves above heated the building. Native limestone, obtained in nearby quarries, was used for walls and tile floor.

The court appropriated for building this court house the sum of $4,000 from the state tax, then in the hands of the county treasurer of Bell County, the balance of the cost to be paid out of the county funds, raised by a special tax, in annual installments of $1,000 each.

The Chief Justice was authorized to advertise for sealed bids for building the court house, to be submitted on the third Monday (17th day) of May, 1858, the work to commence by June 1, 1858 and to be completed by November 1, 1859. On May 19, 1858, the bids were opened and were as follows: Robert B. Foster and Oliver H. Bigham—$14,497; A. M. Keller and Simeon Bramlet—$13,625.

Messrs. Keller and Bramlet, the lowest bidders, obtained the contract, gave the required builder's bond and on June 1, 1858, began the work of construction. Mr. Keller later retired from the enterprise. The building was completed by Mr. Bramlet and was first occupied by the District Court on December 5, 1859. It was formally received and accepted by the Commissioners' Court on February 20, 1860, and served the county for all purposes until 1883—twenty-three years.

In the biennial county election in August, 1858, the building of this court house was a campaign issue and not a single member of the court was re-elected, although Colonel Robertson, Chief Justice, and some or all of the commissioners were candidates. But that is the usual way. The officer who votes to spend public money or to raise the taxes on the people for a public improvement, however necessary and urgent, usually goes down in defeat, a martyr to the performance of his plain duty—especially in such provincial and non-progressive communities as then constituted the majority of the citizenship of the new Texas counties. Things have improved somewhat since those days, we are thankful to say.

Until the levy of the special tax the county had not always been able to pay its bills in cash and had been obliged to issue script. On August 16, 1858, the new Commissioners' Court entered an order forbidding the county treasurer to redeem any county script until November 1, 1858; requiring all holders of script to report to the county treasurer by that date the amount and date of their script which was to be registered by the treasurer and numbered; and ordering that officer thereafter to pay for old script in the order of number and date; and further requiring the county clerk to number every piece of script issued by him. This order was to be published for four successive weeks in *The Belton Independent*.

The meagerness of county revenues and expenditures at this period is illustrated by the report, on August 20, 1860, of Milton W. Damron, assessor and collector of taxes, that he had paid over to the county treasurer, since May 21, 1859, the sum of $2,090.55. On the same date the county treasurer, John W. Scott, reported the disbursements of county funds for the year preceding and the balances on hand, as follows:

Fund	Disbursements	Balance
Common County Fund	$2,035.50	$1,784.26
Jury Fund	1,060.36	551.60
Belton Lot Sales Fund		812.75
School Fund	1,144.41	12.08
Totals	$4,240.27	$3,160.69

Because in rainy weather the deep mud around the new court house had become a great inconvenience, the court decided on a further improvement. On August 20, 1860, the sum of $100 was appropriated to gravel the public square about the court house.

Though not shown by the record, this work was performed by Mr. John Kiser, familiarly known as "Humpback" Kiser. His equipment consisted of a two wheel dumpcart, drawn by a yoke of small steers. The cart was loaded at the gravel bars in Nolan Creek, within the town, hauled up to the public square and dumped. The rather ludicrous operation is well remembered by the old timers. In 1910, when trenches were opened on the public square for laying the sanitary sewer system, this layer of gravel placed there by old "Hump-back" Kiser in 1860 was encountered at a depth of about six or seven feet below the surface at the northeast corner of the square. In 1914 the city pavement was laid down, still further raising the grade level of the court house square.

It would be of some interest, had we the space, to follow the steps, from year to year, of the early Commissioners' Court in laying out the public highways of the county; but we must confine our narrative to a general description of the procedure followed.

With the settling down of a few families in a neighborhood or the erection of a little saw-mill or grist-mill somewhere, a petition came in from the settlers to establish roads connecting the locality with the county seat and other points of business or social interest. The usual "jury of view" was appointed to visit the neighborhood, select the route of the proposed highway, assess the damages to the owners of lands through which it should run and to report their action back to the court, which generally approved the report and ordered the road overseer of that section, or a new one then appointed for this road, to open the road for public use. As most of the lands were owned by non-residents, or by residents who were anxious for the roads, the damages were usually nothing.

Each road or section of a road was denominated a "road district" over which annually the court appointed an overseer and to it apportioned all of the able bodied men, including their men slaves, as "hands" to open and keep up the road. Opening a road consisted of cutting out the timber and brush, plowing one or two furrows through the open prairie to mark the route, removing large rocks and stumps, and cutting down the banks of streams where necessary. There were no bridges of any kind, but sometimes, logs or large stones were placed in the crossings of boggy branches.

The main highway was that crossing the country from north to south—from the "Waco Village" to Georgetown, *via* Belton, and passing the later villages of Old Troy, Howard, Salado, Prairie Dell and Corn Hill (Williamson County). From about Howard this highway followed the Military Road, heretofore mentioned, except that the Childers Mill crossing of the Lampasas River, where high bluffs are encountered on both sides, gradually gave way to the "Shaw Crossing" (just below the present highway bridge) where the river banks were more easily negotiated. This road was a part of the great highway from St. Louis, Memphis and the east to Austin, San Antonio and Mexico, over which the overland mail stages and other through travel passed.

The opening of the roads through the new settlements marked the evolution of the county's progress from year to year and the rolls of the road overseers, as shown by the county records, contain the names of many of the representative citizens of their time. Among the early appointees were: John H. Anderson, N. Beardslee, Joel D. Blair, John Dunlap, John Early, James Fletcher, Granger McDaniel, James Moore, John B. Reed, Arch. Willingham, Silas Baggett, Wm. B. Blair, Geo. W. Chapman, Fleming T. Cox, Wm. B. Cross, Chas. P. Cruger, Samuel Green Davidson, Thos. Duncan, Elisha Embree, Ed. T. Estes, Peter Hardeman, John Keggans, Daniel McKay, Patton Morris, Thos. J. Neighbors, Louis A. Ogle, Newton M. Proctor, Sr., Warren Puett, James R. Sutton, Thos. G. Tomlinson, Thomas J. Trimmier and a great many others.

The following entry made by the Commissioners' Court

on May 22, 1855, is reminiscent of the "old days":

"It is ordered by the court that all the territory included in School District No. 10, according to its original boundaries and School District No. 15, in said County, shall be known as the Belton Patrol District, and it is further ordered that D. R. Hill, Silas Baggett, David Williams, Edward Lee and Frank Thomas are hereby appointed a Patrol Detachment for said Patrol District and that the said D. R. Hill be hereby appointed Captain of the said Patrol Detachment."

Later the whole county was laid off into Patrol Districts and patrolmen were appointed therein regularly.

To the present generation this recital is not very explicit. In all of the slave states—the old South—there were laws providing for "patrols." The Texas statute of May 9, 1846[9] authorized the Commissioners Court of each county to divide the county into convenient patrol districts and to appoint for each district a patrol detachment, with a captain and from three to five privates, to serve three months, and this service was compulsory and without compensation. Such appointments were made from the citizens of each patrol district who were subject to military duty. They were required to patrol their districts at least once a month, oftener if necessary, by visiting the negro quarters and all the other places where slaves assembled; if a slave was found off his master's plantation or strolling about without a "pass" from his master or other authorized person, the patrol detachment could inflict upon the slave not exceeding twenty-five lashes. It was their further duty to search for and apprehend runaway slaves and white persons associating with slaves or participating in any assemblage of slaves without permission of their masters. An amendatory statute of January 13, 1862,[10] enacted during the Civil War, when the men subject to military duty were absent in the Confederate army and conditions were more unsettled, increased the number of patrols so as to consist of from five to twenty privates, to be appointed from among the citizens of the district, and it added other restrictions called for by the exigencies of the times.

When the Civil War ended in 1865 and the slaves were emancipated the patrol became ancient history. The pur-

[9] Gammel, II, 1497.
[10] Gammel, V, 498.

pose of the system was to prevent the organization of uprisings by the slaves, usually led by unscrupulous white interlopers and abolitionists. The patrol was not intended to be oppressive, but entirely disciplinary and defensive. Neither this nor any other precautions prevented the negroes from occasionally paying social visits to neighboring negro quarters in the late hours of the night and elderly people still recall the old ditty:

"Run, nigger, run, the patterollers'll get you!
Run, nigger, run, for it's almost day!"

During the 1850's several changes were made in the boundaries of Bell County. The first was caused by the creation of Coryell County by an act of the legislature, February 4, 1854. As already shown, up to this time Bell County had embraced the territory now comprised in Coryell and several other counties. Many people living in that area had theretofore been counted as Bell County citizens, but thenceforth their names pass to the citizenship roll of Coryell. Among these were: W. P. Arrowood, Thomas Bertrong, Goldsby Childers, Prior Childers, Wm. C. Dalrymple, David R. Franks, John J. Tanner, Richard G. Grant, James J. Joplin, Thomas Mahuron, Horatio M. Morrison, Noah Neff, John Potter, James W. Pugh, Theophilus H. Robertson, Orville T. Tyler and others. Some of them (Prior Childers, O. T. Tyler and others) later moved back to Bell County and here resided the remainder of their lives.

On May 16, 1854, Chief Justice John Danley was allowed $22.60 for services in organizing Coryell County and was ordered to present an account for $12 of that amount to the county court of Coryell. On August 21, 1854, Colonel Hermon Aiken presented to the court the field notes of the survey of the boundary line between Bell and Coryell Counties. At an election held at Fort Gates, March 4, 1854, O. T. Tyler, the writer's father, was chosen as the first chief justice of Coryell County. In 1863 he was elected a member of the House of Representatives of the Tenth Legislature from the 61st District, which was composed of Coryell and thirteen other western counties. In 1864 he moved to Salado, Bell County.

Two other changes in the county's boundaries involved, in one case, a gain and in the other a loss of territory. By an act of the Sixth Legislature, August 30, 1856, "a strip of territory six miles wide on the southwest side of Falls County, adjoining Bell County, including Elm Creek" was cut off from Falls County and "attached to and made a part of Bell County for all county purposes" and it was therein made "the duty of the County Court of Bell County to cause the lines of said county to be run and marked as established by this Act, after giving notice of the time and place, twenty days previously thereto, to the Chief Justice of Falls County."

The provisions of this act were carried out by an order entered on February 16, 1857, by the Commissioners' Court of Bell County, appointing H. E. Bradford, then District Surveyor of Milam Land District, to run and mark the line and make due return to said court. The Clerk was ordered to notify the Chief Justice of Falls County that the survey would be made on March 30, 1857, commencing near the residence of Jack Moore. The survey was actually made on the 16th, 17th, and 18th days of April, 1857, by H. E. Bradford, District Surveyor.

Tradition has given, as the reason for the transfer of this six mile strip to Bell County, the inconvenience of the settlers on Elm Creek in going to and from Marlin, the county seat of Falls County. The greater distance to Marlin than to Belton, the muddy Brazos River bottom, about five miles wide, and the impassability of that stream during long periods of floods, rendered it very difficult for these people to transact their county seat business at Marlin. Most of them were closely allied to Belton by kinship as well as by strong social and business ties. For these reasons the Act was reputed to have been passed by the legislature at their instance.

Another explanation sometimes given for the willingness of Falls County to part with this strip of rich land was that Marlin, then recently chosen as the county seat of Falls County, was too far eastward from the geographical center of that county and there was a fear that the county seat might be removed to a point on the west bank of the Brazos River, about old Fort Milam (old Viesca) near the "Falls," and therefore the promoters of Marlin, then predominant in the sparsely settled county, were quite willing to part with this territory on the west and thus bring the geographical center of the county *nearer to Marlin*. This, too, is merely an old tradition. Anyway it was a very happy arrangement for both counties.

In 1860 the County Surveyor of Milam County, Mr. George Green, made a survey of a proposed new boundary line between Bell and Milam Counties. It cut off a considerable area from Bell County and added it to Milam. We do not know why or under whose auspices this was done originally, unless it was desired by some large land owners along the boundary line. Anyway, the Commissioners' Court of Milam County adopted the proposed new line and requested Bell County to acquiesce in the change. On November 19, 1860, the Commissioners' Court of Bell County adopted a resolution recognizing and adhering to the original boundary line run out and established by William Armstrong, District Surveyor of Milam Land District, in 1850, under the Act of January 22, 1850, creating Bell County and defining its boundaries, and vigorously protesting against a *different* line, as run by Mr. Green.

This disagreement between the Commissioners' Courts of the two counties was ended by the passage, by the Eighth Legislature, of "An Act to define the line between Bell and Milam Counties," approved April 4, 1861, defining the boundary line between the two counties and appointing George Green, of Milam County, and R. P. Bigham, of Bell County, as commissioners and surveyors, to run out and mark the line accordingly and to make and record in the County Clerk's Office of each county field notes of the work. The boundary line thus fixed by this Legislative Act was the identical line previously run by Green and rejected by the commissioners court of Bell County.

It is palpable that this legislative Act was put through without the knowledge or consent of the constituted authorities of Bell County or of any of its citizens. And it will be noted that the Act itself *fixed the line*—entirely different from the original line of 1850—and did not provide for the survey by nor approval of any *official* authority, but designated two persons, one from each county, and vested in them, *personally and individually*, the absolute authority to *run and mark this new line* with no responsibility or accountability to any other authority whatever, and their report of the survey, when recorded in the Clerk's Office of the counties, became *final and conclusive* of the rights of all. Rather a bold way to put over a land grab. But Bell County was represented in that legislature—both in the Senate and House—by gentlemen residing in other counties of the respective Districts, who probably knew nothing of the objections of Bell County nor of the real "lay of the land" and, besides, the politicians were at that time too deeply engrossed in the burning issues of secession and the war to give attentions to a matter seemingly so trivial.

Messrs. Green and Bigham made the survey of the new line and filed their report. And some people went to bed one night in Bell County and woke up next morning in Milam County! Thus the line stands to this day. Bell County lost something like sixteen thousand acres of territory, of little value then but of great value now, for all of which Milam County is doubtless grateful, or should be, to the *enterprise* of Green, the surveyor, and his clients who seem to have engineered the scheme.

4. *The Early District Court*

The first district court ever held in Bell County was opened on April 7, 1851, and was presided over by Judge R. E. B. Baylor. The court held terms in the spring and fall of each year and usually transacted its business in a few days. Much of the litigation related to land titles and land boundaries, especially to conflicting claims between the settlers, who had purchased lands from the Republic or from the State, and the claimants of the "eleven league" surveys made still earlier under the authority of Mexico. Reference has been made to these in Chapter II.

These disputes led to much hard feeling and even to some violence. In the controversy over the boundaries of the Maximo Moreno eleven league grant, the district court, on application of the owners of that grant, entered an order in the cause of Henry B. Andrews *vs.* John Marshall requiring the surveyor of the Milam Land District or his deputy to survey the Maximo Moreno survey according to the field notes thereof (which were set out in full) "made by Frances W. Johnson, principal and scientific surveyor" of the Austin and Williams colony. There is a well-founded tradition that when the surveyor and his chain carriers appeared in the settlement on Little River to run out the lines of the Moreno grant in accordance with the order of the court, he was there met by a number of the settlers, forbidden to set his compass or to search for the lines, and was even forcibly driven out of the neighborhood. A probable confirmation of this tradition is found in the joint indictment presented in May, 1854, of thirteen men who were charged with "aggravated assault and battery" and all of whom resided in the vicinity of the alleged surveyor episode and were interested adversely to the eleven league claim. The presumption is strengthened by the fact that, on December 23, 1856, in several companion suits involving the boundaries of the José David Sanches six league grant, brought by the administrators of the estate of Dr. William Punchard, deceased, against B. Blankenship, Jesse Bryant, Robert Childers and Benjamin Bryant, settlers, respectively, the old-time *posse comitatus* was granted by Judge Baylor, and each case the following order was made:

"At this term came the parties by their attorneys and the cause coming on to be heard and evidence having been introduced showing that the legally appointed and qualified surveyor of Bell County, under the previous order of this court, in attempting to make a survey of the land in controversy, was stopped by force of arms while making said survey;

It is ordered by the court that the said surveyor perform the order of the court, entered at the last term of this court, and that he have authority and be empowered to call upon the sheriff of Bell County, and, if deemed necessary, *to call out the entire power of the County of Bell*, and that the said sheriff be required, *with said posse* to protect and defend the said surveyor in making said survey of the Sanches grant of six leagues and (this) cause (is) continued under said order."

The same order was re-entered in all of these cases on May 11, 1857; but in November of that year the controversies over the Sanches six league boundaries were settled by an agreed or compromise line. The disputes over the Moreno and Manchaca grants lingered in the district and Supreme Courts for several decades.[10]

The court dealt with a variety of other matters which can merely be indicated here. The first indictment for murder ever found in Bell County was on October 15, 1852, when John Franks was charged with the murder of Donald Smith on April 18, 1852, by striking him "with an axe on the

---

[10] See Martin vs. Parker, **26 Texas Reports,** 254; Phillip vs. Ayers, **45 Texas,** 607; Ayers vs. Harris, **64 Texas,** 299 and **77 Texas,** 115; Ayers vs. Lancaster, **64 Texas,** 312, etc.

head above the right ear" etc. The homicide occurred in the southern part of the county. Every year thereafter other indictments for murder were found. One, in 1854, was against James Steelman, charged with the murder of Daniel Alexander, the benefactor of the public schools. The first hearing on *habeas corpus* was that of James Clark and Riley Irwin, charged with the murder of Thomas Trimmier on July 4, 1854. The hearing was before Judge Baylor on June 27, 1855. Bail was refused and the defendants were remanded to the custody of the sheriff, who was ordered to confine them in the jail of Bastrop County. That night they escaped from the little Belton jail.

On November 22, 1853, in the case of Jesse Royall *vs.* Sarah E. Royall, the district court granted the first divorce ever obtained in Bell County. The first naturalization proceedings in our county were on November 19, 1855, when Joseph Seigmond, a subject of the King of Prussia, and John Cook, a subject of the same king and of the Electorate of Hesse-Cassell, renounced their allegiance to their former sovereigns and declared their intention to become citizens of the United States. The next year three other subjects of German princes and two of the King of Sweden took out naturalization papers.

The first bar meeting ever held in Bell County was at Belton on December 23, 1856, when the attorneys in attendance upon the court assembled to pay tribute to the memory of Judge Abner S. Lipscomb, Associate Justice of the Supreme Court of Texas. Judge Baylor was requested to preside, and a committee consisting of Frank Pendleton, Wilson Y. McFarland, Edward H. Vontress, of Georgetown, Nicholas W. Battle of Waco, and Erasmus Walker presented appropriate resolutions. The resolutions, after adoption, were ordered to be furnished to the *Brenham Enquirer, Brazos Statesman* and the Austin papers for publication.

By the Act of December 19, 1857, Bell County was taken out of the old Third Judicial District and placed in the new Nineteenth District. At a special election, held in 1858, Hon. Nicholas W. Battle, of Waco was chosen district judge and James L. L. McCall, also of Waco, district attorney. And thus our county bade official adieu to the venerable Judge Baylor. The old-timers long remembered him with great respect and affection. He not only presided with dignity and ability over our district court but, being also a minister of the Gospel, he also did what he could to promote the moral and religious upbuilding of the communities in which he officiated as judge. Frequently during court terms he preached at night or on Sundays, in the court house or in the shady groves, and he performed many marriage ceremonies. Judge Baylor's name, in Baylor College, named in his honor, is perpetually linked to Belton and Bell County.

5. *New Communities and Settlers in the Fifties*

It is possible to name some of the people who came into Bell County in the early fifties and settled outside of Belton, but the following list is probably incomplete.

In 1851 a large party of immigrants from Tennessee located in and about Belton. In this party were Oliver H. Bigham, Sam W. Bigham, R. Patton Bigham, E. H. Bigham, W. Nix Bigham, M. S. Bigham, Wilson Bates, John H. Bates, ——— Bates, Reuben Curry, John Q. Allen, Ben F. Allen, John M. Morris, Sam Morris, M. W. Morris, James Morris, F. G. Morris, R. P. Morris, John W. Scott, Jere D. Scott, Geo. J. Coop, Jas. P. Coop, and others. Several of them (the Scotts and Bighams) jointly purchased from Col. Hermon Aiken a large body of wild land on the north bank of the Leon River, some three or four miles above Belton, subdivided it among themselves, built houses and opened farms on their several holdings. This community soon took the name of "Tennessee Valley," which it bears to this day.

From about 1852 to 1855, the country about Cedar Creek, Owl Creek, and on the Stampede Creek began to settle up. A number of families from other sections of Texas and from other states located there and made their homes. Among these were Colonel Hermon Aiken, D. D. Rosborough, Cyrus Eastland, Alonzo Beeman, Isaac T. Bean, James A. Graves, Fred Neibling, G. Wat Graves, James Kell, Col. Jacob Nichols, Ed. S. Flint, Dr, C. W. Moffett, Stephen D. May, John D. Mayes, William Mayes, W. F. Breedlove, Cyrus Ellis, Elisha D. Stubblefield, Isaac N. Stubblefield, R. L. Stubblefield, William Patten, John W. Clark, ——— Meadows, John Dean, Fred H. Beene, Jas. K. Beene, Abner Kuykendall, Hiram Christian, James Porter Rice, J. Alex Grimes, Louis P. Grimes, D. T. Boatwright, John Hughes, Silvester P. Kirk, Moses Dunn, James Clark

Blawkenburg, Wm. H. Rice, James Bell, and others. Josiah Hart and Joseph Bishop were there when the county organized.

About the same time came Elisha Embree, who settled on Pepper's Creek, on the Waco road, some four miles northeast from Belton; Silas Baggett, at Howard, about four miles further on; and several other families in that section, on Pepper's and Bird's Creek, including Mrs. Graves, Hugh O'Keefe, Warren Puett, Elisha Puett, Jas. W. Hodge, Alex Hodge, J. A. Clark, John Nichols, Wm. A. Young, Thos P. Dooley and others.

On Elm Creek were Robert Childers (formerly of "Childers Mill") who had moved there from Ft. Gates, Lieutenant Horace Haldeman (late of the U. S. Army), Loss C. Williams, Jas. M. Williams, Sam H. Williams, James Williams, William Williams, J. R. (Dock) Williams, Owen Slaughter, Rufus Anderson, A. Crom Thomson, John Thompson, Ben E. Shipp, Thos. G. Shipp, Robert C. Hamil, Sam H. Hunter, John Keggans, E. H. Bigham ("Ale" Bigham of the Tennessee colony already mentioned), Robert C. Nelson, Francis W. Venable, and others.

On Salado Creek and in that section the new settlers were E. S. C. Robertson—son of Sterling C. Robertson, the founder of Robertson's colony—Dr. W. R. Alexander, Wm. H. Stinnett, Robert Holliday, Jas. T. Sherrod, Geo. M. McWhirter, John Myers, Wm. Hensley, and others.

Others, south of the Salado, were A. J. Dallas, Alfred Evans, John Cates, Edward Clark, Dr. Carroll Kendrick, (Wm. L?) Lumpkin, W. A. Pace, R. B. Halley, A. W. Cearnel, Mrs. Edrington, and —— Pearce.

On the Lampasas were Gordon W. Shanklin, Newton M. Procter, Sr., Wm. L. Pierce, Howell Tatum, Hal Keys, Willis H. Bruce, Sam C. Hannon, Wm. Brookman and his sons, William and Fred C., Wesley G. Ferguson, A. R. Anderson and son, Vachel H. Anderson, and others.

On the North and South Nolan were John McDowell, Ed. T. Estes, J. R. Smith, John P. Blackburn and sons, Jno. G. Blackburn, M. W. Blackburn and W. H. L. Blackburn, Isaac Shriver, Ben Cox, Fleming T. Cox, John W. Cox, Sam H. Cox, Jesse Sutton, Anderson Sutton, J. J. Parker, Sam Wheat, Alex Walters, Tilman Walters, Wm. Potter, Drury D. Potter, David Gray, John M. Perryman, Net R. Clark, and others.

On Cow House were G. W. Walton, Nelson Walton, Joseph H. Hawkins, J. Rough Petty, T. G. Tomlinson, Jesse Pitts, John Hendrickson, John Potter, Sam Evetts, A. J. Fleming, Jesse Scoggin, Isaac Scoggin, Ambrose Lee, John Riggs, David Elms, James R. Sutton, Joseph Spoonts and others whose names we have been unable to obtain.

Among those who settled on the Leon above Belton were Ramsey M. Cox, John R. Chapman, Duncan St. Clair, and ——— McCoin; while below Belton on the same stream were David Ayers, Joe G. Ferguson, John F. Ferguson, Thomas Duncan, Ed. T. Reed, John C. Caddell, Carter Mabry, Ben H. Irby, D. M. Williamson, Andrew Hasley, James Ashley, Wm. Ashley, Andrew Spiva, James A. Spiva, G. F. Giles and J. C. Stokes.

Newcomers on Little River were John H. Griffin, Warner Wallace, M. L. Houston, John F. McAninch, Lewis Taylor, Elisha Penington, John H. Penington, and Joseph L. Wallace.

For several years after its founding, in 1850, Belton was the only town in the county; but, as already shown, settlers were soon pretty well spread all over the county, chiefly along the streams, and new communities began to be well defined. The community later known as Live Oak began in 1854. It could hardly be called a town, as it had no business houses. The village of Aiken, founded in 1857, was an active little business place until the close of the Civil War. Salado came into existence as a school center, with only two or three small stores, in the latter part of 1859. Belton, Aiken and Salado were the only towns in Bell County prior to the Civil War. In 1857, Belton, Salado and Howard, all located on the overland stage route, had the only postoffices in the county. South Nolan was given one in 1858 and Elm Creek (later known as Old Troy) in 1859.[11] Brief accounts of the founding of Live Oak, Aiken and Salado will now be given.

In 1854, Thomas Gilmore, Methodist circuit rider, held a revival at Pecan Grove, on the north side of Salado Creek just below Chalk's Mill, where the neighbors had previously built a little board school and church house, and he there organized a Methodist church and a Union Sunday school. A short time afterwards the Reverend John Clabaugh held

[11] See **Texas Almanac** for 1857, 1858, 1859, and 1860.

Top: Shady Villa Hotel, Salado, Texas. Built 1852. Many famous men of Texas were guests here.
Bottom: Rear view of the old stage barn at Shady Villa Hotel, Salado. The Little Rock-San Antonio stage put up here.

Ten Years of Growth, 1850-1860

a Baptist meeting there and organized "Salem Baptist Church," which soon erected a board shanty for church purposes near the present Dulaney Mill site on the south side of the creek. John Thomas and a Mr. Haggard served successively as pastors and a Baptist Association was later held there. In both these little houses, which were open to all denominations, the Reverend Mr. Hickey, a Protestant Methodist, and Finis E. Foster, Cumberland Presbyterian, held services. The Sunday school at Pecan Grove purchased a library, probably the first in the county, unless Belton had one.

In 1857 the people decided to move their meeting place to a more central location. They selected the large spreading live oak tree on Mr. Wm. K. Karnes' land, near his residence, and gave the name Live Oak to the site. A brush arbor and split log benches, under the live oak tree, served temporarily for meeting purposes. A Methodist quarterly conference was held under the arbor. In 1859, a commodious log building, used for both school and church purposes, was erected at the old tree and served the community for many years. The Reverend John Carpenter was the regular preacher there for a long time after the log house was built; and he married all the couples and buried all the dead.

After Belton, the next village or business place of importance was Aiken, whose beginning and best days are thus described by Mr. Mat J. Kuykendall:

"In 1857 my father (Abner Kuykendall) bought a beautiful little valley in the bend of the Leon River, twelve miles above Belton, where there was a fine water power. There he put in a plant for a steam saw and flour mill which proved a success. And here soon grew up a thrifty village, second in the county to Belton only, in the business done. This is what is now "Old Aiken." It was named for Col. Hermon Aiken, who was the owner of the tract of land on which it was situated . . . .

"When the Civil War began Aiken was a busy little town of about two hundred inhabitants; the variety and volume of business increased with the need of home manufactures during the years of blockade.

"There were four stores, a cabinet shop for making all kinds of furniture from black walnut and some other hard woods indigenous to these parts, two blacksmith shops, together with wood shops, where were made and repaired wagons, etc. Also a tan yard from which was turned out a good quality of leather; in connection with this was a shoe and saddle shop, which finished good work ready for market. Even the saddle trees were made there. There was another branch of industry, a hat factory, where the wool, as cut from the sheep's back, went in and came out a very nice hat. There was no shoddy in these hats, it was the genuine article, and had not wear-out to it though it did not look quite so well as the Stetson hat of today. . . . Wheat was brought from Comanche, Hamilton and Coryell Counties to these mills to be ground or traded. Sometimes there would be half a dozen big ox wagons together, from Comanche County, all loaded with wheat, with hides on top, to exchange for shoes or other goods. We furnished them a market for all they brought. What we could not use was sent to Houston, whence our goods were brought by wagons."

The desire for a high class school somewhere in Bell County had been slowly growing for some time, and by the fall of 1859 was pretty well developed. On the 8th of October, 1859, a tent meeting was held at the Salado Springs to consider the question and resulted in the organization of the "Salado College Joint Stock Company," to which Col. E. S. C. Robertson donated one hundred acres of land, including the two fine springs situated in the lower part of the present village. Stock in the company to the amount of five thousand dollars was at once subscribed and active preparations were immediately begun. The company was incorporated by a special act of the legislature, approved February 8, 1860.[12]

The college tract was laid out in blocks, lots and streets, and a number of families purchased lots and built substantial homes. The village grew rapidly until checked by the blight of the Civil War. A temporary wooden building was erected, in which a primary school was opened on February 20, 1860, with Rev. Levi Tenney (a Presbyterian minister) as principal, and he was followed in July 1861 by Dr. J. H. Anderson.

At the same time plans were made for the erection of

---

[12] Gammel, **Laws of Texas**, V, 191. These statements are based upon the minutes of the Board of Trustees and upon their printed circular announcement of the opening of the school, dated May 15, 1860.

a large two story stone building, upon the brow of the hill overlooking the valley, its springs and the creek below. On July 4, 1860, the corner stone of this building was laid with Masonic ceremony by Mr. Sam Mather, acting Grand Master of the Grand Lodge, Ancient Free and Accepted Masons of Texas, with the assistance of Belton Lodge No. 166.[13] This was the first corner stone ever laid in Bell County or anywhere in this section of Texas. There was a large crowd present, and an old time barbecue was served and everybody had a joyous time.

The members of the first Board of Trustees, chosen by the stockholders in 1859 were: Col. Hermon Aiken, John S. Blair, A. J. Dallas, Dr. William D. Eastland, Dr. Carroll Kendrick, Col. E. S. C. Robertson and Gordon W. Shanklin.

In all conveyances of lots by the company and by individuals a clause was inserted providing for forfeiture of the land to the grantor should the purchaser sell or permit to be sold therein intoxicating liquors in quantities less than a quart; and a special act of the Legislature, approved September 26, 1866, made the sale or gift of intoxicating liquors within six miles of Salado College (except for medical or sacramental purposes) a misdemeanor.[14]

The articles of association and the charter also stipulated that the school should never become sectarian nor should the peculiar doctrines of any religious denomination be taught therein.

The further growth of Salado and of Salado College will be noted in later chapters.

6. *The Early Schools*

Among the early settlers, scattered far apart as they were, schools were difficult to establish and maintain. But wherever they lived close enough together, small tuition-schools were taught for a few months in the year. Of some of them there remains only a faint tradition, and it is impossible to speak of them with certainty. As Belton was the first town to be laid out, it was one of the first communities to have a school. In a little log cabin on the north side of Pearl Street, opposite the west end of the present

---

[13] Minutes of Belton Lodge No. 166 A. F. & A. M., July 4, 1860.
[14] Gammel, **Laws of Texas,** V, 935.

Second Avenue, the first schools in the town, with fifteen or twenty pupils, were taught by E. Lawrence Stickney, Thomas Lucken, Abram W. Richards, James Arnold and others whose names we have not been able to learn. These were "pay schools."

In 1854, Bell County was laid off into fifteen school districts under the provisions of "An Act to Provide a System of Schools," approved by Governor Pease on February 4, 1854. But this law provided for the tuition of indigent children only; and, as the old-timers know, very little was accomplished under this system because the poorer people resented the term "pauper schools" which was often applied to those schools established under this law. The better schools were still maintained by a small tuition fee. But the foundations were being laid for a system of public free schools. By the State Constitution of 1845 each county was to be allotted four leagues of public land for school purposes. In 1856 Messrs. Howeth and Twitty were employed by the Commissioners' Court to locate three leagues in Wise County and one in Archer County. Little income was realized from these lands, however, for many years.

The schools of Bell County were to receive assistance from another quarter. Daniel Alexander, an eccentric but benevolent man, left his native state of Maine, in 1830, lived awhile in Illinois, and came to Harris County, Texas, in 1840. In 1845 he settled on Darr's Creek, Bell County, a few miles below the present town of Holland. There, all alone, he resided, and there he was assassinated in the spring of 1854. He was buried in the John Fulcher graveyard, on Little River. One James Steelman was indicted for the murder, was tried and acquitted for lack of sufficient evidence to connect him with the crime. Among Alexander's papers was found a will wherein he bequeathed two-thirds of his lands, situated in the county in which he should die and be buried, to such county for the benefit of public free schools therein. He owned a large landed estate in Bell County, on Little River, and the county thus inherited a valuable addition to the four leagues donated to the schools by the state. The lands so inherited, denominated the "Alexander Schools Lands," were sold, the principal was added to the permanent invested County School Fund, and the public schools are enjoying the interest to this day.[15] It would be appropriate, we suggest, for those who have enjoyed his beneficence to search for and locate, if possible, the grave of Daniel Alexander and erect a suitable monument to his memory.

By 1855 and 1856 there were several small schools in operation in communities outside of Belton. Miss Bettie Wallace taught the first school at Pecan Grove (later Live Oak), and in the following years a Mr. Freeman, George White, C. E. Maule, Wm. Carroll Sypert and a Mr. Boyd also taught school there. Mention has already been made of the school at Salado. On April 26, 1858, the Commissioners' Court appointed Messrs. Erasmus Walker, Wilson Y. McFarland and Marshall McIlhenney, three attorreys of Belton, as a board of school examiners to examine teachers and issue certificates of competency. This was apparently the first such board appointed in the county, and while the appointment of lawyers to perform this function may be evidence of low standards in the teaching profession, it is at the same time evidence that some care was being taken in the selection of the teachers.

7. Farming, Stockraising and Transportation in the Fifties

The colonists and pioneers of Texas were not impressed with the agricultural possibilities of a great portion of the country. In some of the lower regions, particularly along the lower Brazos, Trinity and Colorado Rivers and on the Caney and San Bernard Creeks, some fairly large plantations were opened up and cultivated with slave labor brought hither from the old States.

The first lands that were put in cultivation in all of the new settlements were along the streams and the "civilization that follows the plow" came up the country gradually in that way. There were several reasons for this. The river lands were generally alluvial deposits of prehistoric floods,

---

[15] Daniel Alexander also gave, by his will, one-fourth of his lands in other counties "to the suffering poor, over the age of forty-five years, living permanently in such counties." As late as 1909, Harris County sold some of the land so inherited. Other counties have likewise benefitted by his munificence, as he is said to have owned at his death lands in Milam, Burleson, McLennan, Falls, and other counties, some of which have claimed the lands so bequeathed.

very rich, easy to cultivate and held moisture better. The stream furnished water for man and beast. Materials for fencing the land and for building the crude homes of the settlers were obtained from the land in clearing it. But, most important of all, the timbered bottoms furnished the best refuge and protection from the unfriendly Indians who dreaded ambush from the cover of the woods and seldom penetrated the bush either in attack or pursuit of their intended victims.

The upper country, including all of our central region, was long regarded as simply a great stock range where the rainfall was too uncertain to justify extensive farming operations. This was true even along the streams where small fields of corn for immediate subsistence comprised at first the only farming efforts. Later on, about the middle of the fifties in Bell County, there was a gradual increase of farm acreage, especially by those owning slaves, as the old time negro was adapted only to the rudest physical tasks and was seldom utilized otherwise. Even with farming thus extended the principal crop was corn, though the lower country early began the culture of cotton. Until the drought of 1855 and subsequent years abundant crops of corn were made in Bell County and were sold at good prices to the U. S. government posts at Ft. Gates, Fort Chadbourne, and Fort Phantom Hill and to the newly arriving immigrants.

The great drought of the late fifties severely affected the farming interests and gave our county and section a decided set-back. It lasted, with more or less severity, several years and was long referred to as the "seven years' drought." The corn crops were either failures or were very short. Though fairly good corn crops of wheat and other grain were produced, the streams were so low that the water mills were nearly all shut down and but little flour could be had. Some people even ground wheat on their old steel mills. Chinese sugar cane (sorghum) was introduced about 1857 and became a general product and much molasses was made from it for home consumption. A species of corn called "Duoro" was planted by some farmers and pretty good results were obtained. There was practically no rain in 1857 before the first week in August and the country had become bare and desolate, but when the rain finally did arrive the farm conditions were improved fifty per cent, especially the cotton crop on Little River, and watermelons were plentiful and luscious. Times were rather dull but people paid cash for their purchases at the stores, very little credit business being done. The first bale of cotton for the year sold in Houston at 15½ cents per pound. Hides, theretofore a waste product, brought a good price at the stores in exchange for goods.

Conditions were much better in 1858. A good corn crop was made, a large wheat crop—5717 acres—was sown and turned out well and the cotton crop in Little River was good. It was claimed that Bell County cotton in that year graded higher and brought a better price in the Houston market than any other.

On November 20, 1857 the "Bell County Agricultural Club" was organized at Belton with fifty-three members. E. S. C. Robertson was chosen president; John S. Blair and Daniel McMillin, vice presidents; Andrew Marschalk, Sr., secretary; Joel D. Blair, treasurer. Standing committees were composed of the following: on corresponcence, Thomas Trimmier, Warner Wallace, Andrew Marschalk, Sr., Henry Harris, R. B. Foster, E. McLaughlin, M. W. Damron, Elisha Embree, G. W. Graves, Cary White; on by-laws, W. Y. McFarland, Joel D. Blair, A. W. Cearnel, John T. Flint, Dred R. Hill, J. M. Phillips. Under the leadership of Mr. Andrew Marschalk, Sr., who seems to have been an enthusiast in advocating better farming methods and in introducing seeds of new varieties of products, the club flourished for quite a while and did some good work in improving the system of agriculture here.

It may be interesting to note that Mr. Marschalk, at that early day, was talking about hulling cotton and about cotton-seed oil, stating that there were two cotton-seed oil mills at Natchez, Mississippi, when he was a boy, that the oil sold at $1.00 per gallon for burning and lubricating purposes and that the cake, superior to linseed, was fed to cows and horses.[16]

Diversification, though urged in the press, was not practiced to any great extent. Potatoes, cabbage, onions, turnips, beans, peas, watermelons, muskmelons, peaches, pumpkins, cushaws, etc., were luxuries that could be found at the homes of the more prosperous who had maintained their settlements long enough to indulge in them. And with

---

[16] For matter relating to the years 1857 and 1858, see file of **The Belton Independent,** May 2, 1857 to April 16, 1859.

the advent of the crude flouring mills in the central and southern parts of the state the farmers sowed some wheat and thus the family was supplied with flour and the surplus was sold to the people around. Oats, rye, barley, millet, hungarian grass, duoro corn and sorghum were also grown for home consumption in the late fifties. The grain was mowed with scythes and for that reason these crops were not very extensive. In 1858 or 1859 the writer's father, Judge O. T. Tyler, brought the first reapers to this section—one upon each of his farms in Bell and Coryell Counties. They were of the original McCormick type, with hand rake held by a man sitting on the machine to the rear of the driver. The bunch of grain delivered to the ground by the rake was then picked up by hand and tied into a bundle with the straw. In harvest time people came for miles around to see them operating. Several threshers came into the country and the grain crops were well cared for in this regard.

In the late fifties, several mills were equipped in this territory for grinding corn and wheat. Among these were the Chalk Mill on the Salado, the Shanklin Mill on the Lampasas, the Gabriel Mill on the San Gabriel, the Clifton Mill on the Bosque—all operated by water power—the O. T. Tyler Mill in Coryell County, operated by an inclined tread wheel and oxen, and the McCoin Mill on the Leon, operated by steam. Ample supplies of meal and flour were thus available to the people of this section.

In the country lying west of the old stage road leading from Waco to Georgetown, *via* Belton, there was very little cotton raised prior to or during the Civil War—practically none in the Bell County section of that country. On Leon and Little River, below Belton, some cotton was produced. None was planted in the Reed settlement lower down Little River. Just before the Civil War, Mr. Dred R. Hill erected an old time cotton-gin, with a tall wooden screw press, on his farm across the Leon, just east of Belton. And the writer, then a small country boy, used to regard that old wooden screw press, sticking up there in the air, as the most gigantic and wonderful piece of machinery on earth.

As already stated, our section was not favorably regarded for agriculture in the early days, on account of the uncertainty of the rainfall. The great black land prairies of Bell County, where lie the splendidly improved and prosperous farms of today, were then considered as almost worthless except to pasture the growing herds of horses, cattle and sheep. People said that this would never be anything but a stock country. Even so the water supply for the stock, away from the streams, was an uncertain proposition. In selecting his land the colonist, and later the immigrant, looked first for water for his family and stock and for timber for building, fencing and fuel. With these secured he cared not who owned the back lands on the prairie, as the frontage on the stream, with timber and water, was the key to the situation, the vantage ground of supreme control which enabled him to keep out all comers, to throw his stock back on the open prairies and to graze them upon the broad acres of the non-resident owners of those unoccupied hills, costing him absolutely nothing but providing him a constant and increasing source of revenue. True, cattle were not worth much—say $10.00 for a beef steer, $5.00 for a cow or for a steer yearling—but that was all clear profit. They had been raised and fattened upon the other fellow's grass. And when the buyers came around and paid the cash for them it was "like a letter from home with a check in it." The buyers would get together several hundred head and either drive them to Alexandria or Shreveport and thence ship them by steamers to New Orleans or they would drive them all the way through to New Orleans. The cattle went through on the grass of the open range without any feed whatever and arrived at the market in good condition. These drives were great experiences for the cowboys and were filled with adventures which served them for big windy stories for the remainder of their lives. Sometimes they sold their cow ponies and returned by way of the Gulf, on board a fine steamer, and it is said that on one occasion when a steamer waiter at breakfast asked one of these big sunbrowned Texas cowboys, with boots and spurs, whether he wanted his beef "rare or well done," he replied, "Let it rear and be d—d, I can ride anything that wears a hide."

Cattle and horses, running at large upon the open range, were rounded up every spring. Each stock-owner furnished a hand or two, and with this co-operative force, well mounted and provisioned, the country was hunted out and the calves marked and branded for the respective owners of the mother cows. Likewise with the breeding of horses, though they usually ranged near the owner's home and were handled at his own corral. There was generally no attempt to train a horse to the saddle or harness until he was about four years old. Then he was caught up and turned over to an expert "horse-breaker" who kept charge of him until he was sufficiently gentle for general domestic use. The pitching, floundering and bucking of these young prairie-raised horses, especially if they were mixed with the tough and enduring Spanish (Mexican) blood, as most of them were, was a supreme test of the horse-breaker's skill in riding, and the fame of these men, many of whom made this a vocation, was as far extended as that of a professional *toreador* of the Spanish bull fight. A good horse breaker was esteemed quite a hero by his friends and neighbors.

The stock industry too suffered a severe blow from the great drought of 1855 and subsequent years. Nearly all of the smaller streams and springs dried up completely and most of the larger streams stood in isolated pools or tanks. The grass was poor, the cattle and horse on the range drifted in upon the few remaining watering places and lingered about there, consumed the range, and toward the winter season became so poor and weak that large numbers of them died from cold and starvation. The calamity thus visited upon the farming and stock interests—the most productive resources of our people—was keenly felt and it very much retarded the general financial development in the period of the late fifties.

There was a considerable movement of cattle, work oxen, horses and mules from Texas to the southern and northwestern states—Louisiana, Missouri, Kansas, and Illinois—in the late fifties. Some 25,000 horses and mules and 1800 beef cattle passed through Belton in 1857 and about 10,000 horses and mules, 7,000 beef cattle and 800 oxen passed here in 1858.[17]

In 1857 Mr. A. M. Wheat bought 500 beeves in Bell County at $12.50 per head, drove them to Chicago on grass alone, with seven hands, and sold them at $36.00 per head. He and his men camped out all the way and lost only eight or nine head. The herd started in April and reached Chicago

[17] **The Belton Independent** for period of May 2, 1857 to August 14, 1858.

in October.[18]

In 1858 two men passed through Belton who had driven a herd of cattle to St. Joe, Missouri, and sold them at $35.00 per head, making a profit of $15.00 per head.[19]

Back in those good days the cattle tick was getting in his work. The citizens of Vernon County, Missouri, held a mass meeting and resolved that Texas cattle could not pass there because they communicated Spanish of Texas fever to their native cattle. Our editor, Mr. Marschalk, denounced the actions as ridiculous, claiming that Texas cattle were free from disease and citing the fact that the Mobile and New Orleans butchers advertised that *they killed none but Texas cattle.* The actions of the Missouri people was imputed to the competition of the Texas drovers with their home breeders.[20] But we have learned now that the Vernon County people were right in their contention and for some years our State government and our cattle breeders have been fighting the "fever tick" with the dipping process under State laws administered by the Sanitary Live Stock Commission.

Before the days of railroads in Texas our nearest market was Houston and our transportation was by ox-wagon. All of the people in the country watered by the Brazos and Colorado Rivers marketed their surplus products there until the Houston & Texas Central railroad extended to Hempstead and later to Millican. This surplus consisted principally of flour, meal, hides, honey, chickens, eggs, butter, and cotton, of course, where that was produced. The transportation was accomplished with large, heavy wooden-axled wagons, the tar bucket swinging on behind, drawn by teams of four to six and sometimes eight yokes of oxen. Many persons engaged in this occupation. On the return trip they hauled goods for the up-country merchants and farm supplies of sugar, coffee, salt, tobacco, jeans, domestic, etc. The teamsters usually traveled in trains of two or more wagons and kept together. At a bad hill or boggy stream (there were then no bridges on the streams) they assisted each other by doubling up the teams to each wagon and thus pulled it up the bank or over the bog. At night they camped

---

[18] **The Belton Independent** for period of May 2, 1857 to August 14, 1858; November 5, 1857.
[19] **Ibid,** August 14, 1858.
[20] **Ibid,** October 16, 1858.

together for protection and around the jolly roaring campfires smoked their pipes and told their yarns—and, possibly, played a little poker or seven-up. A caravan of those old freight wagons, covered with white sheets, with six or eight yoke of oxen hooked up in each team, strung out along the prairie trail was an inspiring scene—the vestibuled palace-car train of the pioneer days. The plowing as well as the teaming, in those days, was nearly all done with oxen and no one pretended in either case to feed them. They subsisted upon the grass in the open range. At nights the oxen were turned out, two "necked" together, one of them "hobbled" and wearing a large ox-bell that could be heard a mile or more away in the stillness of the early dawn. Otherwise most of the teamster's time would have been spent in hunting for his oxen in the morning. And some of those old oxen were very cunning. They would graze around in open glades till three or four o'clock in the morning, meantime getting as far away as possible, and then they would crawl into a dense thicket of briers and vines, lie down, put their heads down so that the bell sat noiselessly on the ground and then keep as still as death! Cunning? Instinct? Accident? What was it? The teamsters might ride or walk all around that thicket without finding them. But, perchance, a hungry fly came buzzing around and bit the belled ox so deeply that he threw his his head around to scare the fly away and then he was promptly retrieved for another day's work on the farm or in the freighter's team.

A trip from Bell County to Houston and return with an ox wagon usually required about two or three months, unless the Yegua got on a rise, and then the teamster was lucky if he got back home at all during the season with his complete outfit. This stream rising, with many tributaries, in the sand hills of Bastrop, Lee and Milam Counties, forms the west and south boundaries of Burleson County to its confluence with the Brazos and crossed the old direct route from this upper country to Houston. Its waters at high tide, like those of the Platte river, are said to be "six inches deep and a mile wide." The mud and quicksand in its valleys, after the water runs down or rather soaks in, are bottomless. To the teamster waterbound on the further side of the Yegua the early return to his up-country home was hopeless. He had to wait for the mud to dry. And the folks back home awaiting his return frequently ran out of coffee, sugar, etc., and that explains why so many up-country people in those days learned to do without sugar. In the folk-lore of the time "they lived above the Yegua." Later on, when the railroad reached Millican and Navasota, there were other routes to these terminals with ferries over the Brazos and conditions were not so bad.

CHAPTER X

INDIANS, FRONTIER RANGERS, AND GOLD HUNTERS, 1850-1860

1. *Indian Raids*

We must now turn back to the story of the Indian frontier insofar as it affected Bell County during the fifties. The older sections of the county, protected by the newer settlements which had spread westward up the streams, soon became immune to Indian attacks; but throughout this decade the venturesome settlers on the upper Leon, the Cowhouse, Nolan and Lampasas suffered from Indian raids. To what tribes the marauders belonged is very difficult to determine, for the settlers did not easily distinguish one tribe from another and almost invariably referred to the raiders simply as "Indians"; but they were most probably Comanches. The tribes which had formerly lived along the lower Brazos and had given so much trouble to the early settlers on Little River—such as the Caddoes, Anadarkoes, Keechies, Ionies and Wacoes—were now so weakened by war and disease that their feeble remnant dared not provoke the white men, although some of their younger men may have ventured to steal a few horses now and then. But the powerful Comanches, who lorded it over the western plains from Kansas to Mexico and were to dispute the possession of western Texas with the white men for twenty years longer, made periodic raids on exposed portions of the settlements all the way from the Red River to the Rio Grande. It is likely that nearly all the depredations in Bell and adjoining counties after 1850 were the work of the Comanches.

As related in an earlier chapter, the United States army had, in 1849, built Fort Gates on the upper Leon as one of a line of posts to protect the frontier. In 1852 the War Department ordered this line abandoned and a new one established much further west. The news of this alarmed the settlers in western and northwestern Bell County who in January, 1852, sent a petition to Governor Bell describing their danger and asking for protection. Before the petition was actually dispatched they supplemented it with the statement that a band of seven Indians had already appeared on

[1] Petitions and Memorials, State Archives, Austin, Texas.

the Cowhouse and had murdered and scalped Mr. Moses Meek. They asked the Governor to authorize them to raise an efficient ranging company for immediate protection. There is no evidence available that Governor Bell complied with this request. The State had some small ranging forces of its own, but relied chiefly upon the army of the United States in order to avoid the expenses of maintaining independent volunteer companies. It must be said, however, that the army did not give adequate protection. The garrisons stationed at the frontier posts at that period were either composed of infantry or of heavy dragoons, and in either case were wholly unable to prevent the wily Comanches from slipping around them and down into the settlements or to catch them as they came out. The Indian method of attack was to work their way down between the posts in small bands just before the full moon, hide in the woods or mountains during the day, mark out the cabins of the settlers, steal the horses or mules during the night, and then strike out with the stolen herds straight for the plains. Although their main purpose was to steal horses, they seldom failed to murder any unprotected family or traveler who fell in their way, or to kidnap small children. If closely pursued, they scattered in order to confuse their pursuers and united at some point already agreed upon. They fought only when the odds were in their favor or when they were overtaken and could not escape otherwise.

In February, 1853, a band of Indians made a raid in Nolan Valley and in Wilkerson Valley, on the Lampasas, within three to five miles of Belton, and stole a lot of horses from Dave Williams, Riley Irvin, Melville Wilkerson and others. Charles Curtis came in haste to the village of Belton and reported. By the following morning a pursuing party, consisting of Dave Williams, Robert M. White, Joe Townsend, John Potter, and Isaac Williams, started in pursuit and, going up the Lampasas River, soon struck the trail, which they followed for two or three days, passing the Indian camp fires and finding their foot prints and the tracks of the stolen horses. From these it appeared there were seven Indians in the band, one of whom had a very large and peculiar "big toe," fully two inches wide, whom they called "the big-toed chief." They finally discovered the Indians in a grove of timber on a creek or ravine, and when Dave Williams, in command, gave the order, "Charge 'em boys," they put spurs to their horses and rushed upon them. The Indians, surprised, sprang to their feet and the main body of them fled into the thick wood down the creek, with Dave Wiliams and White in hot pursuit. But one Indian, with fleet foot, fled in the opposite direction, pursued by Isaac Williams on horseback, through the thick brush for about 250 yards to a deep ravine in which the Indian was lost to sight. Mr. Williams, dismounting, saw the Indian rapidly running up a small hill some 150 yards distant, on the opposite side of the ravine. He instantly fired and brought down the red man—dead. And he proved to be the "big-toed chief." Returning to find the remainder of the pursuing party, from whom all the other Indians had escaped, he told them of his adventure, showed them the dead Indian, took off his scalp to show the folks at home, and the party, gathering up all of the stolen horses, returned to their homes, restoring the stolen horses to their owners on the way.[2]

In the fall of 1853 Indians made a raid down Nolan Creek and stole a lot of horses, the heaviest losers being the Coxes and Suttons.[3] The further particulars of this affair are not available.

The gold rush to California, which began in 1849 and continued for several years to that state and to other parts of the far West, brought hundreds of immigrant wagon-trains across the plains, and stirred up the plains Indians. The United States Government then began to consider the advisability of placing these Indians in reservations on government land as it had formerly done with the Indians who had got in the way of white settlement east of the Mississippi. Texans, also, wanted the Indians removed from western Texas, but there was no federal land in Texas on which to place them. Therefore, on February 4, 1854, the Texas legislature ordered twelve leagues of land to be located and set aside for Indian reservations. Captain R. B. Marcy of the United States Army and Robert S. Neighbors of San Antonio, the U. S. Indian agent for Texas Indians, were appointed to locate the reservations and induce the Indians to settle on them and learn to live like the whites.

[2] **Reminiscences of Isaac Williams, MS.; Reminiscences of John M. Roberts, MS.;** E. L. Deaton, **Indian Fights on Texas Frontier,** pp.14-15.
[3] **Reminiscences of Jno. M. Roberts, MS.**

These two men, with an escort of soldiers and guides, examined the region of the upper Brazos and Wichita in the spring of 1854, and located one reservation near Fort Belknap, now in Young County, and another about forty miles further west near Camp Cooper on the Clear Fork of the Brazos. The smaller tribes then living further down on the Brazos agreed to settle on the first reservation and did so. The Comanches and Kiowas were to be invited to stay on the upper reservation. The Comanches, who were in several divisions or sub-tribes, were called to a great council at Fort Chadbourne, now in Coke County, northwest of Ballinger. Some of the southern bands, who had begun to fear the power of the white man, agreed to go; but their wilder kinsmen of the upper plains refused to be confined and went back determined to resist the further advance of the whites.

Mr. E. L. Deaton, known to many of the old-timers as Elias Deaton, was at the council and later wrote an interesting account[4] of the "pow-wow." Being a young man, full of curiosity and "with but little to do, he took in the whole situation."

> The Indians began to come in about the last of March and continued to come till sometime in May, bringing all they had with them, women, children, horses, and dogs. They could be seen in trains strung out for miles, each tribe travelling to themselves and when all were in and reported by tribes, a compilation of all showed that there were in all about 26,000 men, women, and children, horses and dogs not counted, which would have equalled if not exceeded the Indians in number. They pitched their camps all along up and down Oak Creek for miles. The writer, for curiosity's sake, spent several days in their camps passing hither and thither for no other purpose than to see the customs and modes of Indian life. They had for their sport the war-dance, the sun-dance, the horse race, the foot race, the shooting match, all in day time; at night the general ball or big dance. Men, women and children, and sometimes the dogs, would take part in these amusements. I saw Indians there that they said were over one hundred years old . . . .
>
> We will now come to the Council. It would open in the morning. You could see them coming by the hundreds. They would fill the fort full but none but the chiefs or great men were allowed to enter the council house. Propositions were made them by the government to settle them on the Brazos, near Ft. Belknap, and, after a parley of three or four weeks, some of the tribes agreed to it, but the treaty did not stick long as the future will disclose.
>
> The Comanche chief, Yellow Wolf, never did agree to go on the reservation. I heard him make several speeches in favor of his people. He said it was impossible to make white men out of Indians; said

[4] E. L. Deaton, **Indian Fights on the Texas Frontier**, 181-184.

that you had as well try to make a dog out of a wolf; and Yellow Wolf proposed to the council that if the government would strike a line commencing on Red River at or near the upper line of Grayson County and run to the mountains at or near Austin or San Antonio, thence to the Rio Grande, and give his people all north of said line, he would make a peace with the whites, but if not he would instill it in the minds of his people to contend for their rights as long as they lived. He contended earnestly for this country, saying that his people had been driven from the eastern shores by the whites to the plains where they could not make a living, and promised that if his men trespassed across the line that we could deal with them according to our law, allowing him the same privilege to deal with our men when they trespassed across the line on his side. But our agents had their orders from Washington and could not vary from them. So, Yellow Wolf took his tribe and went to the mountains and the other tribes accepted the proposition from the government and went on the reserve.

Yellow Wolf did not live long after this. He still kept up stealing horses. He stole a bunch from the Lipan Indians and was followed by them and overtaken on a little creek now in Coke County that bears the name of Yellow Wolf, and there a hot fight ensued between the two tribes in which the Lipans were successful, killing chief Yellow Wolf and recapturing all their horses.

The reservation system proved to be no solution of the Indian problem. The lower reserve was not an entire failure, for the small tribes which settled there—the Caddoes, Anadarkoes, Keechies, Ionies, etc.—had mostly come originally from the eastern wooded area and knew something about raising such crops as corn, beans and melons. With the aid of the white agents they opened farms, began raising small herds of cattle, and sent their children to agency schools. But during the first few years droughts damaged their crops, their cattle were not sufficient to sustain them, and they persisted in hunting off the reservation. This the white settlers, who were already pushing up near the reservation, did not like. On the upper reservation the situation was more dificult. The Comanches who settled there—only a small portion of the great tribe—knew nothing of agriculture and the warriors scorned an occupation which had never been a part of their system of living. Some of the wiser old chiefs tried to persuade them to take up the white man's way of living, but the young bloods preferred the wild free life of the hunt and the glory of the warpath. They could not be held continuously on the reservation. To make matters worse, the western and northern Comanches frequently enticed these young warriors away from the reservation. The peace which had been made with the wild Comanches in 1854 lasted about two years, when white pressure upon their hunting grounds in Kansas, Colorado and northern Texas had thoroughly angered them, and the temptation to steal horses became too great to resist. In 1856 and 1857 they began raiding again, often coming by the upper reservation where they were joined by some of the reservation Comanches, and swooping down on the exposed settlements all the way from the Red River to the Guadalupe, murdering and pillaging. Although Bell County was not so exposed to attacks as it had been a few years before —since settlements and new counties had been established further west—some of the raids penetrated into the county and Bell County citizens often formed companies of minute men or rangers to repel attacks and pursue the marauders.

Since no record seems to have been kept of the horse-stealing raids of this period, the memory of most of them has died out with the passing of the old settlers; but some of the tragedies and narrow escapes have not been forgotten. According to the late Mr. Baldwin P. Lee, a very reliable man, "An old man by the name of Wilson or Wilkson, his wife and little grand-daughter were overtaken while in a buggy on the road about ten miles northwest of Belton, killed and scalped. The minute company (of Belton) gave chase, but the Indians scattered in the Lampasas roughs and escaped."[5] The exact date of this occurrence is not known, but it was evidently during this period.

The last, and the best remembered, of these murderous incursions into Bell County was in March, 1859. On March 14, Judge John M. Perryman, who resided in Coryell County on Cowhouse Creek, only a few miles from the Bell County line, was returning on horseback from Gatesville to his home. When near his home, he was discovered by Indians and they put out after him. As he approached a thicket his horse attempted to jump a boggy branch but stuck in the mud. The Judge leaped or was thrown to the farthest bank and made the thicket on foot before the Indians did. The latter came up and rode around the thicket many times, but were afraid to penetrate it. He had only a single-barreled pistol for defense and expecting, of course, to be killed, he wrote an account of the attack and his will, upon a scrap of paper torn from his pocket memorandum

[5] Sketch of B. P. Lee in **Hunter's Frontier Magazine** April, 1912, pp. 9-11.

book and hid it in the leaves, in the hope that it would be found by his friends. Here he remained many hours, and until near night, when he crept to the edge of the thicket and, looking all around, he could see no Indians. Venturing from one thicket to another he finally reached his home. The Indians carried away his horse—a fine animal—with them.[6]

Two days after the above episode of Judge Perryman, the Indians (presumably the same band) appeared in the neighborhood of Sugar Loaf Mountain on the western line of Bell County. Mr. John Riggs and his wife, Jane Riggs, had but recently settled upon a new place there. A log cabin and a shed-room of green "raw hide" lumber (lumber sawed from native timber) had been hastily thrown up, the shed not completed nor closed in, and Mr. Riggs, who owned a small herd of cattle, was hauling cedar rails from the cedar-brake, not far away, to build pens for his cattle. Their home was in Bell County near the Sugar Loaf Mountain and not far from Cow House Creek and on a little stream called Post Oak branch. His family consisted of himself, wife, two daughters, Rhoda (9), Margaret (5), two sons, William C. (3½), and John (9 mos.).

Mr. Young Pierce lived about one-fourth mile west of the Riggs cabin. He was also hauling cedar from the cedar brake on the day of the occurrences now to be related. On the morning of March 16, 1859, Mr. Young Pierce, on his way, with his wagon, to the cedar brake, was attacked by some sixteen Indians, was killed, and stripped of his clothing; but this murder was not discovered until after the Riggs tragedy.

A little later on the same morning, ignorant of the murder of Pierce and of the presence of Indians in the country, Mr. John Riggs and young David Elms (a lad of about fourteen years old, in the employ of Mr. Riggs) started to the cedar brake with two wagons for rails, Elms being in front. Before they were out of sight of the house, the Indians came upon Elms and began whipping him with ropes and quirts. He pulled off his shirt and gave it to them. They then came to Riggs and began to whip him. Thomas Riggs (a brother, who had just arrived at John Riggs' home), seeing the Indians whipping John, ran toward him, whereupon the Indians desisted and left him. Thomas

[6] Judge J. H. Chrisman, "Early History of Coryell County," in **Old Settlers Association of Bell County, 1903,** p. 45.

Riggs immediately put out to the neighbors to give the alarm of Indians and to obtain help, particularly of Mr. Ambrose Lee, a fearless old frontiersman and a good marksman with a trusty rifle, who lived a mile away. David Elms had meantime escaped. John Riggs, wounded in the hand with an arrow, started back toward his house. His wife and children, having witnessed the whole occurrence and feeling that, unarmed as they were, their house was too open for protection against an attack, became greatly alarmed and had started away, either for Young Pierce's house or for Mr. Mack Whitehead's (a brother-in-law about a mile away west toward Sugar Loaf Mountain); and when John Riggs saw them fleeing he cut across the prairie and joined them about 200 yards from the house. The Indians, seeing that all the family had left the house, charged upon them in the open with an unearthly yell, surrounded them and began shooting Mr. Riggs with arrows, which he pulled out and threw back at them, at the same time throwing rocks with all his might but without avail. They shot him eleven times and he fell lifeless to the ground. Then they attempted to capture Mrs. Riggs, doubtless to lead her away into captivity, but she fought them so desperately, with rocks and anything that came to hand, that they speared her under the left arm, and she died trying to defend herself and her helpless children. Two Indians grabbed the two little girls and held them up behind them on their horses. Going to the Riggs home they plundered it of everything they could carry away on their horses, emptied the feather beds in the yard and wrapping the bedticking around their bodies, danced in merry mockery. They burned all the plunder left and tried to burn the house, but the timber was too green to burn.

Mr. Ambrose Lee came soon afterward and found the two little boys, whom the Indians had somehow, in their hurry, overlooked in the high grass. The infant boy was trying to nurse at the bloody breast of his dead mother, and the dead father lay but a few steps away, mangled with many mortal wounds. It was a sight to make a brave man sick and faint. He took the boys to their aunt, Mrs. Mack Whitehead.

The neighborhood was aroused; the families gathered together at "Fort Scoggin" (so-called), the home of Mr. Jesse Scoggin, which afforded the best protection in the neighborhood. Immediately the news was heralded to the surrounding country and posses for pursuit of the Indians were formed in this and neighboring settlements and at Belton.

The Indians, departing from the Riggs home, went south, crossed the Nolan about one or two miles below where Killeen now stands, and came to Little Nolan Creek, where they secured some of Charlie Cruger's horses by rounding them up under some trees and roping or "snaring" them. Mr. Cruger, returning home from Salado, rode up within 300 yards of them before discovering that they were Indians, turned to run, and was pursued by some of the Indians, but fortunately he was riding a fleet horse and outran them. He sped away for Belton, with a Paul Revere warning as he passed each house, halloaing "Indians," but not stopping to explain.

The Indians, having gathered up quite a herd of horses, moved south to the Douglas Mountain, on the divide between Nolan and the Lampasas, and there stopped to eat their dinner, stolen from the Riggs home, but they didn't offer a bite to the little Riggs girls. Here they spied a Mr. Peevy riding on horseback some distance away. Mounting their horses, they at once rushed upon and killed him, and, while holding a war dance around his dead body, they discovered, in the distance, several men riding in scattered formation, whom they took to be cow hunters but were in fact members of one of the posses started in response to Cruger's alarm who had scattered out in order to find the trail of the Indians. The latter became suddenly frightened, remounted, and fled westward in great haste.

The two little Riggs girls had been carried with them all the while and when the Indians began their flight, after killing Peevy, the one who was carrying the younger girl, Margaret, in trying to hand her over to another Indian (both mounted and running at full speed) accidentally dropped her and they did not stop to pick her up. Her older sister, Rhoda, riding behind another Indian, saw this and jumped down from the horse she was on, but was held in a dangling position till she managed to grap a bush, or something, and wrenched herself loose and she fell, stunned, to the ground. Recovering soon, she hastened back to her little sister and found her, badly bruised and crippled from her fall. The Indians were gone and were seen no more.

The little girls, barefooted, their clothes nearly stripped from them, sore and crippled from rough handling, grass-burrs torturing their little unshod feet, made out to follow back the way they had come and finally found a dim trail which led them several miles to an unoccupied house, the chimney of which they had seen in the distance when first freed from the Indians. Reaching it about dark they spent the night there. The weather being cool, Rhoda took what remained of her own dress, wrapped it around her little sister and nursed her all night. Next morning they followed a road around the mountain to Bates Renick's house, which was abandoned on account of the Indian excitement. Here they went inside the yard and stood awhile, when Mr. John B. Slack, an old Texas veteran, came along, having started out to see what he could learn about the Indians. He found the little Riggs girls there, took them on his horse to the home of Captain Milton W. Damron on the Lampasas, near Comanche Gap, where they were taken care of. The good women of the neighborhood made clothes for them, and they were soon returned to their aunt, Mrs. Whitehead, at Sugar Loaf. When found they had eaten nothing since their last breakfast at their home and were nearly starved.

Posses were made up in several neighborhoods to pursue these Indians. Major John Henry Brown, Capt. M. W. Damron, Ben Cox, James R. Sutton, Ambrose Lee, Charles P. Cruger, John Carmack, John Allcorn, Joseph Murrell, Isaac Shriver, J. J. Meek, C. B. Roberts, Sr., X. B. Saunders, J. Swan Bigham, Wm. B. Blair, Joel Blair, Thomas Trimmier, John B. Slack, Jesse Sutton, old man Harrell and his son, and Bates Renick were members of the posses. The names of the others—there were a number of others—are not available. They pursued the Indians as far as the Santa Anna Mountain and then went to Camp Colorado where they learned that ranger Captains John Williams and McMillan, of that post, were already out on the trail of the Indians. Their horses exhausted, the Bell County posse, after a brief rest, returned to their homes. The rangers recovered Judge Perryman's horse and some others which had been abandoned by the Indians on the Jim Ned Creek, but the Indians were not overtaken.[7]

---

[7] Jas. T. DeShields, in Wilbarger's **Indian Depredations in Texas,** 593. The above narration is based upon the statements of Captain **M. W. Damron** in **Belton Journal,** March 11, 1886; Wm. C. Riggs

There seems to have been a strange sequel to this raid. "While the four Riggs children and other families were at "Fort Scoggins" "a certain white man," says Mr. Wm. C. Riggs, "paid visits to that place and one day asked Rhoda (Riggs) if one of the Indians hadn't a very large nose. She replied, 'Yes,' wondering why he should ask such a question. He told Rhoda that he was acquainted with the Indians and that they were Comanches and came from the Reservation. She was afraid of him and thought she knew his features and reported what was said to her. He was immediately caught, confessed to being one of that cutthroat mob, gave the names of two other whites, who also took part in the murdering of our parents. This villain, whose name was Page, was hung by the people. The others were also executed, but their names were never known to us."[8]

Throughout 1858 and early 1859 similar raids were being made on the counties to the west and northwest of Bell. At many exposed points the settlers either abandoned their homes and moved back into older and more secure sections or "forted up" together at some neighbor's home for the safety of their wives and children. But this meant they must abandon their little crops and stock and, unless relief should soon be given, they must ultimately leave the country. Some of the stolen horses were found on the upper, or Comanche, reservation and there is other strong evidence that the Indians of that reservation were guilty, but the angry and excited settlers came to believe that the Indians of both reservations were implicated. They now began to demand that the Federal Government remove all Indians out of Texas. Bands of frontiersmen under such leaders as John R. Baylor and Peter Garland organized and

---

(son of John and Jane Riggs) in **Belton Daily News,** February 17, 1886; Margaret Benton (daughter of John and Jane Riggs) in **Belton Daily News,** March 2, 1887; MS. Statement of James R. Sutton, and other traditional sources.

[8] Wm. C. Riggs' statement published in **Belton Daily News,** March 18, 1886. He was a son of John and Jane Riggs and was one of the little boys whom the Indians "overlooked in the high grass." In his mature manhood he returned to Bell County and while many of the participants in and contemporaries of this tragedy were still living he interviewed them personally, examined the ground on which the same occurred and from these sources composed the published statement mentioned above.

marched on the two reservations threatening to exterminate all the Indians there. Some of the older frontier leaders, like George B. Erath, tried to prevent collision because they did not believe the Indians of the lower reserve guilty and because they feared the consequences would be a general Indian war. For a time there was danger of a fight between the U. S. forces stationed at the reserves and the citizens. Governor Runnels appointed a special commission of five men—George B. Erath, Richard Coke, John Henry Brown (of Bell County), J. M. Smith and Dr. J. M. Steiner—to look into the situation, while he appealed to the federal government to remove the Indians of both reservations across the Red River into the Indian Territory (now Oklahoma). This was agreed upon and the Indians were removed in the late summer of 1859. Captain John Henry Brown, in command of two detachments of volunteers from Bell, McLennan and other counties followed them to Red River to guard against straggling and thieving.

The removal to the territory did not stop the depredations along the Texas border, for there were in 1860 as many or more murders committed in the counties west of us as before. The depredators were the Caddoes, Wacos, Tahuacanos, and Keechies, formerly friendly but now hostile, both reserve and wild Comanches. A Belton paper of 1860[9] gives blood-curdling accounts of their atrocities in the border counties extending across the State, including Coryell, Hamilton, and Comanche, and notes the arrival in Belton of Mr. Lon Price, of Comanche, on his way to Austin, as an express messenger from that County to ask of Governor Houston relief for these people, from the open attacks of the hostiles. The latter, stealing away from the new reservations and knowing the Texas frontier so well, came down in force, scattered out all along the border counties and pursued almost with impunity their weird and bloody carnival. The poor, unorganized, unequipped settlers were powerless to meet them and each stood in his cabin home, with his gun in hand, to protect his wife and children or, as often happened, to die in the attempt.

These conditions, in Comanche County, continued until the settlers were exhausted and finally forting themselves up at the towns of Comanche, South Leon and Cora (a vil-

[9] The **Belton Democrat**, March 10, 1860.

lage now extinct), without horses, and almost without provisions and ammunition, they were forced to appeal to the outside world for help. In this extremity the good people of Bell County sent them five ox-wagons loaded with flour, and Ben Cox, with a squad of forty Bell County men, well mounted and well armed, went to their rescue and joined them in the defense of their homes and in the pursuit of the savages.[10]

2. *Bell County Volunteer Rangers,* 1859-1860

After the establishment of the first army posts in 1849, our State government, relying upon the obligation of the Federal authorities to furnish adequate protection against the Indians, did not attempt any thorough system of guarding the frontier. From time to time in the fifties, the legislature authorized the governor to raise companies or small troops of mounted rangers, to serve at his discretion; but these were strung out across the State from Red River to the Rio Grande, a distance of more than six hundred miles, and were quite insufficient to afford much protection. The Indians, as we have seen, frequently slipped around the Federal garrisons and the ranger stations and surprised the unprotected settlers in their homes. Consequently, in all the counties subject to Indian raids, the people, for their own protection, organized volunteer squads or companies of scouts, minute men, or rangers. These elected their own commanders, equipped, mounted and supplied themselves, and acting without governmental authority and without pay, did pretty effective work in guarding their communities against the incursions of the red men. Usually these organizations divided themselves up into squads, and the squads took turns in making their scouting trips along the frontier border, each squad being out eight or ten days during the light of the moon, which was the favorite time for the Indian incursions.

Although some sparsely settled counties, such as Coryell, Lampasas and Brown, with county organizations, intervened between Bell County and the great unoccupied west, the Indians, as we have already shown, came into our county on several occasions, stole horses and murdered some of our

[10] E. L. Deaton, **Indian Fights on the Frontier,** 80-81.

people. Following upon the shocking massacre of the Riggs family and other outrages, citizens of Bell County formed themselves into small bodies of volunteer minute men and rangers and scouted the upper country. Several such are here acounted for in the chronological order cf their organization and service.

a. "The Independent Blues." 1859[1]

This company, organized on March 29, 1859, under the leadership of John Henry Brown, then residing in Belton, was composed of the following Bell County citizens: William H. Bell, James D. Bell, J. Swan Bigham, Oliver H. Bigham, Robert C. Bigham, R. Patton Bigham, Wm. Nix Bigham, John S. Blair Jr., Charles Bock, William Bock, John Henry Brown, John C. Clark, James P. Coop, John W. Cowan, Benjamin Cox, Solomon B. Cox, Milton W. Damron, Samuel Green Davidson, James M. Draper, Dr. William D. Eastland, Elisha Embree, Dr. Jno. W. Embree, James Holcomb, Henry Jordan, Marcus A. Keltor, Edward W. Kinnan, George Kuykendall, Matthew J. Kuykendall, Frank Marschalk, Oliver B. Morris, R. P. Morris, John McDowell, William McDowell, Robert Nichols, J. I. Northcutt, John T. Pope, Drury D. Potter, Dr. A. K. Ramsey, Geo. D. Richard, Jas. Leonidas Riggs, William S. Riggs, Cornelius B. Roberts, A. K. Sandlin, X. B. Saunders, Jerry D. Scott, Jesse G. Scott, Isaac Shriver, Jas. A. Stringfellow, Geo. W. Wade, David Williams, Isaac Williams, Robert M. White.

The officers of the company are not named but a safe guess would include Major John Henry Brown, Robert M. White, Benjamin Cox and Samuel Green Davidson.

On April 1, 1859, the "Independent Blues' received as a loan from the State of Texas (on the bond of Major John Henry Brown, Lieutenant Robert M. White Dr. Jno. W. Embree, and Oliver H. Bigham, for their safe return), forty Colt's Navy Revolvers, which were distributed to the members of the company. Otherwise, the members of the company furnished their own outfits, which included mounts,

---

[1] Data obtained from private journal of the late Major John Henry Brown, a copy of which was furnished to the author by his daughters, Misses Lizzie C. Brown and Marion T. Brown, of Dallas, July 28, 1921. Also verbal statements to the author by Captain J. Swan Bigham, Lieutenant William S. Riggs and others.

provisions, guns, ammunition and camp equipage, and they served without pay.

These rangers went out in squads, usually of six men each and remained in the field about eight days each. The service lasted from March 29 to May 17, 1859. At Pidcocke Ranch, on the upper Cow House in Coryell County, they kept an extra supply of guns and ammunition, and two squads—one going out, the other coming in—usually camped together there one night. Not always did the same men form the personnel of a particular squad: some fell out, others came in, according to their engagements at home. Major John Henry Brown, Lieutenant Samuel Green Davidson, Lieutenant Benjamin Cox, Dr. John W. Embree and David Williams were generally in command of the respective squads. They ranged over the western portion of Bell and Coryell Counties and all over the counties of Lampasas, Hamilton, Brown and Comanche, including the present county of Mills.

As already stated, when the Reserve Indians were removed from the upper Brazos to Fort Cobb, Indian Territory, in 1859, Captain John Henry Brown commanded a company which followed them as far as Red River. In this command there were about twenty-five Bell County men, mostly old rangers. A complete roll of these Bell County men is not at hand, but the following is a partial roll: Major John Henry Brown commanding: James D. Bell, Thomas Bell, J. Swan Bigham, Joel D. Blair, Julius Brown, John C. Clark, C. W. Danley, Henry C. Denny, Milton Hodge, Marcus A. Kelton, Hulsey Parker, John Pierson, Wm. J. Venable, Geo. W. Warren, Sterling B. White, W. Alex White, Wilson H. White, Wm. B. Whittington, Columbus Wood.[12]

b. Bell County Minute Men, 1859

While Major Brown and several other members of the "Independent Blues" were absent on this service, the "Blues" organization seems to have relaxed somewhat, if it did not cease to function altogether.

There is evidence, however, that the citizens' volunteer scout service was continued throughout the summer of 1859,

---

[12] Verbal statements to the author by the late H. C. Denny and C. W. Danley, and by J. Swan Bigham, Wm. S. Riggs, and others.

during the light of the moon in each month, by the remaining members of the "Blues" and by some additional volunteers who joined in this work, viz: J. S. Bigham, Albert S. ("Trig") Blair, Joel D. Blair, Pat Bone, Dr. Hamilton Bradford, S. Green Davidson, Dr. Jno. W. Embree, Andrew J. Fleming, Thomas Leath, Wilson Patterson, Drury D. Potter, James Leonidas Riggs, William S. Riggs, Robert M. Scott, James R. Sutton, William Twomey, Alex Walters, Tilman Walters, David Williams, Eli Williamson, and others.

These rangers were known generally as "Minute Men." They mounted, equipped and supplied themselves, and, of course, served without pay.[13] No records of their services, nor detailed lists of the squads, are available.

c. "The Bell County Rovers," 1859-1860

Believing that the troubles with the Indians were not over, John Henry Brown, on his return from the Fort Cobb expedition, at once set to work to organize another ranging company. Some one (doubtless Captain Brown) published the following call in *The Belton Independent*:

"Frontier Meeting.

The 'Bell County Blues' and all citizens of the county willing to aid in protecting the frontier, are requested to meet in Belton at 1 o'clock next Saturday, September 17th, to consult, re-organize the old company, organize a new one, or do whatever may be deemed best. We can at least send out a good scout in the light of each moon.

MANY CITIZENS

Belton, Sept. 14, 1859."

The meeting was held; twenty-four names were enrolled and they adjourned to Saturday, the 24th. On September 24, the company met to organize, elect officers, and adopt rules. Thirty-eight names in all were enrolled. Following is the list of officers and privates:[14] Captain John Henry Brown, 1st Lieutenant Robert M. White, 2nd Lieutenant Sam G. Davidson, 3rd Lieutenant Benj. Cox, Privates A. J. Anderson, R. Patton Bigham, J. Swan Bigham, Robt.

---

[13] Verbal statements to the author by Lieutenant William S. Riggs, Drury D. Potter and others.
[14] Data obtained from Journal of Major John Henry Brown, **supra**.

C. Bigham, Wm. Nix Bigham, Wm. H. Bell, Jas. D. Bell, Wilson Bates, Albert S. Blair, Dr. Hamilton Bradford, John C. Clark, Solomon B. Cox, Elisha W. Cox, Dr. Jno. W. Embree, Ed J. Estis, Jno. T. Flint, Milton Hodge, Sam C. Hannon, A. J. Heise, James C. Holcomb, Henry Jordan, Mark A. Kelton, Chas. H. Kingsbury, E. W. Kinnan, Matt. J. Kuykendall, Henry Ludlow, Robert P. Morris, Oliver B. Morris, Hamilton McDowell, Drury D. Potter,[15] Dr. A. K. Ramsey, William S. Riggs,[16] C. B. Roberts, Jr., Jeremiah D. Scott, Sr., Jeremiah D. Scott, Jr., Jesse G. Scott, J. M. Townsend, J. E. Townsend, Martin L. Walker, David Williams.

It was agreed that the company should be divided into scouts of 10 each, including the captain or a lieutenant; that a scout should range on the frontier for ten days each, commencing six days before the full of each moon, and that the company should be called the "Bell County Rovers." The scout service of "The Bell County Rovers" extended from October 5, 1859 to January 13, 1860.

d. Bob White's Ranging Company, 1860

Under authority of Governor Sam Houston, a number of ranger companies of twenty-five men each, commanded by a lieutenant, were organized under the Act of January 2, 1860 "For the protection of the Frontier."[17] These formed a cordon extending across the western border of the state to prevent the incursions of hostile Indians into the settlements. Early in February, 1860, Dr. John W. Embree, of Belton, received a commission to organize such a company, to be known as the "Texas Mounted Rangers from Bell County," and on February 20, 1860, the men were sworn in at Belton, for a twelve months service, by Captain J. M. W. Hall, of Austin, representing Governor Houston. They were mustered out, however, in July, 1860. The following volunteers enlisted with the rank given:

Officers: Lieutenant Robert M. White, commanding, Wilson H. White, 1st Sergeant, W. Alex White, 2nd Sergeant, Albert S. Blair, 1st Corporal, J. Swan Bigham, 2nd Corporal. Privates: Jesse Blair, Joel D. Blair, David C.

---

[15] Added on statement of Drury D. Potter to the writer.
[16] Added on statement of Wm. S. Riggs to the writer.
[17] Gammel, **Laws of Texas**, IV, 1375.

Bowles, Don A. Chamberlin, John R. Chapman, Edward M. Clark, Stephen P. Clary, James P. Coop, Andrew J. Fleming, Geo. W. Fry, Joseph Halpain, August J. Heise, Milton Hodge, Chas. H. Kingsbury, Henry Ludlow, Joseph W. Murrell, Paul Newman, Robert Nichols, Wm. Perkins, Wm. J. Venable, Geo. W. Warren.

Later, on information that the company was in trouble with the Indians, a party went from Belton to their relief, composed of the following: Dr. John W. Embree, commanding, John Baker, Pastor Burrows, Ed Tom Cox, Jno. F. Ferguson, Joseph G. Ferguson, William Garner, David Hirsch, E. W. Kinnan, John F. Smith, Joseph Townsend and possibly some others.

When not on the move, the company bivouacked at the mouth of Partridge Creek, on the upper Cow House, in Hamilton County.[18]

All along in the fifties there were volunteer organizations of citizens, unofficial companies or squads, who mounted, equipped, armed and supplied themselves, served without pay, and took turns in guarding the mountain passes to the northwest and west against forays of the Indians, in the light of the moon in each month, especially during the spring, summer and fall. It would be pleasing to record here the names of all these dutiful citizens of our frontier but the lapse of time and the oblivion of death have effaced most of them from the memories of people now living and no records whatever of their service were ever made, so far as we know. It will never be known how many lives were thus saved and how much property was thus protected from savage hands.

3. *The Gold Hunters from Bell County, 1858-1859*

In March 1858, a party of about one hundred men, made up chiefly in Bell and Brown counties, organized an expedition to cross the plains and search for some rich gold mines alleged to be on the Pecos River, of whose location they had what were deemed to be accurate maps, field notes and other data.

[18]. Don A. Chamberlin, "Bob White's Ranger Company," **Old Settlers' Association of Bell County, 1902,** p. 21. Mr. Chamberlin had in his possession the original muster roll of the company and exhibited the same to the writer.

Among the members of this expedition were: Isaac T. Bean, S. H. Bell, Hilary M. Bouldin, John B. Constantine, Robert Cox, John Danley, John Early, James Epps, D. Griffin, J. A. Grimes, Wm. P. Hardeman, Silas Hare, John Keggans, Ishmael Kyle, Sam Miller, Wm. Perkins, J. L. and Warren Puett, Dr. A. K. Ramsey, G. W. Rector, James P. Reed, D. D. Rosborough, R. S. Stockard, J. A. Stringfellow, Wm. Wade, and Dave Williams.

The party left Belton late in March and proceeded to San Saba where it was organized, on April 6, as a military company by electing Wm. P. Hardeman captain, Silas Hare first lieutenant, J. B. Hardeman second lieutenant, J. S. Steen third lieutenant, H. M. Bouldin orderly sergeant, and D. D. Rosborough second sergeant. Thence they proceeded by way of Richland Creek, Pecan Springs, Antelope Creek, the South Concho, the Main Concho, up Kioway Creek to the North Concho, and out across the plains to the Horse Head Crossing of the Pecos, which they reached on April 27. Then they moved up the Pecos and spent the month of May searching for the fabled mines. Although they searched diligently, they failed to find them, and early in June most of the party returned home.[19]

Silas Hare and some twenty-four others, however, proceeded to El Paso, and Hare himself and a few others went on to New Mexico. Colonel Hare settled at Rio Bonito among the wild Indians, where he became a government contractor and speculator. Within less than four years he acquired a small fortune (if not a gold mine); but when the Civil War came on he lost all that he had made and beat a hasty retreat to the Confederate lines. Soon afterwards he entered the Confederate army.[20]

In 1859 the reports went over the country that gold, in rich quantities, had been discovered in the foot hills of Pike's Peak, in Colorado. People began to trek thither from all parts and many successfully made the perilous journey. The roads west of the Missouri River were lined with these bold adventurers. Many of them painted in large words, on each side of their wagon sheets the legend: "Pike's Peak or Bust!"

[19] **The Belton Independent,** March 27, April 24, May 29, June 12, 19, and 26, 1858, contains accounts of this expedition, including a portion of a diary kept by J. B. Hardeman.
[20] Letter of Hon. Silas Hare to the author, November 30, 1904.

Top: This house was one of the first built in Salado, and is typical of the architecture of the day.

Bottom: The old Robert Cox place in the cedar brakes north of Belton. This place is an interesting example of the way early settlers put native materials into use in their building. The stone is native limestone. The house is plastered inside with materials dug from the hills, and colored with the ground rock found near the house. The wood is native oak and cedar.

So, in this year 1859, a party of Bell County men caught the infection. They were old man John Hughes, of Hughes Mill, Wm. W. Spoonts, Mack Chambers, Wyman, Jones and Donley (a Scotch-Irishman), all from the northern part of the county, and perhaps a few others. They equipped three wagons, drawn by six or seven yoke of oxen, and went down to Milliken, then the terminus of the Houston and Texas Central Railway, loaded their wagons with groceries and other supplies, and started for Pike's Peak. Arriving in Grayson County, near Red River, they were there told that the report of the gold find was false. The party then disbanded, and most of them returned. William W. Spoonts found carpenter work at the village of Whitesboro, then just starting up, married there, and settled down until he entered the Confederate army. After the war he moved back to Bell County.[21]

[21] Verbal statement of W. W. Spoonts to the author.

CHAPTER XI

BELL COUNTY IN THE CIVIL WAR

1. *Ante-bellum Politics and Secession*

For ten years after annexation the politics of Texas had been conducted mostly along personal lines, although the candidates and voters inclined generally to the Democratic party since it was that party in the old states which had led the fight for annexation in 1844. The Whig party was small and its strength was confined to some of the eastern counties. Partly because there was little opposition to the Democrats, but more because of the size of the State and the difficulties of travel, the efforts to hold party conventions during the first ten years of statehood had not been very successful. Candidates for State offices were brought out by their friends, or announced themselves without party nominations, and the public honors were generally bestowed upon those who had been prominently identified with the Texas Revolution or with the war with Mexico. Although both Democrats and Whigs accepted the national platforms of their respective parties, the questions which had become burning issues in the other states of the Union —such as those involved in the Compromise of 1850—had not greatly perturbed the people of Texas.

In 1854 the controversy over the Kansas-Nebraska Act aroused some interest in the State and the next year the appearance of the American, or "Know Nothing," party in Texas had the effect of making party divisions sharper. General Sam Houston, the most important political figure in Texas, had voted against the Kansas-Nebraska bill in the United States Senate and in 1855 he espoused the policies of the Know Nothings. These acts brought him into conflict with the "regular" Democrats who began to work against his re-election to the Senate. In 1857 General Houston announced himself a candidate for the governorship. The regular, or southern, wing of the party held a State convention in Waco in that year and nominated Hardin R. Runnels for governor and Francis R. Lubbock for lieutenant-governor.

In this campaign of 1857 General Houston delivered a speech in Belton on Tuesday, July 14. He had a strong and influential following in Bell County. A large audience from all parts of the county and even from adjoining counties assembled in a beautiful shady grove where the Post Office and the Park Hotel now stand. The speaker's stand was under some large live oak trees on the exact spot now occupied by the Post Office. After General Houston's speech, Judge W. S. Oldham of Austin replied on behalf of the Democratic nominees. The occasion was a notable one and was never forgotten by the citizens of that day. Although Houston made a vigorous campaign he was defeated by Runnels.

In 1859 the regular Democrats nominated Runnels and Lubbock for re-election and Houston again became a candidate for governor with Edward Clark as his running mate for lieutenant-governor. By this time the sectional conflict between the North and South over the slavery issue had become bitter and many of the southern Democrats were already advocating the secession of the southern states. Although the campaign in Texas turned on several things, the question of union or disunion was one of them and Houston had declared for staying in the Union. Although most Texans were state rights men and believed that the State had the right to secede, they had not yet made up their minds that it was desirable. This time they elected Houston and Clark.

During this campaign Thomas N. Waul, the Democratic candidate for Congress from the western district, and his opponent, Andrew J. (Jack) Hamilton, candidate on the Houston, or independent, ticket, spoke in Belton. They were both able men. They travelled together, slept together, and spoke against each other all over the district. They were guests one night of Mr. Gordon W. Shanklin on the Lampasas four miles south of Belton. Hamilton was elected.

During these two campaigns the only newspaper in Bell County was *The Belton Independent,* founded by Andrew Marschalk, Sr., in 1857, but which had passed to the control of E. W. Kinnan. It supported General Houston and its influence was so strong that Houston sentiment predominated in the county, especially in the northern portion. In March, 1860, some of the regular Democrats started the publication of *The Belton Democrat* with James W. White ("Printer Jim") as publisher and John Henry Brown as editor. Naturally, it was opposed to Houston and advocated not only state rights but, if necessity should arise, secession from the Union.

By this time interest in national politics was thoroughly aroused and, as 1860 was to be a presidential election year, a Democratic mass meeting—said to be the largest ever held in the county up to that time—assembled in the court house in Belton to elect delegates to the Democratic State Convention which was to meet in Galveston, and, in turn, select delegates to the National Democratic Convention at Charleston, South Carolina. Mr. R. B. Halley, of Salado, was chosen to preside, and Wm. H. Bell and G. W. Wade to act as secretaries. A committee on resolutions was appointed, with John Henry Brown as chairman; and this committee reported a lengthy set of resolutions which reviewed the political history of the country and of the Democratic party, and defended the rights of the South under the Constitution. R. B. Halley, Robert Childers, Dr. A. K. Ramsey, S. G. Davidson, Daniel McMillin, and Major Horace Haldeman were appointed delegates to the state convention at Galveston. R. B. Halley was substituted for Major John Henry Brown at the latter's request.[1]

Other prominent leaders in the county among state rights Democrats were: E. S. C. Robertson, W. S. Rather, Thos. C. Tucker, Judge Wilson Y. McFarland, H. E. Bradford, Robert M. White, Dred R. Hill, D. D. Rosborough, Dr. John W. Embree, William Reed, and John Marshall. On the Houston, or Union side, were ranged also some of the best men in the county, nearly all of whom patriotically accepted the will of the people after secession was adopted and performed their full part in the support of the Confederate cause.

It is unnecessary to recite here the well known facts pertaining to the presidential campaign of 1860. In Texas a large majority of the voters were for John C. Breckinridge, the candidate for the southern Democrats, with most of the Houston men supporting John Bell of Tennessee, the candidate of the Constitutional Unionists. Few votes, if any, were cast for Douglas, the northern Democratic leader, and none at all for Abraham Lincoln, the candidate of the anti-slavery Republicans, who were a northern sectional party.

When the people of the South learned in November,

[1] **The Belton Democrat,** Vol 1, No. 1, March 10, 1860.

1860, that Abraham Lincoln had been elected to the presidency by the sectional vote of the northern states, the long pent-up excitement flamed up everywhere. They believed, because of the declarations of the Republican leaders, that the powers of the Federal Government would be used by the victorious Republicans to strike at their rights of property in slaves and that neither the Supreme Court of the United States nor the Constitution itself would be able to protect them. For a time opinion was divided as to the best course to follow. While some thought that safety for the South could be found only in immediate secession from the Union, others wished first to try for compromise or to wait for Mr. Lincoln to disclose his policy. But it soon became clear that the Republicans would agree to no compromise of the matters in dispute. Thereupon South Carolina withdrew from the Union on December 20, 1860, and was followed in January, 1861, by Alabama, Mississippi, Florida, Georgia and Louisiana. The other southern states, except Texas, waited to see what the incoming president, Lincoln, would do.

Although somewhat slower than the other states just mentioned, Texas was moving. One reason for the delay was that Governor Houston had refused to convene the legislature for the purpose of calling an election for a convention which should decide the question of secession. Thereupon early in December a group of some seventy-two citizens issued a call for an election of delegates on January 8, 1861, to assemble in Austin on January 28. Two delegates were to be elected from each legislative district. The call was generally approved and the election was held by the regular election officials. This district composed of Bell and Lampasas counties elected John Henry Brown of Belton and E. Sterling C. Robertson of Salado as delegates.

Governor Houston, in the meantime, had decided to convene the legislature. When it met, January 21, he sent in a message declaring his belief in the right of secession, but not in its expediency, asserting that the convention soon to assemble was not legally called, and asking for an election of delegates to represent Texas in a general convention of southern states. The majority of the legislature, however, refused his request and promptly recognized the legality of the convention.

The convention assembled on January 28 and on February 1 adopted an ordinance of secession by a vote of 167 to 8. Both of the Bell county delegates voted for this ordinance. The ordinance was to be submitted to a vote of the people on February 23, and if ratified, was to go into effect on March 2, the twenty-fifth anniversary of the Texas Declaration of Independence from Mexico.

The Convention appointed a Committee of Public Safety to attend to the defense of the State. John Henry Brown, of Bell County, was a member of this committee. He was also chairman of a committee to prepare an address to the people of Texas setting forth the causes of secession. At the second session of the convention he was a member of a committee to prepare and publish an address to the people of the state setting forth the proceedings of the convention and the reasons therefor. The convention also elected seven delegates to represent Texas at a convention of the seceded states at Montgomery, Alabama. Before these delegates arrived there the Confederate Government had been organized with Jefferson Davis of Mississippi as President and Alexander H. Stephens of Georgia as Vice-president. The Texas convention recessed on February 5 to wait the verdict of the people. It was to reassemble on March 2.

On the question of the ratification of the ordinance of secession there was a brief but vigorous and acrid campaign. Many of the ablest men went on the stump in advocacy of ratification. Governor Houston made a number of speeches against it in what proved to be his last participation in a political campaign. Bell County shared in the general excitement. Governor Houston had made a speech at Belton somewhat earlier, on January 5, when he was trying to prevent the election of a convention. He spoke from a stand improvised of dry goods boxes on the north side of the court house square, about the middle of the block. A large crowd, for those days, had assembled from far and near to hear him, and feeling ran high. He conceded the doctrine of state rights and the right of secession from the Union, but he advocated the peaceful settlement of the sectional issues within the Union. He predicted that war would result, pointed out the disadvantages which the South would labor under because of the greater strength and resources of the North, predicted the disastrous results of war and urged the people to desist from such a ruinous course. That all of Governor Houston's predictions came true is well known to every candid student of history. Most of his hearers were opposed to his views, but so great was their personal admiration of General Houston that they listened to him with respectful attention. There was evidently some disturbance, however, for according to one account a few excitable and over-zealous persons far out on the edge of the crowd resented something the Governor said and threatened to interrupt the proceedings. General Houston noticed them and assumed a defiant attitude; but a number of citizens interposed and effectually quieted the disturbers so that General Houston was able to conclude his address without further incident.[2] According to another account the interruption came from a man some ten or fifteen feet away from the speaker's stand who arose with some show of hostility. Immediately there was a commotion in the audience and the ladies arose from their seats, when General Houston looked the disturber straight in the eye, placed both hands on his Derringer pistol which was belted around him under a cat-skin vest, and said: "Ladies and gentlemen, keep your seats. It's nothing but a fice barking at the lion in his den. If he should shoot at me he couldn't hit my brisket, if it was as wide as a barn door," at the same moment rearing back and spreading out his arms.[3]

Another rather exciting episode which occurred in the campaign of February over the ratification of the secession ordinance illustrates the feeling that was sometimes engendered. A public debate had been arranged at the little village of Aiken between Major John Henry Brown, a champion of secession, and Colonel Alonzo Beeman, a Union man who was a resident of that community. Colonel Beeman, an educated and accomplished man, pleaded eloquently for remaining in the Union and portrayed so graphically the sad results of the war which he said must inevitably follow secession that many of his unbelieving critics of that day have since pronounced his utterances as nothing less than prophetic. When he concluded his speech and came down from the stand, he was set upon by some of the most excited and rabid secessionists with abuse and threatened with personal violence. Although nearly all his neighbors were strong secessionists, they gathered around him in an

[2] Oral statement to the author by the late Don A. Chamberlin.
[3] Oral statement to the author by William S. Riggs.

instant, forming a complete circle facing outwardly, and protected him until the crowd cooled off and order was restored. Major Brown not only had no part in this but in chivalrous fashion expressed regret for it. And it should be recorded that Colonel Beeman, when the war came, although born and reared in the North, did all he could for the southern cause. Too old for military service himself, he said to his two boys who were just of age, "This is my country." They both promptly volunteered for service in the Confederate army.

Notwithstanding the efforts of the conservatives, the people of the State ratified the secession ordinance by a vote of 46,129 to 14,697. The vote in Bell County was 495 for and 198 against the ordinance. The State Convention reassembled, declared the result of the election, ratified the Constitution of the Confederate States, and required all public officials to take an oath of allegiance to the new regime not later than March 16, 1861. When Governor Houston failed to appear on that day to take the oath, the convention declared his office vacant and installed the Lieutenant-governor, Edward Clark, as Governor. General Houston retired to private life and died at his home in Huntsville, July 26, 1863.

Texas participated honorably and gloriously in the War of Secession; but that story does not belong here. We must confine ourselves to the part played by the soldiers and citizens of Bell County.

2. *The Bell County Volunteer Companies*

After a decade of slow but healthy pioneer progress, the development of our county was to be interrupted by the shock of war. The realities of war first struck home to our people when the soldier boys assembled in crudely organized companies, recruited by local leaders, and marched away to the training camps of the armies of the Confederacy, thence soon to be advanced to the lines of hostile military contact between the two sections of the country. At the call of the State for volunteers our young men hastened to join the colors and company after company went out

[4] E. W. Winkler (editor), **Journal of the Texas Secession Convention,** pp. 88, 90.

from Bell County long before there was any mention of a draft or conscript law by the Confederate Congress.

The home people generously turned over to the soldiers whatever needed equipment they were able to supply. The cavalrymen provided their own mounts and those not having them were mounted by horse raisers and other citizens, who trusted for their reimbursement to the fortunes of war, but who never received any compensation. Our local merchants handed out blankets and camp comforts from their stocks of goods, trusting to be reimbursed by the county.

To every company that was enlisted here a beautiful silk flag, made by our good women, was presented on the day of the company's departure for the front. Before the company, drawn up in parade formation, some young lady of the county presented the flag to the captain in an address full of tender affection and patriotic inspiration. The captain received it with an appropriate response on behalf of the company. On these occasions there gathered the mothers, fathers, wives, sisters and younger brothers of the departing soldiers, as well as their friends, neighbors and well-wishers and many other interested citizens. The occasion was one of sentiment and pathos. Every heart was filled with love for the Southern cause and every eye held a tear for the splendid young soldiery of our county, thus generously offering their lives in defense of loved ones, home and country.

Bell County, at the beginning of the war, did not exceed four thousand in white population,[5] yet the muster rolls of her soldiery credited her with more than one thousand men and boys who donned the Confederate gray. No county or country, we believe, ever made a better showing of loyalty to home and fireside.

In his Centennial Address delivered at the Court House in Belton on July 4, 1876, the late Judge X. B. Saunders stated that Bell County sent out thirteen companies to the the Confederate army,[6] but this writer, after the most diligent search for several years past in all available sources of information, and particularly among the old soldiers

[5] The United States Census for 1860 gives the white population as 3,805.
[6] Printed in the **Belton Journal,** July 13, 1876.

themselves, had been unable to locate more than ten companies.

There are in Texas no official archives showing the personnel of her Confederate soldiers. The records of the Adjutant General's Office of Texas, which contained the original muster rolls, were destroyed in the accidental burning of the old State capitol building at Austin in 1881. Some ten years ago the writer undertook to make up from private sources company rolls of the soldiers who went from Bell County to the Confederate army. He invoked the aid of the few soldiers then surviving, and from them and from other sources he compiled *unofficial* rolls of ten companies—some of them fragmentary and very incomplete, and also a list of men from Bell County who joined companies organized elsewhere. He published these rolls in the *Belton Journal* on January 31, and again on February 7, 1918, with an urgent request for corrections and additions, to which request he has received many responses. As thus revised they will be referred to herein as the "Unofficial Rolls of 1918."

Correspondence with the Adjutant General of the United States at Washington elicited the fact that there are on file in that office, in the Confederate Archives, fifty four official quarterly muster rolls of seven companies from Bell County. These were among the records captured at Richmond, Virginia, at the fall of the Confederacy in 1865. But copies of these could not be furnished on account of the stress of demand upon the clerical force of the Department, and the writer thus found himself "up against a blank wall."

Later on, in 1925, Mr. Ernest W. Winkler, Librarian of the University of Texas, procured for the Library of that institution, complete photostatic copies of these fifty-four muster rolls and kindly placed them at the service of the writer, who was thus happily able to compile for this work complete consolidated official muster rolls of each of the seven companies, with officers and their highest ranks attained during their service, and a list of the casualties as shown upon the official rolls of each company. To these official lists he has appended, separately, the names of those shown on his revised "Unofficial Rolls of 1918." He here acknowledges his obligation to Mr. Winkler for this valuable assistance and congratulates himself upon the good fortune of such timely cooperation.

Thus authentic official muster rolls of seven Bell County companies have been obtained for this work—those commanded by Captain J. Swan Bigham, Robert M. White, H. E. Bradford, Milton W. Damron, X. B. Saunders, John F. Smith and Robert B. Halley. Of three other companies—those of Captains G. Wat Graves, Jas. W. Weathersbee and Wm. S. Rather—unofficial fragmentary rolls, compiled from memory by surviving members of the respective companies and from other sources, are the only available data.

Some names appear twice or oftener in the successive rolls. At first the Confederate soldiers were enlisted for a definite period—three, six, or twelve months—at the expiration of which some came home and later enlisted in another company, while the main body of the company reinlisted at the front for the period of the war under their old company organizations. And occasionally there were two men with the same name.

It will be noted that during the latter part of the war no muster rolls of the Bell County companies serving west of the Mississippi seem to have ever reached the Confederate War Department at Richmond or the United States War Department at Washington. A probable explanation is that after the Federals gained control of the Mississippi River open communication between the army west of the river and Richmond was cut off and that thereafter their muster rolls were retained at the headquarters of General E. Kirby Smith, in command of the Trans-Mississippi Department with headquarters at Shreveport. What became of these archives at the "surrender" is not known to the writer. One tradition is that they were destroyed at Shreveport, another is that they were carried away to old Mexico by General Smith and his entourage and were there ultimately destroyed or lost.

With these preliminary explanations the rolls of these ten Bell County companies, official and unofficial, are now presented in the chronological order of their departure for the service, as well as an incomplete list of Bell County men who enlisted or served in other organizations, as above mentioned.

a. Captain J. Swan Bigham's Company

This company grew out of a ranging company, whose brief history, as best we can put it together, is here given.

While delegates were being chosen to the Secession convention Captain Robert B. Halley, foreseeing the early need of some sort of military force, recruited a company in Bell County styled the "Salado Mounted Troops," a quasi-ranging company, and tendered their services to the Secession convention on February 4, 1861, through Major E. S. C. Robertson, one of the Bell County delegates.[7] This was the first organization in Bell County and among the first in Texas of its character. The tender was referred to the Committee of Public Safety appointed by the Convention. This committee commissioned Colonel Henry E. McCulloch to take command of the northwest frontier—in co-operation wth Colonel Ben McCulloch and Colonel John S. ("Old Rip") Ford, who were assigned to other portions—and to seize for the State, or for the Confederate Government then organizing at Montgomery, Alabama, the United States military garrisons located along the Texas frontier from Red River to the Rio Grande, with their mounts, army transportation wagons and teams, arms, ammunitions, equipment, military stores and supplies. Colonel Henry E. McCulloch accepted the services of Captain Halley's company and ordered it to join other companies—under command of Captains T. C. Frost, J. B. Barry, H. A. Hamner and D. C. Cowan, respectively—and some citizen forces under Lieutenant Cunningham, amounting in all to less than two hundred men, at a rendezvous near Camp Colorado, on the Jim Ned Creek in the present county of Coleman. While bivouacked here Colonel H. E. McCulloch, on February 22, received from Captain E. Kirby Smith of the 2nd U. S. Cavalry, the peaceful surrender of Camp Colorado, which he left in charge of Captain T. C. Frost, and proceeded with the remaining force to Ft. Chadbourne, in the present county of Coke. Here was arranged with Col. Morris, the commanding officer, the capitulation on March 1st of this garrison, which was left in charge of Captain Halley. Colonel McCulloch went on with his remnant force, recruited by some other companies, to Camp Cooper on the Clear Fork of the Brazos, lately commanded by Captain S. D. Carpenter, U. S. Army, but which had already been turned over on February 21 to Colonel Wm. C. Dalrymple of the State troops serving under Governor Sam Houston, and this post

---

[7] E. W. Winkler, (Editor) **Journal of the Texas Secession Convention,** p. 80

was taken over by Colonel McCulloch on March 9.[8] A large quantity of arms, ammunitions and other military equipment and supplies was thus obtained from the Federal garrisons along the frontier for the ultimate use of the Confederate army.

Their special work having been accomplished and the term of their enlistment (three months) having expired, Captain Halley's ranging company was automatically disbanded and he and a number of his men returned to their homes, and thus ended the career of the "Salado Mounted Troops." It was not officially in the Confederate service but most of its members joined the Confederate army later on and their names appear upon the muster rolls of Bell County soldiers in the great conflict.

The names of the other officers of Captain Halley's ranging company are not known to the writer, but they doubtless included most of those mentioned in the official roll of the company of Captain S. Green Davidson.

Under call for enlistment in the Confederate service on the frontier, issued meantime, the remainder of Captain Halley's men together with others, recruited from home reorganized in May, 1861, at Fort Chadbourne with Samuel Green Davidson as captain, and were accepted into the service in May, 1861, as Company K, 1st Texas Volunteer Cavalry, Confederate States Army, a regiment of some ten companies under command of Colonel Thomas C. Frost of Comanche. In a fight with Comanche Indians on the upper Colorado in the latter part of June, 1861, Captain Davidson, commanding a special troop of seventy-five men from different companies, was killed in action while leading a charge. His body, borne by his comrades back to camp where Big Spring (Howard County) now stands, was buried there with military honors. The command of the company then fell to First Lieutenant Robert C. Myers. He was soon promoted to the rank of Major, then to Lieutenant Colonel. Second Lieutenant James Swan Bigham then became captain of the company and commanded it throughout the war. For sometime this company served on the lower Rio Grande section and on the San Bernard under Colonel Augustus Buchel, but was transferred early in 1863 to the Louisiana-Arkansas front. The U. S. War Department possesses only

[8] E. W. Winkler, (Editor) **Journal of the Texas Secession Convention,** 370-380.

one official muster roll of this company of which a transcript from the photostat copy is here utilized.[9]

Roster of Company K, First Texas Cavalry, Colonel Augustus Buchel—Enlisted May, 1861. Compiled from official Muster Roll of February 29, 1864, at Camp Sidney Johnston (Louisiana).

James Swan Bigham, Captain, Commanding; Jas. D. Bell, 1st Lieutenant; Mat J. Kuykendall, 2nd Lieutenant; David W. Woodruff, 3rd Lieutenant; A. Crom Thomson, 1st Sergeant; Wm. B. Marshall, 2nd Sergeant; Duncan McNair, 3rd Sergeant; W. H. Griffith, 4th Sergeant; Robert A. Rich, 5th Sergeant; Samuel W. Bishop, 1st Corporal; J. McThomson, 2nd Corporal; F. N. Holcomb, 3rd Corporal; Wm. B. Morris, 4th Corporal; O. L. Bishop, 1st Bugler; Drury D. Potter, 2nd Bugler; Nat J. Franklin, Blacksmith; Wm. R. Holcomb, Farrier.

Privates: John T. Alexander, John J. Anderson, J. H. Aynesworth, Thos. J. Bell, Wm. H. Bell, Asa F. Bellamy, Robt. C. Bigham, Wm. Nix Bigham, Lycurgus Bishop, Jesse C. Blair, Richard T. Brown, Wm. H. Brown, Gaston B. Cabler, Quincy Cabler, Henry N. Cantrell, Caruthers P. Coble, Thos. M. Cosber, Martin L. Crass, Simeon W. Crass, J. C. J. Christian, A. W. Davis, Geo. S. Dawson, James C. Elliott, Milam Gallatin, Samuel Gallatin, David C. Griffin, Edward Harmon, Hubbard S. Heard, Jas. A. Holcomb, Calvin Hughes, W. J. G. Johnson, John G. Kelley, Robt. B. Kuykendall, James M. Lane, Thos. M. Leach, Henry Ludlow, James C. Marshall, R. P. Marshall, Thos. McCoy, James McDonald, Daniel E. Moore, Edward J. Morris, James Moseley, Columbus Nailor, Elihu D. Northcut, Edward D. Pace, James A. Polk, Samuel G. Pullen, Edwin J. Rancier, Robert Randolph, Abram M. Roberts, Wade G. Roberts, Jere D. Scott, Larkin C. Scott, R. M. Scott, W. W. Scott, James H. Slaughter, Geo. W. Warren, John R. Whitley, Allen J. Whitney, James R. Williams, James W. Williams, James W. Williams ("Red Jim"), W. A. Williams, Noah T. Wise, Hastings Young.

At this writing (June 4, 1926) Captain Bigham, though much enfeebled by age, still survives and is the only one of the Bell County Captains now living.

Additions from "Unofficial Roll of 1918"

Names included in roll compiled by Captain J. S. Bigham, James A. Polk, Jas. A. Holcomb and from other sources, but which do not appear on the official muster roll of February 29th, 1864. This list doubtless includes a number of those who returned home on the disbanding of Captain Halley's first company at Fort Chadbourne, as above related.

[9] No casualties are noted on this roll.

Bell County in the Civil War

Wilson Bates, Thos. Bales, Gus A. Beeman, "Granny" Bell, Thos. L. Berry, James W. Bigelow, Isaiah Broussard, John Clark, Jas. P. Coop, Andrew Cox, Benjamin Cox, David Cox, Allen Craighead, John Evans, Martin V. Fleming, ———— Graves, W. R. Halmark, Thos. Holcomb, F. Newton Holcomb, Thos. Kelley, Boaz Kuykendall, Will Kuykendall, John Lane, Columbus McKey, James McNair, James Moore, John Morris, Oliver Morris, R. P. Morris, Sam Morris, C. B. Roberts, Sr., C. B. Roberts, Jr., James T. Roberts, James Robinson, Sam Shelton, Riley Smalley, Ance Stevens, Henry Stokenberry, Jerry Walker.

b. Captain Robert M. White's Company

About the first of July, 1861, Captain Robert M. White took out the next company from Bell County. It was really the first company that went from our county directly to the fighting area. Miss Victoria Bradford, on behalf of the ladies of the county, presented the company with a flag on the day of their departure from Belton. Captain White, who had served as commander of many ranging companies and Indian Scouts on our frontier, had much valuable military experience and was a brave and popular commanding officer. The company bivouacked first at old Bosqueville, near Waco, then at Camp Stone near Lancaster and at Dallas, while training and equipping; but was early assigned to active duty in Arkansas, Choctaw Nation and Southwest Missouri. Crossing the Mississippi River in the early spring of 1862, it saw arduous service in Tennessee, Mississippi, Alabama and Georgia for the remainder of the war—perhaps the most severe fighting of any Bell County company. On the promotion of Captain White to the rank of Major of Sul Ross' regiment on May 26, 1862, the company reorganized and Lieutenant Wm. B. Whittington became captain of this company and commanded it to the end of the war. It went out as a cavalry company but was dismounted at Des Arc, Arkansas, in the spring of 1862 and the horses were sent back to Bell County. Major White was killed in action on the Tennessee River April 26, 1863. His remains were brought back to Belton and buried here.

Dr. Hamilton Bradford was appointed surgeon of the regiment; M. M. Vanderhurst was elected chaplain and John J. Baker became Quartermaster of the Brigade. All of them went out with this company.

From the photostat copies from the U. S. War Department of fifteen official muster rolls,[10] the following consolidated roll of this company is compiled.

Company H, 6th Texas Volunteer Cavalry, Colonel B. Warren Stone, later Colonel L. S. Ross; General Ben McCulloch's Brigade. Enlisted July, 1861. Robert M. White, Captain Commanding; Wm. S. Rather, 1st Lieutenant; W. B. Whittington, 2nd Lieutenant; E. M. Clark, 3rd Lieutenant; R. Henry Baker, 1st Sergeant; Martin L. Walker, 2nd Sergeant; Chas H. Kingsbury, 3rd Sergeant; William S. Riggs, 4th Sergeant; John A. Miller, 1st Corporal; James Hamilton, 2nd Corporal; Wm. H. Nichols, 3rd Corporal; Robert Nichols, 4th Corporal; A. W. Hannah, 1st Bugler, S. G. Bramlet, 2nd Bugler; George W. Coots, Blacksmith; O. H. Bigham, Farrier.

After reorganization, May 26, 1862: Wm. B. Whittington, Captain Commanding; R. Henry Baker, 1st Lieutenant; William S. Riggs, 2nd Lieutenant; E. Rusk Collard, 3rd Lieutenant; A. M. Keller, 1st Sergeant; S. G. Bramlet and John Clary, 2nd Sergeants; Robert Nichols, 3rd Sergeant; Robert N. Wright, 1st Corporal; Albert A. Dumas, 2nd Corporal; M. M. Haggard, 3rd Corporal; James Lambert, Blacksmith; O. H. Bigham, Farrier.

Privates: Alvis Ashley, Matthias Armstron, James A. Arnold, Giles W. Arthur, John J. Baker, Thos. F. Bean, Ronaldo R. Beeman, James W. Bigelow, Matthew W. Blackwell, Albert S. Blair, John S. Blair, John Henry Bond, Ben J. Bradford, Ambrose Bramlet, John C. Brookman, Wm. E. Bruce, William Carl, John W. Christian, John H. Church, Ephraim E. Clark, Nathaniel C. Corley, James H. Cox, Henry Crawford, Chas. Wesley Danley, James M. Day, Alex Austin Freeman, Frank (Scott) Goodsell, James W. Graham, 3rd Sergeant, R. Newton Graves, Henry R. Hakelton, Boykin Hall, John M. Hall, August J. Heise, Fred H. Helleman, James W. Hodge, John M. Holt, Haywood Hughes, Geo. D. Kelley, Matthew Keyes, Wm. C. Kuykendall, Larkin C. Locke, John T. McDonald, Wm. P. McGill, Artemus T. McNeil, Branick Middleton, James H. Miller, Langston Miller, B. H. Montgomery, James W. Moore, John Music, Fred Neibling, Washington Neibling, Wm. M. Olden, Jacob A. Perkins, Wm. M. Perkins, James Leonidas Riggs, Abram M. Roberts, Cyrus A Rosborough, John W. Shanklin, Edwin A. Smith, James M. Smith, Lewis Stacy, John H. Staples, E. Stephenson, A. L. Teagarden, Thos. H. Teagarden, John W. Tucker, Thomas C. Tucker, M. M. Vandenhurst, J. Armstead Vanness, William J. Venable, Geo. W. Wade, Robert A. Walker, Henry J. Warren, Peter R. Warren, Michael C. Westbrook, Nim S. White, Wm. Alex White, Abram O. Williams, Jesse Williams, Wilson Willingham, Richard J. Wright, Peter Wynn.

[10] Official muster rolls of September 7, 1861 at Dallas, Texas; October 31, 1861 at Flat Creek, Mo.: December 31, 1861 at Fort Gibson, Choctaw Nation; February 28, 1862, at Camp Lee Creek, Ark.; April 30, 1862, at Camp McIntosh, Miss.; June 30, 1862, at Camp Maury, Miss.; August 31, 1862, October 31, 1862 and December 31, 1862, at Camp Boggess, Miss.; February 28, 1863, at Spring Hill, Tenn.; April 30, 1863 and June 30, 1863 near Brownsville, Tenn.; August 31, 1863, at Ebenezer, Miss.; October 31, 1863 and June 30, 1864 at Braith's Field.

Casualties

Matthew W. Blackwell, died at Iuka, September 19, 1862.

John Henry Bond, died at Cantonment, Washington, no other particulars.

Benjamin J. Bradford, died at Stony Point, Ark., April 22, 1862.

Ambrose Bramlet, wounded, no details given.

William Carl, killed at Davis' Mills, December 21, 1862.

John Clary, wounded and in hospital, at Pulaski, Tenn.

August Heise, killed by accidental discharge of gun, November 16, 1861.

Chas. H. Kingsbury, wounded and at hospital, Columbia, no other particulars (1863).

Wm. C. Kuykendall, killed at Corinth, October 4, 1862.

John Music, died of wounds received at Davis' Mills, December 21, 1862.

Washington Neibling, died of disease in hospital at Holly Springs, Miss., May 22, 1862.

Wm. H. Nichols, wounded at Davis' Mills, no other particulars. (1862?)

Wm. S. Riggs, wounded, left at hospital, no other particulars.

Cyrus A. Rosborough, died in hospital at Okolona, Miss., no other particulars.

James M. Smith, died near Mooresville, Miss., July 5, 1862.

Martin L. Walker, wounded and prisoner at Corinth, Miss., October 4, (1862?)

Robert A. Walker, died at Cantonment, Washington, March 28, 1862.

Peter R. Warren, died in hospital at Fayetteville, December 10, 1861.

Nim S. White, killed at Davis' Mills, December 21, 1862.

Jesse Williams, died in hospital at Fayetteville, December 12, 1861.

Robert N. Wright, wounded, left in hospital, no other particulars.

J. Armstead Vanness, wounded and prisoner at Davis' Mills, December 21, 1862.

Additions from "Unofficial Roll of 1918"

Names included in an unofficial roll compiled by Lieutenant Wm. S. Riggs and Frank (Scott) Goodsell, but which do not appear upon the official muster rolls above mentioned: B. F. Gassaway, Wm. Gassaway, Thomas Graves, James McCorcle, Geo. W. Watte.

c. Captain H. E. Bradford's Company

The third company from Bell County was recruited for infantry service and commanded by Captain Henry Eugene Bradford. Officers were elected and organization was completed one afternoon in September, 1861, in a vacant lot on Pearl Street, just north of the present county jail, in Belton. On the day of their departure a company flag was presented for the ladies, in the old District Court room, by Miss Kate

Ludlow and was accepted by Captain Bradford on behalf of the company. Marching away to Camp Henry McCulloch, near Victoria, Texas, they trained there until the spring of 1862, when they moved to Camp No. 25 in Smith County, Texas. In August, 1862, they advanced to the Arkansas field and later went into winter quarters at Arkansas Post, where in an engagement on January 11, 1863, a large number of this company, as well as of others, were captured by the Federals and imprisoned at Camp Butler near Springfield, Illinois. The remnant of the company saw active service in hard fought battles in Tennessee and Georgia.

Dr. Thos T. Williamson, assistant Regimental Surgeon, had enlisted in this company.

From photostatic copies of sixteen official muster rolls[11] of this company in the U. S. War Department the following consolidated roll is compiled.

Company F, 6th Texas Volunteer Infantry, Colonel R. R. Garland; Brigadier General, Earl Van Dorn. Henry Eugene Bradford, Captain, Commanding; Ben F. Church, 1st Lieutenant; Levi T. Methvin, 2nd Lieutenant; Mark A. Kelton, Junior 2nd Lieutenant; Collins L. Kinnan, John Shelton, 1st Sergeants; Porter L. Ellis, 2nd Sergeant; Garrett W. Seay, Sylvester Burley, 3rd Sergeants; John B. B. Supple, R. L. Chalk, 4th Sergeants; Stephen A. Sinclair, 5th Sergeant; Wm. H. Meredith, Thos. B. Shelton, Wade W. Hampton, Cornelius M. Atwood, 1st Corporals; Wm. T. J. Hartriek, Richard T. Blackburn, Josiah L. Polk, 2nd Corporals; James E. Petty, 3rd Corporal; James M. Chambers, James P. Ashford, Musicians.

Privates: Bartlett Aiken, James Anderson, Mitchell Anderson, Jackson Baker, Wm. H. Bawcom, Christopher A. Berry, Samuel W. Bigham, Benjamin F. Birch, James D. Blodgett, Francis E. Bond, Geo. A. Bonner, Roland R. Boyd, Willis W. Boyd, Wm. H. Brown, John W. Brown, Henry S. Cearnel, W. Price Cearnel, John D. Chapman, James W. Cowan, Rueben Crow, John B. Davis, Wm. B. Denton Wm, T. Dodson, D. W. Dollar, Christopher C. Doss, Harmon W. Doss, Francis M. Drake, Henry Elms, W. R. Everett, Wm. C. Evetts, Louis L. Fewell, Charles Fleming, Juan Francisco, Amos B. Griffith,

---

[11] Official muster rolls of November 3, 1861, December 31, 1861, February 28, 1862, and April 30, 1862, all at Camp Henry McCulloch, Texas; June 30, 1862 at Camp No. 25, Smith County, Texas; August 31, 1862 at Camp Holmes, Jefferson County, Ark.; October 31, 1862 and December 31, 1862, at Arkansas Post, Ark.; April 30, 1863, June 30 1863 and August 31, 1863, at Harrison, Tenn.; October 31, 1863, at Missionary Ridge, Tenn.; December 31, 1863, at Tunnel Hill, Ga.; February 29, 1864 and April 30, 1864, at Dalton, Ga.; June 30, 1864 near Marietta, Ga. Note on muster roll of June 30, 1863: "This company was in the battle of Arkansas Post January 11, 1863, in which the greater number were captured together with the Company books, Muster Rolls, etc."

David Glowner, Charles Hagerton, Josiah A. Hall, Woodie T. Hamilton, Robert S. Hannon, Green E. Hulsey, Alonzo F. McLaughlin, Daniel Mayes, Harvey McKenzie, David B. Merchant, Albert Methvin, Alfred Methvin, Wm. D. Murray, Pleasant A. Cakley, Aaron E. Oliphant, Jas. M. Oliphant, Stephen O'Neal, Joseph A. Pace, Hamilton Parks, Henry T. Parks, Isom S. Petty, Warren Reed, Jesse Royal, James B. Scott, Jesse G. Scott, Dred D. Shelton, Jas. J. Shelton, Jas. A. Sinclair, Wm. W. Smith, James R. Snodgrass, Sidney Stanley, John A. Stone, Andrew Sutton, Jesse Sutton, Nathan Vaughn.

Casualties

James Anderson, died at Camp Butler, Ill. (prisoner) March 28, 1863.

Wm. H. Bawcom, died at Camp Butler, Ill. (prisoner) February 1, 1863.

Christopher A. Berry, died at Tullahoma, Tenn., May 31, 1863.

James D. Blodgett, died at Camp Butler, Ill. (prisoner) February 10, 1863.

Geo. A. Bonner, died at Camp Butler, Ill. (prisoner) March 27, 1863.

Roland R. Boyd, died at Petersburg, Va., May 9, 1863.

Rueben Crow, died at Camp Butler, Ill. (prisoner).

D. W. Dollar, died at Navasota, Texas, June 15, 1862.

W. R. Everett, died at LaGrange, Ga., June 16, 1863.

David Glowner, died at Camp Butler, Ill. (prisoner), March 31, 1863.

Josiah A. Hall, died at Camp Butler, Ill. (prisoner), March 31, 1863.

Woodie T. Hamilton, killed in battle at Arkansas Post, January 11, 1863.

Robert S. Hannon, died at Camp Butler, Ill. (prisoner), February 18, 1863.

Daniel Mayes, died in hospital prison at St. Louis, February 12, 1863.

Alonzo F. McLaughlin, killed in battle at Arkansas Post, January 11, 1863.

Albert Methvin, killed at Arkansas Post, January 11, 1863.

Alfred Methvin, died of wounds received at New Hope Church, January 12, 1863.

Aaron E. Oliphant, died in hospital at Arkansas Post, December 4, 1862.

Jesse Royall, died at Camp Butler, Ill. (prisoner), February 6, 1863.

James B. Scott, died at Petersburg, Va. (no other particulars) —— 25, 1863.

James G. Scott, died in hospital at Benton, Ark., August 23, 1862.

Garrett W. Seay, died in Saline County, Arkansas, August 19, 1862.

Dred D. Shelton, died at Arkansas Post, November 16, 1862.

James J. Shelton, died at Camp Butler, Ill. (prisoner), February 19, 1863.

Thomas B. Shelton, died at Camp Butler, Ill. (prisoner), February 25, 1863.

J. A. Sinclair, died at Camp Butler, Ill. (prisoner), April 4, 1863.
Stephen A. Sinclair, died in hospital at Arkansas Post, October 2, 1862.
John A. Stone, killed in battle at Arkansas Post, January 11, 1863.
Andrew Sutton, killed in battle at Arkansas Post, January 11, 1863.

Additions from the "Unofficial Roll of 1918"

Names included in roll compiled by Sergeant Porter L. Ellis but which do not appear upon the official muster rolls above mentioned: —— Bailey, Lon Carlisle, Mat Everett, Milton Evetts, —— Finn, —— Halmark, Eph Jordan, Thos. McKnight, Richard Parks.

d. Captain Milton W. Damron's Company

In January, 1862, Captain Milton Wesley Damron led out another company of cavalry. The members of the company, mounted, and in military formation on the west side of the court house square in Belton, elected their officers. Miss Etta Shanklin on behalf of the ladies, presented the company flag in Belton on the day of their departure and the company rode away to the training camp. A leather belt and scabbard, worn by each man, secured and housed as a side arm, a short sword or "bolo" forged from a large steel file, the craftmanship of our local smithies, James Lambert, John Danley and Jas. P. Coop. It was rather a vicious-looking weapon!

The first roll here presented is compiled from photostat copies of the official muster rolls of January 20, 1862 and June 30, 1862, on file in the U. S. War Department and from "Blair's Private Muster Roll of 1862"[12] to which is appended some additional names from the "unofficial roll of 1918" as explained later on.

The second roll presented comprises the names of those members of the company who were captured at Arkansas

[12] This roll is privately owned by Mr. Jesse S. Blair of Belton, Texas, a son of Lt. Wm. B. Blair, among whose private papers it was found. It is not a photostat copy but is apparently an original muster roll, made out on the regular official Confederate printed blank form, listing the full company, with the usual notations as to each individual soldier. One fourth of the sheet, the part which should have contained the date and signature of the commanding officer, is torn off and gone, but as the **full company** is listed it must have been made in 1862 or before the fall or Arkansas Post which occurred on January 11, 1863. It is here designated as "Blair's Private Roll of 1862," though it may have been an official muster roll that was never sent in to the Confederate War Department at Richmond.

Post on January 11, 1863, imprisoned at Camp Douglas, Illinois, and on being exchanged served east of the Mississippi River under command of Lieutenant Blair until the latter lost a leg in the battle of Atlanta, Georgia, in the late spring of 1864, after which no more muster rolls appear.

The remnant of the company who were not captured or killed at Arkansas Post were subsequently consolidated with a similar remnant of Company E, from Ellis County, of the 17th Texas Cavalry and served under Captain Damron west of the Mississippi River, but there is no muster roll of this remnant nor of the consolidated company available.

Company D, 18th Regiment Texas Volunteer Cavalry, Colonel Nicholas H. Darnell, enlisted in fall of 1861 and "mustered in" on January 20, 1862.[13]

Officers: Milton Wesley Damron, Captain, Commanding; William B. Blair, 1st Lieutenant; Samuel W. Bishop, 2nd Lieutenant; John Brown and Andrew Morris, Junior 2nd Lieutenants; James H. Graves, 1st Sergeant; Hamilton McDowell, Frank T. Fulcher, John Trentham, 2nd Sergeants; John McDowell, Francis M. Blankenship, 3rd Sergeants; Benjamin F. Allen, Wm. D. Jordan, 4th Sergeants; Nathaniel P. Fulcher, 5th Sergeant; Willis Stanley, Geo. W. Blevins, James Fisher, 1st Corporals; William Bock, Thos. U. Robinson, 2nd Corporals; William F. Grey, Wm. J. Wheat, 3rd Corporals; William M. Townsend, Wm. J. Carter, James W. Lee, 4th Corporals; Thomas J. Bates, Chas. C. Holcomb, 1st Buglers; Charles C. Holcomb, George M. Spence, 2nd Buglers; Wilson Bates, Farrier; Thomas L. Berry, Blacksmith; Geo. J. Nimmo, Ensign.

Privates: Elisha Allen, Alfred Anderson, Henry C. Anderson, Jno. C. Anderson, Merritt J. Bailey, Wm. R. Baker Thomas Bates, Robert P. Bigham, Samuel Bivens, Amos J. Blackwell, Joel D. Blair, Isaac S. Boren, John Boren, David Brimner, Nathaniel L. Bryant, N. M. Bryant, Jacob W. Burks, John Burks. Samuel Burks, William Burks, Wm. A. Burks, Thos. H. Carroll, Hiram B. Caves, Geo. W. Clour, Andrew P. Cox, John W. Cox, Samuel H. Cox, Allen Craighead, James W. Cross, Wm. B. Cross, Virgil A. S. Cross, James W. Dallas, Orlton R. Day, James H. Denson, Edward H. Draper, Thos. B. Draper, Pendleton Duke, Thos. Early, William Early, Samuel M. Eaton, Henry C. Edrington, H. W. Elliott, Thos. W. Elliott, Benjamin F. Ellis, James T. Epps, George Fisher, James Fisher, Andrew J. Fleming, Wiley W. Foster, Nathaniel P. Fulcher, Robert Gage, Wm. M. Garrison, Mois Gradrohl, Thomas B. Graves, Wm. F. Gray, James A. Griffin, Wm. Hamilton, Wm. P. Haynes, Jas. M. Holcomb, Wm. T. Holcomb, Wm. Harrell, Wm. E. Karnes,

[13] Compiled from official muster rolls of January 20, 1862, at Camp Dallas, Texas and of June 30, 1862, at Camp Searcy, Ark., both signed by Milton W. Damron, commanding the company, and from "Blair's Private Muster Roll of 1862."

Albert A. Kendrick, Marshall F. Leatherman, Wm. M. Martin, Elisha F. McCray, Joseph J. Meeks, Isaac Miers, Joseph W. Murrell, Jr., John Pennington, Alexander Reid, Cornelius B. Roberts, Jr., James T. Roberts, Jose M. Rodriguez, Jeremiah D. Scott, George W. Shipman, Wm. B. Shipman, James H. Slaughter, Richey Sneed, Daniel Sparks, Wm. R. Spurlin, Edward Stalcup, Anderson Sutton, Doctor P. Thompson, James M. Townsend, Andrew J. Vanwinkle, Henry C. Wallace, Samuel D. Wheat, Andrew Wilkins, Andy Willis, Geo. A. C. Wills, Joseph P. Wood, William Wood.

Casualties

Benjamin F. Allen, died at Camp Douglas, Chicago, Ill. (prisoner), March 5, 1863.

Alfred Anderson, died on board S. S. "Nebraska" near Memphis, Tenn. (prisoner), January 15, 1863.

Henry C. Anderson, died at Camp Douglas, Chicago, Illinois (prisoner), March 28, 1863.

Wm. R. Baker, died at Camp Douglas, Chicago, Ill. (prisoner), February 28, 1863.

Thomas Bates, died at Bonham, Texas, March 11, ———.

Thomas L. Berry, died at Camp Douglas, Chicago, Ill. (prisoner), February 2, 1863.

Samuel Bivens, died at Camp McCulloch, Indian Nation, May 8, ———.

Joel D. Blair, wounded and in hospital since September 20, 1863.

Isaac S. Boren, died at Camp Douglas, Chicago, Ill. (prisoner), March 31, 1863.

David Brimmer, died at Camp Douglas, Chicago, Ill. (prisoner), April 2, 1863.

William Burks, killed at Missionary Ridge, Tenn., November 25, 1863.

Wm. A. Burks, died at Camp Douglas, Chicago, Ill. (prisoner), February 23, 1863.

James W. Cross, died at Camp Douglas, Chicago, Ill. (prisoner), March 28, 1863.

Thomas Early, died at Camp Douglas, Chicago, Ill. (prisoner), February 14, 1863.

Thomas W. Elliott, died at Camp Douglas, Chicago, Ill. (prisoner), February 23, 1863.

Wm. E. Karnes, died at Camp Douglas, Chicago, Ill. (prisoner), April 8, 1863.

John Pennington, died at Camp Douglas, Chicago, Ill. (prisoner), April 26, 1863.

Additions from "Unofficial Roll of 1918"

An unofficial roll of Captain Damron's Company, compiled by the author from information furnished from memory by Lieutenant Sam W. Bishop, Corporal Wm. J. Wheat, Privates George Fisher, Samuel H. Cox, Henry C. Edrington, Jesse Sutton, C. B. Roberts and others, all of whom, except Corporal Wheat, have since passed on, contains a number of names which do not appear upon any of the official Muster Rolls on file in the U. S. War Department nor upon "Blair's Private Roll of 1862." They are as follows:

Officers

*Dr. John W. Embree, Regimental Surgeon; *Lieutenant John Edmonson; Lieutenant Pink Thomas.

Privates

Jas. M. Barnhart, Jno. S. Barnhart, Theo Barnhart, *J. C. Boren, *Lafayette Box, M. D., A. F. Boyce, *Fayette Bryant, *Sam H. Carter, Jap Clanton, *James W. Cowan, William Cox, Thomas Dallas, William Dallas, Abe Dalton, Sam Dalton, Wm. Davis, —— Dykes, James Felts, *George Fleming, *Martin V. Fleming, Thos. Forehand, George Gentry, *G. Wat Graves, John (or Gus) Haynes, *Milton Hodge, Pink Irvin, "Bat" Lane, David Lane, —— McAuley, *Moncie McDaniel *Stacie McDaniel, *Wm. McDowell, Jno. McFadden, Dr. Wesley McGuire, *Paul Newman, Harvey Oatman, Thos. Owens, George Seymour, Sam Sims, Steve Sinclair, *Barton Smith, *Gabe Smith, Gid Smith, Wm. A. Smith, Sam Sneed, Noah Sorrels, Sam Storey, *Jesse Sutton, Frank Wharton, Wm. Whitsell, *Arch Wills, —— Witt.—

A number of the above named soldiers were doubtless members of Company E from Ellis County. Those marked with a star are known to the writer to have been from Bell County—perhaps there were some others.

Roll of the Arkansas Post Captives Who Were Exchanged

A notation on the muster roll of June 30, 1863 states, "Captain M. W. Damron, of this company, was absent on furlough at the fall of Arkansas Post. Lieutenant John Brown and five men made their escape after the surrender. Of this company there were forty-one men and two officers captured. The remainder are still west of the Mississippi River."

Of the men captured at Arkansas Post one died on the steam boat "Nebraska" en route to prison, twelve died in the prison at Camp Douglas, Chicago, Illinois, and one was left sick in the prison hospital there. With two exceptions, the remainder were exchanged and served through the last year of the war east of the Mississippi River under command of Lieutenant Wm. B. Blair, as before stated. All subsequent muster rolls on file in the U. S. War Department relate only to these captives, and are signed by Lieutenant Blair, and are dated respectively, June 30, 1863, at Tyner's Station, Tenn.; August 31, 1863 and October 31, 1863, at Missionary Ridge; December 31, 1863, at Tunnel

Hill, Ga., February 29, 1864 at Camp Near Dalton, Ga.; and April 30, 1864 at Dalton, Ga. From these the following roll of those captured is compiled.

Officers

Lieutenant Wm. B. Blair; Ist Sergeant James H. Graves.

Privates[14]

(2) Benjamin F. Allen, (1) Alfred Anderson, (2) Henry C. Anderson, (2) Wm. R. Baker, (2) Thos. L. Berry, Joel D. Blair, Francis M. Blankenship, (3) Geo. W. Blevins, (2) Isaac S. Boren, (2) David Brimmer, Jacob W. Burks, William Burks, (2) William A. Burks, (2) Jas. W. Cross, Virgil A. S. Cross, (2) Thos. Earley, Wm. Earley, (2) Thos. W. Elliott, George Fisher, James Fisher, (4) Andrew J. Fleming, Wiley W. Foster, Frank T. Fulcher, Wm. M. Garrison, Wm. P. Haynes, Wm. D. Jordan, (2) Wm. E. Karnes, Albert A. Kendrick, Marshall F. Leatherman, James Y. Lee, (1) Joseph W. Murrell, Jr., (2) John Pennington, Alexander Reid, Jose M. Rodriguez, (4) Richey Sneed, Edward Stalcup, Doctor P. Thompson, Henry C. Wallace, Samuel D. Wheat, Wm. J. Wheat, Andrew Wilkins.

e. Captain X. B. Saunders' Company

This company of Infantry went out in the late fall of 1861 and trained at Brenham and Hempstead, Texas. Its active service was on the Louisiana-Arkansas front and, toward the close of the conflict, on the Texas coast. Captain Saunders was promoted to the rank of Major in the latter part of 1863 and thereupon Lieutenant James W. White became captain of the company, which he commanded to the end of the war.

Company A, 16th Texas Volunteer Infantry, Colonel George Flournoy, commanding.[15]

Officers: Xenophon Boone Saunders, James W. White, Captains;

---

[14] The numerals prefixed to names in this list indicate: (1) those who died on Steamboat Nebraska en route to prison; (2) died in prison at Camp Douglas, Chicago, Illinois; (3) Left sick in hospital at Camp Douglas; (4) furloughed to report to the command west of the Mississippi River.

[15] Muster rolls dated November 26, 1861; February 28, 1862; June 30, 1862 at Virginia Point, Texas; August 31, 1862, and October 31, 1862 at Camp Nelson, Ark.; August 31, 1863; February 29, 1864, Simsport, La. Notation on Muster Roll dated August 31, 1863: "This company was in the affair at Perkins Landing on the 31st of May. It was also in the Battle at Milliken's Bend on the 7th of June, 1863." On Muster Roll dated February 29, 1864: "This company was detached as Post Guard at Simsport, La., February 20th, 1864."

Milton Hodge, 1st Lieutenant; Ishmael Kile, Thos. J. Graves, Milton Eastland, 2nd Lieutenants; Joseph Furnace, Wm. P. Hancock, L. W. Surghnor, 1st Sergeants; Abram W. Richard, Don A. Chamberlin, W. W. Miller, 2nd Sergeants; John T. Wiseman, George Vandiver, James A. Payne, 3rd Sergeants; Simeon Wiseman, Marcellus C. Bramlett, 4th Sergeants; L. W. Hyatt, 5th Sergeant; C. R. White, C. A. Moore, Wm. Pevehouse, W. R. Wilkins, 1st Corporals; William Noel, 2nd Corporal; Geo. D. Richard, James P. Steel, 3rd Corporals; A. H. O'Keefe, James Bingham, 4th Corporals.

Privates: Ellis Anderson, Gibson Anderson, Wm. Anderson, Wm. Ashton, Wm. H. Ault, A. J. Barker, Geo. W Barker, James Boring, Aaron Bowden, J. Thos. Bramlet, Fred C. Brookman, J. I. H. Burnet, Wash F. Carpenter, A. L. Castleman, Wm. Caviness, W. Price Cearnel, S. G. Clarke, T. J. Cole, J. J. Cornwell, James Cox, C. S. Crawford, J. W. Daniel, N. L. Daniel, N. B. Danley, Wm. P. Dodson, E. P. Dyches, Ben French, J. G. Gammons, Geo. C. Garner, W. B. Halbrook, A. C. Hargiss, L. A. Harper, Wm. H. Herndon, Fred Hoerholdt, J. J. Hudson, J. W. Humphries, J. R. Jones, Wm. Laxson, Turner Lee, C. P. Lemmons, Henry Linney, Lemnel L. Moore, Jacob T. Mundin, M. V. New, Wm. D. Northcut, S. P. Osgood, Chas. D. Richard, Jno. Shamblin, Albert Schultz, Jno. D. Smith, Geo. Spencer, Terry Spencer, D. Steeneken, Wm. J. Stokes, E. C. Stringer, J. A. Stringfellow, H. S. Surghnor, Jno. B. B. Supple, L. Thompson, G. Vandever, J. L. Voorhies, Geo. A. Wallace, John Welch, Thos. Welch, Wm. P. White, Alfred Wilkins, Alford Williams, A. O. Williams, W. R. Williams, Wm. Wiseman.

Casualties

S. G. Clarke, died (no particulars) June 10, 1862.
William Noel, died at Natchitoches, La., August 3, 1862.
A. H. O'Keife, died (no particulars), April 12, 1862.
C. R. White, died (no particulars), April 5, 1862.
Simeon Wiseman, died at Shreveport, La., June 7, 1862.

Additions from "Unofficial Roll of 1918"

An unofficial partial roll of this company was made by the author from data furnished by Fred Holt (Hoerholt), M. W. Blackburn and from other sources, in which the following names appear which are not included in the official rolls on file in the U. S. War Department:

Lieutenant J. F. Estes; Privates Thomas Atwood, M. W. Blackburn, W. H. L. Blackburn, Joe Blackwell, Joe Carter, ——— Garrison, Jas. Alex Grimes, Louis P. Grimes, Jas. A. Hardin, ——— Hodge, Bain Hodges, Geo. W. Lyell, Jno. A. J. Lyell, Hugh Miller, Thos. L. Miller, W. A. Ricketts, Mat Trousdale, Asa H. Wilkes.

f. Captain John F. Smith's Company

Early in the spring of 1862 a company of volunteer infantry was recruited by Captain Hilary M. Bouldin who was duly elected to command the same. The company went to Camp Terry near Austin, Texas, for training and was later transferred to the Arkansas-Louisiana front, where it served throughout the conflict.

Captain Bouldin, having become incapacitated on account of physical disability, tendered his resignation and was honorably discharged from the army on December 5th, 1862; and Lieutenant John F. Smith, who was then elected captain, commanded the company during the remainder of the war.

Company I, 17th Texas Volunteer Infantry, Colonel R. T. Allen, 3rd Brigade, Gen. Theophilus H. Holmes commanding, enlisted April 11, 1862.[16]

Officers

June 30, 1862: Hilary M. Bouldin, Captain; John F. Smith, 1st Lieutenant; Robert C. Miller, Isaac Jalonick, 2nd Lieutenants; Theo. A. Supple, 1st Sergeant; John T. Pope, 2nd Sergeant; Louis P. Grimes, 3rd Sergeant; E. S. Anderson, 4th Sergeant; Elijah Sparks, 1st Corporal; Thos. L. Miller, 2nd Corporal; S. H. Carter, Isaac N. Casey, 3rd Corporals; Jas. H. Ferrall, 4th Corporal; Jas. S. Evans, James Sweet, Musicians, T. B. Dooley, Color Corporal.

December 31, 1862: John F. Smith, Captain; Isaac Jalonick, Robb H. Taylor, 1st Lieutenants; John N. Houston, Gus J. Hendrick, 2nd Lieutenants; Theo. A. Supple, 1st Sergeant; John T. Pope, 2nd Sergeant; R. O. Reed, 3rd Sergeant; E. S. Anderson, 4th Sergeant; Thos. Atwood, W. A. Ricketts, Alex Bearn, 5th Sergeants; Felix E. Gresham, Elijah Sparks, 1st Corporals; T. L. Miller, C. H. Boyd, 2nd Corporals; Isaac N. Casey, 3rd Corporal; Caleb W. Marshall, Jas. H. Ferrell, 4th Corporals; Jas. S. Evans, Musician; T. B. Dooley, Color Corporal.

Regimental officers appointed from this Company: Quartermaster, David D. Rosborough; Quartermaster's Clerks, Chas. A. Bigelow, Henry C. Denny, Henry Austin; Wagon Master, Vachel H. Anderson.

Privates

Miles W. Adams, James S. Allen, F. Henry Austin, Geo. H. Austin, James Thomas Austin, Isaiah Baise, James C. Ballard, J. C. Barclay, J. K. P. Barclay, W. Beard, C. C. Berry, Thos. R. Berry, Chas. A. Bigelow, Joseph Bishop, M. W. Blackburn, Charles Bock, William Bock, F. E. Bond, H. R. Bowles, A. J. Box, M. D. L. Box, B. A. Brundidge, Elijah Birch, John C. Caddel, R. J. Caddel, Thos.

---

[16] Muster Rolls dated June 30, 1862, at Camp Terry near Austin, Texas; October 31, 1862, at Camp Nelson, Prairie County, Ark.; December 31, 1862, at Camp near Little Rock, Ark.; February 28, 1863, at Camp Wright; August 31, 1863, at Camp near Alexandria, La., February 29, 1864 at Camp Norwood Place.

C. Casey, G. W. Cathey, Wm. J. Cathey, John R. Chapman, Jno. W. Clark, Jno. P. Clary, Stephen Clary, Samuel R. Coggin, Robert L. Cox, Nick B. Daugherty, Geo. W. Dennis, Henry C. Denny, T. B. Dooley, Cyrus Eastland, Benjamin Ellis, W. H. Fewell, John M. Fewell, Richard Fitzpatrick, P. F. Gates, Charles R. Graham, James A. Gresham, Jno. H. Griffin, J. J. Haggard, Jno. S. Hannon, Thos. T. Hannon, Henry Harris, A. C. Harvey, W. L. Hawkins, Newman Heard, Wm. G. Hillyard, David Hirsch, C. C. S. Hoerholt, Dan Hollingsworth, Thos. J. Howell, Jno. L. Hughes, John Kegans, Sylvester P. Kirk, John Koch, Michael D. Light, T. L. Mabry, Noble L. Majors, Jno. L. Marshall, Owen Marshall, David E. Martin, J. T. Martin, D. M. McDaniel, Stacy McDaniel, Wm. M. McKinzie, W. A. Meador, N. Meeks, Neal B. Messer, E. D. Miller. C. N. Minnix, J. E. Moore, E. E. Morgan, John Nichols, Hugh O'Keefe, Levi Paulk, Geo. D. Perkins, W. H. Perry, Jno. T. Phillips, Green I. Pope, James S. Pope, Tazewell W. Powers, John W. Prewett, Ed T. Reed, David S. Reed, Michael R. Reed, Geo. W. Reeves, Eugene L. Rich, Jno. F. Shaw, Stephen Shelton, G. W. Shipman, Jno. M. Simmons, A. A. Smith, Nathaniel H. Smith, Wm. Smith, W. B. Smith, J. A. Stringfellow, Jno. B. Supple, Jas. R. Sutton, Wm. Sutton, L. Y. Swan, C. Templeton, James E. Townsend, John A. Tyler, Geo. F. Vickery, Wm. S. Vickery, James M. Wallace, Simeon L. Walton, J. L. Welden, Wiley S. White, Elmer M. Whittenburg, R. A. Whittenburg, G. W. Williams, Isaac Wilson, J. A. Witte, H. H. Wofford, J. I. Wood, J. P. Wood.

Casualties

Thomas Atwood, died in Texas. (No other particulars).

Joseph Bishop, died at Camp Nelson, Prairie County, Ark., October 25, 1862.

Nick B. Daugherty, died at Austin, Ark., November 16, 1862.
Chas. R. Graham, died at Austin, Ark., November 26, 1862.
W. L. Hawkins, died at Austin, Ark., November 13, 1862.
John L. Hughes, died at Austin, Ark., November 23, 1862.
John L. Marshall, died at Austin, Ark., December 16, 1862.
Hugh O'Keefe, died at Austin, Ark., November 12, 1862.
James S. Pope, died at Austin, Ark., November 22, 1862.
W. A. Rickett, died (no particulars), November 23, 1862.
W. B. Smith, died at Austin, Ark., December 12, 1862.
Elijah Sparks, died at Camp Nelson, Ark., November 11, 1862.
Isaac Wilson, died at Austin, Ark., November 26, 1862.

All of these deaths were due to typhoid and pneumonia, except that of Atwood (unknown) and, possibly, that of Daugherty.

Additions from "Unofficial Roll of 1918"

An unofficial muster roll of this company, made by the author from various sources, contains the following names which do not appear upon the official muster rolls on file in the U. S. War Department: W. H. L. Blackburn, Richard Blackburn, Moody J. Coggin, Ed Tom Cox, Ben S. Decherd, Alex. E. Gresham, ——— Gresham, Cap Heard, Y. Heard, Wm. Light, ——— Towsend.

g. Captain R. B. Halley's Company

Late in the fall of 1862 this cavalry company was enlisted, elected Robert Bonner Halley as captain and bivouacked during the Christmas holidays at the gushing Salado Springs, where the citizens gave them a big dance. Here was made the first and only muster roll that reached the Confederate War Department at Richmond and the files of the U. S. War Department. The company served on the Arkansas-Louisiana front.

Company G, Unorganized Battalion, Arizona Brigade Volunteer Cavalry, Commanded by Lieutenant Colonel John W. Mullins. Muster roll dated at Camp Salado, Bell County, Texas, January 1, 1863, signed by F. H. Hoyle, brevet 2nd Lieutenant.

Officers: Robert B. Halley, Captain commanding; Elisha Embree, 1st Lieutenant; Thos. G. Tomlinson, 2nd Lieutenant; Forney H. Hoyle, 2nd Lieutenant, brevet; Joseph E. Long, 1st Sergeant; Carr B. Sherrod, 2nd Sergeant; Geo. D. Caskey, 3rd Sergeant; Andrew J. Chapman, 4th Sergeant; John G. Walker, 5th Sergeant; Ridley B. Thomas, 1st Corporal; William E. Bruce, 2nd Corporal; Nathan B. Holder, 3rd Corporal; Wm. M. Hamilton, 4th Corporal; Theodore T. Wilmott, Bugler; Wm. A. Pace, Farrier; David P. Lowrie, Blacksmith.

Privates: H. C. Applewhite, Joseph F. Berry, Wm. F. Billingsley, Jacob Bishop, Nathan B. Bunting, Wm. J. Bunting, John Burks, Geo. W. Chapman, Ephraim Clark, Geo. W. Clure, Louis Columbus, Thos. C. Duncan, John A. Foreman, Joseph Furnace, Albert L. Gallatin, Wm. D. Hall, John Hallmark, Archie V. Harris, Saml. L. Hasley, Frederick A. Heileman, Geo. H. King, Wm. C. Kirk, Sam Kuykendall, Simeon Kuykendall, Hubbard M. Long, Carter Mabry, Henry P. Mainard, John McDowell, Wm. McDowell, Marshall McIlkenney, John Meeks, Wm. W. Monk, Alexander Moore, McCay Moore, Alex P. Moss, James H. Murrell, John N. Nesbit, Warren Puett, James G. Santlen, Lem Shelton, Sam Shelton, George Sherrod, Isaac Shriver, Wm. H. Smith, William Tanner, John Vannoy, John W. Weldon, Abel R. White, Geo. J. Whiteley, Jas. C. Whiteley, James Wilkinson, Samuel L. Williams.

Additions from "Unofficial Roll of 1918"

A private unofficial muster roll of this company was made up by Sergeant Wm. Alex White and private James Holcomb (neither of whom appear upon the official roll of January 1st, 1863), and was revised by Private Wm. D. Hall. There is no doubt that the Company was recruited and increased in members subsequent to the official muster roll of January 1, 1863, the only roll of the company on file in the U. S .War Department at Washington and made while the company was in fact recruiting at Camp Salado in Bell County. The additional names are:

Sergeant Wm. Alex White, Ben Adams, Theodore Armstrong, James Banton, K. Banton, Hugh Casey, John Casey, "Bill" Caviness, Wm. Caviness, Lewis Chambers, James Chambers, James Chapman, Ed Clark, Thos. A. Cockrell, James Duncan,———Epperson, W. Graves, D. Gravey, Isaac Hamilton, A. Hasley, Thos. Haynes, James A. Holcomb, Joseph Holcomb, Thos. Holcomb, T. Hughes, H. E. Keyes, Wm. Kuykendall, Joe Long, John O'Keefe, Presey K. O'Keefe, Ed Pace, Murrell Ratliff, Amos Rowland, Joe V. Shriver, Ellis M. Sprott, M. V. Townsend, Joseph E. Townsend, Bart Wales, James H. White, Thos. J. White, Sam Whitley, S. M. Whitley, George Whittenburg, George Williams, Richard Wiseman, Thomas Wiseman.

h. Captain Geo. W. Graves' Company

A company of cavalry, of which Geo. W. Graves, familiarly known as "Wat" Graves, was elected captain, went out from Bell County in the early part of 1864 and was assigned to the Rio Grande frontier where it was stationed during the remainder of the war. There is no official muster roll of this company, so far as known to the writer. His "Unofficial Roll of 1918" compiled by Lieutenant Samuel W. Bishop, Privates J. Frank Carter, John W. Aiken, Eli B. Baggett and others is the only available data and is here offered as the best that can be done. It is doubtless substantially correct, though incomplete.

Company A, 4th Texas Cavalry (also listed as Company D, 2nd Arizona Cavalry), Colonel Daniel Showalter, Commanding.

Officers: G. Wat Graves, Captain; John N. Damron, 1st Lieutenant; Samuel W. Bishop, 2nd Lieutenant; Joseph Smith, 3rd Lieutenant; Sam A. Sparks, Daniel McMillin, Silas Baggett, Lieutenants; James Petty, Orderly Sergeant.

Privates: John W. Aiken, V. Armstrong, J. Floyd Arthur, J. Monroe Baggett, Eli B. Baggett, Pits Bishop, Jno. W. Black, Jno. G. Blackburn, Ewing Blair, Alex Baker, J. Frank Carter, Lem Carpenter, John Chalk, Sam Christian, Hez Clark, Dutch Carpenter, M. L. Crawford, Taylor Clark, Wilford Dawson, Henry Damron, William Dennis, Mike Dawsey, Neal Dennis, James Dobbs, William C. Evetts, James J. Franklin (detailed as State Armorer at Austin), Alfred Ford, William Ferrell, Joseph Furnace, Jack Fisher, George Grimes, Bill Gage, John T. Garrison, V. Graves, E. J. L. Green, Joseph B. Harris, Bud Hamilton, A. J. Hamilton, William Hawk, Elijah Hannon, Euk W. Henry, Sylvester Hodge, Nep Horne, ——— Horne, Sanders Height, Alfred G. Hall, George Horton, Richard Jeffries, John J. Jordon, Ed F. Lee, Thomas Light, Jno. F. McAninch, Dock Morris, John McKenzie, Alf Morris, John Neal, Robert Neal, Pleas Nichols, Alf Polk, Asa Reed, David Reed, Mike Reed, ——— Roberson, —— Roberson, Tol Roberts, William Sandlin, John Shackelford, Will Shipman, Sam Short, George Stubblefield, Rans Smith, George Server, Sam Steel, Pleas Steel, Mike Terry, Robert Taylor, Pink Taylor, Mike Turney, Tom Vickery, W. M. Vickery, G. W. Wakefield, George Walker, Joe Walker, George Watkins, Jeff Wells, John Wells, J. C. Whitley, Jack Willingham, —— Word, Henderson Wyatt.

i. Captain James H. Weathersbee's Company

In 1864 Captain William Howeth raised a company of cavalry to serve in the "Home Guards Battalion," composed mostly of men over and under the draft age (18 to 45). About the time the company was ready to go into service Captain Howeth was promoted to the rank of Major, whereupon Lieutenant James H. Weathersbee was promoted to the captaincy and commanded the company during the continuance of the war. It served in the interior or central part of the State (in several detachments), preserved order, arrested deserters, draft-dodgers, bushwhackers, thieves, lawless and suspicious characters. Excepting a few of them who were stationed at Galveston under Captain McMillin, on detached coast guard service, none of these men were sent to the battle fronts.

There is no official muster roll of this company, so far as known to the writer. His "Unofficial Roll of 1918" compiled with the assistance of Privates W. E. Rosborough, John D. Bassell, James W. Estes, E. W. Scott and others is here offered as the only available source and is believed to be approximately correct.

Company B, Battalion Home Guards.

Officers: James H. Weathersbee, Captain; William Redmond, 1st Lieutenant; John Kegans, 2nd Lieutenant; John H. Griffin, 3rd Lieutenant; Joseph P. Wood, 1st Sergeant; John McAuley, Corporal.

Privates: Ben Anderson, Geo. A. Allen, John D. Bassel, Green Berry, M. Swan Bigham, Oliver H. Bigham, Martin Blodgett, Pleas Boyd, Silas Burk, John C. Burris, Dock Cargle, John M. Cathey, Robert Childers, Net R. Clark, Richard Cook, James P. Coop, Jack Darwin, William Dean, Audley Dennis, Otho S. Durant, John Early, Cyrus Eastland, Ed T. Estes, James W. Estes, Berry Fleming, John T. Flint, John Ellis Fulcher, W. Scott Garner, William Gordon, Worth Graves, Samuel C. Hannon, James Hash, Dred R. Hill, Anton L. Hodges, Pleas Howeth, Wesley Howeth, Will W. Howeth, "Yank" Hughes, James Irby, Reddin Johnson, James B. Kegans, Felix N. Lancaster, J. B. Lowery, J. W. Lowery, John P. McKay, Arthur McKnight, John McLain, Ro Miller, Sam H. Miller, James Oliphant, John M. Payne, J. Rough Petty, J. Alf Polk, Jack Potter, William Potter, Newton M. Proctor, Sr., Ed Quinn, —— Queen,

Wm. E. Rosborough, William Royall, E. W. (Ale) Scott, Jerry D. Scott, James Slaughter, Owen W. Slaughter, Sam H. Summers, Anderson Sutton, Green Taylor, A. J. (Jink) Vickery, John W. Vickery, G. W. (Wash) Walton, Nelson Walton, Jas. K. Warrick, Wm. R. Warrick, Sam Whiteley, H. Williams, John Willis, Martin L. Wiseman, Wm. Wrial (or Rial).

j. Captain William Samuel Rather's Company

This was a cavalry company which was recruited in the late spring of 1864 and entered the Confederate Service from Bell County in the early fall of the same year. No muster roll of this company, official or otherwise, is available, but the late Mr. Geo. H. Gassaway furnished the writer with the names of twelve members of the company:

Company B, 4th Texas Cavalry, William S. Rather, Captain.

Privates: J. Bishop, Julius Brown, Dr. A. J. Embree, Geo. H. Gassaway, Uriah Gould, W. Graves, Obe Harris, Jack Huffman, Pope Peevey, A. J. Willingham, Sam Young.

The company camped the first night at Salado and on the next morning Mr. Geo. H. Gassaway received an order detailing him and others to buy beeves for the Confederate government, to be sent to the soldiers on the fighting front. Most all of the men above named worked with Mr. Gassaway in this beef gathering work and were not with the main company any more. The company itself, while nominally a military organization, seems to have been really a *beef supply* company, though some of the company may have engaged in some military duties and some fighting. The field of their operations was mostly in central, south and southwest Texas. These observations are based upon the verbal statements of Mr. Sam Young of Abilene (the only survivor of the twelve men named) to the writer's friend, Mr. O. E. Radford at Abilene, who interviewed him on the writer's behalf. Mr. Young says that the "men were detailed from time to time on detached service of gathering beeves"; that he was with Mr. Gassaway all the time and, never being with the company, is unable to give any further information concerning the operations of the company or to add any more names to the above fragmentary roll of its members.[17]

[17] Letter of O. E. Radford, of Abilene, to Geo. W. Tyler, dated July 28, 1926.

k. Other Bell County Soldiers and Service Men

The following list, made up from information furnished by surviving soldiers and from other authentic sources, comprises Bell County soldiers who do not appear on any of the preceding rolls and many of whom enlisted in companies organized elsewhere. Some were on detached or special service for the Confederate Government. This list is also a part of the writer's "Unofficial Roll of 1918." No claim for absolute accuracy is made for it—there are doubtless errors and omissions which are unavoidable.

Miscellaneous Roll

Birg (or Virg) Armstrong; Dr. James M. Arnold; Isaac T. Bean; Charles Bock; Henry (Bill) Bock; J. Calvin Bonner; David C. Bowles (in Chas. deMontel's Company, McCords Frontier Regiment); H. R. (Hi) Bowles; W. F. Breedlove (Downs' Waco Company); James Brown; Pierre Brown; Gid J. Buck; J. C. Bullard; Beal Bunyon (Co. E, 17th Infantry); Wm. Burns; Thos. S. Butler (Co. G, 2nd Texas Mounted Riflemen); W. C. Carmack (Co. F, 21st Cavalry, 1863); James M. Carpenter (Co. E, 17th Infantry); John W. Carpenter (Co. E, 17th Infantry); Thos. F. Carpenter (Co. D, 21st Cavalry); Joseph Cater (Co. E, 17th Infantry); Wm. S. Chapman (Downs' Waco Company); Wm. P. Childers; Amos Clark (Downs' Waco Company); John Clark; Pedro Contreras; Jasper N. Crass ,21st Cavalry); S. W. Crass; F. Marion Cross (McCord's Frontier Regiment); Charles Cruger; A. C. Danley; Glenn Davis; Frank Drake; J. Dow; Ben Ellis; David L. Elms (1862, Dick Graham's Co., Frontier Service); J. W. Evans (Co. F, 23rd Cavalry); Sam Evetts; Dr. J. A. Ewing; Jno. F. Ferguson (Downs' Waco Company); Joseph G. Ferguson (Downs' Waco Company); Ed S. Flint (Ross' Waco Company); A. B. Ford; James S. Freeman; John T. Freeman; Sam Grimes; Chas. A. Halbert; J. T. W. Halmark; M. D. S. Halmark; Robert C Hamil; W. R. Hamilton; Mike Hampton; Rile Hampton; James Hannon; Thomas Hannon; T. N. B. Harmon (Graham's Rangers); J. J. Harbour (1862, Co. C, 20th Infantry); Silas Hare; Joe H. Hawkins (1861, Co. G, 5th Infantry); Robert Tate Henry; Bain Hodge; J. J. Holcomb; J. P. Holcomb (1862, Co. D, 21st Cavalry); Sam Holcomb (Freeman's Austin Company); Frank Houston; M. Luther Houston; T. J. Howell; Hub Hunt (Freeman's Austin Company); Sam H. Hunter (Co. D, 21st Cavalry, Freeman's Austin Company); James H. Isbell; Ben Jackson (Downs' Waco Company); Sim Kegley; Joseph J. Kendrick; Julian Kendrick; R. D. Kinney (on detached service as shoemaker at Austin); Sylvester P. Kirk; Ben A. Ludlow (1864, Cobb's Waco Scouts); Moritz Maedgen (Co. D, 4th Cavalry); Willis W. Mangham (Co. D, 21st Cavalry, Freeman's Austin Company); Joe Marshall; D. E. Martin; John D. May; J. W. McBryde (Co. E, 19th Cavalry; Andrew T. McCorcle; Reuben McCray (Downs' Waco Company); I. A. Meadows; J. L. Miller; Wm. Mixon (or Nixon); James Moore (Cobb's Waco Scouts); Jonathan E. Moore; Levi Moore; Tom Moore; Wm. M. Moore (Down's

Top: The home of the late W. T. J. Hartrick on the bluff overlooking the Leon River about eight miles from Belton. The one story wing at the left is known as the "preaching house," for it was here that the first Baptist church in the east side of the county was founded and met for many years.

Bottom: The home of the Shanklin family who bought and operated the Childers mill, the first water mill in Bell County. This home originally stood on the main Nacogdoches and San Antonio stage road just above the ford of the Lampasas River known as Shanklin's crossing about half way between Salado and Belton. It was considered an exceptionally luxurious place in its prime.

Waco Company); Willis Moore (Freeman's Austin Company); D. W. Morris (1862, Co. F, 17th Infantry); J. F. Morris (Co. I, 12th Cavalry); J. S. Morris (Co. G, 4th Cavalry); John Myers; Robert Nelson (Freeman's Austin Company); Wm. T. Nelson (Freeman's Austin Company); G. A. Norman (Val Verde Battery); John Norris; Arthur H. O'Kiefe; Porter Parks (Co. C, 24th Cavalry); John Phillips (Freeman's Austin Company); Thomas Phillips (Freeman's Austin Company); Joe H. Plasters (1861, Co. G, 4th Infantry); C. N. Porter (Co. E, 17th Infantry); Richard Marion Potter (Herring's Waco Company); James T. Pryor (1861, Co. A, 7th Infantry); Dr. A. K. Ramsey (enlisted in Alabama); James Michael Reed (Co. E, 2nd Infantry, Milam County Company); R. Bates Renick; Lewis Riddle (Co. D, 16th Infantry); F. M. Robertson; Lewis Robertson (Cobb's Waco Scouts); Isaac Scoggin; —— Scoggin; Garrett Seay; Jesse Smalley (Freeman's Austin Company); A. A. Smith; Henry Smith (Co. E, 17th Infantry); John Smith; Moses Smith; (Co. E, 17th Infantry); Wm. Smith (Co. F, 6th Infantry, Downs' Waco Company); Wm. C. Sparks (Co. E, 2nd Infantry, Milam County Company); Wm. W. Spoonts; Ben Swayne (Freeman's Austin Company); Reuben Swayne (Freeman's Austin Company); Seban Sweat (Freeman's Austin Company); C. B. Thompson, (Co. A, 8th Cavalry); Dr. James H. Tucker; Theo. E. Vanness (enlisted in Missouri); Hugh Walker (Downs' Waco Company); James Walling; R. M. White (Co. I, 21st Cavalry); T. B. Whitely (1863, Co. D, 16th Infantry); E. W. Whitten; Dr. A. C. Willingham; John Yancy.

Davidson's Beef Squad

This was a small number of men serving on special detail to gather and purchase beeves for the Confederate Army on the fighting front. The beeves were driven in herds to Shreveport, Alexandria and other concentration points in Louisiana, Arkansas or eastern Texas. An incomplete unofficial roll of the squad, compiled by the writer from sources deemed reliable here follows: Wilson T. Davidson, Captain commanding, —— Allison, Rufus Anderson, Bill Ellis, Abe Fallon, J. A. Grimes, —— Light, Jesse W. Renick, Irving Stewart, Jas. B. Wilkerson.

1. Staff, Regimental and Other General Officers from Bell County in the Confederate or State Service

Major John Henry Brown served during the first three years of the war in Arkansas, Missouri and Northeast Texas, on the staff of General Henry E. McCulloch. At the close of the war he was in command of some two hundred state troops in West Texas, guarding the frontier and arresting deserters.[18]

[18] Brown, **History of Texas,** Vol. II, p. 429-30.

Colonel E. S. C. Robertson served in the early period on General Henry E. McCulloch's staff, but was retired home on account of ill health.

Major Horace Haldeman (former 1st Lieutenant of the U. S. Army, resigned in 1858) commanded Haldeman's Battery, Walker's Division, throughout the war. He always said he had never "surrendered" but having previously sunk the guns in Red River brought his men with him to his ranch on Elm Creek (old Troy) and there "honorably discharged' them.[19]

Other officers from Bell County were

Colonels: Silas Hare; Peter Haldeman.

Lieutenant Colonel: Robert C. Myers, 1st Texas Volunteer Cavalry.

Majors: Robert M. White, 6th Texas Volunteer Cavalry; X. B. Saunders, 16th Texas Volunteer Infantry; William Howeth, Battalion Home Guards (Cavalry).

Regimental Surgeons: Dr. Jno. W. Embree, Surgeon 18th Texas Volunteer Cavalry; Dr. Thos. T. Williamson, Assistant Surgeon, 6th Texas Infantry.

Regimental Quartermaster: D. D. Rosborough, 17th Texas Volunteer Infantry.

Regimental Wagon Master: Vachel H. Anderson, 17th Texas Volunteer Infantry.

Chief State Armorer at Austin: James J. Franklin, on special detail from Company A, 4th Texas Cavalry (G. W. Grave's Company).

3. *Official and Private Aid to the Soldiers and Their Families*

The records of the Commissioners' Court contain brief mention of the activities of that body from time to time in promoting the war and in aiding the soldiers and their families.

On June 24, 1861, the Court met in special session to devise a plan for supporting and maintaining Captain Robert M. White's volunteer company raised in Bell County and ordered to the encampment for training. A committee, composed of Captain Robert M. White, Geo. W. Wade, Isaac Shriver, John S. Blair, Sr., James W. Moore, Constan-

---

[19] Mrs. Eugenia Haldeman Openheimer in **Old Settlers Association of Bell County** for 1904, p. 11.

tine Hardeman, John T. Flint, John S. Thompson, Owen Slaughter, Daniel McKay, T. G. Tomlinson and Elisha Embree, was appointed to solicit and collect contributions for the support of the company for forty days in the encampment. The funds thus raised were to be repaid by the county through a special tax. Mr. Joel D. Blair was appointed as Commissary and Agent for Bell County to receive the contributions, to purchase and forward supplies to the company's quarter-master and to report at a future meeting of the court. On August 19, 1861, Mr. Blair reported the contributions and the disbursements, which amounted to $491.40. The Court then levied a special tax of ten cents on the one hundred dollars assessed valuations to reimburse the county and a like tax of eight cents to reimburse the contributors to whom, meantime, script receivable in county taxes would be issued. This script was issued on November 19, 1861, to the following contributors to this fund: Norman Austin, John Carpenter, Mr. and Mrs. Chalk, Ramsey M. Cox, Milton W. Damron, John Darley, Wm. D. Eastland, Elisha Embree, Frank & Hirsch, Mrs. Garrison, Halley & Eubank, Robert C. Hamil, Jno. C. Henry, Jalonick & Smith, Henry Keys, Silas A. Kingsbury, E. W. Kinnan, Marshall McIlhenney, Miller & Baker, E. Mills, James W. Moore, Powers & Co., N. M. Proctor, John B. Reed, Gordon W. Shanklin, John Sparks, James A. Stringfellow, Theo A. Supple, Henry J. Warren, R. S. Willingham, Martin V. Wiseman.

On subsequent dates (in 1862) similar script, backed by a special tax of twelve cents, was issued to those contributing to the outfitting of other companies, to-wit:

Contributors to Captain H. E. Bradford's company: A. Clark, Joseph Dennis, Frank & Hirsch, E. Mills, J. W. Scott, Nelson Walton, M. V. Wiseman.

Contributors to Captain X. B. Saunder's company: Norman Austin, Charles P. Cruger, A. J. Dallas, John Danley, A. V. Harris, D. R. Hill, Jalonick & Smith, Miller & Baker, E. Mills, J. W. Scott, Theo. A. Supple, R. H. Taylor, R. S. Willingham, John S. Wiseman, M. V. Wiseman.

Contributors to Captain Milton W. Damron's company: Norman Austin, Milton W. Damron, John Danley, Frank & Hirsch, Jalonick & Smith, John C. Henry, D. R. Hill, Miller & Baker, E. Mills, Powers & Co., C. B. Roberts, N. T.

Roberts, J. W. Scott, Mrs. Shelton, J. A. Stringfellow, R. S. Willingham.

On October 28, 1861, Mr. John W. Scott was appointed by the Court as Commissary to purchase cloth, and have same made into clothing, for the companies of Captains Robert M. White and H. E. Bradford, then in the Confederate service, and to purchase corn and other supplies for the cavalry horses of Captain White and to forward same to them at Camp Stone, near Lancaster, in Dallas County.

The county also provided the expenses of transporting the camp supplies of Captain X. B. Saunders' company from Belton to Brenham, where they were stationed, awaiting orders. Special taxes were levied to cover these expenditures, advanced by the county.

On January 6, 1862, Captain Milton W. Damron was vested with authority, as Commissary, to purchase and outfit for his company then enlisting for service in the Confederate army. Clothing made up by the home people was transported to the members of the companies of Captains X. B. Saunders and Milton W. Damron, in Arkansas, the sum of $100 being appropriated by the court for this purpose, November 17, 1862. The Court, on October 31, 1864, provided transportation of clothing forwarded to the members of Captain R. B. Halley's company in the army.

The assistance thus extended by the county to the soldiers, especially in the early stage of the war, was necessary because the governments of the State and of the Confederacy were not yet thoroughly organized for war, and their arrangements for the supply and equipment of the soldiers, now rushing in great numbers to the training camps, were incomplete and inadequate.

A most pathetic chapter in the progress of the great war between the States is the story of the poor soldier's unfortunate family, left alone at home, often with slight provision for physical support, sometimes none at all. It was enough for them to be deprived of his companionship and protection, but for them to want for the comforts and necessities of life while husband and father was far away, fighting for his country, touched the tenderest chords of human sympathy and patriotic appeal.

It therefore devolved upon the counties and upon the old men, above the fighting age, to go to the relief of the soldier's family. And well did they do their part, all over the country. Our story will briefly record some of the work performed by our county and by its citizens during this period of trial and stress.

On August 18, 1862, the war having actually existed for about a year, the Commissioners' Court of Bell County constituted its members as agents for the county, to ascertain the needs of families of soldiers absent in the service of the Confederacy, and to draw warrants on the County Treasurer for such an amount, in each case, as might be needed. The Chief Justice was assigned to these duties in Belton, and the four Commissioners were to act within their respective beats, outside of Belton. These warrants were to be paid out of the proceeds of a special war tax of 12½ cents upon the one hundred dollars assessed valuation.

To assist the members of the Court in supplying the families of the soldiers with food, clothing, fuel, etc., the following named citizens were appointed November 17, 1862:

Captain Hilary M. Bouldin, to assist the Chief Justice.
Beat 1—King Fisher, Samuel G. Leatherman, Alfred Evans, John Leach.
Beat 2—Melville Wilkerson.
Beat 3—Isaac Nichols, Abner Kuykendall, James Morris.
Beat 4—John Blair, John S. Thompson.

On March 28, 1863 a special war tax of fifty cents on the one hundred dollars assessed valuation was levied by the Commissioners' Court for the support of the families of Bell County's Confederate soldiers, and Captain Hilary M. Bouldin was appointed Commissary for Bell County, at a salary of $2000 per annum. His duties were to purchase and concentrate, at Belton and at other convenient locations, bacon, beef, corn, corn-meal, flour, rice, salt, sugar, wood and Penitentiary fabrics, in wagon load lots, for the use of the families of Confederate soldiers, preference to be given to the indigent families who were to be supplied free of cost, the others at actual cost. The County Treasurer was ordered to supply to Captain Bouldin, at once, for this purpose $2000 of Confederate States Treasury Notes, then on deposit in his office, and Captain Bouldin was required to make monthly reports to the Court, with proper vouchers.

The Chief Justice of Bell County was, on May 18, 1863, ordered to purchase from the Military Board of the State the number of cotton and wool cards (for hand carding) allotted to this county and to distribute them: first, to indigent families of Confederate soldiers free of cost; secondly, to other soldiers' families at cost; thirdly, the surplus, if any, to others at cost. On August 17, 1863, Captain Carey White was appointed as Commissary, vice Captain Bouldin, who had resigned.

On September 22, 1863, the Commissioners' Court subdivided the county into ten commissary beats, for better supplying the needs of the families of soldiers in the Confederate army, and appointed superintendents in each beat, as follows:

Beat 1—Abner Kuykendall and Alonzo Beeman.

Beat 2—Ramsey M. Cox.

Beat 3—Alex E. Hodge and Rev. John Carpenter.

Beat 4—John B. Reed, G. W. McDonald, J. W. Moore and N. B. Nelson.

Beat 5—Dr. A. B. Davis, James C. Armstrong and S. G. Leatherman.

Beat 6—Dr. William R. Alexander.

Beat 7—Ben Ellis and Samuel Burks.

Beat 8—John Hamilton and C. B. Whiteley.

Beat 9—Joseph Hawkins, Thomas Trimmier and Alex Walters.

Beat 10—John S. Blair, Norman Austin and R. S. Willingham.

The special war tax for the support of the families of Confederate soldiers, for the year 1863, was increased October 10, 1863, to seventy-five cents on the one hundred dollars assessed valuation; but this tax, for 1864, was, on February 6, 1864, fixed at twenty-five cents on such valuations in pursuance of the State laws.

On August 20, 1864, it was ordered that each Commissioner should make up and return to the Commissioners' Court a census of the indigent families of Confederate soldiers within their respective beats. On the 29th of the same month each Commissioner was ordered to employ wagons and teams to haul wood and supplies to these families. And on October 31, 1864, orders were made by the Court for the winter's supply of beef to indigent families of soldiers and for butchering and delivering the same to them—150 lbs. beef, with tallow, etc., and 7½ lbs. salt to each person—and for full report of the distribution to be made at the June term, 1865.

On November 28, 1864, the Commissioners' Court ordered that the special war tax for 1864 be collected at once in specie (coin), except that the following articles, in good merchantable condition and delivered to John W. Scott, receiver at Belton, would be received in payment of such tax, at prices named, to-wit: corn-fed pork at 6½ cents per pound; mast-fed pork at 5 cents per pound; salt pork at 6 cents per pound; sole leather at 50 cents per pound; upper leather in proportion; cotton at 12 cents per pound; shelled corn at 60 cents per bushel; ear corn at 50 cents per bushel; beef (25% of tax) at 12 cents per pound; wool (20% of tax) at 20 cents per pound; wheat at $1.25 per bushel.

All soldiers from Bell County in active service and all widows whose taxable property did not amount to $1500, were exempt from the payment of this tax. The Commissioners were authorized to contract with reliable parties to furnish wood to the indigent families of soldiers, to do their hauling, milling and all other things necessary for their comfort, on the best terms and with as little delay as possible, all at the county's expense.

On May 1, 1865, the Commissary was ordered to dispose of the surplus Penitentiary cloth on hand at 60 cents per yard and receive in payment either specie, or shell corn at 60 cents per bushel, good fall wheat (by weight) at $1.25 per bushel, good bacon at 12½ cents per pound, all delivered at the Commissary at Belton.

The several principal acts of the Legislature, under which the Commissioners' Court proceeded in the levying of special taxes and other measures for the aid of the families of our soldier boys in the field are cited in the foot note hereto.[20]

A special term held on June 5, 1865, was the last assemblage of the war-time Commissioners' Court, elected by the people. The old regime was no more—the Confederacy had fallen! And the members of this court were soon afterward replaced by appointees of the Federal military government set up throughout the South.

Efforts to sustain the soldiers at the front and to amel-

[20] Gammel, **Laws of Texas,** V, pp. 601; 617; 675; 680; 682; 816; 818; 819.

iorate the condition of their families at home were not confined to governmental agencies, such as the Commissioners' Court. Every facility at the command of our citizens—of both men and women—was placed unreservedly at the disposal of the soldiers and their loved ones.

Clothing for the soldiers was made by the faithful women of each community, and the county, as we have seen, had it transported to the soldiers at their camps. We had no Red Cross organization then, but the women, in their war work organizations, functioned just about the same. They had a regular sewing-fest going on most all of the time and every woman gave all of her spare time to this noble cause. In Belton they assembled in the District Court room, when it was not otherwise in use, and there pursued their labors for days and weeks. Mrs. John Henry Brown had the only sewing machine in Belton—an old Grover and Baker—and "it was taken to the court house where the ladies gathered. It made so much noise that, when in use, all the ladies had to cease talking."[21]

Every good citizen, with generous heart and willing hands, went to the relief of our soldiers' families in every possible way and supplemented the efforts of the county authorities in supplying them with the necessities and comforts of life. The farmers and their hired help or slaves (as was the case) planted, worked out and gathered their crops for them, butchered their hogs, attended to branding their calves and colts, if any, and were ever ready to (and often did) divide with them their last pound of flour, meal, bacon, lard, sugar, or salt. The good doctors "rolled their pills" and administered them to the sick in the soldiers' families and were ready, by day or night, to go to the relief of suffering and distress. Nearly all of the young physicians were in the army functioning as surgeons. Not only these services but others were rendered freely and generously and people were glad to do them. No greater contempt or opprobrium could have been heaped upon any citizen than to charge him with failing to help a "war widow" and, in the few exceptions to this universal generosity, the individual was not deemed worthy of the notice of a mongrel dog!

During 1861 and 1862 hundreds of beeves were slaught-

---

[21] Miss Lizzie C. Brown, in letter to writer, July 28, 1921.

ered at Belton for the Confederate Army in the field. Strong stock pens or corrals, with wings and shoots and some sort of abattoir were erected in the shady grove near what is now known as the Confederate Park, and fat beeves, wild and vicious, were driven into the pens and, one by one, were trapped into the chute and killed. The carcass was skinned, cleaned, and the meat was cut into strips and barbecued or "cured" by some process of preservation and made into "dried beef." There may have been some other details of "treatment." The idea was to "cure" this meat to be hauled on wagons to the Confederate armies in the field. The writer does not know under whose authority this slaughtering was done, but it was probably under that of the State of Texas, as the county records make no mention of the matter.

The beeves were delivered by contractors and it seems that Judge D. T. Chamberlin had general charge of the operations as commissioner of the government, and that Mr. John Q. Allen and others were concerned in the enterprise in some way. The writer's understanding is that the process of curing the meat was a failure and that the meat was all lost. There was no artificial ice here in those days and the process of the modern meat packers was then unknown to our people.

4. Civic Activities During the War

The demands of the war drew heavily upon the energies and resources of the people and of the governmental authorities, so that but slight attention was bestowed upon the ordinary civic affairs of the county. Progress, development, advancement of the general interests of the country were halted completely. It is almost literally true that not a house was built, not a fence was put up, not an acre of new land was broken—that nothing new was undertaken—during the four years of the war. In a civic and industrial sense "the clock stopped" and these four years must be deducted as lost time in the march of the county's growth.

Public functionaries and private citizens—thoroughly engrossed in the war work—performed only the merest routine duties of the hour and awaited—anxiously, patiently, patriotically, hopefully—the outcome of the great fratricidal conflict along the battle fronts of the Old South.

The first notice of the revolutionary movement to appear in the minutes of the Commissioners' Court was the order of February 18, 1861, to pay "The Belton Democrat" for publishing a notice of the election for delegates to the Secession Convention. On November 18, 1861, the Tax Collector and County Treasurer were ordered to receive Confederate money or Confederate bonds in payment of taxes.

The appointment, periodically, of election officers, road overseers, patrols, etc., was not neglected, and the Commissioners' Court—about the only body representing the collective will and civic activities of the people—held its regular sessions for the performance of this and other duties. But it must be admitted that, aside from those functions which had to do with the war, with the soldiers and with their families, the civic duties thus assigned by the court to our citizens sat lightly upon their shoulders and their appointments were merely nominal in most instances.

On May 19, 1862, the Commissioners' Court ordered the issuance of Bell County treasury warrants, to the amount of $668.79, "payable to Simeon Bramlet or bearer," in denominations running from twenty-five cents to three dollars, in lieu of and to take up a County Court House Bond for that amount, due January 1, 1863, held by him, the warrants to mature at the same time as the Bond, and redeemable in Confederate or State Treasury Notes when presented to the County Treasurer in sums of $20 or more, and to be receivable for all sums due the county, and when so received, to be cancelled and not reissued. The warrants were to be signed by the Chief Justice, countersigned by the County Clerk, and endorsed by the County Treasurer.

As there were no facilities at hand for engraving these warrants, they were printed at a local newspaper printing office with common newspaper type, on cheap thin paper and each little warrant was separately autographed, by each of the oficials. The cost of printing them and the time and *per diem* charge of the officials, in performing this work of "making money," are here given from the minutes:

Printing Warrants		$26.50
Daniel McMillan, Chief Justice	10 days	30.00
E. Mills, County Clerk	5 days	15.00
Ro. Miller, Deputy County Clerk	10 days	30.00
J. W. Scott, County Treasurer	10 days	30.00
Totals	35 days	$131.50

On August 18, 1862, similar warrants were ordered to issue to take up the balance of the Court House Bonds, amounting to $5,967.45.

These county warrants came to be known as "shinplasters." Similar paper warrants were issued by all of the counties, so that the country soon became flooded with them. As the war came on, specie—gold and silver, real money—fled from sight, as always happens in calamitous times. There was but little in circulation. The money of the Confederate Government was not generally distributed and there was no medium of exchange, especially in the small, everyday transactions of the people. Hence it was necessary to create a circulating medium of small denominations, and these outstanding court house bonds were utilized as a basis for such issue. The shinplaster depreciated steadily in value until toward the last it was hardly "worth a continental." But although our Confederate money likewise depreciated, even as late as May, 1863, it received some attention from counterfeiters, for at that time the County Tax Collector turned up with $294.50 and the County Treasurer with $430.00, of *spurious paper currency*, received in the due course of their official business, and for which relief was kindly granted to them by the Commissioners' Court.

Here is a copy of the Bell County Treasury Warrant, alias "shinplaster";

No. 6. $1.00

BELL COUNTY SCRIPT

The Treasurer of Bell County, after the 1st day of Jan., 1863, will pay to Simeon Bramlet or bearer, ONE DOLLAR, in Confederate Notes when the sum of Twenty Dollars is presented.

Belton, May 31st, 1862

E. Mills   *Dan McMillin*
Clerk   Chief Justice

Endorsement on back: *J. W. Scott.*

The Chief Justice was, on November 17, 1862, authorized to act as agent for the county in purchasing powder, lead and caps, to the amount allowed to each county. These articles were controlled and distributed by the State Military Board and were apportioned to the several counties for domestic and defense purposes.

At the same time, five thousand dollars of Bell County Warrants, issued in September preceding, were exchanged for Confederate States Treasury Notes—a measure intended to give more purchasing power and confidence to the circulating medium.

The quarterly report of the County Treasurer, filed January 13, 1864, indicates a total of $9,901.75 of Bell County Treasury Warrants then outstanding but required by a recent law to be redeemed within a few months, and on April 16, 1864, the County Treasurer was ordered to advertise in the *Weekly Telegraph* (of Houston) that said Warrants would be redeemed, according to law, by June, 1864.

The county taxes during the war period were, on each one hundred dollars assessed value, for general purposes 12½ cents; for war purposes 18 cents in 1861, 20 cents in 1862, 75 cents in 1863, 25 cents in 1864.

Doctors A. B. Davis, William D. Eastland, John W. Embree, William Goode, and Alexander M. Headley were, by an order of the Commissioners' Court, made January 13, 1864, exempted from State military duty on account of their professional services being needed by the people. The law authorized such exemptions.

5. Conditions among the People during War Time

When the war began, there were two weekly newspapers in Belton—*The Belton Independent* and *The Belton Democrat*. It is not known to the writer when they ceased publication, but they did not issue later than 1862 or 1863.

In June, 1861, the Confederate government took over the existing mail contracts of the United States government in the South. The weekly overland mail coach continued its service through Belton, as a part of the trans-state route from Red River to Austin and San Antonio, while the horseback mails connected Belton with Gatesville and some other nearby towns.

The merchants, having no reliable source of supply

after the blockade of our Gulf ports, with the country upset by war and its financial blight, and most of them enlisting for service in the Confederate army, soon disposed of their stocks and closed their doors. The few who held on had only the remnants of their goods and soon were completely without the staple articles in general demand

The country was very soon thrown upon its own productive resources and the people learned to do without many things formerly deemed indispensable. When coffee gave out, substitutes made of barley and other things were used. Occasionally a small lot was brought in by a speculating peddler from Matamoras, across the Rio Grande. It was the same with sugar, salt, rice, jeans, calico, shoes, hats and many other articles of prime necessity. So people had to make the best of a bad situation.

Barley coffee without sugar; sorghum molasses and honey, peach and wild plum preserves, garden truck, sweet potatoes, etc.; fresh beef, bacon, mutton and wild game; cloth spun and woven in the homes or in the country and made into clothes; leather tanned and made into boots and shoes; wool hats made in little factories about the country, straw hats plaited at home out of wheat straw, caps made of cloth, coon skins, etc.; ropes made of raw hide or horse hair, saddles and bridles made at home or in little shops here and there; nubias and comforts beautfully knit by mother or sister; buttons made out of "any old thing"; and so on through the list—with all these "luxuries" the people still lived.[22]

In every home was a spinning wheel, and in many of them were looms to weave cloth for the family. Some women wove cloth for the public. There were little tanneries, hatteries, shoemaker's shops, saddle shops, cooper shops, blacksmith shops—oh, everything required. Texas could have "carried on" for a hundred years, if there had been enough soldiers to keep up the fight. But we were far removed from the battle front and were not seriously disturbed in the pursuit of our ordinary efforts for the support and maintenance of

[22] The writer, in 1864, then a mere boy, tanned leather, made shoe lasts and shoe pegs and fabricated some pretty good coarse shoes. Tools were made by the blacksmith. Shoe thread was obtained from passing peddlers from Matamoros, Mexico. This illustrates the way we managed. Many others did more and better things in the struggle of home economies.

our section of the country. It was sadly different in the other Southern States, where their fields were overrun, their stock and other property destroyed or carried away, their homes occupied or burned, their very lives often jeopardized. Here, in Texas, with fairly good crops, with ample herds of cattle, sheep, goats, hogs and much wild game, our labors unaffected by the clashing of armed contenders in great military operations, we did not, could not, feel the strain and stress of the war as did our fellow countrymen in the active war zones. Our most serious heart-burdens were in thinking of the absent soldier boys in forced marches, mounting guard at midnight, falling wounded or killed in the rush of battle, and the tears of their loved ones about us. These were our nearest *personal* contacts with the war.

Our people learned to get along with such comforts as could be provided at home and, at every opportunity, were sending clothing and other things to the soldier boys far away in the armies of the Confederacy. And it should be remembered that, as there were not many people in Bell County in the war period, it required but little to maintain them. They were mostly pioneer people too, and were accustomed to the gaff of hard times, rough habit, coarse diet and severe labor.

During the war Mr. Thos. A. Epps operated a tanyard at a fine spring some seven miles north of Belton, at the head of a canyon which runs into the Leon River below the mouth of Cedar Creek. He had ten or twelve vats, treating probably 300 beef hides, besides pelts of smaller animals, per year. Five or six cabins, constructed of cedar logs, housed the men who operated the plant and their families. The tanning was done with cedar tops and the leather produced was of very good quality and found ready sale in the county for the manufacture of boots, shoes, harness, saddlery, etc. The plant was operated for a short while after the war by Mr. Hutton and later by Mr. Sam Whiteley, but was soon closed and permanently abandoned. During Hutton's time boots and shoes were also made there. The place is yet known in the country about as the "Tanyard Spring".

There is a well-supported tradition that a number of men who were opposed to the War, claiming that they were unwilling to take up arms against the Union, even after Texas had seceded by an overwhelming popular vote, gathered in a well-protected camp at a large spring at the head of Bell Branch, in the northern part of Bell County, surrounded for miles about by a dense cedar-brake and a very rough mountainous country in which there were no settlements. These men did not all belong to Bell County, but some of them came from other counties and even from other states. Among them, too, were a number of deserters from the Confederate army, outlaws, renegades, horse thieves, murderers and other bad characters. They were so strong in numbers and so well armed as to be able to protect themselves in this strategic position against any probable local force coming against them. They obtained their subsistence from relatives, friends and sympathisers on the outside whom they visited at will under cover of night. These outside friends would take corn to the mill nearby, and (so the tradition goes) instruct the miller to grind it and place the meal on the outside of the mill and not to bother should the meal disappear in the night. The truth of this tradition was positively confirmed by the late Mr. Sam W. Bishop who stated to the writer that in recruiting men for Captain Wat Graves' Company for Confederate Service on the Rio Grande border in 1864, he set out for this rendezvous to see if he could convert these men to the Confederate cause and enlist them in the service. As he started into the cedar brake, on a trail, he was challenged by a picket on guard who demanded of Mr. Bishop what he wanted there. After stating his mission, Mr. Bishop was told by the picket to return to the same spot at the same hour next day and he would get an answer. On his return, five of the men were awaiting him. They enlisted with Mr. Bishop and, overtaking the company at San Marcos, all proceeded to the Rio Grande, where the five Bull Branch recruits immediately jumped over into Mexico and were seen no more.

After the war Mr. Bishop pre-empted this identical tract of land, including the spring, deserter's camp, etc., for a stock ranch, obtained a patent to the land from the State and resided there for many years.

Another account corroborates the above traditions of the camp at the noted spring mentioned, with the additional feature that at or near the camp was a rock bluff, that there was a small opening in the abrupt face of this bluff, reached by a large tree that grew up from the bottom of the gulch below, and that once within the small opening, the cave became quite a good-sized room and that one hidden therein would not likely be discovered and could put up a good defensive fight.

Mr. Bishop, P. L. Ellis, J. H. Reese and others, visiting this secluded spot soon after the war, found abundant evidence of the place having been used as a camp. There were burned logs, smoke-colored rocks, and the usual indications that the place had been long occupied. During its war-time occupancy by deserters and other outlaws, and for sometime afterward, this rendezvous was humorously named "Camp Safety" by the people living in that part of the county.

The administration of the civil law was, of course, much relaxed and many things occurred which at other time would not have been tolerated. All portions of Texas received many refugees of all sorts from other states, of whom some came to escape the horrors of the war, some to evade service in the army, some to escape impending retribution at the hand of neighbors for past conduct and some others who came, in the regular course of events, to found a new home in our imperial State. Then there were deserters from the army (as there are in all wars) who took up their abode in the mountains, the cedar-brakes and other places of safety. And the light of the moon frequently saw the dreaded Comanche Indian peeping through the mountain passes on our western border and making a dash into the valleys for good horses and an occasional attack upon the unprotected settlers. Some of the elder men, too old or infirm for army service, and youth too young for regular military duty organized themselves into squads under the State Laws and were designated as State troops of "Home Guards." They were also known by other names, "heel flies," "vigilantes," etc. While accomplishing some good they were credited with taking the law too much into their own hands and with visiting summary vengeance upon otherwise innocent men who had incurred the displeasure of some of the home guards. Then there were squads of men, detailed from the regular army and sent back to arrest deserters. So that, with all these elements operating simultaneously over the country, the home people, especially in certain disturbed localities, were kept pretty badly stirred up and some inexcusable outrages were committed.

In this connection, the old timers will recall the famous

Lige Bivens who deserted from the Confederate army and, returning home, gathered about him a bunch of outlaws who maintained themselves in defiance of the authorities in the mountain fastnesses and cedar-brakes along the line of Bell and Coryell Counties, on Owl Creek, Bear Creek and the Cow House, from whence they made their descent, unheralded and unwelcome, to the peaceful abodes of the women and children, whose husbands and fathers were away in the army. The writer's friend, Col. G. A. Beeman (a son of Mr. Alonzo Beeman, who settled on the Stampede Creek, in Bell County, on 1852) thus described the tragic incident which ended Lige Bivens' career:[23]

"When I joined the army I attached myself to the First Texas Cavalry, Buchel's Regiment, then at San Antonio. We moved from there to the San Bernard, in Wharton County. While encamped there Bob Kuykendall, a messmate, received a letter from his sister, Minnie, says that Lige Bivens was in the cedar brakes near Aiken and that he had abused both her father and mine and threatened death in case they took any part against him. He and his men were deserters from the Confederate Army and were depredating upon the surrounding country. Bob and I read this letter and boy-like * * * determined to go home and see about it, with the Colonel's consent, if it could be secured, *and without it if we must*. We went to see the Colonel and stated our purpose; he asked us to be patient until eight o'clock the next morning, to which we consented. We were booted and saddled for the road and at eight o'clock called on the Colonel, as we had promised, when he told us he had started one company of the regiment during the night and that they were fully fifty miles on the way; that, if we went there, it would arouse local trouble that would last many years after the war ended; that the men he sent lived in another part of the state and they would settle the matter for all time. I state this fully to show how important history may be affected by apparently trifling incidents. The company went there, they killed Bivens and six of eight of his followers and ended the menace to the community."

Only a few days before this, Bivens had appropriated one of the best and fastest horses from the ranch of Major

---

[23] Letter of Col. G. A. Beeman to the author, September 19, 1919. Subsequently reiterated in an article by Col. Beeman in **Frontier Magazine** for July, 1926, p. 10.

Haldeman on Elm Creek (Old Troy) and had sent word to the latter's wife "that he would return the horse when he found one as good." When brought home by the soldier company the horse was wounded, there were bullet holes in the saddle blanket and the saddle was covered with blood.[24]

Education was not entirely neglected during the war. The school at Salado (Salado College) was maintained without interruption during the entire period and steadily gained in patronage and prestige. Its history is given elsewhere in this book.

At Aiken a very good school was taught during a considerable portion of the time, but the name of the teachers and other particulars of the school are not available to the writer.

A few other little schools were kept open and the teachers were regularly paid the portions accruing to them for tuition of indigent pupils. There were no separate schools for indigent pupils. They attended private schools along with other pupils who paid their tuition in full. It may be of interest to some old people who as children attended these schools, either as pay pupils or indigents, to name the list of teachers who drew their pay from the county in November, 1861, the first year of the war, though some of the schools had been taught during preceding years:

A. T. Bagley, John Brown, Thos. K. Cartmel, J. W. Clark, Joseph Dial, Mrs. A. S. Isbell, Miss Ellen D. Leach, Columbus M. Mackey, Thos. G. McWhirter, E. D. Miller, Andrew Morris, John Shelton, J. C. Stokes, John B. B. Supple, Rev. Levi Tenney, Erasmus Walker, George White.

The only other distribution of the indigent school fund, during the war, was on May 18, 1863, and was participated in by Mrs. Amanda S. Isbell, Miss Ellen D. Leach, G. W. McDonald and Thomas Willingham.

The mention of Mrs. Amanda S. Isbell reminds the writer that from the spring of 1861 to the spring of 1862 (barring the summer vacation period) he was a pupil of Mrs. Isbell's little primary school, on Main Street, in Belton, the only school in the town during that year. He then resided in Coryell County, but boarded in Belton for the purpose of attending this school. With the aid of Miss Lizzie C. Brown of Dallas, and the late Mrs. Emily G. Austin, of Bel-

[24] Mrs. Eugenia Haldeman Openheimer in **Old Settlers Association of Bell County for 1904**, p. 10.

ton, the following nearly complete roll of the pupils is made up:

Girls: Bettie Arnold, Mary Blair (Mrs Frank P. Justice), Kate Blair (Mrs. I. B. Warren), Tennie Bouldin (Mrs. Z. C. Law), Clara Brown (Mrs. Thos. B. Mitchell), Alice Edmondson (Mrs. R. M. Bigham), Lizzie C. Brown, Nattie Embree, Addie Jalonick, Emma Jalonick, Mary Kingsbury, Hattie Lee (Mrs. Richard Graves), Mary Lee (Mrs. Thos. F. Carpenter), Emily G. McFarland (Mrs. F Henry Austin), Annie McFarland (Mrs. W. F. A. Ellison), Bettie Rather (Mrs. Robert NelsonNelson), Mary Stringfellow, Effie Sutton, Frances Minnie Tyler, Annie R. Washington (Mrs. D. B. Withers), Myra Willingham. Boys: James S. Blair, Jno. E. Blair, Eddie Church, John Edmondson, James Isbell, Geo. W. Jalonick, Willie McCorcle, James Mitchell Smith, Wilson D. Smith, Geo. W. Tyler.

The writer remembers that it was war time, that these boys played soldiers and, with paper caps and wooden guns and swords, they marched up and down the little campus at recess, while the girls sang the Southern war-songs for them to march by.

CHAPTER XII

RECONSTRUCTION, 1865-1874

1. *The Fall of the Confederacy*

On April 9, 1865, General Robert E. Lee, the great commander of the Confederate army in Virginia, surrendered his ragged, half-starved forces to General U. S. Grant, the general-in-chief of the United States army. With Lee's army gone, it was useless for the other Confederate forces to continue resistance; therefore, by the last of May all of them, from North Carolina to Texas, had surrendered. Their officers and men were paroled and allowed to return home. The Confederacy was no more! The southern soldiers, ragged, ill-fed, often barefoot, straggled back to their desolate homes and loved ones to begin life anew.

On April 14, 1865, only five days after Lee's surrender, Abraham Lincoln, President of the United States, was assassinated by John Wilkes Booth, and Andrew Johnson, the vice-president, assumed the office of President. On May 10, 1865, Jefferson Davis, President of the Confederate States of America, and Postmaster General John H. Reagan, Ex-Governor Francis R. Lubbock and others, were captured near Irwinville, Georgia, and cast into Northern prisons on charges of treason to the government, but for which they were never put on trial. Governor Pendleton Murrah, of Texas, broken in health and discouraged in spirit, abandoned his office and, with other prominent Texas leaders, repaired to Monterrey, Mexico, where he died of tuberculosis in the following August.

For a short time, while Texas was without any authorized government, confusion and apprehension prevailed. The whole South hung on the precipice of uncertainty, doubt and distrust.

About the first real demonstration of the changed conditions was the appearance, one after the other, of remnants of Confederate cavalry from eastern Texas, Louisiana, Arkansas and Missouri. When the war ended these men, unwilling to surrender to superior force on the Union side, marched through Texas, crossed the Rio Grande into Mexico and there aligned themselves with Emperor Maximilian or with the native revolutionary forces who opposed and finally overthrew him. The largest of these forces was led by General Joe Shelby, a famous cavalry officer from Missouri. As they, at different times, passed through Bell County on their way to the Rio Grande, the necessity of provisioning themselves on their hasty marches, ahead of the incoming Federal troops, led them into some excesses. At Belton and at Salado some of the soldiers entered stores and helped themselves to such articles of food and clothing as they chose to commandeer from the small stocks, and, while some resentment was naturally felt, no organized effort was made to prevent or restrain their marauding activities. In fact we could not but sympathize, to some extent, with their plan to escape the humiliation of surrender, and we all wished them success in their new enterprise. But in due time most of these men came back, submitted to the conditions then existing, and again started life in their old homes, or in new ones to which they emigrated. Some of these men subsequently came to Texas and to Bell County to be numbered among her good citizens.

After the southern soldiers returned home they manfully faced the task of providing for their families, rehabilitating community life and restoring the prosperity of their stricken country. Poverty-stricken as they were, surrounded by social and political confusion, and hampered by the petty annoyances and impediments thrown in their way by hostile and suspicious northern politicians and their local minions, they nevertheless won their way back to self-government and prosperity. All honor to them!

It is necessary to recount some of the disappointments and indignities which they had to endure during the nine long years of "Reconstruction" which followed the close of the war. In order to give the setting for what happened in Bell County, we must first review briefly the general situation in Texas and the rest of the South immediately after the close of the war.

2. The First Period of Military Rule, 1865-1866

As fast as the Confederate armies surrendered and disbanded the Union armies took over the control of each of the southern states and, under the orders of President Johnson, established garrisons in all the important towns for the purpose of maintaining order. The existing state governments were refused recognition and quietly dissolved. There was for a time no law but military law. President Johnson wished to restore civil governments, however, and early in the summer of 1865 he began appointing provisional governors over the respective states. These governors were to cooperate with the military officials in maintaining order, but their chief function was to reorganize the state governments. First, they were to give the men of voting age an opportunity to take the "oath of amnesty"— an oath of allegiance to the United States—which act would restore to them the right to vote. Men who had held important offices, civil or military, under the Confederate government were required to obtain special pardon from the President before they could become eligible to vote or hold office. After the voters were registered, the provisional governor was to call an election to a constitutional convention which was to frame a new constitution for the state. Thereafter, when the voters had ratified this new constitution and had elected state and county officers, the new state government was to take over control and direction of civil affairs within the state. The war would then be over and the Union "restored." This was President Johnson's plan; but, as is well known, vindictive northern radicals overthrew it within less than two years and imposed a second period of harsh military rule and corrupt civil government. We must now refer to what happened in Texas after the break-up of the Confederate armies.

General Gordon Granger, of the United States Army, with a large force, landed at Galveston on June 18, 1865. The Confederate forces had surrendered or disbanded. On June 19, he assumed military command of the State and issued his famous proclamation, liberating the slaves, a day still observed by the negroes of Texas as their "emancipation" day or "Juneteenth."

On July 25, 1865, Andrew J. Hamilton arrived in Texas with the commission of President Johnson as Provisional Governor of the State and assumed his duties. He was an old Texan, an able and good man and was representing our District in the United States Congress when Texas seceded. Being a Union man, he had gone to the North early in the war. He at once proceeded to replace the existing civil regime of the secessionists with Union men wherever they could be found. It is believed that Governor Hamilton tried to select the best available material. In some instances he even tendered appointments to ex-Confederate soldiers; and, for patriotic reasons, some of them accepted, although they were not in political accord with the Governor. Although Governor Hamilton headed the civil government, his authority was really that of a military official. He had not been elected by the people but had been appointed by the President to assist the military. He was therefore obliged in all respects to conform with the policies of General Granger wherever the military were directly concerned, although General Granger had been instructed by the President to assist the Governor in restoring order. The civil appointees of Governor Hamilton were also subject to the orders and supervision of the military officials.

The first apparent purpose of the military rule set up all over the State in 1865 was to protect the ignorant negroes in their newly acquired freedom and to repress disorder by means of soldiers instead of by the peace officers elected by the people.

Bell County, of course, shared the general fate and our people were, in due time, greeted with a new set of officials —virtually military appointees—agents set up over us by foreign rulers to collect our taxes, to handle our public funds, to administer our affairs. We were now treated as people of a "conquered province" and must "pay the price of our folly!"

On August 21, 1865, the new radical Commissioners' Court, appointed by the Governor, first assembled and subsequently held other meetings at which the court transacted some routine duties such as appointing road overseers and election officers, levying taxes, drawing jurors, allowing accounts and, more important than all, qualifying the appointees to the various county officers. All of the old experienced and trusted officers—such men as David T. Chamberlain, Chief Justice; A. W. Richard, District Clerk; James Leach, County Clerk; O. H. Bigham, Sheriff; John W. Scott, County Treasurer—were set aside. The individual members of the new commissioners court were men who had theretofore stood well in our county, though inconspicuous, and their *minutes* do not disclose so very much amiss, but the truth is they didn't make many records and their activities—especially those of the chief justice—were most conspicuous in matters *not entered of record*.

A squad of Federal soldiers, stationed here soon after the military "occupation" of the State, were camped for a long time in the beautiful grove on the bank of Nolan Creek in the eastern part of Belton. They were commanded by Lieutenant C. C. Kauffman of the First Iowa Volunteer Cavalry. They seemed to take orders from Judge Christian and his county officials and they were a menace to the whole county. The citizens would wake up in the morning to be told that a good man, perhaps a near neighbor, had been arrested during the night and rushed to the Austin bastile.

And during all this time these men were putting the wildest notions into the heads of the emancipated negroes and doing all in their power to widen the breach between the whites and the blacks. The latter left the farms and congregated in town, ready for any wild adventure, and abandoned all idea of working to earn a living. There were a few fine examples of faithful old former slaves to be excepted from this general statement. But the mass of them, especially of the younger generation, were thoroughly inoculated with the idea that each negro family was to be given a farm, and that the Yankee soldiers and the scalawag office-holders would soon turn it over to them! They were haughty and insulting as far as they dared to be.

It would be tedious and unpleasant to catalog the many indignities and outrages put upon our people by this bunch of political adventurers. They affected, in some way, every community and almost every individual.

Among the poor and prostrate people here and there was some abandoned property of the Confederate Government or property captured from the Federal forces and brought home by the Confederate soldiers. Wheat, bacon and other things collected by the Confederate tithing or "tax-in-kind" officers; salt and other things intended for soldiers' families; some horses and mules owned by the Confederate Government or captured from the Federals; and a few bales of cotton—these and like things were thus held, and it was the general sense of our people that they should be retained by the Confederate soldiers and their families and that such of it as was held in the bulk in the county commissary should be equitably distributed among them. Their need for these aids in their efforts to rehabilitate their homes and to make a new start in life was very great. And thus it might have been but for the vengeful spirit of Hiram Christian. He journeyed down to Austin, the mecca of the new order in Texas, where he engaged and contracted with one F. H. Coupland, Assistant Special Agent of the U. S. Treasury Department, on December 16, 1865, to return to Bell County, to seize all such property and turn it over to the U. S. Government at Austin, for which service he was to receive one-fourth of its value. Not content with the usual peaceful methods in his unworthy undertaking, he invoked the military power to assist him. In a letter to Coupland of January 3, 1866, he stated:

"I found great difficulty in obtaining possession of the above described property and made but little progress in the performance of my duties as contractor as aforesaid previous to the arrival of Lt. C. C. Kauffman with his detachment of soldiers. The object of this communication is to earnestly solicit you to request the Commanding General at Austin to permit Lt. C. C. Kauffman with his detachment of Cavalry to remain in the county of Bell until the collection of Government property is completed. It may not be out of place for me to state that there has been more government property reported to me since the appearance of the soldiers in our town than probably would have been reported in the next twelve months to come had it not been for their appearance. The presence of U. S. troops in our midst keeps our town in perfect peace and order and prevents disturbances that no doubt would occur in their absence. I therefore, not only in behalf of the best interests of the government but also in behalf of the loyal men of my county, earnestly beg that you do all in your power to have the request granted."

Accordingly, on same date, Coupland, who seems to have then been in Belton, thus addressed Lt. Kauffman:

"I would most respectfully request that while you remain in County of Bell that you aid H. Christian, the Contractor for the collection, etc., of Government property in the county aforesaid, in every manner not inconsistent with your duties as an officer of the U. S. Army. You are acquainted with my authority for collection of all captured and abandoned property and must be well aware that a cheerful co-operation of the military with the agents appointed for that purpose will greatly expedite its collection."

Thus Judge Christian, backed up by the military, stripped every poor family and every Confederate soldier of the last vestige of property for which any claim could be made of its having technically belonged to the Confederacy—old broken-down horses and mules, which were being used to make the crops, and supplies collected by the county for the support of the families of our soldiers—all was gathered up by this *benevolent* Contractor, under military protection, and appropriated by him and his associates.

And these soldiers were not only wanted to uphold him in his official grabbing of the property, but also, and probably most important of all, to prevent disturbances and to protect the "loyal men" of the county, which meant himself and the other scalawags and negroes who were running rough-shod over the rights of the people. Certainly no one else needed the protection of United States troops, and there were no disturbances except such as were caused by their own excesses in the abuse of their "little brief authority."

These and many other outrages upon the people are not shown upon the written public records, but their victims, most of whom have passed away, carried the memory of them to their graves.

3. *Disturbances in Bell County; the Early-Hasley Feud; the Murder of Duncan and Daws*

The military and reconstruction period, succeeding the War between the States, brought along its train of evils in our county as it did everywhere throughout the South. And these conditions are difficult, if not impossible, to fairly and fully describe from memory or tradition, after the long lapse of years and the sensitive silence which has brooded over the deplorable events. The story here told is made up from many sources, including statements from some of the persons actually identified with different events, and although we have tried to get the real facts, it may contain some unavoidable but honest errors.

The Confederate Government, for the support of the war, had levied what was commonly called "a tax in kind" upon all of the products and active resources of the country, and every one was required to deliver to the government collector of this tax, at a designated place in each county, one-tenth of his produce, i. e. one-tenth of the corn, wheat, oats, cotton, etc. Under the operation of this system a large amount of corn had been accumulated by the Confederate Government in cribs at the home of Mr. John B. Reed, near Reed's Lake, in Bell County, and some five hundred head of Confederate cavalry horses were sent down from Missouri, Arkansas, or elsewhere, to be fed on this corn, during the winter of 1864-65 in order to put them in good condition for the spring and summer campaign. Something like two companies of Confederate soldiers were in charge of these horses. Along came a squad of the "Texas Home Guards," having in charge three prisoners, deserters, from the Confederate army, whom they had captured in the cedar brakes in Bell and Coryell Counties, and they camped for the night at or near Reed's Lake. During the night the prisoners were taken away from the guard and hanged to a pecan tree near Reed's Lake. These prisoners, it appears, had influential Union friends in the North, who, after the close of the war and the resulting investment of the South by the United States military forces, undertoook to procure the punishment, by court martial, of those concerned in this hanging. Somehow, their suspicions fell upon a number of the oldest and most substantial citizens of the county and soldiers were sent here from Austin to arrest them in the winter of 1865-66. John B. Reed, and his son, Ed. T. Reed, old man Drew Hasley, Dr. Bell and some others were arrested and carried to Austin to await trial by court martial. Others were suspected, but, being warned, escaped arrest by hiding out or fleeing the country for a time. Those imprisoned at Austin were finally released, without a trial, and permitted to return to their homes. There was not a scintilla of proof against them nor against the others suspected. These prisoners, some of them harmless old men, whom the soldiers arrested, were placed in cold, damp dungeons in the dead of winter and in chains! Old man Hasley contracted an illness, while in prison, from which he died soon after his return home. And thus was planted the seed of a vendetta—and in the same way originated many of the most regrettable, but unavoidable chapters of our post-war history throughout the South. Samuel L. Hasley, eldest son of Drew Hasley, was a quiet but determined youth, and brooding over the ill-treatment and consequent death of his father, he resolved upon revenge and is said to have "settled the score" with one or more of the Federal soldiers who were concerned in his father's arrest and ill treatment. Meantime he had gathered about him several friends and sympathizers, including his brother-in-law, Jim McCray, and was prepared to resist arrest. In fact, almost every one sympathized with him in avenging the cruel and undeserved treatment of his old father. But there were exceptions even among his old-time friends and neighbors. From having been a "fire-eating" secessionist Mr. John Early suddenly went over to the other side and became identified with the county officials whom the military and "carpet bag" authorities had set up over the people, and he, with Dr. Carroll Clark and some others, took sides against Hasley and charged him and his followers with serious and infamous crimes. And now the vendetta was complete. One side was designated as the Hasley-McCray party, the other as the Early-Clark party. Incomplete rolls of the members of these factions are before us, but we see no good reason for reviving them at this late day. They included a number of good men and worthy citizens, who post-war conditions had cast into unfortunate conflicts which were deeply regretted by every one. The names of the leaders above mentioned are so well known in the traditions of the county that there can be no harm in the reiteration of them here.

When the Federal soldiers stationed in Belton let it be known that they had orders to arrest Sam Hasley and others, the latter party, to the number of about thirty men, well mounted and well armed, collected and prepared for resistance—their rendezvous being the old Moses Griffin home, near Three Forks. The Early-Clark party, of about equal number, with the Federal soldiers set out to hunt up and arrest Sam Hasley and his followers. Early's home on Friar's Creek (on the Cameron road) was the headquarters of that faction. All of the country between Belton and Reed's Lake up and down the north side of Leon and Little River was in a state of semi-war—the two factions hunting each other in force—for several months. Their only meeting was a fight in the Post Oaks near Three Forks, in which James McCray, of the Hasley-McCray party, was killed and Bob McDaniel of the Early-Clark side received a wound of which he soon afterward died. This feud finally died out and most of the parties to it have long since moved away or have gone to the great beyond.

Another dark episode in this period of our history was the assassination of Duncan and Daws. It followed as an aftermath of the violent deaths of young M——, a Belton youth, and a young man by the name of L——, a stranger here, but intimately associated with M——. These young men were openly and generally charged with being horse-thieves. It was generally talked over the county that they perpetrated a number of bold thefts of horses in the Little River and Three Forks settlements and carried on their deviltries to an extent that became intolerable. At last, the communities struck back, it is supposed, in self-defense, and one day the bodies of M—— and L—— were found floating in the water near Three Forks. Examination showed that they had been shot to death and, presumably, thrown into the river. In due time, a squad of Federal soldiers, sent up from Austin, accompanied by the father and brother of young L——, appeared on the scene with orders to arrest the slayers of M—— and L—— and to take them to Austin for trial by court martial. The squad went out from Belton at night and arrested Mr. Thomas Duncan and his sheep herder, an old Englishman by the name of Daws. They were arrested at Mr. Duncan's home about six miles southeast of Belton. With these two prisoners (both unarmed) the squad started off, intending to arrest others in the neighborhood, and as they passed under the shadow of a large live-oak tree about one-half mile south of the modern residence of the late Mr. William T. J. Hartriek, two men (admittedly L——'s father and brother, who were with the squad) rode up on either side of Duncan and Daws and shot both of them dead! The Lieutenant commanding the squad turned to the L——s and angrily said: "If you are going to murder my prisoners that way, I will not arrest any more for you," or words to that effect. The squad turned back and camped for the rest of the night on the Leon at the Waco crossing and next day left the country. The only ground of suspicion against Duncan was the fact that a fine horse had been stolen from him during the M—— and L—— horse-stealing operations. As for Daws, he was an absolutely harmless, inoffensive old man. The news of this outrage—the killing of Duncan and Daws—spread like wildfire over the country. A number of the best citizens, innocent of any crime but informed that they were suspected by the L——s, left their homes, took hiding places, and a condition of chaos prevailed for some weeks, but gradually the excitement subsided and those affected resumed their usual vocations.

Behind these and other acts of violence and outrage, too numerous to chronicle here, there stood the vengeful shadow and threatening attitude of certain citizens of Bell County, who had opposed secession and had sulkily bided the termination of the war. When the Confederacy finally went down, they promptly sought and obtained places of official authority and power under the military arm of the Federal government, and in revenge for past injuries, real or fancied, used their official influence to bring about the arrests of these citizens and of many others under trumped-up charges of disloyalty to the United States and of insubordination to the newly installed military authority. The most rabid of these perhaps, was Judge Hiram Christian who became the leader of the scalawag and negrophile element of the county. He seemed to have a plentiful supply of bitterness and vengeful spite against his fellow citizens of the secession days and, turning informer, busied himself with their persecution and arrest. He was openly charged with having instigated all of the outrageous affairs here recorded and many others. He not only brought about the arrest and incarceration, at Austin, of old man Hasley, the Reeds and others, but he and one Dr. Carroll Clark were charged with responsibility for the things that led up to the Early-Hasley feud and to the Duncan-Daws murders and others.

The military appointees held on with their high carnival of misrule until the summer of 1866 when the Throckmorton administration and local officials, chosen by the people, were about ready to step into power. But the time had now come at last when, bereft of the support of the Federal military, they could no longer pursue their vengeful course with impunity nor brave the gathering wrath of their fellow citizens.

On July 2, 1866, the military Commissioners' Court began its last session, with said Hiram Christian, presiding as Chief Justice. But he did not stay to sign the minutes at its close. Between the setting and rising sun he and his henchman, Clark, took their departure. Thus they disappeared finally and forever from our records and the haunts of Bell County knew them no more!

And tradition informs us that their deeds followed them —also that someone else followed them in due season—and that both of them were killed, the former in Missouri, the latter in Arkansas, by an unknown stranger in those parts. The reader may be able to pick out the nemesis of their crimes from those whose provocations are most conspicuously set forth in these annals. His identity was well known to many of the old timers of Bell County but they never revealed his part in this regrettable chapter of his tragic career.

Later on the L——s—father and son—were indicted by the grand jury of Bell County for the murder of Duncan and Daws, arrested, at San Antonio and brought to Belton where they were placed in jail, from which a mob very promptly removed them and hanged them in the woods north of town.

4. *A Brief Return to Local Self-Government under Governor Throckmorton, 1866-1867*

President Johnson, a Tennesseean, was disposed to be conciliatory to the South, and taking the view that secession and the laws enacted thereunder were unconstitutional and void and that no state had the power to secede, he regarded the seceding states as still members of the Union. As we have seen, he advised the people to take the oath of allegiance to the United States, to hold sovereign conventions, to retrace their steps, to repudiate secession and their war debt, to elect their senators and congressmen and to resume their places in the national government.

In conformity with this pacific policy of President Johnson, an election was ordered by Provisional Governor Hamilton, of Texas, to be held on January 8, 1866, for delegates to a constitutional convention to assemble February 10, 1866. To this convention Bell and Lampasas Counties, forming a District, sent Major X. B. Saunders as their delegate. The body adjourned on April 2, submitting a new constitution which annulled the ordinance of secession, repudiated the war debt, and provided for the resumption of a normal State government within the Union At the general election, held on June 4th following, this constitution was ratified and state, district and county officers, therein provided for, were chosen. James W. Throckmorton was elected Governor and Geo. W. Jones, Lieutenant Governor. They were inaugurated August 13, 1866. Congressmen were chosen with the Governor, and United States Senators were elected by the Legislature. They were not, however, admitted to their seats at Washington.

The Throckmorton administration lasted about one year. Public affairs were well conducted, the people forgot strife and bickerings, the industries and agriculture of the state were beginning to recuperate from the blight of war and military rule, and the prospects were bright and encouraging for the return of prosperity and happiness to the people.

The county officers elected with the Throckmorton administration were delayed until August 25, 1866, in taking office by the failure (or refusal) of the military commissioners' court to meet and qualify their successors. Under the constitution of the Republic of Texas, the constitutions of 1845 and of 1861, the presiding member of this court had been designated as Chief Justice and the body itself as the Commissioners' Court; but the constitution of 1866 changed the titles to County Judge and Police Court.

By an order entered in January, 1867, the court authorized the town of Salado to vote on the question of incorporation and for town officers. It drew grand and petit juries for the district court; appointed twenty road overseers and assigned hands to them; laid out and defined twenty-three school districts and appointed a board of school examiners, consisting of W. Y. McFarland, Mark A. Kelton, and A. B. Manion; and employed Erasmus Walker as county attorney. The court held only a few meetings but it was faithfully endeavoring to reorganize the county machinery on a normal and workable basis after four years of war and one year of military misrule. While but little economic recovery was yet visible in the county, yet, if allowed to go on in the hands of our chosen public officials, its public affairs would have been gradually put in proper condition.

When the war closed in 1865 the country was prostrate, commercially and otherwise. For a while the stock business was the principal source of income, supplemented by farming on a limited scale. A railroad had extended westward from St. Louis to Abilene, Kansas, and the large cattle raisers began driving cattle overland to that terminal, grazing them and fattening them on the way. These men made up their great droves from their own herds and by purchases from their neighbors. Horses, also, of which there was a large surplus, were in good demand all through the states, South and North, whose supply had been depleted by the war. Many were purchased and driven to Louisiana, Arkansas, Missouri and elsewhere, and were sold

Top: The Robertson home in Salado. Completed about 1864 by Colonel E. S. C. Robertson. Courtesy of Davidson Studio, Belton.

Bottom: The old slave quarters at the Robertson home in Salado. Courtesy of Davidson Studio, Belton.

at good prices by dealers and drovers. Thus a ready market was offered for the surplus stock. The farming operations gradually drifted almost exclusively to corn, wheat and cotton, and the small farmer gained a support for his family. Such cotton as was on hand at the close of the war sold for a high price—from thirty five to forty cents per pound in the Southern market towns, and still higher in Liverpool, England. But we had no cotton here. Our county, up to that time, had produced but little and that was consumed at home in making the clothing for our people and for the soldier boys or it was used to purchase supplies from across the Rio Grande. A few merchants opened up in a small way, but the people, having little ready money, and trained during the war to rigid economy and self denial and to producing at home many of the necessities of life, were not very liberal patrons of the stores. So the mercantile business was slow in recovering its normal activity.

Mr. Robert C. Miller, of the pre-war mercantile partnership of Miller and Baker, is said to have had a few thousand dollars in specie, which he had carefully preserved in a safe place during the hostilities; and with this capital, he opened up a small stock in the old store on the north side of the square in Belton, as soon as the blockade was lifted and goods were obtainable. This was the fall of 1865. As money was very scarce in the country he kept only staple articles of prime necessity and operated on a very moderate scale. Thus beginning, he later associated his two brothers, Wm. A. Miller and Col. J. Z. Miller, from Bastrop County, and Don A. Chamberlin, of Belton, and formed the firm of Miller, Chamberlin & Co., who in a few years became the leading wholesale and retail merchants and jobbers in Central Texas. They did a considerable jobbing trade with the merchants in the counties to the west, and their business is said to have run in the early seventies to about a million dollars per year.

Among others who engaged in merchandising in Bell County soon after the war were the following:

At Belton: (besides Miller, Chamberlin & Co.) H. C. Denny; John C. Henry; S. W. Wybrants & Co.; McWhirter & Venable; Dr. J. W. Embree; Embree & Miller; Embree & Keyes; John H. Powers; W. S. Rather; Constantine Hardeman; Long & Reese; Pendarvis & Reese; Potts &

Brother; Norman Austin & Son; Reed, Methvin & Bigham; Wright & Hughes; Ellis Brothers; E. Sinclair; F. K. Austin; M. E. & S. W. Miller; McGuire & Son; T. E. Smith & Bro.; J. Beringer; Jno. Q. Allen & Co.; Julius Tobler; Ed Rancier.

At Salado: Jno. T. Eubank; E. S. C. Robertson & Son; H. H. Parker (drugs); Giles, Barbee & Coulters; Jake Tinnin; E. Guthrie; W. D. Copeland.

Small stores were opened in the late sixties at Mountain Home, Youngsport, Palto Alto, Moffett, Elm Creek, Harrisville, Moore's Gin, Howard, Griffin's Crossing on Little River, Sulphur Spring, Prairie Dell, Ragsdales, Oenaville, Volo—one store at each place.

As the people received returns for cattle and horses sold, and the output of farms with expanding acreage increased, the merchants enlarged their stocks and did more and more business. In the decade succeeding the war several men made moderately comfortable fortunes in the mercantile and allied businesses.

Restaurants, saloons, livery stables and other such things appeared with the business revival. It was during this period that *The Belton Journal,* a weekly, made its appearance (probably) on January 6, 1866. It was published by Major J. H. Davenport and James T. Longino. It elicited much interest, soon enjoyed a good circulation, and contributed much to the general progress.

5. *The Return to Military Rule,* 1867

But meantime the radical Republicans in Congress, urged on by the Northern fanatics and so-called Southern "loyalists," rejected and overthrew President Johnson's plan for the peaceful restoration of the Southern States and entered upon a mad course of bitter proscription and persecution of all those concerned in the secession movement by enacting, over President Johnson's veto, those infamous statutes known as "the Reconstruction Laws of Congress." The Southern States were divided up into five military districts and placed under the control of army officers, with very full and arbitrary civil as well as military powers. Louisiana and Texas were placed together as the 5th Military District and General Phil Sheridan was put in command, with his headquarters at New Orleans. He at once dispatched to Texas some four thousand troops under the immediate command of General Charles Griffin, who took up his headquarters at Galveston. Under these laws also our Constitution of 1866 was nullified and every man who had ever held an office, even the pettiest, and had participated in the war on the Southern side was disfranchised. To make the situation even worse, the ignorant negro men were given the right to vote.

During this period of "reconstruction" there developed a political terminology which has been and should be preserved in our traditions. These were the terms "scalawag," "carpet-bagger" and "radical." The scalawag was a southern man who joined or gave political support to the reconstruction policies of Congress against the sentiment and interests of his fellow-southerners. Usually he had been a Union man at the beginning of the war, or had been a noncombatant during the war; but sometimes men who had been open secessionists turned scalawags. They were looked upon with aversion as traitors to their people. The carpet-bagger was a northern man who had come South after the war, and especially after the passage of the Reconstruction Acts, to enter politics and with the aid of negro votes to raise himself to a position of power and profit. Most of the carpet-baggers were mere adventurers, men who had failed at everything in the North and who had brought with them all their worldly possessions in a old-fashioned "carpet-bag." Some of them were, as indeed were some of the scalawags, men of ability and honor; but so many were of low character that the group as a whole was despised and disliked. The term "radical" was applied to all those who supported the extreme policies of those northern men who wished to impose heavy penalties on the South—such as military rule, negro suffrage, the disfranchisement of whites, and, in general, the subordination of the South to northern control. One of their purposes was to build up the Republican party in the South on the foundation of negro votes. The southern radicals comprised the white scalawags and carpet-baggers as well as such negro leaders as rose to political prominence. The power of the whole group rested, first, upon the military rule established by the Reconstruction Acts of the radical Congress; later, upon the block of votes cast by the ignorant, credulous ex-slaves. It proved to be a shaky foundation.

On July 30, 1867, not quite one year after the inauguration of Governor Throckmorton's peaceful administration, there came, like a storm in a still night, the famous sweeping order from General Sheridan removing from office Governor Throckmorton and the other high civil officers of the State on the charge that they were "impediments to reconstruction," and appointing Ex-Governor Elisha M. Pease as Provisional Governor, but subject in all respects to the military authority of General Sheridan. All subordinate officers who could not take "the iron-clad oath" of allegiance, in which one had to swear that "he had not taken up arms against the government of the United States nor given aid or comfort to its enemies," were to vacate their offices and give place to military appointees. As very few men of Southern sympathies could take this oath, the offices were generally, as intended, swept clean of the incumbents elected by the people in 1866, and their places were taken by the renegade scalawags and the carpet-baggers, now come into their own, and in some cases by ignorant negroes. In fact, the latter predominated in the counties of South and East Texas and along the Trinity, Brazos and Colorado Rivers.

In the latter part of 1867 General Sheridan was removed from command of the 5th Military District by President Johnson on account of his high handed partisanship and was succeeded by General W. S. Hancock. But Hancock was altogether too just and generous to the people of the South. So his removal was demanded by the radicals and, in 1868, General J. J. Reynolds, another bitter Northern partisan, was given the command by General U. S. Grant. He was relieved for a while, in 1868, by General Canby, whom our people greatly respected; but in 1869 General Reynolds was returned to the post and continued the arbitrary work of General Sheridan to the end of the reconstruction period.

The county officers, elected for four year terms under the constitution of 1866, were all ousted and replaced by military appointees by January, 1868, and faces unknown in public affairs, some of them new to the entire county, confronted the citizen when he entered the courthouse to transact his business there. If some one of our representative citizens holding an office had been overlooked by the military and was not replaced, his official surroundings were so distasteful and impossible that he resigned or abandoned the office. A man named Lewis Elgin, an entire stranger, moved into the county to be appointed County Judge and took the office on February 10, 1868, but he so disgusted his own crowd that the place became untenable for him and his last official act is dated October 17, 1868. Whence he came, whither he went, we knew not, and when "his hour struck" he did not tarry long enough to bid anyone farewell!

His successor, Judge James W. Moore, a military appointee, was a good man. He did not seek the office but consented, at the request of conservative Republicans, to accept the appointment.

As our county was sparsely settled and contained but a small negro population, we were not subjected to so many of the political hardships of military "radical" negro rule as were the people of those counties in which the negro population predominated—the large plantation counties along the valleys of the Brazos, Colorado, etc. where large numbers of slaves were liberated in 1865.

As all business of the county was under the immediate direction of the military, including even the distribution and expenditure of the various county funds and other routine matters, the records of those days disclose nothing of real importance, and in a public or municipal way our county made no progress whatever. Nothing was done to advance the general interest. Taxes were levied, road overseers appointed, and some other perfunctory things were done, but all under military orders and supervision. A little captain or lieutenant of the United States Army, stationed here, directed the administration of our county affairs. There was no accounting of public funds, no responsibility for official conduct except to this military officer. The courts, also dominated by the military, were a farce and citizens had little or no redress for their grievances.

Outside of the record these "county administrators" busied themselves with registrations, elections, freedmen's bureaus, loyal leagues, running down and arresting their ancient enemies, and generally made conditions as unbearable as possible for the people who had espoused secession and the Confederate cause—the so-called "unrepentant rebels."

6. *The Old Ku Klux Klan in Bell County,* 1867-70.

Almost every one has heard something about this once famous institution which flourished in the Southern States during the dark days of reconstruction. Soon after the passage of the infamous Reconstruction Acts of 1867 social and political conditions in the "black belt" of the South became almost intolerable. Led on by unscrupulous carpet-baggers and scalawags (while the Southern whites were largely disfranchised) and supported by the power of the United States Army, the negro voters dominated the elections and filled the offices, high and low, with a motley crew of white rascals, and an occasional negro office holder to preserve the semblance of the negro power.

The debauch went further. Not only did the ignorant negroes exercise all the suffrage or political functions of their late masters but, encouraged, incited and backed up by the mongrel white crew then in charge of affairs, many of them assumed an attitude of overbearing insolence that was rapidly becoming intolerable. The responsibility for this threatening attitude was wholly upon those contemptible white elements who then controlled the negroes, who (with a very few exceptions) would never have attempted or even thought of such things if left alone.

The white people of the South, driven from political control of their own country, disfranchised, financially and physically prostrate, and overawed by coarse and ignorant white swashbucklers from the North, in the uniform of United States soldiers, were helpless, in the circumstances confronting them, to invoke or apply any *legal* protection. The radical forces had organized everywhere "loyal leagues" for securing and maintaining their control of the negroes. The latter, in droves, were herded into membership in these leagues, which were secret societies set up ostensibly to instruct the negroes how to assert their "rights," but really to maintain, through the negro vote, the political supremacy and power of the scoundrels who were exploiting the Southern States like conquered Roman colonies. It need not be told that an *appeal* for protection by the Southern white people to these political ghouls or office holders was quite useless, even absurd. But it was not destined that Anglo-Saxon white people, with the blood of their freedom-loving ancestors coursing through their veins, should forever be lorded over by ignorant negroes, coached and incited by a lot of unprincipled adventurers.

When the war ended the younger men who came home from the army became restless amid the general devastation and gloom and must have diversion, some reflex of their soldier habit. First at Pulaski, in Tennessee, and then at some other towns, they happened to organize themselves into social clubs, of a quasi-military form. Mounted and equipped they might again disport themselves over the hidden trails, through the woods and over the hills of the back country, as they did in the cavalry service of the Confederacy. But as all citizens were forbidden to appear in military dress, or with arms, and as the watchful eye of the unfriendly authorities were to be avoided, these clubs, from necessity, drew off into secrecy and disguise. And, intending at first only to give zest and humor, to their diversion, they made their disguises grotesque and ghostly and, thus arrayed, it was the most natural thing for them to have their fun out of the ignorant negroes in the neighborhood. But to their surprise, their appearance in negro settlements, clothed in these ghostly habiliments, struck terror to the poor creatures, who fled in panic from the sight. A discovery was unexpectedly made! Here was the answer to the "loyal league!" Here was the defensive weapon of the subjugated white people. No army, no government, no loyal league, no amount of carpetbag and scalawag persuasion and cajolery could stand up against the negroes' superstition and fear.

The Ku Klux Klan then found that it had a mission. It was to protect society, to put the carpet-bagger and the scalawag out of business, to restore the negro to his sober common sense and to readjust the country to normal social conditions. The order spread rapidly all over the South. There may have been a general or central organization with directory authority over the scattered units, but generally, it is believed, the movement was spontaneous and local. Some said they had a Grand Cyclops, Grand Magi, Grand Turk, etc., as officers, and that each unit or Lodge was called a Den, but most of them in each locality were a law unto themselves. The radical Congresses made extended investigations of the operations of the Ku Klux Klan and published volumes of reports and so-called testimony—all, of course, for political effect in the North—and passed "force acts" for the punishment of the Klan, but it accomplished little.

But the Ku Klux Klan accomplished a great work and in an orderly way. If there was an occasional act of physical violence, *someone else* forced the issue and the event.

What did they do? Why, their procedure was the simplest and the funniest possible. The Ku Klux Klan, both rider and mount disguised in white costumes, and with high pointed caps, with large mock eyes and mouth, so as to resemble the popular negro idea of ghosts, would ride up to a negro cabin in the dead of night, call the negroes out, claim to be the spirit of Southern soldiers of the vicinity who were killed in some great battle of the war, come back to haunt bad negroes. They performed acts seemingly supernatural, such as one man apparently drinking a whole bucketful of water, *all at once,* and calling for more, with the statement that it was the first water he had drunk since he was killed at Shiloh. "They sent forth dismal wails and made dreadful sounds of rattling bones." They did many other equally awe-inspiring and ghostly stunts, until the badly scared negroes were ready and anxious to do whatever they were told. The ghosts would then warn them against further impudence to white people and order them to go to work, to behave themselves, to attend to their own business, and to quit trying to run the government, and these warnings were coupled with threats of dire consequences for failure to heed them. They promised good treatment and friendly assistance if the negroes behaved themselves.

The result was wonderful. The negroes, really not intending to do wrong but misled by scoundrels, and believing that the *ghosts were right after them,* improved their conduct, ceased their insolence, and conditions were greatly improved. The Klan in many places also paid their respects to the white carpet-bagger and scalawag, with the result that he would decide to go elsewhere, "while the going was good."

Bell County had her Ku Klux Klan, and the reports of their visits, as told by the negroes down in the bottoms of Little River and other localities, used to be amusing in the extreme, notwithstanding the seriousness of our political situation. All of the stories were exaggerated and no two negroes could tell them alike, but all gave wide sweep to their imagination and superstition. We were all "fed up" on "hants," ghosts, and hobgoblins.

The old Klan was disbanded by the official orders of its

reputed commander or leader, General N. B. Forrest, in 1869, and by the anti-Ku Klux laws of Congress passed in 1870 and 1871.

A recent organization calling itself the Ku Klux Klan and claiming to be a revival of the old Order, was the subject of much discussion in the press for several years after 1920—in fact it became an important factor in politics and community activities.

It is quite apparent that the modern Klan has no connection with its predecessor and namesake of 1867, either in purpose or method, and more than this, the conditions which brought the latter into play have long since passed away. There is not even an imaginary necessity in this day and time for the existence of such an organization in our country, North or South.

7. *The Constitutional Convention of* 1868-1869

A state election was held, under military orders, at the county seats only and under guards of United States soldiers, beginning on February 10, 1868, and lasting four days, for delegates to another constitutional convention. The voters—scalawags, carpet-baggers and negroes, plus a few conservative whites who had not been disfranchised under the reconstruction laws of Congress—had previously appeared before the county "Board of Registrars" for registration. This same Board held the elections, and was usually composed of two white men and a negro. This constitutional convention met on June 1, 1868, and after several months (including a recess), during which they did a great many other things besides writing a constitution, they adjourned in confusion, without a quorum; and while it was supposed by the public that no constitution was framed, yet *"an incompleted, undated, unsigned" document, purporting to be a constitution*, was laid before the people by the Commanding General of the District and was ratified by the same voters at a four day military election beginning November 30, 1869. In this election also, Edmund J. Davis was declared chosen as Governor, with other state and local officers throughout the State, including senators and representatives in the twelfth legislature and four members of Congress. In this constitutional convention A. J. Evans, Wm. E. Oakes and Nathan Patten, all of Waco, appeared as delegates from the district to which Bell County was assigned in this military "scramble." Oakes died and Shep Mullens, a Waco negro, took his place in the convention. The Bell County scalawags were either not mean enough to sit in this mongrel assemblage, or they could not be spared from the fleshpots back at home.

On September 30, 1869, Provisional Governor Pease had quit his office in disgust and for a while the executive functions of our State devolved upon Adjutant General James Davidson, a military subaltern of General Reynolds.

8. *The Regime of Governor E. J. Davis, 1870-1874*

On January 8, 1870, General Reynolds appointed E. J. Davis, victor in the recent election, to serve as "provisional Governor" of Texas until his inauguration for the full term. The newly elected legislature assembled under military orders in February, ratified the XIVth and XVth Amendments to the United States Constitution, as required by the Reconstruction Acts of Congress, and recessed. On March 30, President Grant approved an act of Congress which declared Texas once more entitled to representation in Congress. The 12th legislature, controlled by carpet-baggers, scalawags and negroes, again assembled in April and on the 28th Governor Davis was duly inaugurated for the regular four year term.

But the troubles of Texas were not ended. There were to be nearly four years more of misrule and turmoil. Although civil government was nominally restored, the people were still subject to the military authority of the governor exercised through his state police and militia (both composed in part of negroes), to the declaration of martial law and the imposition of heavy fines against the people of whole counties as punishment for the acts of a few irresponsible individuals. Numbers of law abiding citizens were arrested and fined or imprisoned upon mere rumor or at the instigation of personal enemies. Excessive taxation, extravagant and wasteful appropriations, bribery of legislators and other officials, the appointment of incompetent and often corrupt persons to the judiciary, the corrupt and scandalous distribution of county funds among dishonest officials under various pretexts, the unjust and exorbitant exaction of official fees, the restriction of voting to one place in each county, the county seat, and that guarded and overawed by armed soldiers—these were some of the things which the people of Texas had to endure during the administration of Governor Davis. It cannot be charged that Governor Davis was personally dishonest in financial matters, but it is well known that he was surrounded by a crew of corrupt politicians whom he too often appointed to positions of trust and power. Nor were all the other radical leaders corrupt. A few of the despised carpet-baggers and scalawags were personally honest, but they could not control the dishonest and time-serving rascals who worked their way into office.

Long before Governor Davis' term was over it became evident that the rule of the radicals could not last. By 1871 a considerable group of Republicans deserted him. In that same year the Democrats, or Conservatives, as they were then called, elected all their candidates for Congress. In the next year they elected a majority of each house of the legislature; and this 13th Legislature repealed the worst of the laws passed by the notorious 12th Legislature. In 1873 the Democrats nominated Richard Coke and R. B. Hubbard for governor and lieutenant-governor, while the Radical Republicans nominated Davis. The Democratic ticket swept the State in the November election, although the Republicans still held control in a few counties where the negroes were in large majority. In January, 1874, when the 14th Legislature assembled, Coke and Hubbard were inaugurated and Davis was forced to relinquish his office. Texas was "redeemed."

With this brief review of State affairs during the radical regime, we now return to conditions in Bell County. As there were relatively few negroes in the county at that time, the white radicals were never able to get complete control and such as were elected were usually good men. Like most of the frontier counties, in local matters Bell was governed, for the most part, by her own people.

The constitution of 1869 made some changes in the local machinery. The office of county judge was abolished entirely and the probate jurisdiction was vested in the District Court. The Police Court now consisted of five justices of the peace, elected from defined subdivision of the county. The justice from the county seat (or central precinct) was styled the "Presiding Justice," the other four as "Associate Justices." When assembled they constituted the Police Court and performed the functions of the old Commissioners' Court.

Within his own precinct each member was a justice of the peace and the assessor of taxes, and their combined rolls constituted the county tax roll, there being no longer an assessor of taxes for the county. The sheriff collected the taxes.

The new Police Court held its first meeting on July 4, 1870. It placed the courthouse in charge of the sheriff and allowed him $150.00 to expend in its repairs. At the meeting on September 26, a special road tax on one-eighth of one per cent was levied for 1870 and the following were designated as first class roads: (1) Belton and Waco road; (2) Belton and Austin road, via Shaw Crossing; (3) Belton and Marlin road, via John Keggans; (4) Belton and Gatesville road, via Cedar Creek; (5) Belton and Cameron road, via Bunting's and Bryant's; (6) Belton and Sulphur Springs (Lampasas) road; (7) Belton and Lexington road (added February 1, 1871). The court appointed W. J. Long, the sheriff, to be road overseer for the county at a salary of $500 per annum, payable quarterly, and authorized him to employ hands at $1.25 per day to work the first-class roads. Repairs on the old "log jail" of 1855 to the amount of $100.00 were authorized. The petition of Sidney N. Marques for license to erect a toll bridge across big Elm Creek at the crossing of the Belton and Waco road (now old Troy) was granted and the toll fees were fixed. This was the first bridge of any sort ever *authorized* by the county, but it does not appear that this one was ever built.

An order entered February 1, 1871, commanded the county treasurer to pay the *per diem* and fees of the members of the Police Court—the five justices and the clerk— *in preference to all other claims* against the county. The job of county road overseer was advertised to be let to the lowest bidder on sealed proposals, to be opened on February 25, 1871. It fell to W. J. Long at $200 per annum.

On June 3, 1871, a franchise was granted to William A. Miller, Elisha Embree, Silas Baggett and John T. Flint (of Waco), already incorporated by the Legislature as the "Belton Bridge Company," to erect and maintain a public toll bridge over the Leon River at the crossing of the Belton and Waco road (the old "military road" of 1848). This bridge, of the steel truss type, was completed and authorized to open for business on March 25, 1872, and was the first wagon bridge ever built in Bell County. But the free suspension foot-bridge at Salado, built in 1869 by the town of Salado, was the first bridge of any kind ever built in the county. On July 31, 1871, a franchise was granted to William York to operate a ferry on Little River in the Reed and Fulcher Settlement.

After several revisions, the tax rate for the county was finally fixed for 1871, at 62½ cents on the $100 valuation and distributed as follows: common county, 25 cents; county indebtedness, 12½ cents; paupers, lunatics, etc., 12½ cents; repairs of court house and jail, 12½ cents; A poll tax and occupation taxes were also levied.

The sheriff was limited, September 9, 1871, "to five policemen as registration and election guards, except in case of a riot." An order was made, September 25, 1871, for the erection of a fence of cedar posts and pine plank around the courthouse, $200 appropriated therefor and a committee appointed to have the work done. On November 27, 1871, the Belton and Austin road, via Shanklin's Mill, was discontinued as a public road. This was a section of the old "military road" laid out in 1848 by the United States soldiers, which crossed the Lampasas at the Childers' Mill of those days, as previously described.

On November 29, 1871, a committee, consisting of Rev. Jas. E. Ferguson (a member of the Police Court), Rev. Bythel H. Biard and Captain A. J. Harris, was appointed to audit the books and accounts of the offices of the county clerk and of the county treasurer from 1865 to date, to ascertain the receipts and disbursements and the outstanding indebtedness of the county and to make full report. On January 27, 1872, this committee filed a report which showed that, from August, 1865 to December, 1871, county script had been issued by order of the county court to the amout of $22,215.77; that jury script for the same period amounted to $10,418.50; and that the district judge had allowed to the officers of the court $1,368. The total of script issued was, therefore, $34,002.27. In addition, some $362.56 had been expanded, while the commissions charged by the county treasurer amounted to $3,114.61. Thus the total disbursements plus commissions were $37,479.44. The receipts of the treasury for the same period were $39,439.64, leaving a balance of $1,960.20. The treasurer had on hand, however, on $1,791,72, showing an apparent shortage of $168.28. The committee was careful to point out that the discrepancy "may result from our own miscalculation occasioned by the irregular character of the papers we have had to examine." Of the disbursements, $2,815.49 had been paid on the court house bonds. The report did not show how the rest of the county script had been expended. There was still due on the court house bonds some $1500, and other obligations brought the total debt of the county to $3,952.93.

By orders entered November 29, 1871, and March 25, 1872, the records of files and surveys contained in the books of the former "Milam Land District," so far as they relate to the lands situated in Bell County were transcribed into new and well bound books by Mr. Ed. T. Rucker, deputy county surveyor. The original records were old and were wearing out and it was therefore necessary to make a complete transcription of them.

The county surveyor was ordered to make a new map of the town of Belton, showing the names of present lot owners. It seems that for the preceding twenty-two years the county had continued to use the original map, made by E. Lawrence Stickney when "Nolanville" was laid out, and adopted as the official map in 1851.

The road fund of the county was apportioned as follows: Precinct 1, $231; Precinct 2, $163; Precinct 3, $272; Precinct 4, $326; Precinct 5, $122; total, $1,114.

An appropriation of $50 was made to build a bridge over a ravine on the Belton and Gatesville road, between the town of Moffett and the river. This little bridge, doubtless a wooden affair, was the first bridge ever built *by the county*, at least so far as is shown in the records.

The county tax levy for 1872 was 54 cents on the $100, as follows: common county, 20 cents; roads and bridges, 12 cents; paupers, 10 cents; court house and jail, 12 cents. Also poll and occupation taxes.

On April 1, 1872, plans and specifications for a county jail, to be bult of stone, two stories in height, with steel cages, etc. were submitted by Mr. James P. Reed, and adopted by the court. After advertising for bids, the contract was awarded on May 27, 1872, to James P. Reed, N. M. Whitson and Geo. M. McWhirter, composing the firm of Reed, Whitson & Co., at $6,850, the lowest bid. The jail was completed and received by the Police Court November 25, 1873. It was erected on the same lot as the old "log jail" which the sheriff had been ordered to sell at auction to the highest bidder.

As elections were again permitted to be held in various communities of the county, under laws passed by the Democratic legislature in 1873, our Police Court, on June 21, 1873, established fourteen election precincts and appointed a presiding officer for each precinct.

The tax levy for 1873 was 55 cents on the $100, as follows: common county, 25 cents; road and bridge, 5 cents; court house and jail, 12½ cents; pauper fund, 12½ cents.

The following order made by the Police Court, November 24, 1873, but rescinded on January 27, 1874, because palpably illegal, throws an interesting side-light on the important business of stockraising and the unsettled condition of the lands and population of the county at that time.

"Whereas it appears from the petition of L. C. Williams and others that there are a large number of estray beeves in Big Elm Creek bottom in Bell County, which annoy and injure the people living contiguous thereto; and whereas it is impossible to deal with said beeves in the manner pointed out by the statute, in making sale of estray cattle.

It is therefore ordered that said beeves may be gathered and driven to market by any person who desires to do so by paying into the County Treasury ten dollars specie for each beef so gathered and having one of the Commissioners hereinafter mentioned to take the marks and brands of the same, provided that no estray beef under four years old shall be driven under this order. And it is further ordered that L. C. Williams, J. H. Plasters and Seaborn Sweatt be and are hereby appointed Commissioners to take the marks and brands of the beeves hereinbefore mentioned and to receive pay therefor and said Commissioners shall pay over to the County Treasurer the money they or either of them may receive for any of said beeves and shall cause to be recorded the marks and brands thereof in the Records of Marks and Brands for Bell County. Said Commissioners shall take the Treasurer's receipt for any money they may pay over to him under this order."

This Police Court, elected with the Davis administration, held its last term on December 20, 1873, when it was succeeded by a new county regime elected December 2, 1873. No reflection upon the personnel of the retiring Police Court is intended. They were good men and with the handicaps of radical laws and the E. J. Davis overlords they did as well as they could.

9. *The Honey Incident,* 1873

In the late summer of 1873 there came to Belton from Austin the Rev. Geo W. Honey, a Northern Methodist carpet-bag preacher, formerly State Treasurer of Texas in the E. J. Davis Republican Administration. His mission here was to preach to the negroes. The negro church, a wooden shanty, was situated on East Water Street. near the present City Hall and Fire Station. He had been here once before on the same mission. On his former visit he stopped with old "Uncle" John Bell, a good old negro blacksmith and preacher, and he had at first put up with "Brer" Bell again on this second visit and was seen several times riding around town with him in a buggy. At the suggestion of some peace-loving white citizens, however, he had changed his boarding place to the old St. Charles Hotel, on the northeast corner of the Court House Square.

After preaching to the negroes several nights he came to the white Methodist Sunday School on Sunday morning and took his seat in a Bible class, composed of nearly grown girls and boys, taught by Judge X. B. Saunders. From there he went to lunch with the white Methodist preacher—the pastor of the church.

Some of our young men could not stand for all this, and they counselled together as to the best way of showing their contempt and indignation for the reverend Honey, without doing him any serious bodily injury.

That night he was not to be found at the negro church, but they soon learned that he was attending service at the white Methodist Church, and there they waited for him. As he came out they heard him remark that he had left his umbrella at the white Methodist preacher's house and would have to return there for it. As he came out of the preacher's house, the "committee" took him in charge and escorted him—*nolens volens*—to the old swimming hole above town, back of the Supple place and there flung him into the limpid waters of the classic Nolan. He started across to the other side, but the "committee" compelled him to return to their side, when they flung him in again. They then ordered him to remain there for five minutes while they "faded away," and they further advised him not to allow another sun to set upon him in Belton.

Accepting the treatment and the advice of the "committee," he returned, bedraggled and dripping with water, to the hotel and took the morning stage for Austin.

Honey went before the Federal Grand Jury, at Austin, and instituted an investigation of the case. He claimed

The O. T. Tyler home in Salado. From a recent photograph. Courtesy of Davidson Studio, Belton.

(so it was reported) that the perpetrators were all grown men, six feet tall and masked and that it was a Ku Klux outrage, while in fact the committee were all (as it appeared in later years) mere boys ranging from fifteen to eighteen years old, and none of them were masked. Honey's lurid description threw the authorities clear off the track and not one of the "committee" was ever identified or suspected until years afterward.

The affair created quite a sensation in those days ot political persecution, bloody-shirt sectionalism and recent carpet-bag rule, but the excitement gradually subsided. The press of the State poked a good deal of fun at Honey, and the incident was eventually forgotten.

The writer does not positively know the personnel of the "committee," but he surmises that M. M. (Bud) Methvin, Sam Rather, Jr., Wilson Trotter, Lon Gentry (of Houston), Tom Batte, and Steve Davenport could have thrown some light on the dark mystery.

10. *The Last Indian Raids*

When the Civil War ended, the military forces which the State and Confederate governments had kept on the western frontier were disbanded. As the State was not allowed to maintain armed forces of any description—and, in fact, had no money to pay for them—the only means of protection was the United States Army. But the army stationed in Texas was not sent to the frontier; it was kept in small detachments in the older sections for the ostensible purpose of maintaining order and protecting the negroes. The wild Indians were quick to discover their opportunity to attack the exposed western settlements and raided so fiercely and in such numbers that some of the counties between the Red River and the Colcrado were almost abandoned by the despairing people. When the legislature in 1866 provided for raising several companies of rangers and Governor Throckmorton offered their services to General Sheridan, that officer refused them, nor would he agree to send any of his own troops to the frontier. It was not until 1868 that the army made any move against the Indians. From that time until 1875 campaigns were carried on which resulted in forcing the Indians to go to reservations in the Indian Territory (now Oklahoma) and stay there.

Bell County was, of course, fairly well protected from attack by the counties west of her; but small bands of Indians now and then succeeded in pentetrating into the western portions of Bell in horse-stealing operations. A few of these affairs are here recounted, but of some others it has been impossible to get any reports.

During Christmas week, 1867, when one of the heaviest snows that ever fell in the country was still on the ground, a squad of five to seven Indians came into Bell County and stole twenty-one head of horse from the George brothers (James, William and Freeman) and from other persons. There was no pursuit of the Indians.

During the light of the moon in either May or June, 1869, another squad of Indians came down into Nolan Valley as far as the present site of Nolanville, and stole sixty or seventy head of horses from Chas P. Cruger, Berry Fleming, Ira Fleming, and others. They were pursued by a party of settlers consisting of Captain James M. Cross, commander, Will Blackwell, ——— Davis, ——— Davis, Freeman George, William George and Robert Arch Renick. The Indians, discovering that they were being followed, abandoned the horses on a mountain near Brushy Gap, some twenty miles beyond where Copperas Cove now stands. Their tracks indicated that there were some five to seven Indians in the squad. They scattered, each going in a different direction, and therefore could not be trailed or pursued by the small party of settlers. The latter rounded up the stolen horses and brought them back to the owners.

During the light of the moon in July or August of the same year, about the same number of Indians came down over the same route and stole some forty or fifty head of horses. A party composed of Lieutenant Wade Hampton, commanding, Will Blackwell, Burrell Etheridge, Dennis Etheridge, Freeman George and William George followed these Indians to the present site of Copperas Cove and there recovered the stolen horses, the Indians having again abandoned them and scattered in different directions, as before, to evade further pursuit.

In 1870 Colonel Beaumont, with a small troop of United States soldiers, was encamped at the Hancock Spring, in the town of Lampasas, where Captain James M. Cross, of

Crossville, Bell County, called upon him and apprised him of the renewal of Indian raids in this territory. Colonel Beaumont, in writing, commissioned Cross to raise a local ranger company to patrol the frontier of Bell, Lampasas, Coryell and Hamilton Counties, against raids of Indians. Captain Cross returned, assembled his rangers at Crossville, and after explaining to them his arrangements with Colonel Beaumont and stating that the men would probably be paid for their service, turned over the written commission to Lieutenant Wade Hampton. The company was divided into four squads, each squad serving one week, when it was replaced by another. Their meeting place was Sugar Loaf Mountain, whence each squad started on its respective scout service.

In those days the present site of Copperas Cove, or rather the mountain nearby, was the usual rendezvous of the Indians on their way out of the country. There, if not pursued, they camped for a day, rested up, killed a beef and prepared for their outgoing journey.

This ranger service was continued till sometime in 1871, though Freeman George resigned at the end of four months (October, 1870) to go with a cattle drive to Baxter Springs, Kansas.[1]

Mr. F. M. Cross, an old Bell County man (son of James M. Cross), gives an interesting account of what he says was one of the last Indian raids in Bell County.

"In the early spring of 1870 the Indians made a stealing raid in Bell County, in the neighborhood of Youngsport. There were four Indians in the bunch and they secured fourteen head of saddle horses, or thirteen horses and one mule, and killed one mare belonging to Uncle Dee Lane. Being unable to either catch or drive her, they shot her and left her lying with the arrow in her, within five hundred yards of the house. They got the mule out of old Parson Henry Cosper's lot. It was locked by a chain around its neck and the other end around a snag of a limb which had been blown off some three or four feet above where it forked from the tree. They slipped the loop up until they pushed it over the end of the snag and got off with the mule. Its mate was locked around the body of the tree

---

[1] All of the foregoing accounts were given the writer by Mr. Freeman George on March 7, 1923.

and they could not get it. When the news got out next morning a posse of eleven men got together to follow the Indians. There were: Mr. Turnbo, Will Cathey, Mitt Parker, Don Tankersley, Tuck Boone, Jake Cosper, Jack Wilcox, Abe Ray, Dock Cosper, Hiram Teague and my brother, G. B. Cross, of Brownwood.

"These men got mounts and started about 11 o'clock in the morning but the Indians had evidently scattered out some yards apart in order to avoid being trailed, and it was impossible to make any headway following them, so the men decided they would ride straight ahead for fifteen or twenty miles and probably would find where they had gathered more horses and could trail them better. When they reached where Copperas Cove now is, finding no sign on the north side of the mountains, they returned and went due south through the gap. When on the south side of the range of mountains, they struck the trail of the Indians evidently driving the horses, as some ropes were dragging. The Indians were at that time only one mile from them, on the mountain where they had remained all day, waiting to make another haul when night came on, as there was a thick settlement a few miles away on the Lampasas River. Having a spy on the edge of the mountain they discovered that our men had struck their trail and would soon be on them. (They) pulled up camp and left in a full run. When down on the level prairie the wily Indians scattered out some yards apart, leading or riding all the horses, and then grass being high and dry, it was impossible to trail them faster than a walk. The Indians running and having at least three fourths of an hour the start, it was useless to follow their trail. Brother and some others in the crowd having followed the Indian trails out before, knew the route they would go for twenty miles or more, and they decided to make a straight run for points twenty miles ahead. In so doing they frequently came onto the trail. Jake Cosper was riding the mate to the mule the Indians had stolen; this animal, when it came to its mate's trail, would put his nose to the ground and follow like a dog for some distance, then raise his head and bray. This twenty mile run was through practically open country, with scattering small hills and groves here and there. They reached a chain of mountains and stayed close to it, keeping on the north side. The boys reached those mountains about half an hour before sundown, and where the Indians had crossed one of those little streams running down from the mountain, the bank was so wet it looked as if they had not been gone ten minutes. Two of the boys' horses gave out at this point, and one man was suffering with a pain in his side, so they had to leave them. These were Mr. Turnbo, Will Cathey and Abe Ray. The other eight began to crowd their horses to the limit, knowing that what they did must be done in the next hour, as it would be dark by that time, and the men had no provisions for themselves or food for the horses, and there was nobody living within miles that they knew of. During the next four or five miles of the run four more horses were failing and the other four had to leave them. This left only Jack Wilcox, Dock Cosper, Hiram Teague and G. B. Cross. They whipped through some four miles further, when two of their horses gave out, leaving only Hiram Teague and my brother in the chase. By the time the large stars were showing these two caught a glimpse through the scattering timber of what they made sure were the Indians, and made a hard run across a post oak flat to the open prairie; when they reached it, however, nothing was in sight for a mile ahead. It was bright moonlight and they were satisfied the Indians had seen they were gaining fast and had taken to the roughs of the mountains which lay just on the left. The two waited a few minutes, when they were joined by Dock Cosper and Jack Wilcox, and a little later the other four, that had dropped out, came up. Teague and my brother told the boys what they had seen and they also believed the Indians had taken to the mountains. Jack Cosper said "We'll see if we are right or not," and began to ride old Pete around, and in a few minutes Pete put his head to the ground and started right up the mountain, braying, so all were satisfied that the Indians had seen the pursuing party, whom they avoided by keeping little mounds and groves of timber between them. As the posse were without rations and forage and as the Indians would get an all night start on them, they returned to their homes."[2]

And, now, in this story, we bid adieu to the red man in Bell County. For nearly forty years (1834-1870) he had stood across the pathway of the paleface who was all along

[2] F. M. Cross, **Early Days in Central Texas,** pp. 105-8.

endeavoring to seize this land for himself. The Indian had "minded the gap" and stood with bow and arrow taut and tomahawk uplifted. In the words of the immortal Petain, at Verdun, he had said, of the white men, "they shall not pass." The one represented a great people armed with every device that science could produce, the other was a poor savage defending his ancient home with crude and impotent weapons. But behind both, there was the same spirit, the same courage, the same patriotism, the same stoic sense of race injustice and national wrong!

We have ever classed the Indian as an enemy, but he had much cause for his quarrel. His methods were brutal because he knew no other. With places reversed would we not have fought every inch of the ground, with the best weapons at our command?

Many Indians were treacherous and brutal; but there were others who, until betrayed or goaded to retaliation by unthinking and reckless white men, were kind, trustful and the most loyal of friends.

PART III

MATURITY AND MATERIAL PROGRESS

MAP OF BELL COUNTY, 1885

CHAPTER XIII

THE OLD ORDER CHANGES, 1874-1890

1. *The Return to Self-Government*

When Governor Richard Coke and the other Democratic state officials elected with him were inaugurated at Austin in January, 1874, despite the protests of the radical governor, E. J. Davis, the harsh period of reconstruction was over and the control of Texas was once more on the hands of her own people. There was yet one thing more to do—to replace the defective and obnoxious state constitution of 1869 with one in harmony with the traditions and sentiment of the people.

The 14th Legislature called a constitutional convention to meet in Austin on September 6, 1875. In this convention Colonel E. Sterling C. Robertson of Salado represented Bell County. There was a very spirited contest for this position between Colonel Robertson, Dr. A. K. Ramsey and Mr. Ramsey M. Cox; and Mr. Cox bolted the nomination of Colonel Robertson and ran as an independent, but was defeated. The convention met as ordered and finished its labors on November 24. The new constitution was ratified by the people on February 15, 1876, and took effect on April 18. At this same election in February a full set of state, district, county and precinct officers, including senators and representatives in the legislature, was chosen. Governor Coke and his colleagues were re-elected and Democrats were chosen for all other offices, state and local, except in a few counties where the negroes were in the majority. The political power of the Republicans diminished rapidly after 1874 and Texas was said to be "solidly Democratic"; but there was for several years a lively faction of white voters, the "Green-backers," who made politics exciting under the leadership of a number of able and prominent men.

Meanwhile the population of the county was growing. Even during the war years a fair number of families had immigrated into what was still a new country, some of them refugees from parts of Louisiana and Arkansas which had been overrun by the Federal armies. After the war there had been a steady immigration to Texas from the older and more poverty-stricken states of the South and some of these people had come to Bell County to start life over again where good land was cheap and plentiful. The population more than doubled between 1860 and 1870, rising from 4,799 to 9,771. The increase was almost entirely among the whites, for while their numbers had risen from 3,794 to 8,667, the negro population had grown from 1,005 to only 1,104. During the seventies and eighties the tide of immigration was even higher, since the census of 1880 shows 18,783 whites and 1,734 negroes, and that of 1890 lists 30,716 whites and 2,661 negroes.

2. The Founding and Early History of Salado

A brief reference has been made in an earlier chapter to the founding of Salado and Salado College in 1859; but the most important part of the history of this town belongs to the period following the war.

The bold, clear, bubbling springs on the Salado Creek at the crossing of the old military road—later the stage route across the state and now State Highway Number 2 —were well known before the organization of the county. It had been a favorite camping place for the Indians for ages past and of course attracted the attention of the first white men who explored this region. So far as is known, the first white settler was an old man, Archibald Willingham, who with his two sons, Jack and Wilson, and J. C. Ballard, was residing there as early as the fall of 1851.

In 1853 or 1854 Colonel E. Sterling C. Robertson, son of the empresario, Sterling C. Robertson, moved from Austin up to the Salado Springs where he owned several leagues of land which included these springs. Colonel Thomas H. Jones, likewise of Austin, also owned a large amount of land in the vicinity. Robertson acquired the Willingham cabin and afterward erected a large two-story dwelling built in the colonial style. Other settlers soon came in, purchased land from Colonel Robertson, opened up farms and built homes. Among them were N. M. Proctor, W. L. Pearce and Dr. Wm. R. Alexander. None of them lived at the Springs, for Colonel Robertson's family was the only one residing there at this time, but all lived within a range of three or four miles. In the neighborhood of what is now Prairie Dell, four or five miles south of the springs, there were in the middle fifties

Dr. Louis A. Ogle, Dr. Carroll Kendrick, A. W. Cearnel, J. C. Bonner, W. R. Warrick, Charles Holsworth, W. A. Pace, Mrs. Edrington, Robert B. Halley and others. A small school house built of rawhide lumber was erected near J. C. Bonner's home and Wm. Carroll Sypert, of Milam County, and possibly others, taught there for a while.

The founding of the town of Salado was the result of and coincident with the establishment of Salado College. A historical sketch of this famous college will be given in a later chapter. It is sufficient here to say that it was first decided upon at a "tent meeting" held at the Salado Springs on October 8, 1859, which was attended not only by residents of that vicinity but by many from Belton and other sections of the county. Colonel Robertson, a moving spirit of the enterprise, donated one hundred acres of land to the college, part of it to be laid out for a town and sold. A joint stock company was organized; the land was surveyed out into blocks, lots and streets, and some of it was sold that fall and winter. On February 8, 1860, the legislature passed an act incorporating Salado College for a period of twenty years. In the meantime a temporary school building had been erected and plans drawn for a stone building for the college. Families began moving into the new town at once and very soon new houses were going up—some of logs, some of the local limestone and a few others of pine lumber hauled from mills near Bastrop. Within a few months after the "tent meeting" Salado had become a promising little settlement.

Among the families there, besides Colonel Robertson's, we may recall those of Colonel Hermon Aiken, Melville Wilkerson, A. W. Cearnal, Captain R. B. Halley, Simeon Bramlet, Horatio Shelton, Amos Rowland, ... McLaughlin, James Anderson, R. B. Renick, J. W. Vickery, ... Moore, Henry Hellerman, and others. During the next year or two came Col. John T. Flint, Dr. J. A. Ewing, Mrs. Abigail Leach, O. H. Bigham Prof. James L. Smith, Wm. B. Armstrong, J. H. Anderson, C. H. Stuart, and others. During the latter part of the War, there came Judge O. T. Tyler, Wm. A. Davis, Capt. A. J. Harris, John T. Eubank, Rev. .... Brown, C. H. Stuart, Mrs. .... Nichols, and others. During the next few years after the war, many other families came, including Rev. .... Brown, Dr. Welborn Barton, William Taylor, Dr. B. D. McKie, ... Kitchen, Rev. Wm. K.

Hamblen, Dr. H. H. Parker, Capt. J. H. Barbee, J. T. Lyles, Morgan Walters, Col. Thos. H. Jones, John H. Orgain, Mrs. .... Jenkins, James Talbot, W. D. Copeland, Judge W. H. Garrett, Alvin A. Walden, E. N. Dunlap, L. A. Griffith, J. H. Stith, S. Guthrie, Dr. D. H. Armstrong, Robert McAllister, M. H. Buckles, E. R. A. Buckles, Cyrus Eastland, John Hendrickson, Jesse Pitts, Jno. E. King, J. E. Mabry, Rev. Jno. W. **Hunton**, Noah Sand, Capt. M. W. Damron, Dr. J. J. Gregory, C. H. Ramsdell, J. W. Redding, Thos. Riggs, Rev. Geo. W. Baines, J. N. Crass, J. F. Fuller, Wm. P. Hancock, Rev. W. T. Bush, Capt. Geo. A. Smith, A. J. Rose, John W. Ray, Rev. W. K. Dickinson, Capt. Fowler, Campbell Longley, Thos. G. Butler, Arthur Maugham, J. M. G. Davis, Mrs. Dean, Willis J. King, A. M. White, Rev. M. W. Blackwell, Rev. W. A. Elledge, Byron D. Bassil, J. L. Bailey, W. H. Harkey, S. H. Harkey, S. H. Walker, ...Creekmore and many others.

These early families of Salado were of excellent quality. Many of them were people of education and refinement; all were appreciative of the value to their children of good schools and good society. They were a sober, honest, industrious and intelligent group who gave to their beautiful little town a reputation for a high character that was unsurpassed at that time by any community of the state.

The history of early Salado is so intertwined with that of the College that it is difficult to write of one without telling of the other; but there are a few incidents and developments with which the College was not directly concerned that deserve attention. But first something should be said of the physical settling of the town. It is situated at the eastern edge of the famous geological line, the Balcones Fault. The creek from which it takes its name,[1] after draining a large area between the hills to the southwest, turns eastward some distance above the town and flows down between high cliffs, from which it emerges at the town. The valley of the creek was orig-

---

[1] The creek has retained the Spanish pronunciation of "Sä lä' o" or "Salow," as more corruptly pronounced. It means "salty" and is supposed to have swapped names in some mysterious fashion with the Lampasas. This seems unlikely; but as the water of the Salado is never salty, it is difficult to explain the origin of the name. The name of the town has been anglicized, thus: "Sa la' do."

inally covered by giant pecan, elm, and oak trees, and the stream itself, fed by perpetual springs, rippled along over its rocky bottom in constant music. The springs were mostly along the south bank a few steps away from the main stream into which they discharged. Of those within the town limits, the farthest down stream was Anderson Spring, named for Dr. Anderson who conducted the school in 1861-1862 and who built his house about seventy-five yards east of the spring. Next above was the Elm Spring, named for a large elm tree which stood near it. Next, just below the military crossing, was the Big Boiling Spring (at first called the Robertson Spring), which came up in a large gushing column more than a foot high and formed a brook six or eight feet wide and eight or ten inches deep that flowed through a rock-bound channel to the creek some thirty or forty feet away. This spring has since been partly choked up and its waters now flow out through several orifices in the porous rock. Some two or three hundred yards still farther up-stream is the one now known as the Robertson Spring which rises in the private grounds of the Robertson estate and flows through a beautiful little tree-bordered brook nearly a hundred yards into the creek. This is the only one which has been protected from the careless ravages of man and still maintains its pristine loveliness. Farther on are other springs, too far away for public use, but well known to all the boys who wandered and waded up and down the crystal waters of the Salado. These springs, coming out through the Balcones Fault, belong to the great series which extends from the Rio Grande at Del Rio through San Antonio, New Braunfels, San Marcos, Austin, Salado, Shanklin's mill on the Lampasas River and the town of Lampasas.

The old swimming holes on the Salado were the joy of the school boys of the old days and a pleasant memory forever. Among them were the "Long Hole" about half a mile below town, the "Blue Hole" just below the Anderson Spring, the "Perch Hole" just below the Big Boiling Spring, the "Calico Hole" and the "Robertson Hole" some little distance above the ford. Just below town on the southeast side of the creek, and a few yards below the Davis mill-dam, Table Rock reared its broad head fully twenty-five feet above the creek bed. It was a favorite resort for picnics and a trysting place for lovers; and its surface became covered with names, initials, mottoes and verses carved through half a century by the hands of generations of young people who found romance there at sunset and by moonlight in the sound of the murmuring waters. But, like most of the noble forest trees that once bordered the banks of the Salado, the old Table Rock is gone. It was swept down by the floods many years ago and now lies prostrate on the stream-bed below.

For several years after the town was laid out the citidens of Salado crossed the shallow creek by stepping from rock to rock, or on logs laid across the wider places. These logs were chained to the rocks and would swing downstream during freshets and be replaced when the flood subsided. But when in 1866 a dam was thrown across the stream at the lower end of the village, the water was backed up over the rocks. Then for a time "foot logs," raised on legs standing in the water and chained to the rocks below were used; but they were very narrow, rickety and unsafe, and pedestrians not infrequently tumbled off into the water. A general demand arose for a bridge. To meet this problem as well as others, it was decided to incorporate the village. Application for incorporation was made under the general law, and the county court, in January, 1867, authorized an election for town officers. On February 23, Judge O. T. Tyler was elected mayor and a board of aldermen was chosen. These officials appointed the other officers, among them Colonel Thos. H. Jones as treasurer. The town officials first tried to raise funds for a bridge by voluntary donations, but finding they could not raise enough by this means, on December 3, 1868, they ordered an issue of bonds. Here is a copy of one of these bonds, printed on blue paper in ordinary type, except that the words underscored were written in with pen and ink:

No. **Twelve** (12)

The Town of Salado, for value received, will pay to........................, or bearer, **fifty** Dollars with 10 per cent per annum interest from date. One fourth of said amount, and interest thereon, payable on the 5th day of July, A. D. 1869, and the balance in three equal installments from that date. Receivable for all Taxes and Dues to the Corporation of Salado. Issued by authority of an ordinance passed December 3, 1868. This **fifth** day of **January** A. D. **1869.**

    Thos. H. Jones   **O. T. Tyler**
       Treasurer   Mayor
U. S. Internal Revenue—5 cents.

The bonds were all purchased by the citizens of the town. Then, with the proceeds and the subscriptions, amounting in all to some $2,500, the municipal authorities proceeded to build a wire cable suspension foot-bridge of substantial construction, of unique design and of graceful proportions. Two large galvanized rope-wire cables, anchored at each end in strongly built stone abutments, were carried over two double-turretted dressed-stone piers of towers. From these suspended cables wire cords extended down to catch and support the ends of sawed cedar cross-bars or joists on which the plank floor was laid. It was one of the first, probably the very first, of its kind in the Southwest and was designed, engineered and constructed entirely by home talent—by Judge Tyler, Colonel Thos. H. Jones, Judge Wm. H. Garrett, Wm. A. Davis, John Hendrickson and others. It swung some twenty feet above the water and although it could be made to sway enough from side to side to frighten timid souls—especially groups of squealing girls when mischievous boys chose this method of teasing them—it served the people well for more than thirty years. After the county built a combination wagon and foot bridge a few yards upstream the suspension bridge gradually fell into disuse. In 1913 it was finally swept away when a cloud-burst in the upper water-shed of Salado Creek sent down a terrific flood that carried away the county bridge as well. The latter was promptly rebuilt, only to be carried away again in the still greater flood of September 9 and 10, 1921.

The annals of Salado would not be complete without some reference to the mill-dam controversy. On August 25, 1863, the board of trustees of Salado College authorized the President of the Board to sell the land belonging to the College on the north side of the creek and to grant the privilege of using the water of the creek for milling or other purposes, provided no dam should be built so high as to overflow the springs along the creek bank from which the people got their drinking water. By a deed dated August 28, 1863, the president conveyed the land, with the privilege and limitation above set out, to Mr. John T. Flint. Mr. Flint afterward sold the land to Wm. H. Stinnett and he to Mr. Wm. A. Davis with the same privileges and restrictions. Mr. Davis, for the purpose of operating a wool carding machine, put in a log dam which was found to overflow the Anderson and Elm springs. When his attention was called to this, he lowered the water by cutting a notch in the log. This dam washed away and a rock dam was constructed, higher than the log dam and this overflowed the springs. The citizens remonstrated, but their complaints were disregarded. A mass meeting appointed a committee, consisting of Rev. Jas. E. Ferguson, N. M. Proctor and D. F. Hair, all residing several miles outside of town, to examine the springs and report to another meeting of citizens how far, if at all, Mr. Davis had violated his privilege. They reported the springs overflowed, at the time of their examination, from 8 to 10 inches. Afterward, Mr. Davis erected another rock dam, lower down the stream, which raised the water at the springs higher than had the preceding one. Again he was requested to lower the dam to the limit of his deed but declined to do so. In the meantime Mr. Davis put in other machinery for grinding grain and ginning cotton, and doubtless required more water power for its operation.

On January 3, 1870, a petition of some twenty-nine citizens of Salado and patrons of the College came before the Board of Trustees, complaining that the erection of this dam was to their great injury and in violation of the terms of the deed. The Board appointed a committee of five members to inquire into the matter, to confer with Mr. Davis, to furnish him a copy of the petition and to report back to the Board. They reported in substance that the lower springs were overflowed two feet when the dam was full, and recommended that Mr. Davis be required to lower the dam in compliance with the restrictions of the deed. The report was adopted February 28, 1870, and the president was required to communicate this action to Mr. Davis. The president reported on March 2 that Mr. Davis had offered to cut the footway off the dam in order to bring it down with a level of the water when running over the water way and to wall up the two springs on the town tract and put a storm cap over them to keep the mud from running into them. Unwilling to accept this proposal, the Board appointed a committee to collect all the facts in the case and to lay them before competent legal counsel for an opinion, and, on September 14, 1870, instituted suit in the District Court of Bell County, on behalf of Salado College against Mr. W. A. Davis for the reduction of the dam. The first trial resulted in a hung jury, the second (October, 1871) resulted in a verdict

Salado in the early seventies. A painting by Mrs. J. D. Law, based in part upon an old photograph. The view is southward down the street which was also the old stage road. Salado College is in the background.

The Old Order Changes

against the College and in favor of Mr. Davis for $750 attorney's fees, as damages for bringing suit. On appeal to the Supreme Court this judgment was reversed and set aside and the case was remanded for a new trial in the District Court. On April 2, 1878, a verdict was rendered for the College, requiring the dam to be lowered eight inches. This judgment was executed by the Sheriff of Bell County under order of the Court, the dam being so reduced in height. Some reports were that the dam was soon after raised again to the same height as before, but this fact is not vouched for. The mill was operated for several years after all this litigation and, passing into other ownership, was finally, in the late eighties, abandoned. In the flood of 1913, the dam disappeared and has never been restored.

Of course, this controversy caused some friction for a time, but when the College was re-chartered, in 1882, all factions agreed to bury the past and work together; and we find members of the old Board of Trustees (who acted for the College in this litigation) and Mr. Davis, sitting together as colleagues in the new Board and the old-time harmony and good will prevailing.

In January, 1874, the Board of Trustees took steps to organize a public free school district for Salado and vicinity, so that the pupils of the College, within the free school age, should have the benefit of that fund, though attending the College. Major A. J. Rose, Judge John E. King and Dr. D. H. Armstrong became trustees of the public school for the district and co-operated closely and harmoniously with the College trustees in carrying out this purpose.

On February 7, 1874, there was a mass meeting of the citizens of Salado, who appointed "a delegation of three citizens to visit Austin and make known to the Legislature," then in session, "the advantages of Salado as an educational point and to secure, if possible, the location at Salado of some one of the State institutions of learning that may probably be located at this session."

Immediately after the mass meeting, the Board of Trustees met at the college and unanimously adopted a resolution "that the Board of Trustees cooperate with the meeting of the citizens of Salado in the contemplated movement and that the President of the Board of Trustees be fully authorized and is hereby requested to visit Austin and make known to the proper committees of the Legislature and members thereof the advantages of Salado as an educational point, as regards centrality to the people of the State of Texas, its accessibility at all seasons of the year by a daily line of stages, its freedom from epidemics and its known healthfulness, its inexhaustible supply of fine stone for building purposes, and its abundant supply of pure and limpid water for drinking, as well as for milling, manufacturing and irrigating purposes, and to secure the location at this point of at least one of the three State institutions that the Legislature may possibly locate at the present session, viz: The State University, The Agricultural and Mechanical College, and the Normal School—and to ascertain upon what terms the above objects may be secured, if at all, and report to this Board at as early a day as possible."

But the Legislature did not act upon these matters. The Sam Houston Normal Institute was located by the Act of April 21, 1879, upon the site, in Huntsville, of old Austin College—the latter having shortly before been moved to Sherman. The Constitution of 1876 provided that the University of Texas should be located by a vote of the people of the State, and the Agricultural and Mechanical College of Texas, established by an Act of the Legislature passed April 17, 1871, and located in the County of Brazos, was therein made and constituted a branch of the University. Under the Act of March 30, 1881, an election for the location of the University was held throughout the State on the first Tuesday in September (September 6), 1881. At this election the town of Salado, having been duly placed in nomination, received a gratifying complimentary vote; but Austin received a large majority of the votes of the State. Waco and other places were also in nomination.

There has been for many years a wide-spread tradition to the effect that "Salado came within one vote of being selected as the capital of the State." There is no foundation whatever for this claim. It doubtless grew out of the fact that Salado competed in the State election for the location of the University, as stated above. The election for locating the State capital was in 1872. The writer resided in Salado at that time and is positive that Salado was not in that contest and could not have received such a vote. Furthermore, the records of that election show that Salado was not among the places voted on.

Until the early eighties Salado ranked next to Belton in both size and importance among the towns of the county. The College gave it prestige and its merchants did a thriving business over a large part of the southern half of the county. But when the Santa Fe and the M. K. & T. railroads came through north and east of Salado the new railroad towns drew away most of this trade and the College itself was forced to close in 1885. Thereafter the town steadily declined. Some of the merchants closed their stores and moved away. Many families, but especially the more ambitious of the younger generation who saw little to hold them in a decaying town, moved to other towns or to western Texas. Many of the farmers near by sold their farms and were replaced by tenant farmers. The once beautiful little village gradually showed poverty; and social decline accompanied economic decay. The traveler who hurries through the place now in his automobile, barely glancing at abandoned or dilapidated houses, the crumbling walls of the old College and the denuded banks of the spring-fed creek, can have no conception of what Salado was like in its best days.

3. *Cattle Drives and the Old Trail through Bell County*

Unitl the late seventies and early eighties, when the introduction of barbed wire enabled the farmers to fence the prairie lands, and the coming of the railroads provided transportation to markets for crops, the chief industry was stock-raising. Cattle and horses could be driven to market. Prior to the Civil War the principal markets for Texas beef cattle had been New Orleans, Alexandria and Shreveport. Even in those days, however, a few herds were driven to St. Louis or Chicago. The late Captain Sam W. Bishop, an early settler of Bell County, used to relate that he once, as a cowboy, before the war, went through to Chicago with a herd of cattle, purchased a buggy with his wages, hitched his cow ponies to it, and drove back overland to his Bell County home.

But the business of driving cattle from Texas to the northwest markets developed after the close of the Civil War and lasted from 1866 to about 1885. Those were the days of the great drives "up the trail" to Kansas and to the new western ranges of Wyoming and the Dakotas. So much has been written in recent years of these great drives that only a sketch is necessary here. The suspension of nearly all business during the war could but result in almost universal poverty. But while the men had been away in the army, the range cattle of Texas had multiplied, and the state was overstocked with them. In the North the supply had been depleted and cattle were in good demand. About 1866 a few of the more important cattle owners began driving beef steers to southern Kansas where new railroads were extending westward into the plains and toward the Pacific. At Abilene, Ellsworth, Dodge City and other new railroad towns, buyers from Chicago, Kansas City and other packing centers bought the herds as they arrived at prices which gave good profits to the cattlemen. Trail-driving soon became a great business. The herds, numbering from one thousand to two or even three thousand, were driven slowly northward in the spring, feeding on the grass, and fattening as they moved along.

The old-time Texas cowboy was then in flower. Nearly every young man in Texas knew how to ride a horse and how to handle cattle. The long drive up the trail had a special lure for him and it was the ambition of every boy to make the trip. Danger and hardship were as nothing to him. The regular cowboy wore bright-colored woolen hunting shirts, high-heeled boots, breeches running inside his bootlegs, a broad-brimmed sombrero, a big red bandana around his neck, spurs with large rowels, a sixshooter and bowie-knife in his belt, and carried a long rawhide or leather plaited cow-whip, while a lariat looped from his saddle horn. He certainly looked like a "bad man"; but usually he was, with all this toggery, a brave kind-hearted generous fellow. The general outfit consisted of a herd boss, some ten or fifteen cowboys, four or five extra ponies to each man, a horse-wrangler, a cook, and a chuck-wagon which carried not only the cooking equipment and staple foods but the extra bedding and clothing. The drive from the Guadalupe River in southcentral Texas to the railroad termini in Kansas normally took about two months, but the time consumed depended upon the condition of grass, water, weather and other factors. High water in the rivers, stampedes of the wild "longhorns" or troubles with Indians might cause unusual delays. Arrived at last at the objective, the herd was held out in the opened range until sold. Then the cowboys, weary of the trail and thirsting for excitement, received their wages and turned themselves loose in the "wild and wooly" cowtown. Saloons, dance halls and gambling houses welcomed them until their money was spent. Sometimes they got into trouble with the town marshals and police, and there was a gun-battle. These affairs were so frequent that something like a feud developed between the Kansans and the Texans. The wild orgies ended, and wages spent, the cowboys rode back to the Texas ranch to work till the next year's drive. Some few had enough foresight to save their money, invest it in cattle back home and eventually become drovers themselves.

The old cattle-trail from South Texas came through Bell County. It entered near Prairie Dell, ran through Salado and Belton and passed out of the county in the direction of Waco—in other words, it followed in a general way the old Austin, Salado, Belton and Waco stage road. At Salado the herd came right through the heart of the town and crossed the Salado Creek at the big boiling spring, just below the present highway bridge. The citizens of Salado erected a stone fence around the spring, in a half-circle, in order to prevent the cattle from tramping and muddying the approaches, for this spring was the principal water supply for the people there. The trail crossed the Lampasas at the old Shaw Crossing, a few hundred yards below the present bridge on the Belton and Austin road—now Highway No. 2. Entering Belton near the southeast corner of the then corporate limits, the trail crossed Nolan Creek at the Confederate Park, and thence passed through the eastern section of the town, about where the compress and oil mill now stand, to an intersection with the Belton and Waco road—now the Belton and Temple Pike—at Sixth Avenue. The section thus traversed was then mostly open and unoccupied. The trail followed the Belton and Waco road across the Leon (fording that stream) and a mile or two beyond, then struck out on the high divide toward the heads of Cedar and Elm Creeks in the general direction of Waco.

The Driscolls, Days, Houstons, Colonel Seth Mabry, the Millets, "Shanghai" Pearce, the Snyders, Major George W. Littlefield and many others are remembered as the owners of numerous great herds that went over this old trail from South and Southwest Texas. Besides these, herds were made up almost every year in Bell County and driven to Kansas. Silas Baggett, Loss Williams and Theodore Vanness were among those who went with cattle up this trail. Their cowboys were Bell County youngsters who knew all the technique of the cattle game. Some of them still linger with us and well remember the thrilling episodes of those great bovine migrations.

Those drives are best remembered for the thrill of adventure that was inseparable from them. But they were an important part of our history for another reason. They brought millions of dollars in cash into Texas at a time when the people were poor and the country in need of money for the rapid development that was coming. Most of the fortunes of that day were founded on cattle. But long after the last of these fortunes has dissipated, the glamor of the old trail will endure for the coming generations who will read of the hardships and sufferings endured in the management of the wild cattle, and the dangers encountered from the Indian, the Jayhawker and the outlaws of the plains—all of which the cowboy had to meet with cool judgment, undaunted courage and vigorous action. The plumed Knight of the Crusades had no more of steady purpose, endurance and courage than the Knight of the Sombrero and the Jingling Spurs!

The building of railroads into the cattle country during the early eighties and the erection of barbed wire fences on farms and ranches as the tide of population rolled westward across the state soon put an end to the long drives. The Texas and Pacific, the Missouri, Kansas and Texas, the International and Great Northern, the Gulf, Colorado and Santa Fe, and the Houston and Texas Central Railroads furnished quicker, if not cheaper, transportation to the northern markets. The "Old Cattle Trail" soon became a mere tradition.

4. *The Spread of Farming: Barbed Wire and Wind-Mills*

In the meantime, Bell County was itself being transformed from a stock-growing into an agricultural community. In its earlier years it had been, perforce, a stock country because there had been no cheap and ready means of fencing in fields on its wide-spread prairie lands. For a farmer to cut cedar rails or poles in the mountains, or to split rails out of the oaks along the streams, haul them to the prairie and build fences—the old Virginia "worm fence, staked and ridered"—sufficient to keep out the range cattle and horses from the growing crops involved the labor of himself and family for many years. Until the fence should be completed the fields had to be guarded from stock day and night. Another impediment to prairie farming was the fact that over large areas there was no surface water supply for man or beast except in the rainy season or during very wet years; and even the range stock during seasons of drought had to go to the streams for water. The old-timers will remember that well-to-do people who had no spring near by built great subterranean plastered cisterns to catch and hold rain-water for drinking purposes, while poorer families placed one or two empty barrels to catch the rain from the roof. Often the "wiggletails" had to be strained out before the water could be used. In times of drought, drinking water had to be hauled from some spring or stream. Under these conditions, therefore, there were but few prairie farms and they were small.

There were croakers and chronic pessimists, of course, who said that Bell County, because of droughts and scarcity of surface water, was unfit for farming and would never be anything but a stock country. But when, in the seventies, barbed fencing wire was invented and came on the market, and machinery for drilling deep wells on the prairies was perfected, a great change began which in a few years turned our open stock ranges into productive farms and dotted the prairies with the homes of a great farming population. The first well drills were small affairs, run by horse power, and were useful only where water could be found at comparatively shallow depths; but in the late eighties heavier drills run by steam came into use and water could be reached in any section of the county. Wind mills and water tanks also became common. With the problems of fencing and water solved, and railroads coming into the county, there was a new rush of immigration.

The new settlers came from the lower counties of Texas and from all of the southern and many of the western states. A large number of families from Washington county settled on the lower reaches of Elm Creek and on Camp Creek and many Germans and Bohemians also came to that section of Bell County. They, or their descendants, are still there in relatively large numbers. Quite a number of German farmers also came into the Bartlett and Killeen sections of the county and have maintained their distinctive communities. All have their own churches —the German Lutheran—and adhere to many of their social and family customs. Nearly all of them are good citizens and live peaceably side by side with their Anglo-Saxon neighbors.

As the unoccupied prairie yielded to the plow of the newcomer, the price of land steadily advanced. It became too valuable for grazing. The stockraiser either disposed of his surplus animals to western ranchmen and became a farmer, or sold his land to newly arrived immigrants, loaded his family and their belongings in wagons and, herding his stock together, trekked to the boundless plains of the great West and there started ranch-life anew. The black-land prairies were rapidly enclosed with barbed wire, and the day of open range and free grass passed in the eastern half of the county. Nevertheless, in the early eighties, there was a great increase in the sheep business on the thinner hill lands in the western half of Bell County.

The expansion of farming in the county is best shown by the following table, which is compiled from the Census of the United States:

	1869	1879	1889
Acres of improved land	27,927	200,034	378,355
Number of farms	640	2,231	4,249
Average improved acreage per farm	43.63	89.66	89.04
Bushels of corn raised	358,360	402,322	1,521,681
Bushels of wheat raised	3,660	84,267	20,936
Bales of cotton	2,896	9,217	37,473

These figures tell much of the story. The reader will note not only the great increase of land under cultivation and of total crop yields (except of wheat during the second decade), but also the average increase in the size of improved farms. This last was doubtless due to the greater use of labor-saving machinery, such as riding plows, cultivators and threshers. The rise and decline of wheat growing, as well as the rapid growth of cotton production, calls for a brief comment. Before the railroads reached into central Texas, Bell County people had grown all their own breadstuffs, as well as feed for such stock as did not run on the open range, and were able to sell most of the surplus to immigrants. They did not grow much cotton, for the expense of hauling it by wagon to the far-off markets of Houston or Galveston was too great. During the seventies numerous small flour mills in the county enabled them to convert wheat into flour, which was hauled to the counties below and sold there. When the railroads reached the county in the early eighties they began to bring in cheaper flour from the great northern mills and the growing of local wheat declined. The same railroads furnished a cheaper outlet for the more profitable cotton, which rapidly became the "money crop."

At this point mention should be made of the numerous small flour and grist mills which were to be found along the streams from the late sixties to the early eighties. They were nearly all run by water power. The Salado was especially well adapted to milling, and had more mills than any other stream in the county. The oldest one on this creek was Ferguson's Mill. It had first been built by Ira E. and Whitfield Chalk in 1849 or 1850 and after some years had been owned and operated by Mr. James P. Reed. The Reverend James E. Ferguson bought it in 1867 and ran it until his death in 1876. It was then carried on for many years by his family. In 1866 Mr. W. A. Davis, formerly of Round Rock, built a mill and dam on this creek a little way below the big springs at the town of Salado. At first it was a wool-carding establishment but was later converted into a flour and grist mill. In the same year John Meyers erected a mill several miles further down on the Salado, which later passed through the hands of several owners but is best remembered as Summer's Mill. Other mills built on this stream were Dulaney's (1867), T. J. Jones' (1869), Stinnett and Orgain's (1874)—later known as Stinnett's and finally as the Highland Mill—and "Ike" (Isaac V.) Jones' Mill (1880). On the Lampasas, after the little pioneer Childers' Mill, built in 1848, which later was improved and enlarged as Shanklin's Mill, came Guthrie's (1870) and W. K. Hamblen's (1871). Before or during the Civil War several small mills had been built on the Leon and Nolan, but they had been abandoned soon after the war closed. The Belton Flouring Mill was erected in 1866 by James P. Reed, N. M. Whitson and George M. McWhirter. A steam saw mill, later converted into a flour and grist mill was built by Major A. J. Rose on the north side of Cow House Creek, about a mile above Sparta, in 1868 or 1869. It was sold to Wm. O'Hair and his son, J. O'Hair, about 1870. A few years later they disposed of it to Robert M. Little. Most of these old mills are now in ruins, their walls tumbled in, their dams broken by floods, their mill-races choked up with debris, mute witnesses of the changes that have come over our county.

Throughout most of this period the crops were good. The prairie soil was virgin and extremely fertile; the boll weevil and cotton flea had not made their appearance and the pestiferous Johnson grass had never been heard of. Cotton proved a more dependable crop than corn for it was less affected by early summer droughts. For instance, after drought had ruined the corn in 1882, late summer rains produced more cotton than could be picked and much of it was plowed under during the winter in preparation for the next year's planting. But good yields even of cotton could not continue indefinitely. All the old-timers will remember the droughts of 1886 and 1887. In the winter and spring of the former year there was no rain. The early summer passed without relief and the corn failed completely. Late in the summer scattered showers saved some of the cotton, but the crop was very short. The drought continued through the next winter and spring. The small streams dried up and those farmers and stockmen who had no wells or windmills found it difficult to get water for stock. The first copious rain, on June 4, 1887, was too late for corn, but ensured a better cotton crop than in the previous year. In the newly settled counties to the west of us, however, there was practically no rain throughout the three years, 1885, 1886 and 1887. For miles no green thing was to be seen except a few shriveled leaves on the trees. Thousands of families were ruined, and most of them moved back to the lower country. Although Bell was in better condition than the western counties, many of our people fell so heavily in debt that they moved back to the eastern and southern sections of the state. But the great drought did not stop the development of the country, for in succeeding years the crops were good and more immigrants came to take the places of those who had moved away.

Top: Stinnett's Mill on the Salado Creek. The wooden structure was added at a later date to store grain. This mill was built from native limestone, and has a large room downstairs with beamed bur oak ceiling and a great stone fireplace.

Bottom: The dam of Summer's Mill. This is all that is left of the original mill which was next to the last mill along the Salado. A new mill building constructed three years ago now stands on the site of the original, and the same dam serves to run it. This was the only rock dam along the stream.

5. *The Grange*

Back in the seventies the farmers had a great national organization, styled the "Patrons of Husbandry." It was commonly called "The Grange," and its members were referred to as "Grangers." The organization covered the farming district of the whole United States, and at one time its membership numbered hundreds of thousands. It comprised a National Grange, a State Grange in each state, a County Grange in each county, and local Granges in the communities.

Bell County pioneered the movement in this State. Salado Grange, No. 1, opened in the summer of 1873, was the first Grange organized in Texas. Among its charter members were A. J. Rose, O. T. Tyler, William P. Hancock, J. F. Fuller, John S. Rogers, L. A. Griffith, N. L. Norton, Wm. J. Caskey, Joe W. Love and many others.

The order soon spread rapidly over Bell County and throughout the State. County Granges were set up and then the State Grange, all in 1873. Wm. W. Lang of Marlin became the first Grand Worthy Patron of the State Grange. By 1878 the membership had become so large and its political power so great that Mr. Lang became a candidate for governor before the Democratic State Convention, on the Grange or farmers' ticket.[1] Lang resigned the leadership of the State Grange about 1882 and was succeeded by A. J. Rose, as Grand Worthy Patron. The order prospered for some ten or twelve years before it was largely superseded by a radical and active organization, the "Farmers' Alliance."

The leading objects of the Grange organization were co-operation among farmers in the marketing of produce and in the purchase of farm supplies, implements, building materials, etc.; the bringing nearer together of the producer and consumer and the doing away with the "middle-man"; better provisions for education—especially agricultural education; the social uplift of the farmer and his family; a strong code of morals; law and order; lower taxes; and

---

[1] The convention became "locked" between Lang, Governor Richard B. Hubbard, Ex-Governor James W. Throckmorton, and Judge Thomas J. Devine. After balloting several days without a choice, under the old two-thirds rule, the contending elements finally compromised on Judge Oran M. Roberts, the "Old Alcalde."

greater participation by farmers in making the laws. And during those days it was the usual stunt for politicians to cater to the Granger vote and to identify themselves with the political demands of the farmers.

The first incorporated Grange store in the State was started in Salado, whence others, too, spread all over Texas. They flourished for a time, but at last, with drouths and hard times, they went upon the financial rocks.

The Texas Cooperative Association, a rather ambitious enterprise, also organized and incorporated at Salado, set up its office in Galveston with Mr. John S. Rogers, of Salado, as manager. Its mission was to receive, by consignment, cotton and other farm products from the farmers (through their local Grange Stores) all over the State; to sell these products direct to spinners' agents and exporters; to purchase, at wholesale prices, the supplies of all kinds required by the farmers, consigning such purchase, in car-load lots, to the local Grange stores, where they were to be distributed among members and customers. To pay its overhead expenses the Association charged a small fixed commission upon all transactions. It was well planned, and for many years was a decided success. Even after the Grange was superseded by the "Alliance," the latter organization used the facilities of the Grange Agency at Galveston.

The local Grange stores and the Texas Co-operative Association were all based theoretically upon *spot cash* transactions, for they had but little capital and could not extend credit. When droughts and other calamities visited the farmers they were forced back to the credit accommodations offered by the regular merchants, and these co-operative enterprises, handling only cash transactions, lost a large per cent of the business of even their own membership. In a one-crop country the cash or "pay as you go" system seems to be impracticable, however well managed.

The Texas Farmer was launched by William P. Hancock and J. F. Fuller, of Salado, about 1880. It was devoted to the interests of the farmers generally and of the Patrons of Husbandry in particular. At first it was printed at the office of *The Belton Courier* in Belton, but later equipped its own print shop in Belton, where it was edited and managed by J. F. Fuller. The paper became the official organ of the State Grange, and enjoyed a state-wide circulation. Later it was moved to Dallas and there it was edited and managed by Wm. A. Shaw, generally known as "Farmer Shaw," who made it an influential factor with the press and with the farmers of Texas.

Such an organization, with an overwhelming farmer vote throughout the State, was, of course, catered to and preyed upon by politicians, within and without the membership; and what with the financial straits of the individual farmers and the arrival of a new organization, the Farmers' Alliance, the Grange gradually disappeared as an active body.

The Order still exists in other parts of the United States and still holds well attended National Grange meetings; but it no longer exists in Texas, so far as is known to the writer.

The membership included all members of the farmer's family—men, women and children (above a certain age)—and all of them participated in the Grange meetings held in halls or rooms prepared for the purpose. The meetings were secret and were conducted on the lodge plan, with a ritual for the initiation of new members and installation of officers. While women as well as men held office in the Grange, the more responsible active duties in that body were performed by the men of the Order.

The Grange did much to promote social intercourse among farmers and their families, brought about a more general habit of reading and investigation, especially along economic lines, and induced broader thinking and a more liberal attitude in the minds of a great body of citizens whose outlook had been too much limited by the hard routine of life on the farm. Though now no longer functioning in Texas, the Grange left its imprint, virile and lasting, upon the period.

6. *The Break-up of an Outlaw Gang*

Some ugly things have occurred in our county as they have in all new communities. On the night of Monday May 25, 1874, was an occurrence which shocked this community and the whole State.

While the transition from the demoralizing effects of the Civil War, with its political and moral chaos, to a more orderly and peaceful state of affairs was going on, there were those who resented the better standards of conduct, who persisted in the defiance of law and order, and who were making their last determined stand against the restoration of normal social conditions. Many of these men were old offenders, comprising all sorts of outlawry in their catalogue of crimes. Thieves, robbers, murderers and ex-convicts were holding high carnival all over the western frontier or border counties and the people stood in awe of them. These troubles grew out of the conditions which followed after the war. There was a chain of outlaws from Red River to the lower Rio Grande, and all along the intervening country there were allies to harbor and protect them. And when a fine horse was stolen by one of the band of thieves it was passed along to another until it could be disposed of at some place far distant. A murderer or robber was harbored, secreted and protected until he could pass down the line beyond danger of arrest, or, if arrested, the gang devised a way, by deception or false swearing or by a mob attack on the prison, to effect his release. Courthouses and jails seemed to be—and indeed were—impotent to bring these infamous rascals to the penalties of the law. The mountainous cedar brakes, then almost a wilderness, extending along the western border of Bell and Coryell Counties—on the Salado, Lampasas, Cow House, Bear Creek, Owl Creek, and the dense thickets along the Leon in both counties—offered them a secure retreat and rendezvous from which it was impossible to rout them—especially with the aid and comfort given them by some unworthy settlers. The good people of all these counties were intensely aroused but were powerless, for their lives and their property were alike at the mercy of these outlaw gangs. At last, by the diligence of our sheriff, Captain Robert B. Halley, and his deputies, ten of these desperate fellows were collected at one time in the jail of Bell County—a very insecure prison. The charges against them included murder, robbery and horse-theft, and against some of them several charges were pending. Of their guilt there was really no question or doubt. On the night of May 25, 1874—when the Sheriff was away on his official duties—the sound of horses' feet, pounding upon the hard roads and streets, was heard by the quiet citizens of Belton. They came by tens and twenties from different directions. It was the work of but a few minutes to bind the jailer, who refused to surrender the keys, to batter down the doors and to riddle nine of the choice specimens confined in the slatted iron cage with a fusilade of bullets. All were shot dead in a moment. Their names were John Alexander (alias Daily), William Henry Grumbles, William S. Smith, J. S. McDonald, Marion McDonald, ... Wingfield, ... Beckneal, ... Crow, Loyd Coleman. All were charged with horse stealing except Coleman, who was accused of having murdered his wife. One of the proscribed gang, Tyre Thompson, being on the sick list, had been placed on a cot in an adjoining room. He was overlooked by the mob and thus escaped death, but he later faced a jury and received a life sentence.

This was, of course, a drastic and regrettable thing. It sent a thrill of horror throughout the State; but it also struck like a thunderbolt in the ranks of the organized outlaws, and they gave Bell County a wide berth ever afterwards. It is not necessary here to justify this action, but it must be conceded that it was in a measure forced by the exigencies of the times upon the better element of Bell and her sister counties—for it is an indisputable fact that this mob came from several counties and that our citizens constituted a minority of the actors in this bloody scene. It is well known that men from as far away as Red River were members and even leaders of the avenging mob.

Two famous outlaws of this period, Sam Bass and Bill Longley, had a slight connection with Bell County, though neither of them operated here. The trap which ended the career of Sam Bass, noted train robber of north Texas, was sprung in Belton. Jim Murphy, one of the gang, had been arrested and, to save himself, had agreed to go back to the band and "give them away." They were en route to Round Rock to rob the bank there and camped for a day or two in the suburbs of Belton. Here Bass sold a pony and while he was arranging the bill of sale in town, Murphy slipped away for a few minutes and mailed a letter to Adjutant General John B. Jones, at Austin, saying: "We are on our way to rob the Round Rock bank. For God's sake be there to prevent it." General Jones quickly assembled his rangers, met the gang at Round Rock and in a rapid fire gun battle in the street on July 19th Sam Bass received wounds from which he died on July 21, 1878. The father of Bill Longley, a notorious desperado who is credited with having killed thirty-two men, lived for a time in Bell County, west of Salado, and Bill used to hang out there. The father, Campbell Longley, was a good man and a good neighbor. Bill had begun his wild career in his native county, Lee, by killing a negro. He is said to have been a young man of engaging manner and it is certain that he had many friends; but he killed without compunction anyone who crossed him. He was finally convicted of murder and hanged at Giddings, October 11, 1878.

7. *Problems of the County Government*

The new Police Court which came into office in January, 1874, although operating under the radical State Constitution of 1869, had been elected by the bona-fide citizenship of the county. It made an audit of the county finances and found that the indebtedness of the county had increased from $2,161.01, as shown by the audit of January, 1872, to $14,190.62 on January 1, 1874. Incoming taxes reduced this by the following March to $10,303.96. This deficit was a great handicap to the authorities in every phase of public business, for county warrants were at a heavy discount, and the county was compelled to pay more for supplies than those who paid cash. This fact and the very defective laws for the collection of taxes were largely to blame for the continuation of the deficit. There was no legal machinery for the rigid enforcement of tax collections, and their payment was almost a voluntary matter. The fight to bring the county warrants to par and to lower the tax rate lasted for four years.

The Police Court fixed the tax rate for 1874 at 60 cents on the $100 valuation. It was distributed as follows: common county rate, 25 cents; court house and jail expense, 20 cents; roads and bridges, 5 cents; paupers, 10 cents. There were also the usual poll and occupation taxes. The financial condition of the treasury seems to have improved, for the tax rate for 1875 was reduced to 45 cents—the common county rate being lowered to 20 cents and that for the court house and jail to 10 cents. The tax rate for 1876 was further reduced to 42 cents.

Under the new State Constitution of 1876 the Police Court was replaced by the Commissioners' Court, composed of four commissioners and presided over by the county judge. On January 1, 1877, the new court placed upon its minutes the following statement of the county's finances:

Expenditures from July 1, 1875, to December 31, 1876 ....$16,979.07
Amount of debt to June 30, 1875 .... 6,131.42
Total debt and expenditures to December 31, 1876 .... 23,110.49
Receipts by Treasurer since June 30, 1875 .... 20,456.13
Balance of indebtedness, January 1, 1877 ....$ 2,654.36

The debt was further reduced during the year and on March 31, 1878, it was entirely wiped out and the county had a cash balance of $5500.03. For the first time in its history the county was solvent, its warrants or script at par, a condition which it was able to mantain thereafter. The better financial condition is shown in the tax reduction. The rate for 1877 had been reduced to 33½ cents, while that for 1879 was lowered to 23 cents. By 1882 it had been brought down to 15 cents on the $100 valuation of property, the lowest point it reached during those years. Beginning with the issue of bonds in 1884 for the erection of a new court house and jail and, shortly afterwards, of bridge and road bonds, the rate rose again until in 1889 it was 37 cents, 25 cents of which was to pay off the bonds.

The spread of settlements and the rapid increase of marketable crops made imperative the opening of new roads and the building of new or better bridges. The roads, except for the few main highways, had been little better than mere trails which twisted about over the prairies or around the hills and sought easy crossings on the creeks and ravines. As the land was gradually fenced in, these roads were forced into narrow lanes which in wet weather, especially on the black lands, became almost bottomless quagmires that were impassable for loaded wagons. After heavy rains the unbridged streams were often likewise impassable and even dangerous. But to build good roads, as we think of them today, was far beyond the financial strength of the county; so the method pursued was still the old one of appointing an overseer for each section of public road and requiring every able-bodied man living along that section to put in a few days of labor each year in "working the road" under the direction of the overseer. It was a clumsy and inefficient ssytem, but it served to keep the roads in better condition than they would have been otherwise.

Providing bridges was a more difficult matter. Obviously, they could not be built by any such casual method, for the larger ones especially cost considerable money and required skill in planning and building. Sometimes private parties were authorized to establish ferries or toll bridges. In 1874, license was granted by the commissioners court to W. T. Anderson, W. G. West and Caston Sawyer to operate a ferry at the Shaw crossing on the Lampasas and also to Dr. J. J. Gregory for one at the crossing of the McMillin and Davilla road on Little River. The next year the Lampasas Bridge Company was licensed to build and maintain a toll bridge over the Lampasas near the Shaw crossing. James P. Reed was president of the company, John G. Batte was secretary, and among the stockholders were J. Q. Allen, H. C. Denny, J. W. Embree, W. K. Hamblen, J. Z. Miller and O. T. Tyler. This bridge, where the one on Highway No. 2 now is, was maintained as a private enterprise for several years. The small stone house which stands near the south end was occupied by the gate-keeper who collected the tolls. Although the county commissioners authorized the building of small wooden bridges from time to time, activity in building on a larger scale did not begin until 1886, when the great stimulation of business by the new railroads had made action necessary. The contract for the first iron bridge ever built by the county itself, across the Leon near Moffatt, was let on June 30, 1886, to the Kansas City Bridge Company for $1798. At about this time the old toll bridge over the Leon at the Waco road crossing was purchased by popular subscription and donated to the county for free service. On June 22, 1886, the county purchased the piers and approaches of the toll bridge on the Lampasas, mentioned above, for $3600, with the intention of placing thereon a free iron bridge. The contract for this bridge was let in June, 1889, at $7000. In August, 1886, contracts were made for the erection of several small wooden bridges in different parts of the county. In July, 1888, the Penn Bridge Company received a contract to build an iron bridge on stone piers across the Leon at the crossing of the Belton and Cameron road. In July, 1889, the Milwaukee Bridge Company was awarded the contract, on competitive bidding, for the erection of eight iron bridges at a total cost of $58,000. Three were on Little River, at the Reed crossing, the Greathouse-Temple crossing, and near Three Forks; three on the Lampasas, near the Three Forks, at the Wilkerson crossing, and at Youngsport; one on the Leon at the Miller crossing; and one on the Cow House at Sparta.

Meanwhile the Commissioners' Court had been providing for better care of the county's official records and for new public buildings. In June, 1875, Mr. Wm. G. Ludlow, the district and county clerk (the two offices were combined under the Constitution of 1869) was authorized to go to St. Louis and purchase a large Hall iron safe for the safe-keeping and protection from fire of the deed records and other books of the county. This was the first precaution ever taken for the protection of these records against fire or theft. On November 24, 1882, the court purchased for $250 the right to use the Campbell patent system of indexing the records of the county and employed Robert H. Turner, Wm. G. Taylor and Wm. P. Blackburn to index the deed records from Book A to Volume 36 under this system.

In September, 1883, plans and specifications for a new county jail, prepared by J. N. Preston & Son, of Austin, were finally approved. The Commissioners' Court purchased a lot on West Central Avenue as a site and advertised in the Galveston News for bids. The contract for construction was awarded to John Hendrickson and John H. Burnet of Belton at the price of $35,000. Pauli Bros., of St. Louis, were subcontractors for the steel cages, iron work, locks, levers, and plumbing. To pay for the building the county issued and sold to the State Board of Education fifteen year six per cent bonds. The jail was completed and accepted on May 26, 1884, and was immediately ready for "guests."

In the meantime, seeing that the county was on the eve of erecting a new jail and probably a new court house, the citizens of the new town of Temple and vicinity had, on June 11, 1883, presented a petition for the rescission of the special jail tax levied by the court. This action was followed next day by a petition of more than two hundred freeholders of the county, presented to the county judge, for an election to determine whether the county seat should remain at Belton or be removed to Temple. The election was ordered and held on August 14, 1883, with the result that Belton received a large majority of the votes.

The Commissioners' Court now resolved to go ahead

with plans for a new court house. On November 12 it passed resolutions in which, after reciting that several grand juries had condemned the old court house, built in 1858-'59, as unsafe repository for the county records and had recommended the building of a new and more suitable structure, they declared that there was a pressing need for a new and better court house. The court thereupon ordered that six per cent county bonds to the amount of $65,000 be issued for this purpose, based upon a special tax of ten cents on the hundred dollars. After advertising in the Galveston News for plans and specifications the plans submitted by J. N. Preston & Son of Austin were accepted. And after again advertising for bids the contract was let, March 4, 1884, to Ben D. Lee of Belton, at $64,965. The old court house was sold, wrecked and removed, and temporary quarters for the officers and courts were procured in various places around town. The cornerstone of the new court house was laid on June 24, 1884, with the usual Masonic ceremonies, by the Grand Lodge of Texas, Ancient Free and Accepted Masons, under the auspices of Belton Lodge No. 166, by request of the Commissioners' Court. A. J. Rose, Past Grand Master of the Grand Lodge of Texas, presided at the ceremonies and Reverend William Carey Crane, President of Baylor University at Independence, was orator of the day. The building was completed and accepted on May 30, 1885. Although far superior to the old court house, it was not fireproof, and in 1898 it was found necessary, for the safety of the records, to expend several thousand dollars in making the county clerk's office fire-proof.

During this period some progress was made in the public school system, but even at the end of the period adequate financial support was painfully lacking. A small amount was apportioned to each school from the State Permanent School Fund on the basis of scholastic enrollment; the county had a small fund of its own derived from its four leagues of school lands and from the Daniel Alexander bequest; and independent school districts were permitted by the State Constitution to impose a small tax for school purposes. But the aggregate of these resources was small. It was difficult to induce districts to vote taxes, and generally it was necessary to supplement the short terms permitted by the state funds by tuition or private subscription. There was no good method of examining and certifying teachers and the result was that some of the teachers, especially in the country schools, were clearly incompetent. They had been selected more for the purpose of giving employment to some local young man or woman who was a friend of the trustees than for the benefit of the school itself. Until 1887 the county judge acted as county superintendent of public instruction but in that year the Commissioners' Court elected to that office the first professional school man to hold the position in Bell County, Mr. T. J. Witt. Back in 1876 the three leagues of school land owned by Bell County but located in Wise County were ordered surveyed and offered for sale at prices ranging from $1.50 to $3 per acre. In the same year the administration of the Daniel Alexander School Lands—referred to previously as a donation to the schools—was placed in the hands of the county attorney, H. M. Furman. In 1877 these lands also were ordered sold. The proceeds of these sales became a part of Bell County's special permanent school fund. During this period several private educational institutions were giving valuable service to the county, but they will be described in a separate chapter.

8. New Enterprises

The first ice-making machine ever operated in Bell County was brought to Belton from San Antonio by Mr. E. Brunet, of Austin, about 1875, and was set up on the south bank of the Leon River about a hundred yards above the present highway bridge on the Temple pike, about where the Riverside Swimming Pool now is. It is said that this machine had been operated at old Point Isabel, at the mouth of the Rio Grande, just before and during the Civil War and that it was the first to be used in Texas. It was very small and Mr. Brunet could make only about 1,000 pounds a day, and he delivered the ice in Belton at ten cents per pound! Later on a larger and more modern plant was installed in Belton and the old outfit was moved to some little town in the West.

In the fall of 1877 a subscription was opened by citizens of Belton for stock in the "Belton Telegraph Company" at $25 per share. On December 20, 1877, the following stockholders met at Geo. W. Tyler's law office in

Belton: H. C. Denny, James P. Reed, W. J. Long, L. T. Methvin, Joe L. Wilson, Geo. N. Austin, Dr. Taylor Hudson, C. I. Bowman, D. L. Russell, J. P. Osterhout, A. V. Harris, Otto Mackensen, I. B. Webb, B. S. Deckerd, Geo. W. Tyler, W. S. Holman, S. M. Ray, J. J. Rackley, W. H. Edwards, Geo. W. Hunt, and J. G. Batte.

Mr. James P. Reed was made chairman of the meeting and Geo. W. Tyler, secretary. Five directors were chosen whose names were to be inserted in the charter of the company: James P. Reed, J. Z. Miller, W. S. Holman, Geo. W. Tyler, and H. C. Denny. The charter was read and adopted and was later executed and filed with the Secretary of State. The board of directors above named met on December 26 and organized by electing James P. Reed president and H. C. Denny secretary and treasurer, adopted by-laws, ordered fifty per cent of the subscriptions paid by January 5, 1878, and instructed the president to proceed at once with the construction of a telegraph line from Belton to a connection with the Western Union Telegraph line at Round Rock, on the I. and G. N. Railroad in Williamson County.[1] Contracts were immediately let for cedar poles (from the cedar-brakes on Nolan and Cow House, in Bell County), for wire and other equipment, and some time in the spring of 1878 the line was completed and offices opened at Belton, Salado, Corn Hill, Georgetown, and Round Rock. Belton and Bell County thus obtained their first wire connections with the outside world.

In the summer of 1879, the business men of Lampasas expressed a desire to have the line extended to that place. Dr. J. W. Embree and Geo. W. Tyler were sent by the company as a committee to negotiate the deal. Lampasas gave a bonus as an inducement and the company very soon had the line completed and open from Belton to that point, with offices at Palo Alto and Lampasas. During the next year the citizens of Gatesville arranged with the company, through its representative, Geo. W. Tyler, sent thither for that purpose, for the extension of the line from Palo Alto to Gatesville. This little home company thus flashed the first wire messages to Belton, Lampasas and Gatesville.

[1] **Belton Journal,** December 27, 1877.

The Old Order Changes

One of the main purposes of the company was to provide for transmission to out-of-the-way towns of daily quotations of the cotton market; and Belton, on the completion of this line, became a very important interior cotton market.

With the coming of the railroads into this territory in 1881 and 1882, and the wire service which always accompanies them, the need of the local line no longer existed and it was sold to the Frontier Telegraph Company, owned and operated by Mr. Robert J. Brackenridge, of Austin. This company's lines extended out of Austin to the western part of the state, but it was in turn absorbed by the Western Union and the Postal Telegraph companies, as the country settled up, in the eighties.

Our first telephones were brought in during the spring of 1884 when the Southwestern Telegraph and Telephone Company entered this territory, and connected Temple and Belton with other cities of Texas, installing local exchanges in both places.

The first cotton-seed oil mill in this part of Texas was erected at Belton about 1879 or 1880 by a northern company, and was operated for a few years under the personal management of Mr. William G. Kay. It was later absorbed by the American Cotton Oil Association of New York, a big commercial trust, which closed down the mill and dismantled and removed the machinery. The building, a large two-story stone structure, stood vacant until it was condemned as a dangerous nuisance by the local authorities, who razed its walls to the ground. Before the coming of the oil mill our farmers had used their cotton seed for stock feed or fertilizer, or had burned it; but from that time cotton seed had commercial value.

In 1883 the business men of Belton formed a corporation styled "The Belton Compress Company" and erected what was for those days a first class cotton compress. It was in operation for some eighteen or twenty years before it too fell into the hands of a trust which has since used the plant only as a cotton warehouse. It has been twice destroyed by fire and rebuilt.

Belton had been the pioneer town of the county in these enterprises because, until the rise of Temple in the eighties, it had been the largest and wealthiest community; but the enterprising business men of Temple were soon in the field. In the middle eighties a large compress and two large cotton seed oil mills were built in Temple, all of which are still (1923) in successful operation.

Until the early eighties the people of Belton, like those of other towns, had depended upon wells and cisterns for their water. Of course, they had no modern sewage system. This situation was not only dangerous to public health but subjected the whole town to fire hazards. In the fall of 1883 the city council of Belton, after much preliminary study by a sub-committee composed of George W. Tyler, F. Henry Austin, and J. E. Terrell, with Mr. M. L. Lynch, a civil engineer, as their technical advisor, drew up plans and specifications for a water-works system and invited bids thereon. They awarded the contract to Messrs. Morgan Jones of Ft. Worth, James H. Britton of Sherman, and Wm. C. Connor of Dallas on the basis of $41,000 for the water-works system, complete, and $3,500 for equipment for the fire department. This latter consisted of a hook-and-ladder truck, two hose carts and twelve hundred feet of hose. The contractors did a thoroughly satisfactory job. They erected on the bank of the Leon River, which was the source of water supply, a duplex set of engines and pumps, built a stand-pipe twenty feet in diameter and fifty feet high on North Main Street at Tenth Avenue and laid eight, six and four-inch mains. The system was completed, tested and delivered to the city on July 1, 1884. These improvements were paid for by an issue of six per cent bonds to the amount of $45,000. In 1891 a private company of citizens brought in three fine artesian wells in Belton. By lease contracts the city connected its mains with these wells and abandoned the Leon as a source of water supply. Later the city acquired the three wells and added a fourth, thus assuring its citizens a plentiful supply of pure water.

9. *The Coming of the Railroads*

We have already referred to the building of railroads into Bell County as an important factor in its development. The decade of the eighties was one of great activity in railroad building in Texas and the people of every section of the State were eager for the quicker and cheaper transportation which these arteries of commerce were expected to bring them. Land-owners, especially, looked forward to higher prices for their property when the new roads had brought increase of immigration and the opening up of new farms; and the merchants, professional men, and property owners in the towns were so filled with expectations of benefits that they were ready to make large donations of cash to any railway company that would build through their towns. The railroad officials were fully aware of this eagerness and were prompt to take advantage of it.

Two railroads across Bell County had been projected in the early seventies. The first, the Missouri, Kansas and Texas, had been chartered by the Legislature on August 2, 1870, to run from the Red River through Waco, Belton and Austin to the Rio Grande, with the view to future extension to Mexico City.[2] The other, the Hearne, Belton and Northwestern, chartered by an act of April 25, 1874,[3] was to build from Hearne, on the International and Great Northern, through Cameron, Belton and Lampasas and thence northwestwardly to intersect the projected Texas and Pacific. Both roads were actually surveyed through the county, but the great financial depression which began in 1873 and lasted until 1879 made it impossible to finance either road.

In the meantime the Gulf, Colorado and Santa Fe, organized by a group of Galveston capitalists in 1873, was building slowly up from the island city toward Bell County. officials had not only built the road largely from donations but were also seeking tax exemptions. On May 15, 1878, at the urgent request of representatives of the company and of many citizens of Belton and of other sections of the county, the Commissioners' Court of Bell County passed an order exempting this company from the payment of county taxes for ten years on condition that it extend its line to Belton within two years. The exact wording of the order was as follows:

That in consideration of the construction of the Gulf, Colorado and Santa Fe Railroad to the town of Belton, in said (Bell) County within two years from this date by the Gulf, Colorado and Santa Fe Railroad Company, the Commissioners' Court does by this order adjudge and decree that the County of Bell exempts from county taxation for a term of ten years the road bed and fixtures that may be constructed by said company within the County of Bell.

[2] Gammel, **Laws of Texas**, VI, 565.
[3] Gammel, **Laws of Texas**, VIII, 312.

It is the judgment of this Court that in view of the foregoing order the County of Bell will be greatly benefitted in the increase of taxable property secured by the completion of the road that would not otherwise be secured and decreasing taxation in the same ratio.

The vote on the order was at first a tie, Messrs. W. S. Whaley and Silas Baggett favoring and Messrs. Wm. P. Hancock and Thomas M. Soape opposing the proposition. County Judge Erasmus Walker, who presided cast the deciding vote in favor of the order. The dissenting commissioners entered a protest against the action of the majority to the effect that the Court had no power, under the Constitution and the laws of the State, to make such an order, and that it was against public policy and was a dangerous precedent. No informed person seriously questioned the constitutional objection to the action or thought the order would stand a legal test; but the act of the Court showed how much the people desired the advantage of railway connection with the outside world. The road did not reach the limits of the county before the two years expired, but it was approaching. Thereupon the Commissioners' Court of February 9, 1880, extended the time for two more years.

By the spring of 1880 the Santa Fe had completed its line to the eastern edge of Bell County at a point near the Knobs, or at the present town of Rogers. Representatives of the company then went to Belton and stated that their funds were running low and that the road would have to stop where it was unless substantial assistance came from Belton. After much negotiation and many public meetings the representatives of the company submitted to the people of Belton, assembled in public meeting in the old district court room, June 12, 1880, a proposition to complete the road to Belton by March 1, 1881, on condition of the donation to the Santa Fe of (1) a right-of-way two hundred feet wide through Belton and Bell County, the company to choose the more practicable of two routes, (2) depot grounds in Belton, (3) $75,000. The citizens accepted the proposal with unanimity and enthusiasm, onerous though it was, and appointed a committee to canvass the people for the required donation and to procure the right of way on both routes.

Two surveys had been made from the Knobs to Belton before this meeting, and the citizens understood that the right-of-way would be along one of these routes. One came up the valley of Little River and the Leon, the other crossed the high prairie by way of old Harrisville and Mount Vernon, a little to the north of the first. Each was as nearly on a direct line from the Knobs as the topography would allow, each crossed the Leon nearly east of Belton, near the Cameron crossing, and each entered the town on its eastern boundary. There was then no intimation of any other route. The bonus was secured by promissary notes and deeds to lands (placed in escrow). The right-of-way *through the county,* not merely to Belton, was secured by a $7,000 bond (ample at that time) signed by many responsible citizens.

At the meeting of June 12 one of the officials of the company said that the terminus of the road would remain at Belton for at least two years, which would make the town an important trade center for all the upper country. At the final meeting, when the bonus and other requirements of the company had been delivered and accepted, this same official, in an affected burst of gratitude, said that they intended "to make Belton the boss town on the Santa Fe road."

What did the Santa Fe Company then do? In the first place, in July, 1880, it abandoned both of the routes already surveyed and located the road on another survey that ran much further to the north by way of old Birdsdale, some seven or eight miles northeast of Belton, then turning sharply to the west, almost at a right angle, crossed the Leon and entered the corporate limits of Belton on its north boundary line about four hundred feet west of the northeast corner of the corporate limits, ran thence about forty feet inside the corporate line for about two thousand feet and then turned outside the corporate limits. In the second place it did not demand of the citizens any depot grounds within the town, nor did it locate the depot within half a mile of the court house, as its charter required it to do, but placed it some three hundred and fifty yards from the corporate limits, over a mile from the court house, on land which the company had already acquired. In the third place, having obtained a deed, in August, 1880, to 187 acres of prairie land near old Birdsdale, where the road made the sharp turn towards Belton, the company proceeded to promote a new town, **Temple**, and to extend the main line from that point to Fort Worth. It placed the company shops at Temple, and the new town began a rapid growth which soon made it the largest in the county.

The citizens of Belton felt that they had been duped, mulct and injured by the disadvantageous location of the depot and the promotion of a rival town so near by. Notwithstanding all this, most of the subscribers paid their donations. When the few remaining ones refused they were sued at Galveston. They employed two able attorneys, Seth Shepard and F. Charles Hume, to defend the suits on the ground that the company had not complied with the contract. The Miller case was agreed upon as a test case and was tried before the district judge without a jury. The company recovered judgment; the defendants appealed to the Supreme Court of Texas and that Court reversed the judgment and rendered judgment for the defendant, Miller, holding that it could not enforce the payment of the notes sued on because "there was in the whole transaction a want of that good faith and fair dealing which the makers of these obligations (the people of Belton) had good right to expect and demand of the company."[4] The testimony of the officials of the company who had conducted the negotiations with the citizens showed that they had deliberately deceived the people of Belton with respect to the route to be followed from the Knobs to Belton and the intended location of the depot, or as they said, they "kept mum" and allowed the people "to deceive themselves."

What is written above is not intended to cast any reflection upon the citizens of Temple for what occurred, for at that time there was no Temple. Nor is any blame attached to the present management of the Gulf, Colorado and Santa Fe—now owned and controlled by the Atcheson, Topeka and Santa Fe—for they had nothing to do with it and probably have never known the inside facts of the case. The writer's only purpose is to clear the citizens of Belton of the charge so often made against them that when the Santa Fe was built they were non-progressives, that they wouldn't help the company, that they "failed to offer an attractive bonus" and other like imputations. The truth is that they met every requirement of the company and were deliberately buncoed by some greedy officials

[4] Miller vs. Gulf, Colorado and Santa Fe Railway Co., **65 Texas Reports,** 664-669.

who were engaged in schemes of land and town-lot speculations at the expense of the people who had donated most of the money with which the road was built.

About one year after the Santa Fe reached Belton the company began the extension of the western branch from that point to Lampasas. A few years later they extended it to Brownwood, Ballinger, and San Angelo. Temple, as already said, became the headquarters for both the north and south divisions of the main line and for the western or San Angelo division. The Santa Fe Company also laid out and promoted other towns on its lines—Rogers, Heidenheimer, Pendletonville, Nolanville and Killeen.

Hardly had the Santa Fe laid down its track to Belton when news came that the Missouri, Kansas and Texas, familiarly known as the "Katy," would extend its line from Denison through Fort Worth and Waco to Taylor. We have seen that this road had been authorized to cross Texas by an act of the Legislature in 1870. As laid out in 1881 this road ran from Waco through Temple and crossed Little River below the Three Forks. The citizens of Belton again came forward with a donation, $30,000, and secured the construction by the M.K. & T. Company of a branch line from Echo, three miles south of Temple, to their town. The depot was located about three blocks east of the court house square. The main line was built through the county in 1881-1882 and the branch line to Belton was completed in September, 1882. This company also laid out and established new towns along its line in Bell County. They were Troy (near the old town of Troy), Echo, Little River, Holland, and Bartlett. Echo never developed and the station there was later abandoned, the branch line trains to and from Belton running into and out of the station at Temple. Bartlett is on the county line and a large part of the town, with the railway depot, is in Williamson County.

The Santa Fe and the Katy are the only railroads that have been built in Bell County—unless we include the Belton and Temple Interurban Railway, operated by electric power, which was completed in 1905. Numerous railways have been projected to run through the central portion of the county, but all have failed to materialize. On December 20, 1887, citizens along the line filed a charter for the Austin and McGregor Railway Company to run a line from Austin via Round Rock, Georgetown, Corn Hill, Salado and Belton to McGregor in McLennan County. H. C. Mills of McGregor, Geo. W. Tyler of Belton, Huling P. Robertson of Salado, A. J. Robertson of Corn Hill, Emzy Taylor of Georgetown, John T. Hayes of Round Rock, and Joseph Nalle, W. H. Tobin and A. P. Wooldridge of Austin were named in the charter as directors. Joseph Nalle was made president. Several directors' meetings were held and much preliminary negotiation was had, but it proved impossible to finance the road and the project was abandoned. Early in 1895 the Belton and Northeastern Railway Company was chartered to run from Belton to McGregor. The line was surveyed and located and some right of way was tentatively obtained. The enterprise was launched on what was supposed to be an assurance from the St. Louis and Southwestern Railway Company or "Cotton Belt" that, if the road was built, the company would operate it on a traffic arrangement. But it developed that the Cotton Belt was not in a financial condition to take over the line and this enterprise also was abandoned. Other railroad projects will be mentioned in another chapter.

The building of the Santa Fe and the M.K. & T. greatly accelerated the development of the county. As these roads offered quicker and cheaper transportation of crops to market many new farms opened up near the new railroad towns. The price of good raw land was still comparatively low in the middle eighties, averaging from eight to ten dollars per acre; but it had nearly doubled by 1890. Most of the older settlers who had been wise or fortunate enough to buy large bodies of land when it was cheap were disposed to hold it now that prices were rising, while many of the immigrant farmers, being too poor to buy land, became renters. It was during the later part of the eighties that farm tenantry began to be common. Cotton became more and more the staple crop, especially on the tenant farms, because it could always be sold for cash and thus returned a fairly sure income to the landlord. Another notable development was the growth of the new railroad towns at the expense of those that had no railroad. Farmers very naturally preferred to market their crops on the railroad where they received slightly higher prices and could buy supplies somewhat cheaper. Some of the older towns, like Howard and Old Troy, soon disappeared under this severe competition, while others, like Moffatt and Salado, which hitherto had been the second largest town in the county, lost much of their trade and steadily declined. Even Belton, although it continued to grow steadily, could not keep pace with its favored young rival, Temple. The small towns, whether on or off the railroad, did more business than they do today because bad roads and slow wagon transportation made it inconvenient for most country people to do their trading more than eight or ten miles from their homes. The advent of the automobile some years later was to change that situation. The merchants, brought into closer connection with St. Louis and Chicago and with Dallas, the new distributing center of north Texas, began to buy good from the wholesalers and jobbers of those cities. They still did much of their business with Houston and Galveston, since most of the cotton was sold there, but they were no longer wholly dependent upon them. Because of the railroads. Bell County's trade, like that of other parts of central Texas, began to shift about towards the north.

10. *The Rise of Temple*

At the beginning of 1880 the greater part of the present site of Temple was owned by Mr. Jonathan E. Moore. In August of that year, soon after they had made their deal with the citizens of Belton, certain directors of the Gulf, Colorado and Santa Fe Railway Company bought some 187 acres of Mr. Moore's land at $20 per acre. Most of his neighbors thought Mr. Moore had received a very high price for it. Soon afterwards the railroad was built up from the town of Rogers and a construction camp was established near the site of the present depot. As most of the occupants of the camp were railroad construction workers and hangers-on, it was a rather "tough" place. It consisted of a number of rough board shacks and tents and three saloons, and was locally known as "Tangle-foot" because many of its inhabitants were seldom able to walk straight.

But the men who had bought Mr. Moore's land had plans for something bigger than a temporary construction camp. As the road was to build a branch line from this point north to Fort Worth and as they knew that the

M.K. & T. was coming in this direction, they had their land surveyed out into streets and town lots and in the early summer of 1881 they advertised a great celebration and sale of lots to be held on June 29. On that day a great concourse of people assembled from miles around to enjoy the excitement and the free barbecue. Many of the lots were auctioned off, some selling for as high as $300, some as low as $45, but averaging about $150 each.[5] Many of the visitors refused to buy because they thought the town "could never amount to much" since it was laid out on the bare prairie where there was no water. They were soon to learn that they had been mistaken.

The promoters of the new town named it in honor of Mr. B. M. Temple who was at that time the chief construction engineer for the Gulf, Colorado and Santa Fe. It began to grow from the start. There was a nucleus of railroad workers to begin with and stores went up rapidly. As it was a junction point it soon became an important trading center. The land around it was extremely fertile and, though thinly settled before the town was laid out, was quickly covered with farms. In 1882 the M.K. & T. came through and made things even more lively. When the Santa Fe made Temple a division point and built its shops there it added to the population several hundred people and a steady pay-roll. Doctors, lawyers and other professional men were attracted to the place and new business enterprises came in steadily. It was evident that the new town was "amounting to something."

Nevertheless the citizens of early Temple were troubled with many problems. The first and most urgent was the lack of an adequate water supply. At first the business men had a well dug where the present First Street and Avenue A intersect. It was known as the "Public Well" and furnished but little water. The people of the residential district bought their water from wagons at twenty-five cents per barrel. Some of them put down wells of their own and others relied upon cisterns, above or below ground, to catch rainwater. A few years later Captain Henry Smith drilled for the city two artesian wells—one down on Knobb Creek, the other at a high point in the

---

[5] The deeds to these lots, which are on record in the county clerk's office in Belton, show the names of the purchasers and the prices paid. All deeds are assigned by George Sealy of Galveston.

Top and center: Two views of the north side of the Court House Square, Belton, in 1870.

Bottom: Texas Veterans Association annual reunion at Belton, April 21, 1883.

northwestern part of the town—but they did not provide enough water. Then the Santa Fe Railway Company, by putting a dam across Bird's Creek west of town, created Lake Polk which it allowed the city to use as a source of water supply. Even this soon proved insufficient and a project was started to get water from the Leon River. Under the slogan "The Leon or Bust!" the enterprise was carried through. There was now plenty of water; but, unfortunately, there was at first neither a filtering plant nor a settling basin, and when the Leon was on a rise what came through the taps was little better than liquid mud. Until the water-works system was put in there was little protection against fires. Most of the early business houses were light wooden shacks which burned easily, and once a fire started it was likely to be disastrous. Volunteer fire-fighting companies were formed, but so long as they had to draw water from wells they could do little after a fire had once got under way. Even after water mains were laid, they were often unable in bad weather to get their hose carts or other apparatus through the deep mud of the streets. The black soil under the town was deep and after heavy or prolonged rains the mud was almost bottomless and it stuck to wheels like glue. Many old timers assert that it was not unusual for wagons or even carriages to bog down in the streets and remain there for days or weeks until the ground dried. Although plank sidewalks enabled the pedestrian to get from one corner of a block to another, getting across a muddy street intersection was both a problem and an adventure. Temple was ten years old before cement walks were laid. Some people in derision called the new town "Mud."

During these early years, despite the fact that the majority of its citizens were of the best quality, Temple had the reputation of being a "tough place." As an important railroad center where property values were rising and business was brisk, it naturally attracted people of many sorts—and some of them were bad. Saloons and gambling joints were numerous and about them gathered not only their local hangers-on but a rough element from far and near. Those transient tourists known as tramps, who before the day of the automobile and paved highway always followed the railroads, were constant visitors and frequent causes of annoyance. And the town was a haven for those young men of retarded minds who cherished the delusion that the surest way to prove their manhood was to carry a six-shooter and a bottle of bad whiskey and to "show off" with a tough crowd. These conditions greatly disturbed the good people of Temple; but it took many years of work through the authorities of the law and the steady pressure of public opinion to bring about a change. Early Temple had the defects of all fast growing towns.

When the town was barely six months old it had grown to such an extent that some of the citizens thought it should be incorporated. On January 18, 1882, a petition, signed by fifty names, was presented to County Judge W. M. Minyard asking for an election in Temple on the question of incorporation. The county Commissioners' Court on June 1 ordered an election to be held on July 8. At this election only 119 votes were cast—many citizens had not been in residence long enough to vote—and the supporters of the measure won by only three votes, 61 to 58. Soon thereafter the first city election was held and J. W. Callaway was elected the first mayor. He was succeeded in 1884 by W. H. Crain who served two years and was in turn succeeded by Callaway.

It was two years after the founding of the town before a public school was organized. Two private schools were established, however, in 1882, one by Miss Jennie McConnell and Mrs. Ida Sebastian and the other by Miss Jennie Gray. After a little while these two school consolidated under a Mr. Lang as principal with the three women founders as teachers. On June 13, 1883, a stock company with a capital of $2,500 organized for the establishment of "Temple Academy." The company erected a building and in August elected Mr. J. Waggoner to head the institution. In the meantime agitation had begun for a public school, and on September 24, 1883, the citizens voted, 114 to 2, to form an independent school district. At another election on December 17 they voted a special tax for the school. Nine days later the school trustees purchased for $4,392 the building which had just been put up to house the Temple Academy. This building, a great barnlike structure, was located on the present site of the Central Junior High School. Mr. Waggoner was kept as principal for that year and was then succeeded to Mr. B. M. Howard. The enrollment during this second year was 274 pupils. Unfortunately, factional controversies retarded the development of the schools and the superintendency changed hands every year until Mr. W. T. Hamner was elected to that position in 1888. He remained in charge until 1893 when Mr. J. E. Blair succeeded him.

The churches lost little time in getting established. The first to organize were the Presbyterians who erected a church building in 1881 with C. W. Peyton, formerly of Belton, as their pastor. In 1882 the Baptists of old Birdsdale moved their church into Temple. Their first pastor in the new location was J. M. Joiner. The Methodists had also had a church near by in the Double File community under the pastorate of J. M. Porter. In 1882 this congregation moved to Temple, but until they erected their first building in 1884 they worshiped in the Presbyterian Church. Their first regular pastor was John M. Barcus who was sent by the conference in 1883. These three were the largest of the early church organizations, but several others became well established during the eighties. The Catholics held masses almost from the beginning of the town, at first in private homes. They soon established a regular mission. The Evangelicals, under the leadership of John Gomer, were organized in 1882. The Protestant Episcopal Church in 1883 set up a mission which was erected into a church in 1889. The Lutherans organized in 1886. The Christian Church was first established in 1889.

The first newspaper to be published in Temple was the *Weekly Times,* owned and edited by W. D. Cox and J. S. Thompson. Mr. Cox had come from Giddings where he had a small printing plant. He tells how he arrived on a bleak October afternoon and made the rounds of the few stores and offices in search of business support, of how he spent the cold night in a tent annex to the sole hotel, and of how he secured a two-room building back of Joe R. Irvin's drug store on First Street for his shop. His equipment consisted of a small Washington hand press, an 8 x 10 Monumental lever job press and a very limited supply of job and "ad" type. "Here . . . was first held up to the light of a dingy little window, on the afternoon of November 21, 1881, the first copy of the *Temple Weekly Times.*[6] Mr. Thompson soon withdrew from the business. In 1886 Mr. J. F. Lewis became half owner but drew out next year to found the *Herald,* the second paper in Temple. In the meantime the *Times* had flourished and put out both

[6] Mr. Cox published his story in the **Temple Mirror** in 1912.

daily and weekly editions. In 1888 Mickel and Hull acquired an interest in the paper but resold to Cox who continued as sole owner until he sold to Mr. J. D. Crow about 1890. After Mr. Lewis began the publication of the *Herald* there was a hot rivalry between that paper and the *Times*. They took opposing sides on nearly every question. About December, 1887, the Temple *Saturday Sun,* a weekly, was established by R. O. Gresham and Jno. S. Perry and continued for several years. The Temple *Mirror* was founded in 1890 by Felix Venney and O. P. Gresham. In later years it was acquired by R. O. Gresham.

In January, 1882, P. L. and F. F. Downs established the first bank, the "Bell County Bank," with $10,000 cash capital, in a small frame building two doors from where its successor, the First National, now stands. Two years later this bank became a national bank with a capital stock of $50,000.

The comparatively rapid growth of Temple is shown by the fact that the U. S. Census of 1890 gave its population as 4,047, while Belton, which in 1880—before Temple existed—had a population of 1,797 inhabitants, had grown to only 3,000. Temple has maintained its lead ever since.

11. *Politics in Bell County During the Eighties*

The experiences of Reconstruction had apparently solidified the Democratic party in our county, as it had in all other parts of Texas, and for many years the leaders of that party were the men who had been most active in redeeming the state from the rule of the radicals. But the "hard times" of the seventies, which had been especially severe on the farmers, had given rise to the Greenback Party, which was very strong in many of the western states and had considerable following in Texas. It had its adherents in Bell, but was never able to make much of a showing. The Grange had flourished from the middle seventies until the midle eighties; but it was not a political organization, although some of its leaders went into politics and exercised considerable influence upon the course of the Democratic party in Texas. The same may be said for the successor of the Grange, the Farmers' Alliance, whose strongest leader was Dr. C. W. Macune. But the unrest which revealed itself in these organizations frequently led to the formation of some sort of "third party" that made a fight against the regular Democrats. Until 1886 the supremacy of the Democrats had never been threatened in Bell County and that party had never made nominations for county offices, although it had held county conventions to select delegates to the district and state nominating conventions. This it had done, as usual, in the early summer of 1886. Somewhat later a group calling itself the Union Labor party, composed of former Greenbackers, Knights of Labor, anti-monopolists and other elements, held a county meeting in Temple and put out a full county ticket on a platform which was then regarded as extremely radical. This movement alarmed the Democrats and at the suggestion of leading members of the party Judge Rufus King, the county chairman, reassembled the precinct delegates of the previous convention. When they met they promptly decided it expedient to make Democratic nominations for the county offices; and they named a full county ticket which was completely successful at the November eelction. After that time the Democrats continued to make county nominations in convention until the present primary election system was introduced.

In the meantime another issue had arisen to threaten the unity of the Democrats—the proposal for State-wide prohibition. Prior to this time the liquor question—or more accurately the licensing of saloons—had been handled as a purely local matter through local option elections. Back in January, 1877, a county vote had been taken on the question with the result that the prohibitionists won by 668 to 652 votes. This did not settle the matter, however, for on January 11, 1878, in another election the anti-prohibitionists won by a very large majority, 918 to 129. Thereafter the several towns or precincts settled the matter for themselves and a number of them adopted prohibition. General interest in the subject had been growing and in 1887 the state legislature, in response to considerable pressure, submitted to the people an amendment to the State constitution prohibiting the sale of intoxicating liquors in the State. An exciting campaign followed and the membership of the Democratic party divided on the question, with much bitterness resulting. In the election on August 4, 1887, the advocates of state-wide prohibition were defeated although they made a strong showing. In Bell County the vote was: for the amendment, 2,742 votes;

against it, 3,501; the majority against it was 759. The feeling aroused by this contest did not disappear for many years. In fact the lines then drawn may be said never to have disappeared, for the Democrats of the State have been divided on this question ever since.

The next year, 1888, came a schism in the ranks of the county Democracy which was largely an aftermath of this contest. The county convention nominated a full county ticket including a candidate for representative to the legislature. Among the defeated were two old officeholders whose friends challenged the action of the convention and refused to accept the results. There was also widespread dissatisfaction with the nominee for the legislature. The two office holders became independent candidates for reelection and one of the nominees of the Union Labor group in the preceding election came out against the legislative nominee. The three independents defeated the regular nominees at the polls. In 1890 there was another contest over the nomination to the legislature on the ground that the regular nominee had received the nomination by unfair tactics in the county convention, and again the independent, or bolting, candidate won.

At the end of this period the general discontent among the farmers over falling prices of farm products and mounting debts, and their demands for a greater volume of currency, the regulation of railway rates, the abolition of monopolies and a more uniform tax system were about to usher the people's (or Populist) party into existence.

CHAPTER XIV

TWENTY-FIVE YEARS OF GROWTH, 1890-1915

1. *"Hard Times" and Agitation for Relief,* 1890-1899

For several years the cotton and wheat farmers of the United States had been faced by the problem of declining prices for their products and relatively high prices for almost everything they had to buy. This seems to have been caused in part by the tendency toward monopolistic control of manufactured products and in part by the one-crop system followed by those farmers who had to purchase their supplies on credit during the year, usually at higher prices than if they paid cash. The credit system was almost universal in the cotton country, and in bad crop years the farmer was likely to find himself still in debt when his cotton was sold. Even in good years there was little cash left to him after his debts were paid. The individual farmer was generally at the mercy of the cotton buyers who organized to get the cotton for as little as possible. Another difficulty was that nearly all the cotton came on the market during about two months in the early fall. As his creditor merchant demanded payment at once, the farmer had to sell at the time when prices were lowest. Another factor was that the withdrawal of large sums of money from northern banks to pay for southern cotton during these fall months caused a money stringency in northern commercial centers which helped to depress all prices. And after he sold his cottton, the grower usually saw its price advance. Naturally there was great discussion of these evils and of possible remedies.

The Grange, the first important organization of farmers, was slowly dying by the middle eighties, but it was soon succeeded in Texas by another, known as the Farmers' Alliance. Like the Grange the Alliance sought to improve the social life of farmers and their families, to train them in the economic principles of their occupation and to bring about better prices and cheaper living costs by co-operative selling and buying. Between 1886 and 1890 the Texas Alliance spread into all the southern and some of the western states after having combined with similar organizations in Louisiana and Arkansas. At a great meeting in St. Louis in October, 1889, its president, Dr. C. W. Macune, of Milam County, proposed the famous "subtreasury scheme" which the organization supported and made a public issue for several years. This plan, in brief, was for the United States Government to erect large warehouses or elevators at convenient points throughout the cotton and grain growing regions in which the farmer could store his crop. The Government was then to issue to him, through substreasury offices, as a loan, treasury notes to the amount of seventy-five per cent of the market value of his stored crop, the cotton or grain being held as security for the loan. He must sell within a year, but the crop sale could be spread throughout the year at better prices than if thrown on the market at once. When he sold he was to repay the Government loan with interest at the rate of one per cent a year. The Government would then cancel the repaid notes in order to avoid a permanent inflation of the currency. It was Dr. Macune's belief that this scheme would enable the farmer to get a higher price for his crop and at the same time provide an elastic currency without danger of undue inflation or contraction. The Alliance was strong in Bell County and most of the members of the order favored the subtreasury plan. It was vigorously debated at public gatherings, for many of the more conservative citizens, especially the bankers and business men, opposed it, saying that it was a radical nostrum and would bankrupt the Government. Bills to carry out the plan were introduced into both houses of Congress but were defeated, so the scheme was never tried out.

Although the leaders of the Alliance tried to keep the order out of partisan politics, the "demands" which they pressed upon the law-makers directed the attention of its members to the attitude of both Democratic and Republican leaders toward the farmers' program. The result was that many members, incensed at the refusal of the old parties to grant their demands, moved toward the formation of a new party for the farmers and laborers of the country. Another group, loyal Democrats, resented this action and made a fight upon the leaders of the Alliance. Thus it split and soon disappeared. It was largely from the radical group that the People's, or Populist, party was formed in 1892.

The People's party adopted another scheme for the relief of the debt-ridden farmer, the free and unlimited coinage of silver at a fixed ratio, "sixteen to one," of gold.

They wished to increase the volume of money in circulation and, by thus increasing prices, enable the debtor to pay his debts. When the terrible panic of 1893 came on, prices fell still lower, credit was difficult to obtain except at high rates, money was scarce and the debtor was in desperate plight. The movement for "free silver" spread all over the West and South and was taken up by the Democrats of those sections and even by many western Republicans. The controversy became heated with most of our people supporting the silver plan as it had then become good Democratic doctrine. Only a few men in Bell County held to the single gold standard. As is well known the silver movement really culminated in the great political campaign of 1896 when W. J. Bryan was the candidate of both Democrats and Populists for the presidency. After his defeat the movement declined, partly because new discoveries of gold so increased the supply that money became more plentiful and prices rose again.

The depression lasted until about 1898 or 1899. Strangely enough, the price of farm lands increased throughout this period. Many small farmers lost their land through mortgage foreclosures while others sold them and moved to some part of western Texas where lands were much cheaper. There was a marked tendency for farm lands to be consolidated into the hands of fewer owners, many of them business or professional men who had foreclosed on mortgages or had invested their profits in farm lands. These large owners usually held the lands for a rise in value and rented them to immigrant farmers from the older southern states. Tenantry was increasing and continued to do so. Even in 1890, according to the Census of the United States, fifty-three per cent of the farms in Bell County were farmed by tenants. By 1900 this percentage had increased to over fifty-six and by 1910 to sixty. Nearly all these tenants paid their rent with a share of the crop, the customary one-fourth of the cotton and one-third of the grain. But this did not pay the owner as much interest as he thought he was entitled to on the increased value of the land and many landlords began to require an additional money rent. This caused much resentment among the tenant farmers and later became a political issue. There can be no doubt that the decreasing number of home-owning farmers was a bad thing both for agriculture and for the community as a whole.

2. Public and Private Improvements in the 1890's

In spite of the hard times of the nineties the county officials undertook a number of public improvements, especially the building of new bridges. In April, 1892, the Commissioners' Court let a contract to the King Bridge Company to build an iron bridge at Salado for $3,500. In September, 1893, it purchased two road graders and two road plows for $565 for use on the county roads. Although the old system of requiring local residents to work the roads was still in use, it had become very unsatisfactory and there was a growing demand that the county take a more active part in keeping the roads in repair. In June, 1894, bridges were contracted for on the Lampasas River at the Burris Crossing and on Elm Creek at Oenaville for a combined cost of a little less than $8,000. In October, 1895, another was provided for at the Whitely Crossing of the Cow House in Tennessee Valley. Several smaller bridges were erected, and by 1900 they had been provided at all the important crossings of streams in the county. These bridges were paid for mostly by the issue of county bridge bonds; but as the county was gradually paying off its old indebtedness, the county tax rate remained at about the same point throughout the period with an average of forty-two cents on the hundred dollars of property valuations.

On December 1, 1894, the new county treasurer, J. J. Lowry, in response to the court's request for a statement of the county's financial situation, reported that of the several bond issues to the total of $180,000, some $53,000 had been paid, leaving only $127,000 outstanding. Of these $30,000 were jail bonds, $50,000 court house bonds, and $57,000 were for bridges. Of this total $15,000 were held for the Bell County permanent school fund. The total of the school fund, including notes for the school lands, sold in Wise County and for the Alexander school lands, amounted to $34,717.59.

During this time private enterprise also contributed a number of improvements of interest to the public. In 1890 the second cotton-seed oil mill was erected in Belton by Mr. William Thatcher and Belton associates at a cost of about $110,000. Several changes of ownership occurred later and finally this mill came to be operated under the name of the Occidental Oil Company which also owned small mills at Bartlett and Granger. In 1891 Belton, Temple, and other towns in central Texas promoted local independent companies for furnishing the then new system of electric lighting. Those little companies pioneered the business that was later taken over by the Texas Power and Light Company which now supplies most of the light and power for this portion of Texas. At about the same time that electric lighting was installed, independent and competing telephone systems were set up in Temple and Belton and operated for many years before they gave way to the present Southwestern Bell Telephone Company. The Postal Telegraph also came in and opened stations not only in Temple and Belton but at some other towns in the county. The Bell County Fair Association, organized about 1891, for several years held interesting and successful exhibits at the Ben D. Lee place about one mile southeast of Belton.

At Temple the Santa Fe Railway Company erected a fine new depot and division office building, the Harvey house, the Railroad Y.M.C.A., and the Santa Fe Hospital. The M. K. & T. Railway Company moved its station from the crossing of the two roads to Central Avenue and there built a modern depot. Temple was still growing steadily and extending its trade territory, as is shown by the extensive jobbing business of the Temple Grocery Company in the early nineties and of its successors, branches of the Rotan Grocery Company and the Cooper Grocery Company, both of Waco. The Mississippi Store also did an extensive dry goods business throughout a wide territory. The foundations were laid early for Temple's subsequent reputation as a great hospital center. The Santa Fe Hospital, for the use of employees of the Santa Fe Railroad only, first opened in a small building on March 2, 1892. It now occupies a large, well-equipped modern structure and serves a wide area of the Santa Fe system. The King's Daughters Hospital began in a little three-room frame house in 1897. In 1900 it moved into a larger frame building at its present location. Five years later a frame addition was built and Dr. J. S. McCelvey donated its first operating room. In 1909 a brick building was added and in 1912 the first fire-proof unit was erected at a cost of $100,00. In 1917 another fire-proof unit was added; and in 1927 all the old structures not fire-proof were replaced by a $300,000 modern fire-proof building with 116 additional beds. In 1904 Drs. A. C. Scott and R. R. White purchased an old building with eight rooms and installed a hospital therein. In 1907 they built an addition with twenty rooms and in 1911 still another with twenty-four beds. Three years later they constructed the present main building with sixty beds. In 1922 they, with Dr. J. M. Woodson, erected the building which houses the hospital clinic and the Woodson Eye, Ear, Nose and Throat Clinic. A modern steam plant was added in 1925 and in 1928 was erected a four-story fire-proof unit with 104 additional beds. These three hospitals cover some thirty acres of grounds and employ about 700 persons. The wide reputations of their skilled medical and surgical staffs attract to Temple approximately 20,000 patients annually. The two general hospitals maintain schools for training nurses and have graduated several hundred of them.

At Belton both the Santa Fe and the M.K. & T. Railways abandoned their depots at the outer edges of the city and came up into town near the business center where they erected new station buildings. The Central Hotel was erected about 1891. In 1895 an up-to-date opera house, "The Grand," opened on the southwest corner of the square and gave Belton a theatre service equal to anything outside the large cities, for which the public often showed its appreciation.

3. *The War with Spain,* 1898

From the beginning of the revolt in Cuba in early 1895 against the authority of Spain our people watched the conflict with growing interest. Sympathy for the Cubans was greatly stimulated by the newspapers and magazines which featured the struggle for "Cuba libre"; and when early in 1898 it became evident that the United States would be involved, patriotic fervor ran high. The news of the declaration of war, in April, 1898, was received with enthusiasm and hundreds of young men prepared to go to war. The Government, however, did not raise a large army and called on Texas for only a few more than 5,000 volunteers. The writer has been able to get the names of only 120 men who went from Bell County, and a few of these may have resided in other counties. The list is as follows:

(1)) Company A, Second Texas Volunteer Infantry, U. S. Army, Colonel Louis M. Oppenheimer (of Austin), commanding, C. G. Bierbower (of Lampasas), Captain.
Sergeants: David C. Randall, Jack H. Roberts, ―――― Sanders.
Corporals: Lon Baker, Joe. H. Lassiter, Colon McMahon, Henry J. Welhausen.
Privates: Herbert E. Cawthon, Wilbur F. Flewellen, Brax Fugate, Jack Fuller, Herman C. Karnes, Thomas Landreth, Robert Mathis, Dickerson Nelson, Charles B. Rucker, ―――― Saunders, Arthur Skipper, Joe Sparra, Ernest Wells.

(2) Company A, "Belton Rifles," Fourth Texas Volunteer Infantry, Oscar E. Cockerell, Captain.
Lieutenant: Lindsey P. Rucker.
Sergeants: Resin S. Farr, Jr., R. L. Drake, S. B. Wheeler, D. A. Platt.
Corporals: S. G. Grimes, E. W. Pohic, H. T. Landrum, Mack Boyd, W. S. Scott, W. M. F. Mullins, Oscar L. Carlock, C. W. Johnson, F. N. Landreth, Talmadge D. Beasley.
Quartermaster: John H. Connell, Jr.; Musicians: James R. Russell and S. Watkins; Artificer: H. Dunborn; Wagon Master: John M. Franklin.
Privates: Karl Bronchle, Chas. W. Bunce, T. J. Chapman, E. F. Crosby, Elijah Jones, J. A. Lamb, Wm. C. Scott, O. R. Stricklin, Sam O. Bates, Joe L. Bland, D. S. Beasley, G. T. Brandon, S. F. Butler, Wm. Bowers, D. B. Bronson, E. W. Britzman, E. F. Barnet, W. R. Baker, Ed Cornelius, Frank Cornelius, Thom. M. Cox, J. H. Cox, E. C. Cato, Jas. W. Crisp, O. A. Demoney, E. E. Dearing, J. F. Davis, A. W. Eaton, J. H. Ferrell, S. D. Foster, Geo. W. Foster, Wm. L. Gibson, Alf G. Hall, Ben L. Haynes, C. M. Hairslip, Hamilton Holland, Sam Hanekamp, George Jung, Henry Johnson, B. H. Lockwood, J. J. Lile, Geo. W. Mitchell, A. B. Mitchell, Joe Marek, Jr., Geo. S. Massey, Monroe McCelvey, R. F. McKey, C L. Newman, Robert Purcell, Robert Pevehouse, R J. Perry, Wm. Robinson, O. Rogers, M. M. Ray, J. H. Schusta, W. F. Slaughter, J. S. Stephenson, L. J. Stafford, G. B. Stover, E. T. Sparks, Jno. S. Thatcher, Lee Tipton, Sam O. Wilson, Jr., Henry Wilford, J. E. Wheeler, G. O. Whiteley, N. L. Wills, Archie Watts, Sanford Yance.

(3) Other Bell County Enlistments.
Assistant Surgeons: Dr. Wilson T. Davidson, Jr., Third Regiment, U. S. Volunteer Infantry; Dr. Henry C. McClenenen, First Texas Regiment, U. S. Volunteer Cavalry.
Hospital Corps: Dr. Robert Walter Smith, Regular U. S. Army; Dr. Rufus Whitten King, Orderly Sergeant, First Texas Regiment, U. S. Volunteer Infantry; Dr. Joe H. Burnett, First Sergeant, Fifth Louisiana Regiment, U. S. Volunteer Infantry, "Hood's Immunes."
Privates: B. L. Appleby, Eugene Appleby, Fifth U. S. Infantry, Regular Army; W. R. Keylich, Barney Thorp, Galveston Artillery; Frank W. Burford, Theo Chandler, Troop I, First Texas Regiment, U. S. Volunteer Cavalry.

4. The Return of Better Times

The depression had run its course by 1899. Cotton prices were better that fall and the next year the crop was unusually large with prices still better. In consequence most farmers in Bell County were able to pay themselves out of debt and business generally was brisk. Even old debts barred by limitation were in many instances paid off by the debtors. With the return of business confidence and prosperity the political agitations, which had marked the preceding decade, died away. Conditions seemed favorable for new business enterprises.

For years there had been much discussion in Texas of the need of cotton yarn and cloth mills here in the cotton country. The success of such mills in other cotton states (the Carolinas and Georgia) seemed to warrant their introduction into Texas, and in fact a few had been built. In 1900 the business men of Belton raised some $65,000 and organized a company which erected a good two-story stone building and installed therein 3,200 spindles and 100 looms for weaving unbleached domestic. Before purchasing their machinery the company sent J. Z. Miller, Jr. and Geo. W. Tyler as a committee to inspect personally the mills in operation at Florence and Huntsville, Alabama. The mill began operations in 1901 with a Mr. Mitchell of North Carolina, an experienced mill man, in charge as superintendent and manager. The cloth produced was of the very best quality, but the competition in this particular product became so keen as to cut off any profit and the mill did not prosper. It was then changed to a strictly yarn mill and the number of spindles was increased to 7,000. Mr. O. A. Robbins, of Charlotte, North Carolina, an expert mill man, became superintendent with a Mr. Oliver as foreman; but Mr. Robbins soon withdrew from the management and that duty fell upon Mr. J. Z. Miller, the secretary of the company. The mill was showing a profit when the money panic of 1907 swept the country. The consignees in the East cancelled their contracts with the mill and even refused to receive the yarns already shipped them. Caught in this unexpected situation with no market for its products, the mill was forced to close. It stood idle for about nine years when it was sold to Colonel Johnson and others, of North Carolina, who enlarged it to 16,000 spindles and have since successfully operated and much improved it.

During the years 1903 and 1904, Mr. J. C. Houser, a young attorney of Lewistown, Pennsylvania, visiting this section for health and for business opportunities, became impressed with the idea of connecting the two leading towns of Bell County—Belton and Temple—with an electric interurban railroad. He discussed the matter with business men of both towns, especially of Temple, and received such encouragement that he decided to go home and try to interest his financial friends and neighbors in the enterprise. He did so and in due time a representative committee of Pennsylvania gentlemen came here with Mr. Houser to look the proposition over. The eastern capitalists offered to build and operate the road provided the two towns would purchase a certain amount of the company's stock and construction bonds. This was finally arranged and the road was built. Construction began in December, 1904, and the line was completed and began operation in March or April of 1905. It included a line connecting the two towns and a loop for local service in each—about twelve miles of trackage, including spurs, sidings, and switches. A power house and car barn was erected at Midway, near the half-way point, and there was produced the electric current to operate the cars.

The company was chartered as the Belton and Temple Traction Company on May 5, 1904, and the first board of directors consisted of eleven Pennsylvanians, and N. K. Smith of Belton, and A. F. Bentley of Temple. One of the directors, Mr. H. E. Ahrens, became the contractor and built and equipped the road. Mr. J. H. Houser served as manager until he was relieved October 1, 1905, by Mr. Walter G. Haag, also from Pennsylvania. Mr. Haag continued in the position until August 2, 1923, when Mr. Houser again took charge.

Unfortunately the enterprise did not have the financial success anticipated by its promoters. This was largely due to the coming of the automobile and the building of a good pike road between the two towns.

The road passed through a Federal receivership in 1909-10 and was then taken over, through trustees, by the holders of the first mortgage bonds sold in the original construction. The original stock-holders were wiped out and the bond-holders became the stock-holders of a new company styled The Southwestern Traction Company, though another bond issue covered one-half the invested capital. These again put the company through a State Court receivership and at the receivers' sale the properties were again purchased and placed in the hands of trustees for the second set of bond-holders and they operated the road for some years. Meantime the road ceased to use its power house, but obtained its electric current from the Texas Power and Light Company.

The owners of the line and the people of both towns had hoped that, in the not distant future, the Dallas-Waco interurban might come this way, absorb the Belton-Temple line and extend it on to Austin and San Antonio, but as the road has now entirely ceased operations this dream has vanished.

Besides the properties mentioned the original company acquired a thirty-eight acre tract of land at Midway, covered with beautiful live oaks and other shade trees and built therein a commodious summer theatre. But this also turned out to be unprofitable, and the premises, known as Midway Park, and used for several years by the Bell County Fair Association for holding its annual fairs, was sold to the society known as the Ku Klux Klan, whose meetings were held there.

The prosperity of the farmers, which had seemed so assured by the great cotton crop of 1900 and the high prices which had come with the new century, was soon threatened by the coming of a new and seemingly ineradicable pest, the boll-weevil. While that crop was being grown, this insect had crossed the Rio Grande from Mexico and it soon spread over the fields of southern Texas. Within two or three years it had reached Bell County and its ravages almost destroyed the crops of 1904 and 1905. The United States Government at once sent trained entomologists to study its habits and to seek means of destroying it; but they have never even yet succeeded in doing to. As is told in the famous boll-weevil song, it seemed to thrive on any sort of treatment. About the best the farmer can do is to plant early, cultivate intensively and hope for a hot sumer and a cold winter. In some sections of the South the weevil has forced the farmers to turn to other things than cotton; but on our black-land tenant farms that has been a difficult thing to do. The reduction in the cotton crop during the first years of heavy infestation was a blow not only to the cotton farmer but likewise to the business men of the towns whose business depended so much upon the condition of the farmers. Every town in this section felt the effects of the ravages of the little insect. Although the weevil did the most damage during the first years of infestation, it continued to cut down production—with the aid of soil erosion and exhaustion from the continuous planting of cotton on the same ground. For these reasons, doubtless, the Bell County crop of 1909 showed only a small advance over that of ten years before—58,050 bales to 56,560 in 1899—although the acreage planted in cotton had increased from 145,784 to 190,217 acres.

The boll-weevil was not the only thing that checked the growing prosperity of the county. In October 1907 occured a money panic in the East which affected the whole country. The banks in New York refused to pay out cash, except in small sums, and banks throughout the interior, even those with large balances in the New York banks, could not obtain their New York deposits in cash. It became necessary in turn for all of the banks throughout the country, however solvent, to suspend cash payments except in small amounts, usually $5.00 per day per person.

The bankers in Bell County promptly met and agreed to issue cashiers' checks as an emergency currency, guaranteed by all of the banks in the county. This paper was issued by each of the banks when money was demanded and it passed current in business, performing all of the functions of government currency during the period of the money disturbance. At the end of some sixty or ninety days, when the crisis had passed, the emergency papers was all redeemed and cash payments were resumed. Of course, business went on as usual, checks being substituted for cash; and confidence was generally maintained in business circles. There had been a fear that cash would be withdrawn in large amounts from the banks, go into hiding and thus cause the suspension of business or bankruptcy in many branches of industry. The system adopted by the Bell County banks saved the day and nobody was seriously hurt, beyond the depression that business always suffers in times of money deflation. Here is a copy of one of the emergency cashiers' checks mentioned above:

No. 1999

THE BELTON NATIONAL BANK
Belton, Texas

$1.00........................Will pay to the Bearer........................$1.00
In Convenient Exchange at Par
O N E   D O L L A R

Belton, Texas, November 18, 1907   W. W. James,
                                          Ass't. Cashier.

On the reverse side:

$1   This Check will be received by this Bank
     as a deposit or for any obligation held by
     it, and by all merchants in business trans- $1
     actions with them.

These checks, slightly larger than government currency, were printed in black type on a blue ground with blue border, and on account of their resemblance to the advertising literature of a certain large mail order house in the east, the people about town facetiously called them "Soap Receipts"!

5. *Agitation for More Railroads*

Large sections of the county which had not been directly served by the railroads built in the early eighties were eager for the advantages that these carriers could bring them. This was especially true of those towns along the old Waco-Austin stage road, like Salado and Corn Hill, which had been seriously damaged by the competition of the railroad towns. Both Belton and Temple, rival towns, also desired to extend their railway connections. In the nineties there was much talk for a while of a railroad to be built from Temple to Salado, but the project, if ever seriously entertained by those who started the discussion, evaporated in mere talk.

About 1908 the business men of Waco, Belton, Salado and Georgetown got together in a movement to build a railroad from Waco to Georgetown by way of Belton and Salado. Several conferences were held and a small fund was contributed with which a reconnaisance survey and a tentative estimate of construction costs were made by an experienced engineer; but efforts to finance the road failed and the matter dropped. The next year the Temple and Northwestern Railway Company was chartered to build from Temple by way of Gatesville and Hamilton to Comanche. The company surveyed and located its line, procured most of the necessary right of way, even did considerable grading and laid a mile or so of track out of Temple, when it exhausted its funds and, unable to procure more, gave up the project.

A more ambitious enterprise with, apparently, a better prospect of success was undertaken in 1910 when a charter was filed for a railroad to run from Quanah, up in Hardeman County, to Rockport on the Gulf of Mexico. Its corporate name was the Quanah, Seymour, Dublin and Rockport Railway Company, but it was popularly known as the "Middlebuster" because it was to pass through the middle of the state and cross a number of the existing railroad lines. The charter did not call for the line to run through Belton but through the western part of the county. Belton business men did not intend to be left off the line, however, and invited Colonel L. E. Walker, president of the company, to visit them and make a proposition. When he offered to bring the road through Belton if the town would donate $100,000, the Commercial Club accepted the proposition in less than a minute! Committees were appointed to raise the subsidy and mass meetings met almost daily to push on the work. Salado citizens also helped and when the subscription reached the sum of $70,000 Colonel Walker said he was satisfied and would waive the balance. Active preparations for building began. The whole line, from Quanah through Belton and Austin to Rockport, was surveyed and cross-sectioned by means of contributions all along the route. Actual construction began at Belton where about $40,000 of cash was actually paid in. Most of the right of way between Belton and Salado was procured and a portion of it was graded. Meanwhile Colonel Walker got in touch with English promoters, visited London in person, arranged for the necessary funds in London and Brussels, contracted for the construction of the whole line and apparently had everything in shape for the consummation of the enterprise when the Balkan War broke out, in 1912, and so disturbed European finances that the promised funds were delayed. After this war ended, active preparations were again going ahead when— Crash!—came the World War. In that maelstrom the "Middlebuster" sank, never to be brought to the surface again.

In later years improved highways, which reach further and further into all important sections of the county and the State, and automobiles and auto-trucks have made the railroad less necessary to the economic life of smaller communities. Moreover, the financial difficulties of the railroads have almost stopped the building of new lines. Unless some great change, now unforeseen, takes place, it is improbable that we shall ever see a renewal of the agitation for building railroads in our county.

6. Population Trends in the County, 1890-1910

As we have already seen, the population of the county in 1890, as reported by the United States Census, numbered 33,377—30,716 whites and 2,661 negroes. Temple then had 4,047 and Belton 3,000 inhabitants. No other town had more than a few hundred. By 1900, according to the same authority, the total for the county had grown to 45,535, of whom 41,723 were whites and 3,812 were negroes. Belton's population had increased to 3,700 while Temple's had risen to 7,065. The next largest town was Killeen with 780, since more than half of Bartlett, with a total of 957, was in Williamson County. The rate of increase, therefore, had been slightly more than 36%, which was pretty good for the hard times of the nineties. In the generally more prosperous ten years from 1900 to 1910 the rate of growth fell off sharply, for the total population of the county in the later year was 49,186, showing an increase of only about 8%. An interesting development is disclosed by the Census for 1910—all the growth was in the incorporated towns. Temple had increased to 10,993, Belton to 4,164, while Killeen and Rogers had nearly doubled their size and now had 1,265 and 1,275 respectively. Bartlett, on the Williamson County line, had also very nearly doubled its population—from 957 to 1,815. While the increase for the whole county had been only 3,641, the incorporated towns alone showed 5,839 additional inhabitants. To put it in another way, Temple's increase had been more than that of the county as a whole; and the areas outside the incorporated towns showed a loss of 2,198 people Although the numbers of acres in "improved farms" had increased by over 5,000 in these ten years, the *number of farms* (each separate tenant holding is counted as a farm) *decreased* by 144. This was probably because the more extensive use of farming machinery had enabled the farmer to cultivate more land and therefore increased the average acreage. But an increase of only 8% in population in ten years was surely less than normal and is to be explained by the fact that a portion of the surplus from the farm was being drained off to the cheaper lands of western Texas—which was then being settled very rapidly—and to the towns, especially to the larger centers outside of Bell County. Another rather interesting thing is that while the white population for the county showed an increase of only 1,161, the black population increased by 2,490. Apparently most of the negroes had come into the towns as laborers, since there was only a very slight increase of them on the farms.

7. *Improvements in the Public Schools*

From time to time in the preceding chapters we have made reference to the public schools in Bell County; but since the greatest development in the schools took place in the period covered by this chapter it may be well to summarize the steps in their progress from the beginning. As already related, our first schools were private affairs conducted by any persons who desired to undertake them. The State, and the county as well, had been too poor to establish a good system nor were trained teachers available. Back in 1854 the State undertook to set up a general system but accomplished little before the Civil War broke out. After the war the poverty of the State and the people again prevented effective action. The radical Republicans, under Governor E. J. Davis, inaugurated a system in 1870-'71, but it was of such a character that it was unpopular and it was swept away by the Constitution of 1876. For the next eight years such public schools as existed were paid for by a very small apportionment from the State school fund, by voluntary contributions and by tuition fees.

The basic law underlying our present system was enacted in 1884 when the counties were allowed to divide themselves into districts in each of which school trustees were to be elected to manage the schools under the general supervision of the county school board. Towns could incorporate themselves as independent school districts and could levy a local tax of twenty cents on the one hundred dollars of property valuations, but only by vote of two-thirds of the property owners. In 1887 county superintendents of schools were provided. Under this law the schools were somewhat better supported, especially in some of the independent districts, although it proved very difficult to get a vote of two-thirds of the property owners for a tax upon themselves. Judged by the standards of our time the schools were still very poor even in the towns. The little country district schools were pitifully inadequate. Housed in cheap, shabby buildings, with virtually no equipment, running but three or four months in the year, under poorly paid and poorly trained teachers, they hardly deserved the name of schools. The teachers were often chosen out of favoritism or to give employment to local boys or girls entirely without regard to their qualifications for the work. The town schools were somewhat better, but few of them would pass muster today. There were few public high schools in the State worthy of the name before 1890. About 1885 the young University of Texas began to try to raise the standards of the high schools in order to insure better preparation on the part of students who wished to enter college, and as the years went by this supervision resulted in steady improvement.

As the general economic condition of the people began to improve, especially after 1900, more money began to be available for schools and communities began to take more pride in them. Moreover, the teachers, better trained and better organized, were working for improvements. In 1908 the Constitution was amended to allow a majority of *all qualified voters* to impose a property tax of fifty cents on the hundred dollars of valuation for the support of the schools. This provided more funds both for buildings and equipment and salaries for better teachers. Before this time the University of Texas, the A. & M. College, the state normal schools (now called State teachers' colleges), as well as the several denominational colleges, were sending their well trained graduates back into the schools as teachers.

What has been said above is applicable to Bell County as well as to the State in general. Naturally, the public schools in the larger towns, Belton and Temple, were the first to develop efficient graded primary schools and standardized high schools. But Killeen, Rogers, Holland, Troy and Pendleton also developed high schools and subordinate grades, and more recently several well organized rural districts, formed by the consolidation of several adjacent school districts, have done the same. Most of them have imposed a tax upon themselves to support these better schools and have introduced many new and interesting features into the curricula. Some of the buildings, such as the Temple High School, are very handsome.

8. *The Agricultural Experiment Station and Its Work*

When the virgin lands of this section were first turned over by the plow they were fertile and grew abundant crops without the use of fertilizers; and as the farms were somewhat scattered they were seldom infested from other areas by the destructive insect pests. Little thought was given in those days to the conservation of the fertility of the soil or to preventing erosion by flood waters. But as time went on the fertility of these farm lands began to decline because of erosion, continuous cropping in cotton and bad methods of cultivation. As the fields spread out until they were separated only by fences or roads, insect pests passed easily from one to another. Along in the eighties some farmers bought from seed dealers in the South Atlantic States small quantities of seed of a new grass which was lauded as a great hay producer and meadow grass. It was the notorious Johnson grass. The farmers discovered that it was a perennial which spread from both seed and roots, that they could not get rid of it without infinite labor, and that it threatened to take possession of the rest of their farms. The railroads, which carried it for hay with live-stock shipments, soon spread it all along the right-of-way and thence it went into the adjacent fields. Then the leaf worm and the boll worm, and finally the worst pest of all, the boll-weevil, appeared. These pests and the increasing impoverishment of the soil reduced cotton production per acre by one-third to one-half of what it had been in earlier years. Agriculture was on the decline in the black-land belt and seemed headed for ruin.

But when the scientifically trained expetrs from the Department of Agriculture came along and tried to tell the farmers the causes of some of their troubles and how to remedy them, they were laughed at and scorned as "book farmers" who couldn't possibly know anything. Some of the more intelligent and progressive farmers, it is true, did listen and try to carry out the recommendations of the experts—usually with fair success—but the conservative old-style farmer clung subbornly to his old ways. It became evident, however, that it was not sufficient to send out experts to lecture to the farmers; it was necessary to put on practical demonstrations of better methods and also to carry out many experiments under careful observation with respect to soils, seeds, varieties of products and methods of combatting destructive pests. The United States Government had for many years helped to maintain an experimental agricultural station at the A. & M. College. It began to extend its support to certain substations located in different parts of the State. In 1911 one was designated for Bell County and was located near Midway, on the Belton and Temple pike, and called the Temple sub-station. A number of persons in both Temple and Belton contributed money for the purchase of the land. The station began operations in 1912 with experiments on various types of crops on different kinds of soil. The experts in charge have invited farmers to visit the experimental farm and have held conferences of farmers and stockmen, and have done a valuable work for Bell and adjacent counties. The farmers who have given most careful attention to what has been demonstrated there are readily recognized as the most successful in the county. Some others have stubbornly stayed away, saying that "book farmers" can teach them nothing. Unfortunately, this seems to be true, but not for the reasons they give. The truth is becoming clearer every year that the successful farmer of the future must be an educated man, a man trained for his work, for farming is likely to become one of the learned professions.

9. *The Good Roads Movement and the Advent of the Automobile*

Early in the present century a number of public spirited men were inspired with the idea that good roads would do much to improve conditions in town and country. They formed a sort of band of evangelists styled "The National Good Roads Association of the United States," with headquarters in St. Lous, Missouri. The railroad companies furnished them free transportation for their personnel and road demonstration equipment and contributed liberally, with other large commercial interests, to the expenses of the campaigns including, of course, reasonable salaries to the field operators. The latter held "conventions" all over the country lasting from one to three days, during which addresses, actual demonstrations, distribution of good roads literature, printed by the government, and other methods of publicity were employed to challenge the attention of the general public to the importance of the subject. These conventions were entertaining and instructive and undoubtedly aroused attention to the gross inadequacy of the transportation facilities of the back country—conditions that, in rainy seasons, placed an embargo upon rural travel and rendered the delivery of farm products to the markets and railroad stations impracticable, as occured in our county during the fall and winter of 1902-3.

Col. William H. Moore, of Chicago, was the general and capable president of this unique organization and he was generally accompanied in his missionary journeys over Texas by Col. T. P. Rixey of St. Louis, Capt. Wm. Bradburn, Civil Engineer of Houston, Texas, and others, who completed a strong team of good road evangels. Local speakers and committees were drafted in the communities of the conventions, especially county commissioners and others who were officially charged with the opening and up-keep of public highways. The main object was agitation and propaganda—and it was well planned and successfully carried on.

This association held a convention in Temple in February, 1905, and another in Belton, March 23, 1907. Both conventions were fairly well attended by progressive citizens from town and country and, without doubt, left a profound impression upon the minds of our people—of those absent as well as those present. The campaign being thus launched upon the public, the agitation went on and in due time an era of good road building was ushered in upon the people of Bell County, greatly stimulated by the grading and graveling of the Belton and Temple pike by our Commissioners' Court under directions and advice of engineers of the Good Roads Bureau of the United States, in 1912.

An object lesson of great force was presented during the early part of the decade. During the entire fall of 1902 and the early winter following, there was a continuous rainfall. It was unprecedented. The roads in numerous sections became impassable. Along some of the lanes buggies and wagons stuck in the mud and remained so for days and some of them for weeks. In the towns, especially in the black-land sections, grocery merchants and others delivered goods to their customers on horseback or by pedestrians, where there was no pavement. Traffic, and business requiring transportation over the public roads and streets, came almost completely to a stand-still. Such an experience increased the agitation for better roads.

The first efforts were confined to grading and ditching the dirt roads and to bridging the streams, large and small. Thus the way was being prepared for something better—graveled roads—later on. Our commissioners went the full limit of their financial resources in these preliminary efforts and conditions were much improved.

The real beginning of good roads construction in Bell County was when Justice Precinct Number One, including Belton, voted a bond issue of $150,000 for good roads on May 16, 1913. This was followed soon afterward by similar action in various other sections of the county—embracing in the aggregate almost every community—until graveled highways extended out from Belton, Temple Rogers, Holland, Killeen and every other important center and penetrated nearly every section of the agricultural area of the county. Eighteen road districts had voted bonds aggregating a little over $1,200,000 when on December 10, 1917, these bond issues were merged, the road districts canceled out, and a new bond issue of $1,900,000 was voted by the people of the whole county, with the proceeds of which all of the previous district bond issues were liquidated in full and refunded, and the surplus of nearly $700,000 was used in new road construction. Steel bridges over the large streams and concrete culverts and spillways over the minor waterways characterized the building plans.

State and Federal aid was obtained on highways of statewide or national rank, such as the King of Trails and the Meridian Highway, which was also designated as the Mexico-Texas Highway.

Commissioner W. P. Denman, of Belton, deserves much credit for his championship and efficient execution of the good roads program endorsed and promoted by the citizens of his precinct and of the county. His service extended from 1907 to 1922, a period of fifteen years.

The early days of the century saw two or three little rattling chain-driven affairs called automobiles, horseless vehicles or "gas buggies," owned and used by physicians. They were "fearfully and wonderfully made" and were not a joy but a nuisance forever—generally they ran down one hill and had to be backed up the next hill. Their day was brief. By 1908, however, there were several standard "machines" rolling around here and during the next five years there were several hundred. Every automobile owner was an enthusiastic good roads advocate and, conversely, the completed good roads set up a yearning in everybody to own an automobile. At this writing (1923) there are more than six thousand automobiles registered in Bell County. With a greater prosperity the number will probably double.

The buggy horse has disappeared almost completely, and the draft horse and mule hitched to the farm wagon are seldom seen on the public highways, for they too have been replaced by the auto truck in consequence of good roads. Even the auto tractor has appeared on the farm. The summer and fall breaking and harrowing of the land, the harvesting of the grain, the operation of the grain separator, the hauling of the farm products to town and many other kinds of farm work—pumping water and sawing wood—are being done more and more each year by the motive power of the tractor, and at a wonderful saving in time and efficiency. But thus far, the horse and the mule are holding their own for the cultivation of the "row crops"—corn and cotton—as all efforts to adapt the tractor to this service have failed.

First the railroad, telegraph, and telephone annihilated distance in travel, transportation, and communication. Now the automobile spans the intermediate spaces of the country, bringing distant towns and communities and farms in close touch; the auto-truck moves the farmer right up to the door of his market; and the farm tractor reduces weeks of labor down to days or even hours. The next author of a history of Bell County will doubtless devote this space to aeroplanes and the like. In fact, it so happens that as this line is penned, an aero engine is singing its song some two or three thousand feet above my head in Belton, in a merry spin probably from Dallas or Ft. Worth to San Antonio—a matter of only about two or three hours' time in these new chariots of the sky.

CHAPTER XV

PRIVATE EDUCATIONAL INSTITUTIONS OF BELL COUNTY

1. *Salado College*

We have told in an earlier chapter something of the founding of this once famous old school, and our readers will recall that it began with a "tent meeting" at the Salado Springs on October 8, 1859, when Colonel E. S. C. Robertson offered to donate one hundred acres north and south of the springs to a corporation to be formed with a capital of not less than $5,000 for the purpose of erecting the College, an offer which was accepted on the spot.

For sometime there had been much talk of the need of a more advanced school than the county afforded. Thus far only a few small private schools for the younger children were in existence and there was no institution of college rank anywhere along this western frontier. Interest in such an enterprise seems to have focused along the Salado, but leading men in Belton and other parts of the county were also discussing it. By the fall of 1859 the movement was coming to a head, but the location first suggested seems to have been the Sulphur Spring, some three miles down the creek from the Salado Springs, probably because this place was looked upon as a future health resort since many famiiles were already in the habit of camping there in the summer to drink its waters. The "tent meeting" referred to was actually called to consider the organization of a school at the Sulphur Spring, but adjourned without taking action and immediately reconvened to accept the plan of Colonel Robertson.

In this new meeting "articles of association" were prepared (perhaps they had already been prepared) and were signed by Dr. Carroll Kendrick, A. W. Cearnal, John Clabaugh, W. L. Martin, John T. Flint, A. J. Dallas, J. C. Lynch, John S. Blair, Newton M. Proctor, E. Sterling C. Robertson, and Dr. T. C. Denson. The capital stock was fixed at not less than $5,000 in shares of $100 each. In addition to those named above some thirty-five others signed the agreement and took one or more shares of the stock. Seven trustees, as provided by the articles, were chosen by the stockholders: Hermon Aiken, John S. Blair,

Carroll Kendrick, A. J. Dallas, E. S. C. Robertson, W. D. Eastland, and G. W. Shanklin. Colonel Robertson was made president and ex-officio secretary and treasurer. The board of trustees received from him by deed of gift, dated October 16, 1859, the hundred acres of land which included not only a high elevation on the south side of the creek for a school site but a portion of the beautiful wooded valley, some of the springs and land on the north side of the creek.

In the meantime the tract was surveyed and subdivided, a small temporary wooden school building provided for, and plans drawn for a two-story stone structure containing one wing 40 x 20 feet in the clear, inside measurement, and the other 20 x 20 feet measured likewise, the two forming an ell. This structure became the eastern portion of the College building when the latter was enlarged. The contract for this first stone building was awarded to S. Bramlet & Son for $4,000. At a meeting of the board of trustees held November 18, 1859, Dr. (and Reverend) Carroll Kendrick offered the following resolutions which were adopted:

"That the Board of Trustees apply to the Legislature for an act incorporating Salado College as soon as practicable;
The said Board urge upon the Legislature the insertion of a clause inhibiting the sale of intoxicating liquors, the keeping of billiard saloons and ten pin alleys on the land donated by E. Sterling C. Robertson for college purposes and for as great a distance around the same as practicable, in the act of incorporating the same."

In response to the application of the trustees, the legislature by an act approved February 8, 1860, duly incorporated "Salado College" for twenty years with full powers to maintain the institution, grant diplomas, confer degrees and perform other corporate functions. The College was to "be open to pupils of all religious demoninations, but should never become sectarian in its character, nor shall the peculiar doctrines of any religious denomination be taught therein."

On November 26, 1859, the board instructed its president to advertise in the Belton *Independent,* the Austin *Intelligencer,* the Waco *Democrat* and the Houston *Telegraph* for a primary teacher. On January 18, they elected Levi Tenney, a scholarly Presbyterian minister then residing in Falls County, to this position and issued a formal announcement that the school would open on February 20.

Although a severe winter hindered building operations of both the school and the new residents of the place, the school actually opened on the date set with the teachers occupying tents. From the first the attendance was good and by the next May there were sixty pupils. On May 20, 1860, the trustees adopted a set of "Rules and Regulations of Salado College, also an Outline of its Organization," of which five hundred copies were printed in a four-page leaflet.

The construction of the stone College building had progressed far enough to lay the corner-stone on July 4, 1860. By request of the trustees, Belton Lodge No. 166, Ancient Free and Accepted Masons, conducted the ceremonies under special dispensation from John B. McMahon, of Seguin, Grand Master of the Masons of Texas, who named Mr. Sam Mather of Georgetown as his representative for the occasion. The corner-stone was laid with the usual Masonic ceremony in the presence of a large assemblage of people, many of whom came from other counties and from towns as far away as Austin and Waco. The Salado people served a great barbecue and entertained their visitors in the old-time spirit of hospitality. The College people held a great sale of lots—of course, some had been sold before this time—and persons from all over central Texas purchased and become identified with the enterprise, and many of them moved to Salado to educate their children. The exact date on which the College building was completed and accepted by the trustees is not known, but it was probably in the fall or winter of 1860-61.

The attendance increased from 75 in the first short term to 125 the next year. In 1862 it was 180; in 1863 it fell off slightly to 150, and in 1864 to 126. Thus even the hardships of the war period did not prevent the new school from carrying on. It must be remembered, however, that not all of these pupils were in the College proper, for some were in the primary department. In those days of thinly scattered population, where money was very scarce, no school could sustain itself from the fees of students of college rank alone. When peace returned in 1865 the attendance shot upward, for there was an enrollment of 307 that year, a mark that was never quite reached again. Between 1866 and 1872 the attendance averaged about 250 —the highest being 289 in 1866 and the lowest, 223, in 1867. In 1873, the year of the terrible financial panic, it dropped to 169. Figures for the subsequent twelve years are not available.

After the war the student body represented all sections of the State and even the larger cities. In a catalog issued in 1873, there were students registered from Alvarado, Bastrop, Bremond, Brenham, Caldwell, Calvert, Cameron, Circleville, Davila, Davisville, Eagle Springs, Florence, Gainesville, Georgetown, Giddings, Marlin, Nelsonville, Orange, Perry, San Saba, Shovel Mountain, Texana, Towash, Travis, Waco, Washington, and from all points in Bell County, and in the five or six preceding years, the patronage was even more widely distributed throughout the State. The good people of the town opened their homes for the accommodation of the non-resident students and thus a wholesome home influence was enjoyed by all of them. There was never a regular "boarding house" in all the history of Salado as a school town.

The founders of the College were determined that no avoidable temptations should surround the students of the school. In all deeds made by the corporation for the conveyance of lots there was this clause:

"It being agreed that should the owner of said lot sell spirituous, vinous or other intoxicating liquors in quantities less than a quart or permit the same to be done by others on said lot, the title or claim to the same is to revert back to said (naming the grantor in the deed)."

and this recital was copied into all the conveyances, from one to another, for many years after the founding of the village. On September 26, 1866, a special act of the legislature prohibited the sale or gift of intoxicating liquors within six miles of Salado College, except for medicinal or sacramental purposes, under penalty of a fine of from $50 to $100.

The testimony of a soldier who passed through the town in July, 1869, may indicate something of the attitude of the people of Salado:

"The village (of Salado) is particularly impressed upon my mind as being the first teetotal, "sure enough," "total abstinence" villages that I ever visited. A female college, or some institution of learning, controlled the place and its surroundings, and neither "love nor money" could induce or produce any kind of spirits—at least so said the boys who investigated the subject as we passed through."[1]

The head of the College was called the "principal" and

---

[1] H. H. McConnell, **Five Years a Cavalryman**, etc., pp. 183-184.

Left: Dr. S. J. Jones, founder and principal of the Thomas Arnold High School, Salado.

Right: The faculty of Salado College, about 1873. Front row, left to right: James L. Smith, Otto Fuchs, W. T. Etheridge. Top row: Miss Mittie Collins, Samuel G. Sanders, Miss Sallie R. Young.

the other members of the faculty were "assistants," (Wherever the word "president" is encountered it refers to the president of the board of trustees.) From the best information available the following list of the members of the teaching staff of the College has been compiled:

Rev. Levi Tenney, Principal, February 20, 1860 to July 20, 1861. Assistants: M. W. Robertson, W. H. Long.

Dr. J. H. Anderson, Principal, July 1861 to October 1862. Assistants not now known

Gideon J. Buck, Principal, October 1862 to July 1863. Assistants not now known.

Prof. James Lowery Smith, A.M., Principal, September 1863 to March 1874. Assistants (at different times): Higher Courses, A. J. Harris, A.M.; Lucius H. Davis, A.M.; W. T. Etheridge, A.M.; Samuel G. Sanders, A. B..; Intermediate, Miss Lou Smith, Miss Letitia Barbee, W. E. Rosborough, Mrs. Lucius H. Davis; Primary, Miss Sallie R. Young; music, Mrs. ―― Rogers, Mrs. Chas. A. Bigelow, Prof. Otto Fuchs. Others not now known.

Dr. Samuel D. Sanders, A.M., Principal, March 1874 to July 1876, Assistants: James L. Smith, A.M.; Samuel G. Sanders, A.B.; Lucius H. Davis, A.M.; Mrs. W. H. Garrett, Mrs. L. H. Davis, Mrs. Martha J. Sanders, Prof E. L. Faupel (music), and others.

Prof. O. H. McQuber, Principal, July 1876 to July 1879. Assistants Mrs. ―― Purdom, Major H. A. Conisins and others.

Prof. James Lowery Smith, A.M., Principal, July 1879 to July 1880; Miss Frances Peace and other assistants not known.

Col. Wm. A. Alexander, Principal, July, 1880, to ―― 1880. Assistants ―― Green, ―― Bradley and others.

Prof. Smith Ragsdale, Principal, 1880 to July 1883. Assistants: C. A. Bryant, Miss Hettie Sublett, Miss Cook (music) and others.

Major Wm. A. Banks, Principal, July 1883 to July 1884. Assistants: C. A. Bryant, A. L. Banks, Miss Hettie Sublett, Miss ―― Ray, ―― Hickman, Miss Lena Williams and others.

Dr. Samuel J. Jones, Ph.D., Principal, July 1884 to July 1885. Assistants: Lucius H. Davis, A.M.; R. B. Halley, Jr., Mrs. Charlotte Halloran Jones, A. L. Banks, ―― Hickman, Miss Emma Halley.

The following is nearly, but not quite, a complete roll of the graduates of Salado College for the years named:

1867: Helen F. Embree (Mrs. George C. Pendleton), Melissa H. Barbee (Mrs. J. H. Barbee), Nannie Wilkerson (Mrs. Robt. N. Wright).

1868: Anna C. Leach (Mrs. F. P. Cooper), Belle A. Young (Mrs. ―― Million), Sallie M. Vickery (Mrs. C. W. Macune).

1869: Wm. E. Rosborough, Geo. Frank Vickery, Wm. Stewart Vickery.

1871: Geo. W. Tyler, Thos. H. Jones, Jr., Fredonia Augusta Halley (Mrs. Charles H. Ramsdell), Bettie S. Mabry (Mrs. Gus Norrell), Lora D. Mabry (Mrs. J. A. Cruse).

1872: Granville N. Vickery, Luella Robertson (Mrs. Z. T. Fulmore), Annie M. Baines (Mrs. W. E. Rosborough).

1873: Mary V. Vickery (Mrs. J. T. King).
1874: Francis M. Ray, Thos. R. Russell, Wm. S. Wolf.
1875: Alice Rose (Mrs. T. R. Russell), Helen Rose (Mrs. A. J. Mackey), Wm. F. Moore.
1876: Addie Barton, Laura Sherman (Mrs. D. E. Patterson), Huling P. Robertson, John W. Dickinson.
1880: Kate S. Crawford (Mrs. Z. C. Taylor).
1884: Albert R. Crawford.

The following persons have served on the Board of Trustees of Salado College from 1859 and contributed much in time, service and money to its beneficent work:

Col. E. S. C. Robertson, Col. Hermon Aiken, Dr. Carrol Kendrick, A. J. Dallas, Dr. Wm. D. Eastland, Gordon W. Shanklin, John S. Blair, Judge O. T. Tyler, Dr. Welborn Barton, Col. Thos. H. Jones, Rev. Wm. K. Hamblen, L. A. Griffith, Judge John E. King, John W. Vickery, Col. N. L. Norton, Wm. A. Davis, Vachel H. Anderson, Capt. A. M. Keller, Wm. J. Caskey, Huling P. Robertson, Rev. John M. Porter, Capt. Henry C. Smith, Major A. J. Rose, Capt. Thos. E. Woods, Dr. D. G. Adams, Prof. Lucius H. Davis, Mc. T. Bush, Wm. F. Moore, Hon. Wm. P. Hancock, A. D.Griffith, W. H. Harkey, J. W. Love, John H. Orgain, J. W. Sutherland, G. C. Love, and others.

The following persons served as presidents of the Board of Trustees: Col. E. S. C. Robertson, Judge O. T. Tyler, Major A. J. Rose, Capt. A. M. Keller, Dr. D. G. Adams, J. W. Love, and perhaps others.

About the later sixties, two literary societies were organized among the older students of Salado College, which made their impress upon the general tone and morale of the school, as well as upon the progress and development of the student body.

The Euphradian Society, fostered and promoted by Prof. James L. Smith, principal of the school, and his assistant, Capt. A. J. Harris, was organized in 1866 for study of parliamentary law and practice and to afford an opportunity to the young men to improve themselves in public speaking and debate. Officers were changed monthly. Debates were held weekly. A question was selected by vote. The president then named three judges and a leader for each side of the question and these leaders at once, by alternate selection, divided the whole society (except the president, secretary and the three judges) into two sides, by "choosing up" and thus the debating teams were lined up for the next weekly meeting. Every one had the chance to discharge the duties of the various official positions, as well as that of participating in the debates. Speeches were limited to a few minutes each. While all had the privilege, in practice, only a limited number, at each meeting, responded with an argument, when their names were called—so that the debates were not protracted greatly. The three judges, not participating in the discussion, awarded the victory to the winning side. In the long years there were some lively and wordy jousts in the Euphradian. At each annual commencement the Society invited some able speaker to address them and appeared with him upon the rostrum on such occasions. Among those who thus honored the Society were B. H. Carroll, D. D., Hon. A. W. Terrell, Rev. Sam P. Wright and others.

A number of prominent men, in the various professions and avocations in Texas, here learned their first lessons in public speaking and had their first experience in friendly contests, that well fitted them for the subsequent conflicts and forensic battles of real life. A roll call of the old Euphradian Society would disclose many names more or less familiar in the subsequent social, professional and political life of Texas.

The other Society, organized by the ladies, was more fortunate than the Euphradian, in that it has enjoyed the advantage of a loyal and devoted historian, Mrs. Kate Alma Orgain, and it is chiefly from her comprehensive account that we draw the facts for our brief sketch

The proposition to form a reading club or society for the young ladies of the College and of the village originated with Miss Sallie R. Young, Miss Letitia Barbee and Mrs. Orgain, all teachers in the College, in 1868. They with several other ladies met at the home of Mrs. E. S. C. Robertson and there organized. The meetings were held at the homes of members, until a room in the College building was assigned to them and was properly furnished for their purposes. Soon after it was started the society held a Fair in the College, which cleared $130.00. This amount was expended for books, which were the foundation of a circulating library. This was increased by purchase of additional books from time to time, and was perhaps the first circulating library in Texas under the management of women. Meetings were held weekly, at which some one usually read aloud from some author agreed upon. Entertainments were given to raise money for the purchase of books. Among those participating in the first institution of the society, besides those above mentioned were Mesdames E. S. C. Robertson, W. A. Davis, Lynch, Welborn Barton, O. T. Tyler, Gavin, Misses Sue Standefer, Rebecca Barton, Melissa Barbee, Augusta Halley, Sallie Vickery, Josephine Aiken, Ann Garrett, Mollie Bonner. Subsequent members were Misses Laura Fowler, Cora Fowler, Alice Rose, Helen Rose, Sallie Hamblen, Mary Hamblen, Addie Barton, Emma Barton, Emma Halley, Mollie Vickery, Lillie Aiken, Pinkie Garrett, Jennie Coulter, Lillie Jones, Ada Davis, Luella Robertson, Annie Baines, Annie Tyler, Alphier Cawthon and many others.

The first president was Mrs. Kate A. Orgain. One of the first books read at the meetings was *David Copperfield* and the last play presented was Dickens' story of "Old Scrooge," in 1876. The society, though, carried on for several years after this.

The name "Amasavourian," suggested by Miss Sallie Young, was, Mrs. Orgain believed, "a coined word, made by uniting *amo* (Latin), "I love," and *savoir* (French) "to know," which a liberal translation might construe into "Love to Know" or "Love of Knowing."

The society accomplished a great work and did much to elevate the standard of womanly refinement and literary culture in the College and in the community.

When the writer matriculated as a student in Salado College in the spring of 1864, the only bell possessed by the institution was the ordinary hand affair. In the fall of 1865 or 1866, Rev. Mr. Brown, a Baptist preacher residing at Salado, returned home from a trip somewhere in the lower part of the State and brought with him a good sized bronze or brass church or College bell, which he offered to sell for some one or two hundred dollars. The citizens promptly raised the money by donations and bought the bell—the first bell the town ever owned. All these matters were stated by Prof. Jas. L. Smith, principal, in his morning chapel talks. Possibly he told where Mr. Brown obtained this bell, but, if so, the writer does not remember the fact. Mr. Ed T. Estes, of Nolan Valley, then residing temporarily in Salado, hung the bell from a scaffolding on the roof of the College building. A rope extending over the roof and down against the south wall near the stair landing enabled one standing on the ground to ring the bell. For a number of years this old bell served not only to call the boys and girls "to books" but to summon the whole citizenship to prayer-meeting, Sunday School, church services and to all other public gatherings, either at the usual hours for day service or "at early candlelight" in the evening, for the College chapel, the only assembly hall in town, served all these purposes.

When the annex of 1869-1871 was built, a large and imposing tower or belfrey was erected over the south entrance and in this was placed a new and much larger bell, donated by Dr. Wm. R. Alexander. For many years the rolling, thrilling tenor-key ding-dong of the old bell reverberated through the village and for miles around, and its echoes ring today in the memories of hundreds of people, now grown old, who as boys and girls dutifully obeyed its summons and wended their way to the sacred halls of old Salado College. In the fire of 1901 it fell and was broken into fragments, which were partally melted by the heat. They were carried away for souvenirs. On the restoration of the building, Major A. J. Rose donated another large bell which went through the fire of 1902 without injury, but in the 1924 fire it fell and was cracked and broken beyond repair.

Sometime after the large bell donated by Dr. Alexander was installed, the first or "Brown" bell was loaned by the College to the public free schools of Salado and was hung in the belfry of their building on the north side of the creek and the writer is informed that it hangs, at this time, in a section of that building, and is held in trust for the College.[2]

An interesting episode occurred in 1868. The different Synods of the Cumberland Presbyterian Church, in Texas, decided to join together in the establishment of a University to be supported by all of them, and appointed a Committee on Location to receive offers from any community desiring the same. On July 1, 1868, a petition was prepared and circulated for signatures asking the Trustees and Stockholders of Salado College to invite the location of said University at Salado and to donate the building and grounds of the College as a bonus therefor and many of the signers tendered additional donations to make the required amount. Eighty citizens of Salado signed the petition.

A stockholders meeting, to consider this petition, was held at Salado October 6, 1868, at which some thirty-four of the forty-eight shares were represented in person or by

[2] Statement of W. S. Rose.

duly authorized proxies. Col. Thos. H. Jones offered a resolution authorizing the president to carry out the purposes of the petition by negotiations with the locating committee of the Cumberland Presbyterian Church, which resolution was advocated in discussion by Messrs. W. A. Davis, O. T. Tyler, Thos. H. Jones and W. K. Hamblen.

Col. E. S. C. Robertson then took the floor in opposition and offered as a substitute a lengthy preamble setting forth the history of the Salado College Joint Stock Company and of the college, emphasizing the agreement originally entered into and the provision of the charter that the institution should never become sectarian, and concluding with resolutions that the agreement against sectarianism was binding upon all and could not be now set aside. Col. Robertson's resolutions wrought a complete change in the views of the majority of those present. Col. Jones immediately withdrew his original resolution and a long discussion ensued upon the adoption of Col. Robertson's substitute, participated in by Messrs. Robertson, Barton, Hamblen and Jones in favor of its adoption and by Messrs. Davis and Tyler against it. The substitute was adopted by 25½ ayes cast by Jno. W. Aiken, W. K. Hamblen, Welborn Barton, A. J. Dallas, E. S. C. Robertson, Thos. H. Jones, and N. M. Proctor, for themselves and those whose proxies they held, against 8½ nos cast by W. A. Davis and O. T. Tyler for themselves and those whose proxies they held.

That killed the proposition. The writer has good reason to state that it is almost a certainty that the Presbyterians would have located their school at Salado, if the latter had made the offer which was originally proposed. The locating committee of the Synods met at Round Rock in February, 1869, and located, at that meeting, the institution since known as Trinity University, at Tehuacana Springs, in Limestone County, where it was maintained for many years until it was removed to Waxahachie, where it is now.

It was the idea of those favoring the location of the Cumberland Presbyterian University at Salado that the original charter forbidding sectarianism could be amended so as to permit of the denominational institution there, and as practically all of the old stockholders, the original promoters of the College, were apparently consenting to the change, there would have been no breach of faith. Had this been done the subsequent history of Salado would have been very different and its fortunes would doubtless have been much brighter than they are today.

But the agitation for the Presbyterian school was not without its compensation. The village of Salado had now grown from one family in 1859 to some one hundred and fifty famiiles, within a radius of three miles from the College, with four well organized religious societies—the Baptist, Christian, Cumberland Presbyterian, and Methodist—all worshiping harmoniously in the chapel or auditorium of the College, using alternate Sundays in each month, and all working together in a union Sunday school, prayer meeting, and other religious and social organizations. The school, with a patronage from all sections of the State, had outgrown the capacity of the existing building, and the time had arrived for an expansion of the facilities of the College. A movement to enlarge the College building crystalized quickly and by subscriptions to stock in the company and by donations from others, the Board of Trustees were soon warranted in letting the contract for a stone addition, 45 x 60 feet, on the west side of the old building. This addition was two stories in height, with two large class rooms on the lower floor and a very large one above which was to be used as an auditorium and chapel, thus releasing the space in the old building theretofore used for that purpose. By 1871, the walls of the new addition were up, and, with a temporary floor and roof, the commencement and graduating exercises of June of that year were held therein. And in the course of time, the work was completed so as to be permanently occupied, although the plastering and finishing were delayed several years for want of funds.

When the addition to the college building was completed, there was an unliquidated debt of some $1500 carried over, with accumulation of interest, in favor of a contractor. He assigned the claim to outside parties and it was extended by a mortgage upon all the property of the company, which was finally sold on foreclosure November 6, 1877. At the sale Col. E. S. C. Robertson became the purchaser and individual owner of Salado College, with its buildings, unsold lots, etc.,[3] but, while the Company and its trustees no longer exercised any control over the same, the school was carried on in the buildings under the pri-

[3] See Deed Records Bell County, Vol. 28, page 607 et seq.

vate arrangements with Col. Robertson and, after his death in 1879, with his succession.

Meantime, on February 8, 1880, the charter of Salado College expired by its own terms and the faculty ceased to issue diplomas to the pupils completing the course of study, which accounts for the hiatus in the list of graduates from 1880 to 1884.

In 1882, a new organization was effected and a private corporation formed under the general laws of the State, under the old name of Salado College; and this new company, by deed of August 13, 1882, purchased from the estate of Col. Robertson some seven acres of the original 100 acres, embracing only the ground on the hill on which the old College buildings stood.[4] Stock in the new company was purchased by citizens of the town and community, trustees were chosen, and the new regime took charge of the buildings and maintained the school, under the management of the several gentlemen elsewhere mentioned, until 1885.

From 1885 till 1890, the buildings, grounds and equipment were turned over to the trustees of the local public free school and, during that period, were operated by them as a free school under the general free school laws of the State. From 1890 till 1913, the Thomas Arnold High School was maintained in the College building by Dr. Samuel J. Jones, under a lease, as elsewhere noted. From 1913 to 1918 the school was maintained in a meager way by the Board under the principalship of Mr.———Doyle and Mr. E. E. Dyess, successively.

On January 18, 1919, at a meeting of the stockholders of Salado College, called for the purpose, it was resolved by unanimous vote to donate the grounds and buildings to the public free schools of Salado and vicinity, to be operated under the public free school system of the State, and the trustees were instructed to convey the property to the County Judge of Bell County and his successors in office, which was accordingly done.

When Salado College was founded in 1859 there were no schools worthy of the name in this part of Texas, either public or private. It therefore served a great need. Although, as in all such institutions of that day, its faculty changed frequently, it gave sound instruction in an old-

[4] **Ibid,** Vol. 17, page 40, **et seq.**

fashioned curriculum based chiefly on mathematics, Latin and literature. The institution never had a dollar of endowment and its only resource for current maintenance was the tuition fees paid by the students. But for many years it flourished and was the source of great pride to its founders and friends because it enjoyed an excellent reputation as one of the best schools in the State. But as the state funds for the support of public schools became larger and public free schools came to be established in nearly every community—though some of them were of little merit—the unendowed private school was doomed. New colleges supported by the several churches were springing up in all parts of Texas and the State itself was at last remembering its duties and entering the field with the A. & M. College, the Sam Houston Normal Institute for teachers and finally, in 1883, with the University of Texas at Austin. Although the friends of the College made a long and hard fight to keep it going, the new competition was too much for their meagre resources. Salado College had an honorable history; but it is now only a fading memory, and with the demolition of the old stone building perhaps even the memory of it will soon be gone.

2. Baylor College for Women

This famous Baptist institution of learning harks back to February 1, 1845, when President Anson Jones approved the "Act to incorporate Baylor University,"[5] passed by the ninth Congress of the Republic of Texas. Its foundation was the work of the Texas Baptist Educational Society which had been organized in 1843. It was named in honor of Judge R. E. B. Baylor, who drew the charter, was a member of the first Board of Trustees and a benefactor of the institution. Independence, in Washington County, secured the location by a bonus of $7,925 in competition with the villages of Travis, Huntsville, and Grimes Prairie.

Baylor University was a co-educational institution until 1851. The female department was then separated, but was governed by the same Board of Trustees as the University. By an Act of the Legislature, approved Septem-

[5] Gammel, **Laws of Texas,** II, page 1130.

ber 25, 1866, the Baylor Female College was placed under the charge of a separate Board of Trustees and was conducted in buildings at Independence detached from the University.

In 1845, Independence was near the frontier limits of the population of Texas, as there were but few people residing above the Old San Antonio Road at that time— mostly at or about Nashville and (by 1846) at Cameron. The movement of population westward and northward and the isolation of Independence in the building of the railroad lines through that section brought on an agitation, in 1885, for the removal of Baylor University and the Female College to more central locations. Removal was decided upon by the Baptist State Convention at Lampasas that year and a number of places entered the competition for each institution. In 1886, the Baylor University was consolidated with Waco University, and Baylor Female College was located at Belton as a result of the raising by the town of a bonus of $32,000, consisting of grounds and new buildings erected thereon for college purposes. Rev. M. V. Smith and Rev. W. R. Maxwell, Baptist ministers, were strong factors in securing the location for Belton.

The corner-stone of the first building at Belton, now known as Luther Hall (in honor of the late Dr. J. H. Luther) was laid by the Grand Lodge of Texas, under the auspices of Belton Lodge No. 166, A. F. & A. M. on April 21, 1886, A. J. Rose, Past Grand Master, presiding, and the College was formally reopened at Belton September 13, 1886. This building was enlarged in 1888. The Wilson Administration Building (named in honor of the late Dr. W. A. Wilson), also known as Alma Reeves Chapel, was erected in 1906-7. The corner-stone was laid by the Masonic bodies above mentioned on April 21, 1906, Geo. W. Tyler, Past Grand Master, presiding—exactly twenty years after the corner-stone of the first building was laid. Since then several other commodious and imposing structures have been added, at a cost of nearly a million dollars, the chief buildings being now as follows: Luther Hall, 1886 and 1888; Wilson Building (Alma Reeves Chapel), 1906; Ferguson Hall in honor of the late C. O. and Mary A. Ferguson, 1914; Heard Hall, 1919; Wells Science Hall, in honor of the late Dr. E. H. Wells, 1920; Burt Hall, in honor of Col. R. E. Burt, 1920; Ruth Stribling Hall, 1921; The Hospital Building, 1922.

Besides the above are the buildings of the Cottage Home, the principal one being the Ely-Pepper Hall. This department of the college work, originally founded by Mrs. Elli Moore Townsend and others, as a collaborator of the main institution, has been incorporated into the College proper and is designed to aid young ladies of limited means to attend the College. The College grounds have been much extended and now comprise a large acreage, all contiguous, on which are maintained the steam heating plant, electric light plant, ice plant, laundry, dairy, etc., all utilized in connection with the College.

The following gentlemen have served as president of Baylor Female College:

Prof. Horace Clark (1851-1864); Prof. B. S. Fitzgerald (1864-1866); Prof. Horace Clark (1866-1871); Rev. H. L. Graves (1871-1872); Col. W. W. Fontaine (1872-1875); Dr. Wm. W. Royall (1875-1878); Dr. John Hill Luther (1878-1891); Prof. P. H. Eager (1891-1894); Dr. E. H. Wells (1894-1896); Dr. Wm. A. Wilson (1896-1911); Dr. E. G. Townsend (1911-1912); Dr. John Crumpton Hardy (1912 to date).

In September, 1895, the College celebrated the fiftieth year of its existence by a "Golden Jubilee." It has held a number of "home-comings" for its former students; and in June 1920 it celebrated the completion of its seventy-fifth year with a Diamond Jubilee.

The remains of Judge R. E. B. Baylor were removed from Independence and reinterred on the campus and the old Independence College bell was set up on the campus on May 6, 1917.

The name has been changed to "Baylor College for Women." It was affiliated with the University of Texas in 1911, as well as with all other institutions for higher education throughout the country. It is especially strong in the department of music and the fine arts. Statistics of attendance during the early years are not at hand, but the increase of late years has been very rapid. In the student body are young ladies from all over Texas, and even from several foreign countries. Its graduates are scattered everywhere, and many of them are serving as missionaries in foreign fields.

The College was founded by the Baptist denomination of Texas, which has exclusive control of its management, elects the Board of Trustees, stands sponsor for the institution, and bestows its patronage and full support. The relations between the College and the citizens of Belton are very cordial and are mutually sympathetic and helpful. Belton and Bell County have a pardonable pride in the high standing and brilliant success of the institution.

3. *The Belton Academy*

In 1886 Prof. Charles W. Wedemeyer, a graduate of Baylor University at Independence, came to Belton and founded the Belton Academy for advanced preparatory training, which he conducted for many years, finally closing it about 1911, when the public free high schools of the county attained such high standards as to render private schools no longer necessary. At different times there were associated with Prof. Wedemeyer, Miss Johnson, Ramon Nichols, James B. Chaffin, and a number of others. Many young men of this county and elsewhere owe their early training to this school, among them Major Walter H. Walker, of the U. S. Army, Justice Mallory B. Blair, of the Court of Civil Appeals at Austin, Chas. M. Campbell, banker, of Temple, Tom DuBose, County Clerk, and many others.

4. *The Thomas Arnold High School,* 1890-1913

As elsewhere stated, the Salado College buildings and grounds were leased, in 1890, by the Board of Trustees to Dr. Samuel J. Jones, a graduate of Vanderbilt University and formerly a brilliant member of the faculty of the University of Texas. At first Prof. Thos. J. Witt was associated with him, but after several years he retired. The new school was given the name of Thomas Arnold High School "in grateful appreciation of the character and work of the great master of Rugby, who made the men who made England." Dr. Jones' aim, as stated, was "to rigidly maintain the high school standard, to supply the gap that exists between the grammar schools of the State and the University and to prepare for active work that young man or woman who finds it impossible to continue study in a higher institution."[6] The school was restricted to high school work and was limited to one hundred pupils.

---

[6] Announcement of Thomas Arnold High School, 1903.

It maintained a very high standard and its reputation spread throughout the State. The student body was drawn from all central Texas, regardless of free schools, and its graduates were everywhere accorded the highest rank in preparatory work and scholarship. It is believed that no secondary school in the State outranked the Thomas Arnold.

The faculty consisted of Dr. Samuel J. Jones, A. M., Ph. D., Principal; Assistants, at different times, Thos. J. Witt, M. C. Quillian, Mrs. Charlotte Halloran Jones, Miss Narnie Harrison, Miss Kate E. White, Mrs. Kate A. Orgain (music), Miss Pearl Harvey (music), Miss Judith Wright, Miss Kate English, and others.

The Thomas Arnold was distinguished not only by the high standards and excellent quality of its work but by the rare personality of its founder and head, Dr. Jones. Those who did not know him well thought him eccentric, but they saw only the surface mannerisms. Of short, compact figure, with a noble head and the eyes of a poet, he added to an exact and wide learning—the fruit of a vigorous mind—an abundance of common sense and a kindliness that endeared him to all who were fortunate enough to know him well. He taught Latin and Greek, and as he enjoyed teaching them he managed to make those dead languages live again for his students; but he loved even better to gather a group of boys about him, either in his class-room or in his home on Friday nights, and to talk of modern literature, current economic problems or of national and international politics. Many a boy and girl discovered through him not only the intellectual treasures of the world of books but a newer and finer attitude toward the practical problems of daily life. The short, sturdy figure, the magnificent head, the smiling face, the rich voice, the dreamy hazel-brown eyes that could be so keen, the twirling cane that he always carried make up a picture that will never fade from the memory of the boys and girls to whom he was ever an inspiring friend. It may be said of him that he made many of the men and women who are making Texas today.

His wife, Mrs. Charlotte Halloran Jones, was a brilliant, wise, witty and kindly woman who was beloved by everyone. She was an ideal help-meet and co-worker, and she made her home a happy gathering place for the students, especially for the boys. Her untimely death in

1905 was mourned by thousands who had felt her beneficent influence. Although Dr. Jones carried on courageously with the school for several years after her death, her loss was a heavy blow to him. Finally his own ill-health and advancing years, with diminished support for private schools everywhere evident, determined him to close the school and retire from the teaching profession. This he did in 1913. In 1915 Governor James E. Ferguson appointed him a member of the Board of Regents of the University of Texas, a position which he filled with great benefit to that institution and credit to himself; but after two or three years he resigned because of ill-health. He died at the home of his daughter in Lynchburg, Virginia, in the spring of 1918 and was buried by the side of his wife in the old Salado cemetery.

After Dr. Jones closed his school in 1913 the people of Salado tried to revive it by employing other teachers; but the real Thomas Arnold was gone, for there was no one who could fill the place of Dr. Jones. After struggling along feebly for a few years they gave up the attempt in 1918. The old College building which had housed two notable schools was turned over to the public school, but in 1924 it was inspected and declared unsafe. Thereupon a new public school building was erected on the site of the W. K. Hamblen home. In the summer of 1924 the old College was for the third time ravaged by fire.

The first fire broke out on one night in the spring of 1901 and burned everything but the bare walls. A mass meeting of the citizens was held under an arbor just west of the Baptist Church, which was attended by the writer, Dr. Thomas Yarrell and others from Belton. A movement for rebuilding was started; and in less than a year the work was done, so that the June commencement of the Thomas Arnold was held in the restored building. The school had been taught meanwhile in the large two-story residence of the late Dr. B. D. McKie. But in a few weeks after its completion, in the summer of 1902, another fire destroyed the rebuilt structure, again leaving only the stone walls. It is pretty well known that both fires were the work of an incendiary who harbored a grudge against the people of the town and who chose this cowardly method of satisfying his malevolent feeling. Nothing daunted, the people made another effort and again restored the building and the Thomas Arnold continued its work therein. After the fire of 1924 the walls began to crumble, and what is left of this old structure stands as a mutilated memorial to the former dignity and influence of Salado.

CHAPTER XVI

IN THE WORLD WAR—AND AFTER

1. *The First Effects of the World War,* 1914-1916

Before the great war broke out in Europe in the summer of 1914 our people generally had no anticipation of what was so soon to occur nor of how it was to affect them. They had heard rumors of war in that section of the world for so long that they had come to believe that nothing would happen. They were moderately prosperous and contented, for the prices of farm products were good, the crops were large and business was brisk. Then, like a clap of thunder, came the war. The stock market broke downward; money became tight, with bankers and other creditors nervous; and cotton prices dropped from over twelve to about six cents per pound. The depression lasted for about one year and was swiftly followed by a war-inflated boom, for soon the warring nations with millions of men drawn away from their farms and factories began buying enormous quantities of American food-stuffs, raw materials and even manufactures. Cotton came into great demand not only for clothing but also for use in manufacturing explosives. European gold poured into the United States and prices rose continuously.

When the war first began, probably most of our Bell County people were neutral in sentiment. They only hoped that it would not last long. Those few who were of foreign birth very naturally sided with their own people and some among them who were reserves of their national armies hustled back to fight for the nation in which they had been born and reared. There were also a few of our young men, bold, restless and adventurous, who hurried up to Canada to join the forces being sent from that country. Gradually, popular feeling began to turn against the Central Powers, especially Germany, and this feeling grew so intense that by the beginning of 1917 the greater part of our people were ready for war. Therefore, when war was declared against Germany on April 6, 1917, our people were unanimous in support of the Government.

2. *The Selective Draft and Its Local Administration*

Under the leadership of President Wilson the Government took vigorous action to raise a large army. In May it established training camps for officers in various sections of the country. At one of these camps, at Leon Springs near San Antonio, a number of Bell County boys received instruction and commissions, mostly as lieutenants and captains. A full list of the men from here who received commissions is not available, but the State Adjutant General credited about sixty to Bell County.

On May 18 Congress passed the Selective Draft Act which made all men from twenty-one to thirty years of age liable to military or other such service as the President should direct. On the same day President Wilson ordered that all men within the ages named should register on June 5, 1917 at a registration place within their respective precincts. Later these men were required to answer in writing a questionnaire concerning every detail of their physical, personal, financial, social, domestic, occupational and other conditions that would enable the local draft board to determine their eligibility for service and their claim, if any, to exemption. In addition, they were called before the board for physical examination. Thus equipped with the personal history and status of each registrant, the board could determine which of the registered men should go to the training camps to be made into soldiers and seamen of the United States. Each registrant of a precinct was given a number. The total number of registrants in Bell County was 4,581.

In the meantime, in accordance with the Selective Draft Act, the President had appointed the local draft boards. Bell County had two such boards. Local Draft Board No. 1, at Belton, was first composed of Dr. A. B. Crain, W. S. Hunter and Neal Bassell. Mr. Hunter resigned and was succeeded by Angus G. Vick, who also resigned later and was replaced by George F. Pierce. Dr. Crain resigned to enter the service and was succeeded by Dr. J. M. Frazier. The members of Local Draft Board No. 2, at Temple, were Dr. L. W. Pollok, W. S. Lemly, and Jno. S. Perry. It was the duty of these boards to determine whether the men drafted should be placed in the service or exemption classes. The first draft was made in Washington on July 20. A series of numbers, each enclosed in a gelatin capsule, was placed in a large glass bowl, and when one was drawn out the man in each registration precinct who had been given that number was called into service, subject to the action of the local board. They were to be ready by Stepember 5. Under this first call nine men from each of the two districts of Bell County were called. Those from District No. 1 were: Chester Guy Burton (Killeen), Joseph Adolph Dusek (Bartlett), Albert Willie Frederick (Bartlett), James Dee Irvin (Maxdale), Jack McFalls (Salado), George Pace (Salado), Charles Weaver Pyle (Belton), Jesse Wilson Sutton (Killeen) and James R. Waldrip (Belton). Those sent from District Number 2 were: Henry Brocker, M. D. Bryant, Arthur C. Cobb, Elmer V. Garrett, Wm. A. Kelly, Emil Machu, William Pappas, A. C. Wells and H. M. Whitlow. In prepaartion for the drafted men the Government had begun the erection of large training camps, or cantonments, in different parts of the country. In Texas were Camp Travis at San Antonio, Camp Bowie at Ft. Worth, Camp McArthur at Waco, Camp Logan at Houston and some smaller camps and aviation fields. The first quota from Bell County was sent to Camp Travis where they were classified into the particular branches of the service chosen by them or to which they were assigned. Thereafter quota after quota was called as more men were needed. A majority of the men from our county went over-seas and were in the American Expeditionary Forces when the end came. That many of them got into action on fighting fronts is evidenced by the fact that twenty-four were killed or died of wounds and forty-six others were wounded in action. Sixty-eight more died of disease, accident or unknown causes.

On July 4, 1918, the Provost Marshal General of the United States issued a circular to the local draft boards requiring them to appoint boards of instruction for the purpose of putting "the selective service men into camp willing, loyal, intelligent, clean and sober and thus fit them better for rapid progress in becoming good soldiers." He required the men to be assembled for such instructions once or twice before their departure for the training camp and again on the day of their entraining. Local Board No. 1, Belton, on July 17, appointed as such board of instruction: A. C. Bauer, Geo. W. Tyler, M. B. Blair, M. M. White, C. C. Countess and Slade Yarrell. On July 22, 1918, by previous appointment with the commanding officer, all the members of this board visited Camp McArthur, at Waco, where they were taken in charge by Brigadier General Lute Wahl, commanding, and his Adjutant General, Major W. S. Biddle, both of whom fully explained in detail its organization and operation, but especially those things of interest and importance to the prospective soldier. From this time on the board engaged strenuously in its duty of instructing the men as they were called to the colors. Local Board No. 2, Temple, appointed a similar board of instruction which included M. B. Blair and Geo. W. Tyler. Though late getting into action this last board did considerable work. On Sunday afternoon, November 10, 1918, they met at Temple the last quota called and gave them the customary instructions. This group did not entrain, however, as the signing of the armistice was hourly expected and they were held over. The next day the great news came with an order for their release from the draft.

3. *Local Civic Organizations in Support of the War*

The advocates of preparedness had secured the passage by the Congress of the United States of the Act of August 29, 1916, seven months prior to our declaration of war, which Act created the Council of National Defense and provided for similar units in the several States and in the counties thereof, under laws to be enacted by the several States.

The Texas State Council of Defense was provided for by the Act of the Legislature of May 14, 1917, under authority of which the Governor appointed thirty-nine leading citizens of Texas to compose such State Council. This Council proceeded at once to the appointment of a County Council of Defense in each county in the State. The members from Bell County were named on July 6, 1917, and when organized, on July 23, the Council comprised the following personnel: Geo. W. Tyler, Belton, chairman; Chas. W. Taylor, Rogers, vice-chairman; J. C. Mitchell, Temple, secretary; Mrs. Sam S. Walker, Belton, assistant secretary; Hugh C. Smith, Killeen, treasurer; Stewart Shaw, Temple; Jno. H. Underwood, Holland.

The Bell County Council of Defense, upon suggestion of the State Council of Defense, proceeded to the appointment of two local leaders—a man and a woman—in each of some fifty-two subdivisions of the County, and named general committees in several branches of the work, such as magazines for soldiers, war gardens, war industries, German language and loyalty, legal advisory committees for soldiers, public health and sanitation, speaker's bureau, woman's work, labor, publicity, food conservation, finance, military affairs, protection, etc.

Mrs. Sam S. Walker, of the County Council, also served as County Chairman of the Woman's Committee of Bell County, under special appointment of the National Council. She organized the woman workers of the county, distributed the war tasks among them and presided at several of their county meetings. It was a fine and efficient organization. Other members of the County Council of Defense served in special capacities when called upon by several departments of the government or of war organizations.

Later, under instructions from the State and National Councils, the Bell County Council of Defense, with the assistance of the several boards of school trustees, organized, in August and September, 1918, a Community Council of Defense in every school district in Bell County, in some districts several councils, reaching a total of one hundred and eleven councils, including three among the colored people. The enrollment of their membership aggregated nearly fifteen thousand people. Hon. Elliott Dunlap Smith, Chief of the Field Division of the Council of National Defense, at Washington, D. C., on October 25, 1918, wrote to our Bell County Council of Defense congratulating it upon this work and stating that it had the best record he had received from any county in the United States.

Thereafter all kinds of war work, such as the Liberty Bond drives, Red Cross campaigns, food conservation, etc., during and after the war, were carried on through the co-operation of these Community Councils under the direction of the County Council of Defense. With only a few exceptions they were functioning admirably and with great efficiency when the war ended. Most of the Community Councils then or soon afterward automatically dissolved, but several of the more progressive communities have since organized Community Clubs or Social Centers which are but the survival and continuation of the spirit of neighborhood cooperation, irrespective of political or religious affiliations, inspired by the brief but educational career of the Community Councils of Defense.

The work of the County and Community Councils extended to every phase of war activity. They cooperated with the Local Draft Board, the Food Administration, the Red Cross, and all other interests as directed by the National and State Councils. As similar organizations existed throughout the whole United States they collectively mobilized the whole civilian strength and capacity of the nation—all acting like an army under one general leadership. Much of their work was done through circulars and bulletins printed in the local papers and by addresses and appeals at patriotic gatherings. For some months after the armistice the County Council of defense was utilized in the demobilization of the army, the search for lost soldiers, the adjustment of allotments, allowances, etc.

The Bell County Council of Defense printed a pamphlet of some twenty quarto pages, entitled "The Home Fires Burning," being a resumé of its two years of war work containing the names of its local leaders and general committees; officers and committees of the Community Councils of Defense; and Bell County's Roll of Honor—the names of all soldiers, sailors, and marines from Bell County who died, were wounded or killed in the World War, as far as known at that time. This publication was tendered as a souvenir of the World War to the first reunion of the soldier boys at Belton on July 4, 1919, at which was organized the first Camp of the American Legion in Bell County. The Council was congratulated by the War Department upon the publication of this pamphlet souvenir.

For the names of the co-workers of the County and Community Councils reference must be made to this publication, as their number—nearly one thousand—is too large for insertion here. They represented the best blood and the purest patriotism of the county. Each did his or her part, at whatever sacrifice, in the great enterprise.

During the week of October 28—November 4, 1917, Hon. Herbert Hoover, National Food Administrator, put on his great drive with "Pledge Cards" which the housewives of the whole nation were asked to sign, pledging their voluntary cooperation with him in conserving food for war purposes. For this temporary organization Geo. W. Tyler was appointed County Chairman for Bell County, and he in turn appointed Mr. Angus G. Vick, County Manager. The members of the County Executive Committee were: Belton, Dr. S. L. Mayo, A. C. Bauer, Mrs. Jesse S. Blair, Rev. W. H. Howard; Temple, A. J. Jarrell, F. F. Downs, Mrs. Thos. C. Hall, Dan H. McKenzie. The local chairmen were: Killeen, M. P. Dalton; Holland, C. B. Starke; Bartlett, D. K. Leatherman; Rogers, Dr. R. R. Curtis; Troy, Mrs. W. L. Maedgen; Pendleton, W. E. Phillips; Heidenheimer, Geo. P. Marshall; Salado, N. L. Shanklin. This novel and remarkable campaign, conducted by personal visits to homes by the committees in each community, resulted in the signatures of several thousand housewives in Bell County.

Mr. E. A. Peden, of Houston, Food Administrator for Texas, perfected his permanent organization in January, 1918, with district and county food administrators throughout the whole State. Mr. James W. Bass, Waco, was made District Food Administrator for our district (the 13th) and the temporary organization for Bell County was made permanent, with new titles and some additions to the personnel.

There was practically no legal way of enforcing food conservation—no legal penalties for violation of the regulations—except by the cancellation of the license of business concerns, all of whom were required to have licenses from Washington. Nevertheless the people, with almost one accord, responded cheerfully to the appeals of the Food Administration and there was everywhere a generous rivalry in the self-imposed deprivations and sacrifices thus enjoined upon them. Who will ever forget the "one month of wheatless and flourless Texas" proclaimed by Mr. Peden and willingly enforced by the great mass of the people of Texas upon themselves? Gladly they denied themselves flour so that more could go to the soldiers and to the allies.

As the war went on, the multiplying duties of Chairman of the Bell County Council of Defense and of County Food Administrator combined became too much for one man, and at his own request, Geo. W. Tyler was relieved of those of County Food Administrator on August 9, 1918, when he was succeeded by Mr. Geo. P. Hunton, of Temple, who ably served, with the same personal organization, till the end of the war.

The Bell County Chapter of the American Red Cross was chartered on May 16, 1917, with the following officers, all residing in Temple: Charles M. Campbell, Chairman; Mrs. Thos. C. Hall, Vice Chairman; Mrs. J. R. Rucker, Secretary; P. L. Downs, Jr., Treasurer. The officers of the County Executive Committee were Charles M. Campbell, Chairman; Mrs. J. R. Rucker, Vice Chairman; H. C. Glenn, Secretary; and C. B. Hutchison, Treasurer. In addition to these officers there were forty-eight members at large representing every community in the county. There were also standing committees on eleven branches of work carried on by the Red Cross. Branch chapters were established in Belton and Killeen, and auxiliaries in many other localities.

The outstanding feature of the Red Cross Work in Bell County was the Woman's Work Department, in charge of the ladies. They made up and shipped out carloads of garments, surgical wrappings and other war necessities. They gave freely of their time and labor in this great work. The money to purchase material for these products was furnished by the business men of Bell County and many thousands of dollars were freely contributed. The organization contributed one of its members, Miss Lucile Scott, of Temple, (now Mrs. Preston Childers of Cotulla), to the work in the camps of the soldiers in France, where she went at her own expense and gave her time unselfishly to the service there.

In the world war, as in the Civil War of 1861-5, the good women of Bell County gave, as no one else could, the work of their hands to the amelioration of the hardships and sufferings incident to the cruel conflict and earned the unbounded gratitude of our people. No civic unit made a better showing in the war work than did the ladies of the Red Cross.

Hon. Mallory B. Blair, County Judge, handled all of the drives in Bell County for the sale of Liberty and Victory Bonds of the United States government, under the supervision of the Treasury Department, through the Federal Reserve Bank of the 11th District at Dallas. He appointed a sub-chairman at each town and these men, with the cooperation of the County Council of Defense and of the Community Councils, carried on the work. In each and every drive Bell County "went over the top" within the time limit and, barring a very few unpleasant episodes, the response of our people was generous and enthusiastic.

The fine morale and the patriotic demeanor of the people of our county are among the most precious and pleasing chapters of the history of those exciting times. There may have been equal devotion to the cause in other parts of the country, but it certainly could not surpass the magnificent bearing of the people of Bell County.

4. *The Armistice and the Return of the Soldiers*

Who that experienced it can ever forget the day and the hour when the armistice was signed? Those whose friends, brothers, or sons were fighting at the front in France had lived in hourly dread that news might come of the death or wounding of a loved one. They had eagerly and fearfully scanned the newspaper reports of the great battles along the front, enthusiastic over the successes of the American and Allied armies, shocked at the terrific cost of lives, painfully anxious to know whether their own were safe. When the news of the armistice came then, our people showed their joy and happiness in their faces. They were not noisy—their hearts were too full of thankfulness for much outward demonstration. Then they began to wonder when the boys would be coming home again.

It was not long before the soldiers who were still in the great training camps, or had not yet gone over-seas, were discharged. Then after a time the great ships began to bring back those in the A. E. F. Our Bell County boys returning from over-seas service came in upon us quietly and modestly. They all wore the over-seas caps, some wore chevrons and others the insignia of officers. When the greetings of relatives and friends were over, they settled back into their pre-war occupations or obtained new employment. Like all real soldiers they talked but little about their personal experiences and adventures on the fighting line. In fact, they seldom spoke of their service except when pressed with questions from their friends and then they related the movements of their units, ignoring their own individual exploits. Their soldierly modesty was admirably maintained and is to this day. But isolated bits of personal prowess have leaked out to us through other sources and Bell County people know that our boys made good and we are proud of them.

On July 4, 1919, a Bell County Post of the American Legion was organized at the Yettie Tobler Park in Belton at a big celebration to welcome the returning soldiers. Major Will R. Brown, of Temple, was chosen Commander and Sergeant Major C. W. Pyle, of Belton, was elected Adjutant, with other officers. Later this became Belton Post and a Temple Post was organized. By mutual agreement, and under the patronage of their respective chambers of commerce, Belton Post celebrates July Fourth and Temple Post Armistice Day, November 11.

5. *Material Conditions During and After the War*

As already noted, crop prices, which had fallen sharply when the war began in Europe in 1914, had begun to rise rapidly by the fall of 1915. They continued to advance during the next year, with cotton going to twenty cents per pound. Of course, with the general price level rising, increasing the cost of everything the farmer had to buy, his profits were not as large as might be expected because it was costing him more and more to grow and gather his crop. When we entered the war in 1917 the prices of farm products were going up rapidly. Then came a hard blow. Through 1917 and 1918, just when the farmers should have been getting the advantages of the extraordinary war prices, a distressing drought fell upon all central and western Texas. In many parts of this wide area there were no crops at all; throughout the section even the best yields were extremely light. Of course the expenses of the farmers continued, so that most of them fell into debt. Further west the drought was more severely felt than here, and the general distress was so great that the State Council of Defense held a meeting in Austin in September, 1918, to which the county Councils of Defense were invited, and organized a general relief committee. This committee solicited and obtained from well-to-do people over the State and by drives in the more fortunate communities, through the county Councils of Defense, the loan of funds which were in turn reloaned to the drought sufferers to enable them to plant and raise the crop of 1919. Bell County declined to ask for any of this relief and was exempted from contributing to the loan fund since she agreed to take care of her own situation without any outside assistance. The Legislature also passed a law, on February 19, 1919, authorizing the Commissioners' Courts of counties to make limited loans to distressed farmers in order that they might purchase seed, feed and other necessities while making the crop year of that year. Only a few applications were made in Bell County under this statute, but in other counties considerable relief was extended under its provisions.

Happily the year 1919 was a very seasonable one and the whole country was blessed with copious rains. All crops, cotton, corn, wheat and oats, yielded abundantly and brought high prices. Wheat sold at $2.20 per bushel—a price guaranteed by the Governmnet—and cotton rose to more than forty cents a pound. Partly because of the higher cost of living, partly because of the withdrawal of so many men into the army and navy, wages had gone to unprecedented heights. Cotton pickers were getting from two dollars to two dollars fifty cents per hundred pounds, common laborers asked and received four or five dollars per day, skilled labor as high as fifteen dollars a day. Despite the high cost of living and the evidence that these high wages were bound to be only temporary, there was a wild riot of extravagance among the wage earners. They spent their money freely for automobiles and fine clothes—silk shirts, silk hose, silk dresses and other high-priced finery. This was especially true of the colored population, men and women alike. Some of the latter, who formerly "took in washing" now sent their own clothes to the steam laundries. For awhile it was almost impossible to obtain household help at any price. Africa had come into its own and was riding a high wave of luxurious indulgence. It was at this time that a lady accosted a colored woman who had formerly hired out as a cook, with the question, "Do you want a job of cooking?" and was promptly met with the reply, "No, do you?"

As there is no white domestic labor here, the situation affected most conspicuously the colored people, but the white unskilled laborers caught the infection and attempted to satisfy all their long repressed desires for luxuries. Wages for skilled labor soared to heights hitherto unknown in this section of the country. Of course, all right-minded people want to see labor well paid, for the honest laborer deserves to enjoy a comfortable standard of living and to be able to provide for the future of his children. The trouble in this instance was that wages went so high that the employers found that it was costing them more than the finished work was worth, so they had to shut down on everything but the most essential industries. Numbers of laborers soon found that employment was declining.

Then came the "deflation" of 1920 when the big banks in the East began to call in loans, stocks were thrown on the market while prices collapsed, numbers of industrial plants closed down, and cotton fell from over forty cents to around twelve to fifteen cents per pound. It had cost our farmers over thirty cents to raise each pound of this cotton and they were threatened with ruin. Unemployment became general and wages came down rapidly. The cotton crop of 1921 proved to be very short, so that the price rose somewhat but not enough to pay off the losses of the year before. Gradually, however, as the cost of production was lowered the farmers found that they could make some profit even with cotton at less than half the war prices. They began to pay out of debt, and as they got back on a more nearly normal basis general business conditions in our section improved.

The U. S. Census for 1920 showed for the first time an actual loss of population for our county, for the total had dropped from 49,180 in 1910 to 46,412, a decline of 2,768. With one exception, the towns had barely held their own. The exception, Belton, had gained 934 inhabitants to rise to 5,098. As in the preceding decade, the loss had been in the farm population and an analysis of the figures shows that it must have been about 3,800. Whether the severe drought of 1917-18 had caused an exodus, or farm youths who had been in the army were disinclined to return to the quiet life of the farm, or high wages in the cities and the new oil fields had lured families away, we cannot say. The proportion of farm tenants to the total of farmers remained about the same, namely sixty per cent.

During this period the State began to play a larger part in the building of improved highways and has since steadily enlarged its control over this important work. It seems probable that in years to come the State Highway Commission may take over the whole task of highway construction and maintenance. It is perhaps idle to speculate what the influence of smooth hard-surfaced roads and swift automobiles may be upon the future of our farm and town populations. On the one hand they may result in concentrating trade and therefore the urban population in the larger centers, since it will be easy for a family to do its trading from thirty to fifty miles away. On the other hand, they may tend to scatter the hitherto congested population of the larger cities by enabling more families to enjoy the greater freedom of life in the country, especially if the wide and cheap distribution of electric power should bring the conveniences of city life into the country. But the answers to these and other questions about the future will be known only by the younger generation.

CHAPTER XVII

SOME INSTITUTIONS OF BELL COUNTY

1. *Freemasonry in Bell County*

The oldest organization of any kind with a continued, uninterrupted existence within the county is *Belton Lodge, No. 166, Ancient Free and Accepted Masons.*

The Dispensation for this Lodge was granted by the Grand Master of Masons in Texas on January 20, 1855, on the petition of twelve brethren who thereby became the charter members. These were E. S. C. Robertson, Worshipful Master, James Porter Rice, Senior Warden, Elisha D. Stubblefield, Junior Warden, and Silas Baggett, Isaac T. Bean, Alonzo Beeman, Hiram Christian, Dr. Jno. W. Embree, Rev. Finis E. Foster, G. Wat Graves, Isaac Jalonick, and Jno. M. Perryman.

The first meeting was held on Saturday, February 3, 1855. The place of this meeting cannot be given with absolute certainty, but is believed to have been the Cumberland Presbyterian Church building which had then but recently been erected where the First Methodist Church now stands.

It was first given the name of "Tom Blakey" Lodge. No one now living knows the origin of this name, but an extensive investigation made by the writer in 1904 disclosed that Colonel Robertson was associated in the early forties, in Milam Lodge No. 11, at Independence, Texas, with Thomas W. Blakey, a sturdy pioneer from Kentucky, who immigrated to Texas in 1832 and had died at Independence on April 21, 1853. Other corroborating circumstances have led to the conclusion that the Lodge was named in his honor at the suggestion of Colonel Robertson.

The Grand Lodge of Texas, in session at Galveston, granted a charter to this Lodge on January 23, 1856, and on January 24, 1857, the same body, on request of the Lodge, changed the name to Belton Lodge.

From the beginning the regular or "stated" meetings have been on the second Saturday of each month.

Two of the Grand Masters of Masons in Texas have been members of this Lodge, though both were members of Salado Lodge No. 296, at the date of their respective elevation to the Grand Mastership. These were Andrew

J. Rose, Grand Master, 1886-7, and Geo. W. Tyler, Grand Master, 1890-1.

The Lodges in chronological order, in Bell County, are as follows:

Names	No.	Organized	Location
Belton	166	1855	Belton
Leon	193	1856	White Hall
Salado	296	1865	Salado
Sunshine[1]	341	1871	Volo
Oenaville[2]	363	1872	Oenaville
Knob Creek	401	1874	Removed to Temple
South Nolan[3]	416	1874	(or 1875) Removed to Killeen
Rogers	602	1884	Rogers
Zerne	615	1885	Holland
Troy	640	1886	Troy
Nolanville	937	1906	Nolanville
Killeen	1125	1917	Killeen

The other branches of Masonry have been organized in the county as follows:

Chapters of Royal Arch Masons

Names	No.	Organized	Location
Belton	76	1860	Belton
Salado[4]	107	1872	Salado
Temple (form. Moody)	199	1893	Removed to Temple
Holland	267	1905	Holland
Killeen	311	1908	Killeen

Geo. M. McWhirter, a member of Belton Chapter No. 76, Royal Arch Masons, was Grand High Priest of the Grand Chapter of Texas for the year 1878-9.

Councils of Royal and Select Masters

Names	No.	Organized	Location
Belton	48	1907	Belton
Salado[5]	66	1907	Salado
Temple	137	1907	Temple
Holland	202	1907	Holland
Killeen	247	1907	Killeen

[1] Demised 1881. [2] Demised 1881. [3] Demised 1915.
[4] Demised 1913.
[5] Demised 1914.

Commanderies of the Order of Knights Templar

Names	No.	Organized	Location
Belton	23	1887	Belton
Temple	41	1903	Temple

Two members of Belton Commandery No. 23, Knights Templar, have been elevated to the position of Grand Commander of Knights Templar in Texas: P. T. Morey, Grand Commander, 1900-1901; Geo. W. Tyler, Grand Commander, 1914-1915.

Chapters of the Order of the Eastern Star

Names	No.	Organized	Location
Selma	72	1900	Troy
Vashti	32	1901	Temple
Killeen	490	1909	Killeen
Nolanville	12	1909	Nolanville
Rogers	148	1911	Rogers
Holland	544	1913	Holland
Belton[6]	589	1915	Belton

Two former residents of Bell County have been high officials of the Eastern Star: Dr. W. B. Halley, Ballinger, Worthy Grand Patron, 1917-1918; Mrs. Velma Bailey Halley, Ballinger, Worthy Grand Matron, 1925-1926. Both were born and reared in Salado.

2. First Odd-Fellows Lodge in Bell County

On the 28th day of July, 1859, by previous appointment, Henry E. Perkins, Grand Master of the Independent Order of Odd Fellows in Texas, met the following named former members of the Order, residing in or near Belton: Sam W. Bigham (Tennessee), Charles Brock (New York), David T. Chamberlin (Vermont), Ben F. Church (Kentucky), Hugh O'Kieff (Indiana), Tazwell W. Powers (Tennessee), and James P. Reed (Missouri).

This meeting was held in the Masonic Hall, on Main Street, in Belton. The Grand Master granted a dispensation for a Lodge and the following officers were then elected and installed:

---

[6] An Eastern Star Chapter was organized in Belton in 1884 and another in the nineties, but both died after a brief existence.

D. T. Chamberlin, Noble Grand; James P. Reed, Vice Grand; Charles Brock, Recording Secretary; T. W. Powers, Treasurer. Belton Ark Lodge was adopted as the name and D. T. Chamberlin was appointed District Deputy Grand Master for the District. A charter was granted by the Odd Fellows Grand Lodge on February 10, 1860.

From December 10, 1861, till February 27, 1866, the meetings of the Lodge were suspended on account of the civil war, the scattering of the membership and the absence of many of them in military service.[7]

Since the resumption of meetings in 1866 the Lodge has with varying fortunes continued its work and is a prosperous institution at this time, with a good membership, a valuable building for Lodge purposes and a promising future.

There are several other Lodges of this order in Bell County, but the dates of their respective organizations and other particulars are not available.

3. Banks in Bell County

A. Banks in Belton

Until late in the sixties there was not a real bank in the county, nor did the word "bank" appear in any advertisement here, so far as known. The only transaction of a banking nature done were the buying and selling of exchange. From about 1854 several firms in Belton purchased drafts on commercial centers and sold their drafts on these points. Prominent among these pre-war firms were Chamberlin and Flint, Attorneys (David T. Chamberlin and John T. Flint); Isaac Jalonick, later Jalonick and Smith, merchants (Isaac Jalonick and John F. Smith); and Miller and Baker, merchants (Robert C. Miller and John J. Baker). There were practically no deposits and no bank loans or discounts. The sparse population, the scarcity of money, and the small volume of business did not call for such facilities. Our principal commodities were cattle, horses, and farm products. The latter were mostly consumed at home. Cattle were sold to cash buyers or traded

---

[7] Manuscript of address by Mr. Jas. P. Reed, delivered before the Lodge, February 1, 1878.

Top: One of the beautiful new buildings of Baylor College is Hardy Hall, the social activities center. Courtesy of Davidson Studio.

Bottom: Presser Hall, one of the newer buildings of Baylor College for Women, now known as Mary Hardin-Baylor College. The Fine Arts Department is housed in this building. Courtesy of Davidson Studio, Belton.

to merchants on account. Horses were usually sold at home for cash or in trade. Cattle buyers drove their purchases to market, mostly to New Orleans, though a few drove as far as St. Louis and Chicago. The proceeds were brought back in merchandise, farm implements, cash with which to buy land and supplies, but occasionally they brought bank drafts. All such drafts were absorbed by the firms before-named and they in turn used them to pay for their merchandise stocks or sold drafts against them. The banks of deposit were generally the time-honored tin can and a hole in the ground. Every man was his own banker in those days.

The exchange business of these firms was gradually increasing with the settlement and development of the county and there would doubtless have been a regular bank opened up in Belton in course of time, but for the great war of 1861-65, during which all commercial transactions were practically suspended and there was no need of a bank. There is a well authenticated story to the effect that a certain prosperous farmer, departing for the army, brought five thousand dollars in gold to Judge David T. Chamberlin for safe-keeping. After the war he called for his money, whereupon Judge Chamberlin fished a sealed metal pot out of a well in his yard on Main Street and promptly handed over the money to the delighted owner. There is another story to the effect that Mr. Robert C. Miller, about the same time, buried eight thousand dollars in gold near the mouth of the Nolan and that after the war he dug it up and started again in business.

About 1867 the mercantile houses of Miller, Chamberlin and Co. (Robert C. Miller, W. A. Miller, J. Z. Miller and Don A. Chamberlin) and H. C. Denny (H. C. Denny, Jno. F. Smith and Ed A. Smith) began to do a small banking business, mostly in the old ante-bellum way of buying and selling exchange. The amount of deposits, loans and discounts was insignificant, as money was scarce in the country and interest rates were high—from one to five per cent per month.

In 1874 the first named firm dissolved. The Millers, with Mr. Jno. Q. Allen, became Miller Bros. and Co.; and Don A. Chamberlin, admitting his brother, Harvey J. Chamberlin, formed the firm of Chamberlin Brothers. Both firms continued in the banking business which by this time was expanding to its normal function, with an appreciable amount of small deposits. The latter firm ceased business early in 1877. In 1880 L. Burr and Co. (Lem Burr, Julius Kaufmann, Julius Runge) opened a wholesale grocery store in Belton with a banking department and operated till about 1882.

H. C. Denny and Co., who had retired from business for awhile, took over the banking interests of L. Burr and Co. and in 1882 opened up the first exclusive banking house in Belton. Mr. Denny died in 1900 and the bank ceased business about 1914. About the same time (1882) Miller Bros. retired from merchandise and did an exclusive banking business. Thus far, all were private banks.

With the building of railroads, the growth of Belton and Temple and the expansion of markets, banks became more essential to business activity. The demand for larger capital and the advantages of incorporation under the Federal laws caused the private banks gradually to be converted into national banks. But it was not until the hard times of the late eighties and nineties had passed and more prosperous times had come that the county generally, especially the smaller towns, became well supplied with banking institutions.

The First National Bank of Belton, the first chartered bank in Bell County, was opened in 1882 with a capital of $50,000. P. N. Boren was president, R. H. Stewart, cashier. The Belton National Bank, the second incorporated bank in Belton, succeeded the private banking firm of Miller Bros. in 1884. Its capital was $50,000. J. Z. Miller was president, and J. Z. Miller, Jr. was cashier. In 1887 it purchased the franchise and bank building of the First National, moved into the new building (at the northeast corner of Court House square) and there still continues the banking business as The Belton National Bank. For sometime Wm. W. James has been president, and Ghent Carpenter, cashier. The Citizens' National Bank of Belton was chartered in 1889, with B. A. Ludlow, president, Louis H. Tyler, cashier, with a capital of $50,000. In 1890 it changed to a private bank, ceasing business in 1902.

The first and for sometime the only savings institution in Belton was the Yarrell Savings Bank, owned and operated by Thomas Yarrell, Sr. It became a part of another bank in 1907. In 1905 the Belton Loan and Trust Company took out the first charter in Belton under the new Texas banking laws with a capital of $10,000. Jas. E.

Ferguson was president and Thomas Yarrell, Jr., was cashier. This was succeeded in 1906 by the Farmer's State Bank of Belton with a capital of $25,000 under Jas. E. Ferguson as president and Wantland Shannon as cashier. This bank voluntarily liquidated and retired from business in 1907.

Thereupon The People's National Bank was chartered in 1907 with a capital of $50,000 under Thomas Yarrell, Sr., as president and Thomas Yarrell, Jr., as cashier. It is still in business (1923) with Thomas Yarrell, Sr., as president and Slade Yarrell as cashier.

The First State Bank of Belton was organized in 1910 with a capital of $25,000 under E. C. Clabaugh as president and W. C. Rylander as cashier. At this time (1923) Charles B. Wade is president and Jesse Wallis Blair is cashier.

So, out of all of these launchings we have (1923) in Belton these three banks: The Belton National Bank, chartered 1884; The People's National Bank, chartered 1907; and The First State Bank, chartered 1910.

B. Banks in Temple

The Bell County Bank, the first in Temple, was opened as a private bank on February 1, 1882, in a small frame building, by F. F. Downs and P. L. Downs, under the firm name of Downs Bros. In 1882 this firm organized the First National Bank of Temple with a capital of $50,000 which was later increased to $100,000. F. F. Downs was president and P. L. Downs was cashier. P. L. Downs is now (1923) vice-president and C. B. Hutchison is cashier.

The Temple National Bank began about 1887 under W. Goodrich Jones as president and C. L. McKay, cashier, with a capital of $100,000. In 1898 the ownership changed and Geo. C. Pendleton became president and W. E. Hall, cashier. It ceased business in 1906. The Bell County National Bank was chartered about 1888 with a capital of $50,000 and C. L. McKay as president and Henry D. Kane as cashier; but it closed in 1894. Miller, Hall and Co. (J. Z. Miller, J. Z. Miller, Jr., and W. E. Hall) opened a private bank in Temple about 1894, which was merged with the Temple National, above-mentioned, in 1898. The City National Bank was chartered in 1902 with a capital of

$100,000; Charles M. Campbell was president and W. E. Moore was cashier.

The Temple State Bank was organized in 1906 with a capital of $100,000 (later increased to $250,000) with Jas. E. Ferguson as president and W. S. Rowland as cashier. It was reorganized and chartered in 1921 as The Guaranty State Bank with a capital of $100,000 under E. W. Moore, president, and L. P. Heard, cashier. The American Bank and Trust Company was launched under a state charter in 1907 with a capital of $50,000 under Jno. J. Cox as president and J. F. Binkley as cashier. The panic of 1907 struck it "amidship" and it "died aborning." The Farmer's State Bank was organized in 1910 with a capital of $100,000. A. L. Flint was president and C. D. Seybold was cashier. The Temple Trust Company chartered in 1912 without banking privileges, does strictly a loan business on real estate mortgages, etc. Its capital is $100,000 and H. G. Glenn is president and W. S. Rowland is cashier.

Thus Temple is shown to enjoy at this time (1923) the advantages of the following banks: The First National Bank, chartered in 1884; The City National Bank, chartered in 1902; The Farmer's State Bank, chartered in 1910; The Guaranty State Bank, chartered in 1921; and The Temple Trust Company, chartered in 1912.

C. Banks in Other Towns

In the eighties John T. Bartlett, in the town of Bartlett, began a private banking business which in 1904 was incorporated into The Bartlett National Bank with a capital of $50,000 under John T. Bartlett as president and T. B. Benson as cashier. The First National Bank of Bartlett was organized in 1900 with a capital of $50,000 under J. L. Bailey as president and C. C. Bailey as cashier. The First State Bank of Bartlett was chartered in 1909 with a capital of $25,000 under J. V. Morris as president.

The Heidenheimer State Bank was opened in 1910 under T. H. Heard, president, and V. Carson, cashier, with a capital of $10,000.

In Holland Dr. Vol. Reed and Wm. M. Reed started a private bank in 1892 under the firm name of Reed Bros., which was merged in The First State Bank of Holland in 1909 with $50,000 capital. Dr. Vol. Reed was president and V. E. H. Reed, cashier. The First National Bank of

Holland was chartered in 1906 with a capital of $50,000 under L. B. Mewhinney as president and Logan Mewhinney as cashier.

Will Rancier and Sam Rancier began operating the Jeweler's Bank in Killeen in the nineties and incorporated it into The First National Bank of Killeen in 1901 with a capital of $50,000 and with Will Rancier as president and Sam Rancier as cashier. This bank was reorganized in 1921 with J. W. Norman as president and J L. Swope as cashier. In 1907 The First State Bank of Killeen was chartered with a capital of $50,000 under Hugh C. Smith as president and M. P. Dalton as cashier. The Guaranty State Bank was launched in 1920 with a capital of $50,000 under Claude McBryde as president and W. F. Wicker as cashier.

For a short while E. Lane and Co. did a private banking business in Nolanville. Will Rancier and E. Lane were proprietors and E. Lane was manager.

The First State Bank of Pendleton was chartered in 1909 with a capital of $25,000 under B J. Carpenter as president and N. M. McHorse as cashier.

In 1896 Joe N. Brooker of Rogers began a private bank which he operated for some years. The First National Bank of Rogers was organized in 1901 with a capital of $50,000 under J. Hugh Wear as president and W. B. Thomas, cashier. The Rogers State Bank was chartered in 1907 with a capital of $50,000 and with M. V. Baugh as president and W. P. Baugh as cashier.

In Salado The First State Bank was opened in 1911 with a capital of $10,000. ─────────(?) was president and J. L. Hearn was cashier. It was reorganized later with W. T. Foster as president and Theo G. Harkey as cashier. It ceased business in 1920.

In Troy for some years D. W. McGlasson, under the name of McGlasson and Co. did a small banking business, which ceased in 1896. The Citizens Exchange Bank began business about 1904 with a capital of $25,000 under C. E. Maedgen as president and W. L. Maedgen as cashier.

On December 31, 1923, the total of deposits in the twenty banks in Bell County amounted to $10,180,532.67, which was an average of $236.74 per capita. The combined resources of these banks was some $13,000,000. What a contrast with the situation fifty years earlier!

4. *Fairs in Bell County*

The first attempt at an agricultural fair and stock exhibition in Bell County was at Salado, whose citizens incorporated the Central Texas Fair Association and held three very successful annual fairs there, one in 1873 on the north side of the creek west of town, the others in 1874 and 1875, about a mile north of town on the Belton road. All were held in the fall of the year and were generously attended and supported by the people all over the county and from adjoining counties. Judge O. T. Tyler was president of the Association and Col. N. L. Norton was general manager and was a splendid man for the place.

In addition to its very creditable exhibits in the departments of agriculture, live stock, machinery and others, the Fair of 1874 was notable for the assemblage or reunions, on different days, of several bodies of men, whose programs gave added zest and interest to the Fair. There were the Veterans of the Texas Revolution and of the Republic of Texas, Veterans of the United States War with Mexico and Veterans of the Confederate Army, and there was also a day for the Patrons of Husbandry (the "Grangers").

The Fair, by mutual agreement between the people of the two towns, was moved to Belton, the county seat, the next year (1876). Here were held several annual exhibits, the site being in the east part of town, or South side of Nolan, on the plat now known as "Mayesville." Governor Richard B. Hubbard delivered the opening address at this Fair in Belton in October, 1877. Dr. Jno. W. Embree, T. E. Smith, A. F. Hicks, and others, successfully managed these functions.

At this time our citizens tendered a fine banquet, at the City Hotel, to Governor Hubbard, Major A. J. Dorn, State Treasurer, Col. John M. Thornton, Austin correspondent to the *Galveston News,* and to Major John Henry Brown, then of Dallas, but a former honored citizen of Belton.

The next effort in this way was the "Bell County Fair Association," chartered about 1890, which held its fairs and races for several years on the Ben D. Lee place about one mile southeast of Belton on the Holland road. These exhibits were considered very good at the time and the horse racing was equal to any in the State in those days. Balloon ascensions, high diving, and other novelties were some of the diversions. The leading spirits were Col. Wm. Thatcher, Ben D. Lee, Col. C. M. Campbell, and others.

In 1915 another Bell County Fair Association held its first fair in the Midway park, on the Belton and Temple pike and Interurban railway line. For several years it held annual exhibits which were quite successful and beneficial. Col. P. L. Downs, L. S. Williamson, Sam H. Cater, Joe Cornish, W. A. Spencer, and others were its principal promoters.

5. *The Sanctificationists of Belton*

The master mind of this peculiar institution was Mrs. Martha McWhirter, who possessed "extraordinary powers" and exercised a "strange influence over her followers." Her maiden name was White. She was born in Jackson County, Tennessee, in 1827, joined the Methodist Church at sixteen, and married Geo. M. McWhirter, of Wilson County, Tennessee, in 1845. They moved to Bell County, Texas, in 1855, first settling on the Salado Creek, at or near the site of the present Armstrong School house, where they were leading factors in the building of the Live Oak Church and in the promotion of that community. Soon after the termination of the War between the States, sometime about 1865 or 1866, the family moved to Belton, where Major McWhirter engaged in the mercantile business and also was interested in a flour mill. The family stood as high as any in the country. Major McWhirter was a prominent and zealous Mason and served, 1878-1879, as Grand High Priest of the Grand Royal Arch Chapter of Texas. He, too, was a member of the Methodist Church and both he and his wife were recognized as leaders in that denomination, particularly in Sunday School work.

For some years after the war there was no denominational church building in Belton and the different church societies held services on alternate Sundays in the Court House or at some other place mutually arranged for the purpose. About 1870, the Methodists erected a separate church building, and proposed to organize therein a Methodist Sunday School. Till then all denominations had worked together in a Union Sunday School, of which Major Mc-

Whirter had been superintendent for some time. Major and Mrs. McWhirter did not approve of the proposal of the Methodists to set up a denominational Sunday School, but favored the Union Sunday School with which they continued their connection. This, apparently, was the beginning of the breach between Mrs. McWhirter and her Church, which gradually became wider and more emphatic. In this schism, the particulars of which it would be difficult as well as useless to recount in detail, several other ladies, friends of hers but members of other denominations, became identified, and they at last found themselves united in a sort of religious band, holding prayer meetings at each other's homes and generally acting outside of their respective denominational organizations. Before the end of the decade they had entirely segregated themselves from their Churches and were concerned as leaders, in cooperation with other citizens, in the building of a non-sectarian meeting house, and in the holding of religious service therein—a union service disconnected with any of the regular church congregations.

Mrs. McWhirter, in the meantime, had come to have a wonderful influence over her followers, all of whom at first were women, and had become their acknowledged leader and director. Not only so, but she claimed to have divine authority, or rather directions, revealed to her in dreams and other miraculous manifestations. For some years before all these events she had claimed in a quiet way to have received evidence, by divine communication, that she had become sanctified—a doctrine taught by her own and some other denominations—and this doctrine she carried into the new association or band of which she was now the dominant mind. Other members sought in prayer, and claimed to have obtained, divine assurance of their own sanctification, till all of the members were so endowed and, in consequence, they began to be referred to by the general public as "the Sanctificationists," and, by the more irreverent, as "The Sancties." This stage of their development occurred about 1875 to 1880. So marked was their religious attitude and so decided their differentiation from the sectarian organizations, that, although they belonged to old, respectable and well-to-do families, yet, as a natural consequence of their peculiar profession and religious conduct, they became to a great extent isolated from their former friends and associates; and the little they had to do with their neighbors or the outside world was almost entirely of a routine business nature.

There were some additions of people from elsewhere, who heard of this band and came to Belton to cast their lot in with the Belton Sanctificationists. At different periods the band numbered probably from thirty to fifty people of adult ages or nearly so.

Passing over the details of their struggles, we come to note some of the outstanding features of this remarkable band. Most of these features had their inception in revelations communicated to Mrs. McWhirter in her dreams or trances.

It was a cardinal, inflexible law, as revealed to her, that a "sanctified" woman could not be the wife of an "unsanctified" man and *vice versa*. As a result, celibacy became the almost universal condition of the membership and, though for a time the married women resided in the homes of their unsanctified husbands, they finally left these homes for others provided by the band, usually taking the children of the household with them. Some of the children, especially the girls, grew up with the band and became members. A few of these girls, breaking away from their bonds, married and went out into the wicked world, never to return. The boys, as they grew up, usually found their way to more congenial environments. Gradually the band became a group of widows and maids, except for the three or four male members, to be mentioned in due course. One member, becoming dissatisfied with the arrangement, and perhaps with the doctrines of the band, quietly (with the help of outside friends) slipped away with her children, and went back to her own people in another state, leaving her husband to the tender mercies of the others. She subsequently divorced him, and he too finally looked out into the world through a different window and took his departure from the sacred circle.

Next, the members grew into a commune, with a common treasury. They began earning money by taking in washing, selling milk and butter, hiring out as cooks, operating a steam laundry, etc., and they put all learnings into the common fund. They opened a hotel or boardinghouse in the old J. C. Henry home and later bought the adjoining lot and built a commodious hotel, which they operated for several years, doing nearly all of the work themselves. All of these enterprises succeeded remarkably well and they accumulated considerable money and property. A part of the band then went to Waco and operated two hotels there, under leases, and finally, in 1899, the hotels in Waco were closed, the one in Belton was leased (later sold) and the whole band moved to Washington, D. C., where they purchased a large brick building, the size of a hotel, at 1437 Kenesaw Avenue, and there resided together for some years, supporting themselves by selling milk and butter, baking bread, cakes, etc. for private families, and doing various other kinds of work.

Mrs. McWhirter died April 21, 1904, and later on the band bought a small farm out in Maryland, a few miles from Washington, and the remnant of them were living there at last accounts.

In 1879 there came to Belton two brothers from Scotland. They were carpenters and did well in their trade. Having been connected with a religious society of the *same name* in their native country, they naturally united with the Sanctificationists of Belton, little dreaming that they were exposing themselves to the wrath and indignation of the men whose homes had been broken up by the adherence of their wives, mothers and sisters to this religious cult. Feeling ran high and, while nothing could be done with a lot of women, it was but a short time till the resentment manifested itself toward these two men, and so, one night in February, 1880, they were taken from their homes by a crowd of men and boys, carried out on the Waco road near the edge of town, and were there stripped and given a severe flogging and ordered to leave the country. As they did not obey this order, they were arrested and tried for lunacy and sent to the Asylum at Austin. The Asylum authorities soon pronounced them sane and discharged them from custody. They obtained employment at Austin in their trade of carpentering and remained there until they were brought back to Belton as witnesses before the Grand Jury, which was investigating the whipping. No indictment was returned. The victims remained in Belton and pursued their trade successfully for years, but never had anything more to do with the Sanctificationists.

The late Dr. George P. Garrison, then Professor of History in the University of Texas, spent several weeks in Belton in the summer of 1893, investigating and studying this freakish religious phenomenon. He boarded, while here, at the hotel conducted by the band and interviewed them personally about their organization, its history, beliefs and practices . He also discussed these matters freely with citizens of Belton. He was thus able to obtain first hand information. His study of the band was incorporated in a paper entitled "A Woman's Community in Texas," published in "The Charities Review" of New York for September, 1893, (Vol. III, No. 1), which is very interesting reading and quite authentic.

Dr. Garrison did not attempt to give a resumé of their religious belief, as it could not be accurately defined or explained. His conclusion was in these words:

"The whole matter is summed up by Mrs. McWhirter in the statement that it is the work of God under whose protection the sisters live and by whom a way will always be opened for them. The people of Belton sum it up by saying that Mrs. McWhirter is the center and soul of the organization, that its prolonged existence and success are due to her really extraordinary powers and to her strange influence over her followers and that when she is gone there will be the end of it."

The band became quite extensively known and advertised through the press, all over the country, and their fame followed them to Washington where they were visited, interviewed, studied and written about by numerous students of psychology and social science.

Major McWhirter never took any interest in the affairs of the band nor sympathized with their vagaries. For some years he patiently tolerated their proceedings, whether enacted at his home or at the homes of other members. But finally his situation became untenable and he left his home and furnished a room over a store building down town, owned by him, and there took up his residence alone. And there, in 1887, he died. Although, for religious reasons, his wife never visited him in his solitary abode, he remained loyal to her to the last. Not long before his death, he made his will, giving his half of their joint estate to his children, but naming Mrs. McWhirter as executrix, without bond, stating that "she was honest and would do right by the children." And she did, for she and every member of her band were absolutely and scrupulously honest.

6. The Temple Stag Party, 1893-1922

This unique affair was formally launched on Thanksgiving Day, November 29, 1893. The idea probably germinated from a general Thanksgiving celebration held in the old Opera House on the public square in Temple in 1892. On a suggestion to repeat this function the following year it was found that the Opera House was not available and so Col. W. Goodrich Jones, the father of the movement, invited his friends to meet at his residence and some seventy-five guests appeared and the Stag Party was born. For six consecutive years the hospitable home of Col. Jones and wife was thrown open to the business and other men of Temple on Thanksgiving in welcome to the Stags and at last the party grew too large for the facilities of the residence and had to meet elsewhere—in hotels, vacant stores, etc. The average attendance was about three hundred. While Colonel Jones was host, the invitation was extended to all of his friends and the feast was free to all and was a good one. Afterwards tickets were sold to cover the expenses. At each banquet a toastmaster and an executive committee, for the next banquet, were chosen. The toastmasters, besides Colonel Jones, have included Hon. Geo. C. Pendleton, W. B. Blaine, T. J. Darling, A. H. Parsons, T. B. Coppage, Chas. M. Campbell, John J. Cox, Jno. D. Robinson, F. F. Downs, F. M. Spann, Rev. P. A. Heckman, Gov. Jas. E. Ferguson, Rev. B. A. Hodges, H. C. Poe, W. O. Cox, Sam D. Snodgrass, Jno. C. Hardy, Dr. O. F. Gober, Rev. M. T. Andrews, H. L. Dailey, P. L. Downs, and others.

A few regular toasts were pre-announced and then followed a general fusilade of impromptu five-minute speeches. Often an amusing and instructive stunt was put on or some surprise for an inoffensive stag.

The speakers have included all or nearly all of the leading men of Temple, Belton and other towns in Bell County and quite a number of prominent gentlemen from other sections. Among the latter may be mentioned: W. B. Scott, J. W. Dickinson, T. B. Coppage, F. G. Pettibone, of the Santa Fe System; Will H. Mayes, Brownwood; Wm. J. Yeager, Readville, Pennsylvania; Mr. Stoddard, New York; W. D. Williams, Railway Commissioner; Dr. Howard Agnew Johnson, Stamford, Conn.; Louis J. Wortham, Fort Worth; Dr. Wm. B. Phillips, State Geologist; Tom L. Mc-

Culloch, Waco; W. C. Linden, San Antonio; Nelson Phillips, Chief Justice Supreme Court; Tom Connally, Congressman; Tom Finty, Jr., *Dallas News;* Morris Sheppard, United States Senator; W. H. Atwell, Dallas; Joab H. Banton, District Attorney of New York; and many others.

The Stag Party, the happy inspiration of its founder, Colonel Jones, became a cherished institution Its purposes were to promote sociability and good feeling among men of every interest, in Temple particularly and in the county generally, and to foster all worthy community activities. All who have enjoyed the annual festivity regret that in recent years it has been abandoned.

7. *The Old Settlers' Association of Bell County,* 1898-1904

In the latter part of 1898 a few old-timers organized the Old Settlers' Association of Bell County for social and historical purposes. A preliminary meeting was held in the office of Captain H. E. Bradford, then County Surveyor, in the lower northeast corner room of the Court House in Belton. Those present were Captain H. E. Bradford, Don A. Chamberlin, Hon. Wilson T. Davidson, P. L. Ellis, Judge X. B. Saunders, Geo. W. Tyler, and possibly one or two others. A temporary organization was made with X. B. Saunders, president; W. T. Davidson, vice-president; H. E. Bradford, Secretary; Don A. Chamberlin, Treasurer. A committee on Constitution was named, consisting of Messrs. Tyler, Davidson and Bradford, and the meeting adjourned to meet in Tyler's office on December 3, 1898, at 7:30 P. M. At this adjourned meeting the constitution reported by the committee was adopted and the temporary organization was made permanent. The charter members were H. E. Bradford, Don A. Chamberlin, Wilson T. Davidson, P. L. Ellis, M. J. Kuykendall, W. S. Riggs, X. B. Saunders, M. H. Shanklin, and Geo. W. Tyler.

During the six years of its active existence the following persons were the officers of the Association:

Year	President	Vice-President
1898-1899	X. B. Saunders	W. T. Davidson
1899-1900	X. B. Saunders	W. T. Davidson
1900-1901	W. T. Davidson	M. J. Kuykendall
1901-1902	Geo. W. Tyler	M. J. Kuykendall
1902-1903	Geo. W. Tyler	J. M. Thomson

Year	President	Vice-President
1903-1904	R. Y. King	P. S. Turner
1904-	R. Y. King	W. T. Davidson

	Secretary	Treasurer	Historian
1898-1899	H. E. Bradford	D. A. Chamberlin	
1899-1900	H. E. Bradford		
1900-1901	M. H. Shanklin		
1901-1902	M. H. Shanklin		
1902-1903	M. H. Shanklin		John D. Robinson
1903-1904	W. S. Hunter		Geo. W. Tyler
1904-	Geo. W. Tyler		H. E. Bradford

The Secretary's book shows the enrollment of the following persons as members:

John C. Anderson, W. L. Armstrong, Theo Armstrong, Geo. N. Austin, Isaac T. Bean, Mrs. L. A. Barton, Mrs. M. A. Blackburn, Mrs. J. A. Blackburn, R. Blackburn, Jno. G. Blackburn, Whit Blackburn, Mrs. W. B. Blair, W. B. Blair, Jas. S. Blair, P. A. Bonner, J. C. Bonner, Mrs. M. Bowles, David C. Bowles, H. E. Bradford, Wm. Brookman, Fred C. Brookman, Wm. E. Bruce, J. R. Bryant, J. M. Carpenter, Thos. F. Carpenter, J. F. Carter, Jr., Wm. J. Caskey, Don A. Chamberlin, W. S. Chapman, Net R. Clark, J. H. Cox, E. Tom Cox, Mrs. Lucy Cox, Wm. A. Craddock, J. N. Crass, C. W. Danley, Wilson T. Davidson, Geo. W. Dennis, Mrs. A. E. Dennis, George Dennis, P. L. Ellis, Mrs. A. J. Embree, Mrs. J. W. Embree, Robert T. Estes, Joseph G. Ferguson, Joe B. Ferguson, Mrs. S. J. Ferguson, Chas. O. Ferguson, James E. Ferguson, J. F. Fuller, Mrs. Elizabeth Fuller, Mrs. N. C. Furnace, Joseph Furnace, Mrs. Geo. H. Gassaway, Mrs. A. E. Graves, Wm. W. Hair, Wm. K. Hamblen, A. J. Hamilton, Wm. P. Hancock, Wm. T. J. Hartriek, Mrs. T. C. Hartriek, E. M. Hatcher, Thomas Hilyard, L. T. Holcomb, F. N. Holcomb, W. R. Holcomb, Mrs. Eve Cockrell Hughes, W. S. Hunter, John W. Hunton, Henry L. Karnes, Mrs. S. A. Kegley, Mat Keyes, Mrs. May Keyes, Rufus Y. King, M. J. Kuykendall, John I. Lamb, Dr. Jarrette D. Law, J. G. Leatherman, A. B. Lewis, Mrs. L. C. Lewis, Mrs. P. H. Mallory, C. W. Marshall, Joe Marshall, J. F. McAninch, Mrs. A. P. McCune, Mrs. R. T. McCune, William McCune, J. P. McKay, Wm. Meader, J. Z. Miller, Sr., Robert Neal, Fred Neibling, John Nichols, Mrs. Susan Nichols, S. L. Oliver, Mrs. M. J. Pearce, S. A. Pearce, Geo. C. Pendleton, Mrs. C. Perkins, Wm. Perkins, Mrs. Seabelle Perkins, Chas. A. Peters, Mrs. E. J. Polk, J. A. Polk, Green I. Pope, Jno. T. Pope, S. J. Pope, Drury D. Potter, Lon Price, Newton

M. Proctor, Mrs. Victoria Rather, Vol. E. H. Reed, Robt. A. Rich, Wm. S. Riggs, Mrs. Sallie J. Riggs, Jno. D. Robinson, Thos. U. Robinson, A. J. Rose, X. B. Saunders, Wm. K. Saunders, M. H. Shanklin, Wm. C. Sparks, J. E. Sparks, Mrs. L. E. Sparks, Ale Scott, Jim Scott, A. P. Sloan, Wm. W. Spoonts, E. E. Stewart, Thos. F. Stockton, W. G. W. Stone, H. C. Surghnor, W. R. Sypert, R. B. Thomas, J. Mc. Thomson, D. P. Thompson, Jno. S. Tulloch, Jno. W. Turner, Pitt S. Turner, Mrs. O. T. Tyler, Geo. W. Tyler, Wm. W. Upshaw, Mrs. Jane M. Ware, S. E. Wills, C. H. Wedemeyer, G. A. Wills, Wm. R. Wills, Mrs. M. V. Wiseman, G. W. Wiseman, L. E. Wood, Thos. C. Wright, J. C. Yarbrough.

Six annual Reunions were held in Belton from July 22, 1899, to November 5, 1904. These Reunions at first consisted of addresses and a basket picnic and a social gathering, renewal of old acquaintances, recital of accounts and traditions of early days and other modes of entertainment.

At the Reunions of 1902, 1903, and 1904 there was added a set program, consisting of the reading of historical and other papers, prepared at the request of the president, which proved interesting to the assemblies and which contained much valuable historical data.

A list of these papers here follows:

Papers Read at the Reunion of 1902

"A Tragic Event at Old Tenoxtitlan" by Hon. Rufus Y. King.
"The History of Old Fort Griffin" by Hon. Wilson T. Davidson.
"A Country Boy in the 'Black Waxy'" by Hon. Geo. C. Pendleton.
"The Pioneer Women of Texas" by Dr. Jarrette D. Law.
"The Pioneers, their Pleasures, Hardships and Hazardous Life," by Hon. A. J. Rose.
"Early Days on the Lampasas" by M. H. Shanklin.
"Bob White's Ranger Company" by Don A. Chamberlin.
"Early Settlement of Brooksville" by Wm. J. Caskey.
"Locating Lands in Old Milam Land District" by Capt. H. E. Bradford.
"Belton in the Fifties" by P. L. Ellis.
"The First Steamboat at Old Nashville" by J. Mc. Thomson.

"History of Washington County" by Prof. C. H. Wedemeyer.
"Reveries of a Bachelor" by Dr. Pitt S. Turner.
"Love-making in the Backwoods" by Jno. D. Robinson.

Papers Read at the Reunion of 1903

"A Tale of Two Texas Towns—Anahuac and Harrisburg" by Mrs. Adele B. Looscan of Houston.
"Causes of the Texas Revolution" by Judge C. W. Raines, State Librarian, Austin.
"History of Old Nashville" by Col. Frank Brown of Austin.
"Gen. Sam Houston—A Character Sketch" by Dr. D. R. Wallace of Waco.
"Reminiscences of James Coryell and Levi Taylor and Short Account of an Indian Massacre in 1837" by Newton C. Duncan of Wheelock.
"History of Old Aiken" by Mat J. Kuykendall.
"Early History of Washington County, II" by Prof. C. H. Wedemeyer.
"Spanish Land Titles in Texas" by Capt. H. E. Bradford.
"The Belton Overflow of 1853" by Capt. Thos. C. Wright.
"Pioneer Experiences in the Early Days of Bell County" by Mrs. John Blackburn.
"Belton in the Fifties, II" by P. L. Ellis.
"The District Judges of Bell County since its Organization" by L. K. Tarver.
"Indian Attack upon the Gregg Family in 1841" by Hon. Rufus Y. King.
"Early History of Coryell County" by Judge John H. Chrisman.

Papers Read at the Reunion of 1904

"Capt. Eli Chandler's Campaign Against an Indian Village" by Newton C. Duncan of Wheelock.
"Old Settlers of Milam County" by M. H. Addison of Caldwell.
"Sketch of Major Horace Haldeman and Pioneer Days in Bell County" by Mrs. Eugenia Haldeman Openheimer of Austin.

"Early Courtship and Marriage in Texas" by Newton C. Duncan of Wheelock.

"The Texas Farmer in Pioneer Days" by Geo. W. Tyler.

"History of Melville Wilkinson and Family" by Mrs. Eva Cockrell Hughes.

"The Victory and Death of Captain Bird" by Capt. H. E. Bradford.

"Sketch of John C. Reid, the First County Clerk of Bell County" by Mrs. Nanna Smithwick Donaldson of Williamson County, Texas.

"Mercantile Business in Belton in Ante-bellum Days" by John F. Smith of Galveston.

"Reminiscences of Old Troy and Oenaville" by L. C. Williams of Beaumont.

"Retaliation of the Caddos in 1835-6 and other Reminiscences" by Newton C. Duncan of Wheelock.

Nearly all of the papers read at the Reunions of 1902, 1903, and 1904, with the official minutes of the proceedings, were printed in a Belton newspaper as a serial and, while thus set up in type, were run into pamphlets for the use of the Association. Those of 1902 and 1903 were thus handled by the *Journal-Reporter,* and those of 1904 by the *Bell County Democrat.* Of late years the demand for these pamphlets from students of Texas local history, both near and far, has nearly exhausted the small editions and their historical value continues to increase. While some of these papers are scholarly and well written, others were crude and presented by the authors only after much urging and with the understanding that they would be re-written and put into readable shape—in other words, the authors furnished the basic facts and expressed them in their own way. But these were valuable contributions and, in re-writing them, we left as much of the original language of the author as possible.

Many of the contributors are no more. "The History of Old Nashville"—the Jamestown of all the upper Brazos and Little River country—written by Col. Frank Brown of Austin, is in itself worth all of the efforts of the Association. His childhood had been spent in Nashville, and he was almost its only survivor, and was certainly the only person then living who could have written its history, and now he is gone. So with many of the other papers—their preservation by the Association was the only chance to salvage for posterity the important historical facts they contained.

There was no meeting or reunion of the Association after 1904. The conditions leading to the cessation of meetings are well set forth in the preamble and resolutions adopted at the Reunion of 1904, as follows:

"Whereas, The organization of this association is imperfect, crude and chaotic and is not sufficiently cohesive and compact to accomplish the best results and purposes, and the Association has no financial resources or revenue whatever with which to pay its necessary and proper expenses, such as printing, postage, stationery, etc., therefore;

"Resolved, That the president appoint a committee of five members whose duty it shall be to devise a more perfect plan of organization, to provide some method of raising a reasonable annual revenue, and that said committee is hereby given full power to proceed at once with such reorganization in cooperation with our regular officers who shall be officers of the reorganized Association and that we pledge ourselves to respect and heartily cooperate with whatever plan of reorganization said committee may decide upon, consistent with the original plans, purposes and practices of this Association.

"Resolved, That we heartily approve of the historical work being done under the auspices of this Association by the preparation and publishing of historical papers, and that we look forward to the development of this Association into a permanent historical society such as have long existed in many of the older communities of the United States.

"Resolved, further, That we tender our thanks to all those who have furnished papers at this and former Reunions and take much pride in the fact that persons living elsewhere have thought enough of our purposes to contribute valuable historical papers to our archives."

In addition, it should be stated that the labors and responsibilities of the Association devolved upon a very few—and they were mostly elderly persons—and one member had thus far paid all of the expenses, such as printing the proceedings and papers. The intention of the foregoing resolutions was to reorganize upon a better footing but this "was easier said than done." The members of the committee appointed to devise a plan were never able to see their way to establishing a better organization, and the officers and working members, discouraged at the outlook and too busy with their private concerns to give any more time to the Association's affairs, simply delayed further meetings and the interest gradually died.

And thus passed into history the Old Settlers' Association of Bell County. Much was accomplished, in its short career, in rescuing from oblivion important historical material relating to Bell County and this section of the State—material that could not now be supplied from any possible source. This writer has realized the great value of many facts preserved in the papers read at the reunions of the Association and has made free use of them in this work, as his numerous citations of sources show, and he recognizes frankly and gratefully their great assistance to him in the performance of his difficult task. He prizes his membership in the organization and is glad to have been thus associated with many of the worthy and revered pioneers of Bell County.

THE END

Marker in front of Judge Tyler's home and the Geo. W. Tyler Park Marker

Index

Adams, Benjamin, 130.
Addison, ..., 27.
Agriculture Experiment Station, 343.
Ahrens, H. E., 335.
Aid, Soldiers, 226.
Aiken, 161.
Aiken, Col. Hermon, 90, 91, 92, 93, 139, 142, 152, 158, 161, 163, 283, 349.
Aiken, Jno. W., 358.
Aiken, Miss Josephine, 356.
Aiken, Miss Lillie, 356.
Alexander, Daniel, 130, 157, 164, 165.
Alexander, John (Alias Daily), 303.
Alexander, Jno. T., 143.
Alexander, Dr. Wm. R., 159, 230, 282, 357.
"Alexander School Lands," 164.
Allcorn, John, 183.
Allen, ..., 86.
Allen, Ben F., 158.
Allen, Ethan, 61.
Allen, George, 71.
Allen, John Q., 158, 233, 258, 306, 385.
Allen, Mrs. Matilda F. (nee Connell), 125.
Allen, Moses, 103.
Allen, Samuel T., 28.
Allen, Thomas J., 114, 125.
Allen, Lieut. Wm. R., 64, 66, 68, 69, 71, 72.
Anderson, Dr. ...., 285.
Anderson, A. J., 189.
Anderson, A. R., 159.
Anderson, David, 23, 24.
Anderson, Dr. J. H., 162.
Anderson, J. H., 283.
Anderson, James, 119, 121, 283.
Anderson, John, 129.
Anderson, John H., 150.
Anderson, Rufus, 159.
Anderson, Vachel H., 159, 226.
Anderson, W. T., 306.
Andrews, Henry B., 155.
Annexation of Texas to United States, 78.

Ante-Bellum Politics and Secession, 194.
Armstrong, Dr. D. H., 284, 289.
Armstrong, James C., 230.
Armstrong, W. B., 283.
Armstrong, William, 89, 113, 121.
Arocha, José Nepomucena, 24.
Arrowood, W. P., 152.
Ashley, James, 130, 160.
Ashley, Wm., 160.
Atkinson, John, 71.
Austin, Mrs. Emily G., 242.
Austin, F. K., 258.
Austin, F. Henry, 312.
Austin, Geo. N., 310.
Austin, Moses, 1
Austin, Norman, 140, 143, 227, 230.
Austin, Stephen F., 1.
Automobile, Advent of, 345.
Ayres, David, 160.
Ayres, William, 64, 71.

Badgett, Wm., 64.
Baggett, Silas, 130, 151, 159, 268, 294, 314, 381.
Baggett, William, 71.
Bagley, A. T., 242.
Bailey, J. L., 284.
Bailey, Jesse, 41, 44, 52.
Bailey, Lige, 9.
Baines, Miss Arnie, 356.
Baines, Rev. Geo. W., 284.
Baker, John J., 141, 191, 207, 384.
Ball, Charles, 71.
Ballard, J. C., 232.
Banks, County, 384; Belton, 384; Temple, 387; in other county towns, 388.
Banta, Peter, 119, 123.
Baptist Church, organization of Salem, 161.
Bar meeting, first in Bell County, 157.
Barbed wire, 294.
Barbee, Capt. J. H., 284.
Barbee, Miss Letitia, 355.
Barbee, Miss Melissa, 356.
Barcus, John M., 323.
Barnard, Joseph H., 71.

Barnes, Roswell, 103.
Barrow, John, 41.
Barrow, Captain Thomas H., 9, 28, 41, 42, 45.
Bartlett, Jno. T., 388.
Barton, Miss Addie, 356.
Barton, Miss Emma, 356.
Barton, Miss Rebecca, 356.
Barton, Sam, 41.
Barton, Dr. Welborn, 283, 358.
Barton, Mrs. Welborn, 356.
Bass, Sam, 303.
Bassell, Neal, 369.
Bassil, Byron D., 284.
Bates, John F., 158.
Bates, Silas, 41.
Bates, Wilson, 158, 190.
Batte, John G., 306, 310.
Batte, Tom, 273.
Bauer, A. C., 370, 374.
Bayley, Winfred, 80.
Baylor College for Women, 361; founding of, 361; removal from old Independence, 362; first building at, 362; additional buildings of, 363; presidents of, 363; removal of Judge Baylor to, 363; name changed to, 363.
Baylor, John R., 184.
Baylor, Judge R. E. B., 120, 129, 155, 156, 157, 158, 361, 363.
Bayne, William G., 73.
Bean, Isaac T., 158, 192.
Beardslee, Nehemiah, 121, 150.
Beardsley, Richard, 126.
Beck, John, 103.
Beckneal, ..., 303.
Beeman, Colonel Alonzo, 92, 158, 199, 230, 241, 381.
Beene, Fred H., 158.
Beene, Jas. K., 158.
Beisner, C., 71.
Bell County, act to create, 107; bids for courthouse of, 126; boundary changes of, 152; Civil War and, 194; creation and organization of, 107; deed conveying land of, 125; deed records of, 121; district court of, 129; early records of, 121; farming in, 165; first bar meeting in, 157; first grand jury of, 129; first marriage record of, 122; first officers of, 118; first session of commissioners' court of, 123; first tax levy in, 127; first transaction in probate court of, 128; highways and roads, 149; minute men, 188; new courthouse of, 146; organization of, 118; probate court of, 128; residents, 1850, 94; revenues and expenditures, 148; "Bell County Rovers," 189; stock-raising, 165; surveying of, 113; transportation in, 165, 171; volunteer companies of, 200.
Bell, Dr. ...., 251.
Bell, James D., 9, 159, 187, 188, 190.
Bell, John, 196, 272.
Bell, Gov. Peter Hansborough, 107, 174.
Bell, S. H., 192.
Bell, Thos., 188.
Bell, William H., 187, 190, 196.
Belton (see also Nolanville), 137; Academy, 364; beginnings of, 115; cotton compress, 311; **Belton Courier**, 300; **Belton Democrat**, 195; early business houses of, 116; early structures of, 115; **Belton Independent**, 195; new name for Nolanville, 139; first mill, 117; Belton and Temple Traction Company, 335; water works system, 312.
Benge, H., 103.
Bentley, A. F., 335.
Beringer, J., 258.
Berry, ..., 41, 42.
Berry, John, 26.
Bertrong, Thomas, 152.
Bettinger, A., 71.
Biard, Bythel H., 269.
"Big Foot," Comanche chief, 73, 74.
Bigelow, Chas. A., 141.
Bigham, E. H., 158, 159.
Bigham, J. Swan, 137, 183, 187, 188, 189, 190, 203, 205; Bigham's Company, 203.
Bigham, M. S., 158.
Bigham, Oliver H., 117, 143, 146, 148, 158, 187, 247, 283.
Bigham, Robert C., 187, 189.
Bigham, R. Patton, 154, 158, 187.
Bigham, Sam W., 117, 158, 383.
Bigham, William Nix, 158, 187, 190.

Index

Bird, Capt. John, 9, 44, 62, 64, 65, 70, 71, 72; muster roll of Bird's company at Bird's Creek fight, 71.
Bird, Corporal Wm. P., 44, 64, 71.
Birdeshaw, William, 119, 120.
Bishop, James J., 111.
Bishop, Josepah, 82, 111, 159.
Bishop, Capt. Samuel W., 110, 111, 112, 239, 240.
Bivens, Lige, 241.
Blackburn, Jno. G., 159.
Blackburn, John P., 159.
Blackburn, M. W., 159.
Blackburn, W. H. L., 159.
Blackburn, Wm. P., 307.
Blackwell, Rev. M. W., 284.
Blackwell, Will, 274.
Blair, Samuel A., 68, 71.
Blair, Albert S., 189, 190.
Blair, J. E., 323.
Blair, James K., 82, 85, 86, 89, 119, 123.
Blair, Jesse, 190.
Blair, Mrs. Jesse S., 374.
Blair, Joel D., 82, 85, 89, 137, 143, 150, 167, 183, 188, 189, 190, 227.
Blair, John S., 86, 117, 137, 140, 163, 167, 226, 229, 230, 349.
Blair, John S., Jr., 187.
Blair, Joshua O., 71.
Blair, Judge Mallory B., 110, 364, 370, 371, 375.
Blair, William B., 71, 83, 85, 86, 89, 117, 150, 183.
Blanc, J., 64.
Blanc, T., 64.
Blankenship, B., 156.
Blawkenburg, James Clark, 158.
Boatler, Grafton H., 71.
Boatwright, D. T., 158.
Bock, Charles, 144, 187.
Bock, William, 144, 147, 187.
Boll-weevil, 336.
Bond issues, 330.
Bone, Pat, 189.
Bonner, J. C., 283.
Bonner, Miss Mollie, 356.
Boone, Tuck, 276.
Booth, John Wilkes, 244.
Bouldin, Hilary M., 192, 217, 229.
Boundary changes, 152.
Boundary disputes, case concerning, 156.
Bowen, Gid, 9.
Bowie knife, 134.
Bowles, Calvin, 9, 28.
Bowles, David C., 190.
Bowles, James F., 130.
Bowles, John, 124, 126, 129; children of, 86.
Bowman, C. I., 310.
Boyd, ..., 165.
Bradford, H. E., 143, 144, 153, 196, 203, 209, 227, 228, 397, 399, 400, 401; Bradford's Company, 209.
Bradford, Dr. Hamilton, 189, 190, 207.
Bradford, Milton, 71.
Bradford, Thomas, 71.
Bradford, Miss Victoria, 207.
Bradley, Daniel, 71.
Bramlet, Simeon, 148, 234, 283.
Breckinridge, John C., 196.
Breedlove, W. F., 158.
Bridges, 268, 305, 330.
Brittain, A., 103.
Brocker, Henry, 370.
Brookman, Fred C., 159.
Brookman, Wm., 159.
Brookman, William, Jr., 159.
Brookshire, James, 64.
Brookshire, Nathan, 62, 64, 66, 68, 69, 70.
Brown, Rev. ...., 283, 356.
Brown, John Dell, 9.
Brown, Lt. John, 215.
Brown, John, 242.
Brown, Major John Henry, 65, 144, 183, 185, 187, 188, 189, 195, 196, 197, 198, 199, 225, 390.
Brown, Julius, 183.
Brown, Littleton, 71.
Brown, Thomas, 71.
Brown, Maj. Will R., 377.
Bruce, Willis H., 159.
Brunet, E., 309.
Bryan, W. J., 329.
Bryant, Allen, 103, 129.
Bryant, Barney, 103.
Bryant, Major Benjamin, 9, 61, 73, 78, 80, 90, 156.
Bryant, Jesse, 103, 156.
Bryant, Fayette, 89.
Bryant, Lafayette, 73.
Bryant, M. D., 370.
Buckles, E. R. A., 284.
Buckles, M. H., 284.
Buildings, methods used in early, 117; stone, of Belton, 140.

The History of Bell County

Burch, Walter, 103, 129.
Burdick, Jackson E., 71.
Burks, Samuel, 230.
Burleson, ..., 91.
Burleson, General Ed., 27, 29, 65.
Burnet, John H., 307.
Burney, Col. Geo. E., 137.
Burns, James B., 130.
Burrows, Pastor, 191.
Burt, Col. R. E., 362.
Burton, Chester Guy, 370.
Bush, Rev. W. T., 284.
Business, improvements in, 331.
Butler, J. O., 71.
Butler, Thos. G., 284.
Buzby, ..., 103.
Byrne, Paton, 28.

Caddell, John C., 160.
Caldwell, H., 103.
Caldwell, William, 103, 129.
Callaway, J. W., 322.
Cameron, Captain Ewen, 80.
Cameron, made county seat of Milam County, 9; new county seat, 79.
Campbell, ..., 9, 72, 73.
Campbell, Chas. M., 364, 374, 375, 388, 391, 396.
Campbell, Daniel H., 23.
Campbell, David W., 28, 41.
Campbell, Nathan, 28.
Canfield, Thomas, 103.
Carmack, John, 183.
Carpenter, Rev. John, 142, 161, 227, 230.
"Carpet-baggers," 259.
Carroll, B. H., 355.
Carter, Wiley, 22, 61.
Cartmel, Thos. K., 242.
Casey, Joel, 124.
Caskey, Wm. J., 299.
Castleman, Michael, 28, 41.
Cates, John, 103, 159.
Cathey, John M., 129.
Cathey, Will, 276, 277.
Cattle, 169, 170; drives, 291; ordinance, 271.
Cawthon, Miss Alphier, 356.
Cearnel, A. W., 159, 167, 283, 349.
Cedar Creek residents, 100.
Chaffin, James B., 364.
Chalk, Ira E., 117, 297.
Chalk, Whitfield, 117, 297.

Chalmers, Albert, 9.
Chalmers, John, 9.
Chamberlin, David T., 119.
Chamberlin, Judge David T., 119, 132, 142, 143, 233, 247, 383, 384, 385.
Chamberlin, Don A., 191, 257, 385, 397, 399.
Chambers, Mack, 193.
Chance, Nancy, 23.
Chandler, Eli, 28.
Chapman, Mrs. Catherine Frazier, 15, 36.
Chapman, George W., 9, 15, 17, 18, 27, 35, 36, 82, 124, 128, 130, 150.
Chapman, Heman, 6, 17, 18, 27.
Chapman, John R., 160, 191.
"Charter Oak" election, 109.
Chatfield, Norman, 103.
Childers, Amanda, 17.
Childers, Caroline, 17, 31, 82, 122.
Childers, Catherine, 17.
Childers, Mrs. Elizabeth Thomas, 17.
Childers, Captain Goldsby, 6, 9, 12, 14, 15, 16, 17, 21, 24, 26, 29, 30, 32, 35, 43, 45, 52, 53, 81, 82, 83, 87, 121; children of, 86; and family, 77; 152.
Childers, Mrs. Goldsby, death of, 54.
Childers, James Franklin, 16, 17, 18, 24.
Childers, Frank, 45, 47, 48, 50, 51.
Childers, Mrs. Julia A., 121.
Childers, Mary Jane, 17.
Childers, Prior, 15, 17, 23, 81, 83, 121, 152.
Childers, Robert, 15, 16, 17, 18, 23, 27, 28, 29, 35, 43, 45, 47, 82, 83, 84, 85, 87, 117, 119, 121, 123, 156, 159, 196.
Childers, Thomas, 16, 17, 18, 23, 26, 121.
"Childers' Mill," 84; residents of, 95.
Childers family, 27.
Childress, Francis M., 28.
Childress, James R., 28.
Chisholm, G. T., 103.
Christian, Judge Hiram, 158, 249, 254, 381.

Index

Civil War, additional list of soldiers, 224; aid for soldiers' families in, 228, 229; anti-secessionists in, 239; in Bell County, 194; Confederate muster roll in Bell County, 202; Bigham's Company in, 203; Bradford's Company in, 209; civic activities during, 233; Confederate desertion in, 241; Confederate officers in, 225; Confederate's equipment for, 201; county treasury warrants in, 234; Damron's Company in, 212; Davidson's Beef Squad in, 225; economic conditions during, 236; first Texas cavalry in, roster of Company K in, 206; Graves' Company in, 226; Halley's Company in, 220; "heel flies" in, 240; "Home Guards" in, 240; home production during, 237; Rather's Company in, 223; Sam Houston's stand in, 194, 195; "Salado Mounted Troops" in, 204; Saunders' Company in, 216; Smith's Company in, 217; Soldiers' aid in, 226; Superintendents for soldiers' aid in, 230; Texas Volunteer Infantry, Company 1 in, 218; Volunteer Companies in, 200; Weathersbee's Company in, 222; White's Company in, 207.
Circus, first in Bell County, 136.
Clabaugh, Rev. John, 160, 349.
Clark, A., 227.
Clark, Dr. Carroll, 252, 254.
Clark, David, 9, 41, 44, 47, 48, 50, 51.
Clark, Edward W., 159, 191, 200.
Clark, Prof. Horace, 363.
Clark, J. A., 159.
Clark, James, 157.
Clark, James C., Sr., 103; Jr., 103.
Clark, John, C., 187, 188, 190.
Clark, John W., 158, 242.
Clark, Net R., 159.
Clary, J. R., 103.
Clary, Stephen P., 191.
Cobb, Arthur C., 370.
Cockrell, John, 9.
Coke, Governor Richard, 185, 267, 281.

Coleman, Col. ...., 42, 43.
Coleman, John W., 119.
Coleman, Loyd, 303.
Coleman, Major Robert M., 9, 41.
College, Salado, Joint Stock Company, 162.
Collins, D. W., 72.
Collins, J. E., 103.
Collins, Willis, 23.
Colonial Grants, in Bell County, 1; land laws pertaining to, 1.
Colter, A. H., 103.
Commissioners' Court, 304; first session of, 123; officers of, 124.
Commissioners, special, of Bell County, 109.
Committee of Public Safety, 198.
Communities, new, 1850, 158.
Confederacy, fall of, 244.
Confederates, Bell County muster rolls of, 202; equipment of, 201.
Connally, Tom, 397.
Connell, John H., 9.
Connell, Mrs. Matilda F., 9, 23, 113.
Connell, Patrick, 28.
Connell, William, 82.
Constantine, John B., 192.
Constitutional Convention, 1868-69, 265, 281.
Convention of Southern States, 197.
Cook, Augustus W., 28.
Cook, Henry, 28.
Cook, Rev. Henry C., 86.
Coop, Geo. J., 158.
Coop, James P., 141, 158, 187, 191, 212.
Cook, John, 157.
Copeland, W. D., 258, 284.
Cordon, Juan, 23.
Cordova, Jacob de, 81.
Cornelison, Moses, 144.
Coryell, James, 9, 28, 41.
Cosper, Dock, 276, 277.
Cosper, Henry, 275.
Cosper, Jake, 275.
Cotton, 167, 168.
Couch, Rev. Isaac, 30.
Coulter, Miss Jennie, 356.
Countess, C. C., 370.

County, debt, 305; government problems of, 304; jail, 307; revenues, 148.
Court, District, 155.
Courthouse, 308; bids for, 126; new, 146.
Cowan, John W., 187.
Cox, Lieut. Benjamin, 159, 183, 187, 188, 189.
Cox, Ed Tom, 191.
Cox, Elisha W., 190.
Cox, Euclid M., 58, 59.
Cox, Fleming T., 150, 159.
Cox, Rev. J. Fred, 59.
Cox, John P., 59.
Cox, John W., 159.
Cox, M., 227.
Cox, Nathan, 103.
Cox, Dr. Ramsey M., 160, 230, 281.
Cox, Robert, 192.
Cox, Sam H., 159.
Cox, Solomon, B., 187, 190.
Cox, W. D., 323.
Cox, William R., 41.
Cox, Ziba, 103.
Coxey, Joel, 103.
Craddock, Mrs. Amanda Childers, 15, 82.
Craddock, John R., 9, 28, 29, 82.
Crain, Dr. A. B., 369.
Crain, W. H., 322.
Crane, Rev. Wm. Carey, 308.
Crass, J. N., 284.
Crawford, Daniel C., 103, 130.
Crawford, T. G., 119.
Creekmore, ..., 284.
Crosby, Josiah F., 129.
Cross, F. M., 116, 117, 275.
Cross, G. B., 277.
Cross, James M., 82, 84, 85, 89, 117, 119, 123, 126, 274; and children, 86.
Cross, Riley, 89.
Cross, Wm. B., 116, 150.
Crouch, Isaac, 9.
Crow, ..., 303.
Crow, J. D., 324.
Cruger, Charles P., 140, 150, 182, 183, 227, 274.
Cruise, Christopher, 130.
Cullins, Aaron, 9, 41, 44, 52.
Cullins, Daniel, 9, 33, 41, 43, 44, 45, 52, 53.
Cullis, John, 103.
Cullis, Wm., 103.

Cummings, Moses, 9, 10, 12, 19, 20.
Curry, Reuben, 158.
Curtis, Lieut. Charles, 22, 41, 46, 47, 50, 52, 175.
Curtis, Dr. R. R., 374.
Cuthrew, John, 103.

Dallas, A. J., 159, 163, 227, 349, 350, 358.
Dalrymple, Col. Wm. C., 87, 152.
Dalton, M. P., 374.
Damron, Capt. Milton Wesley, 129, 130, 148, 167, 183, 187, 203, 212, 215, 227, 228, 284; Damron's Company, 212.
Dancing, 136.
Danley, C. W., 188.
Danley, Judge John, 111, 115, 116, 118, 119, 122, 123, 125, 128, 142, 152, 192, 212, 227.
Darnell, Anson, 41.
Davenport, Maj. J. H., 258.
Davenport, Steve, 273.
Davidson, Dr. Robert, 6, 7, 9, 15, 16, 18, 24, 30.
Davidson, Samuel Green, 150, 187, 188, 189, 196.
Davidson, Captain Wilson T., 6, 15, 44, 45, 225, 397, 399.
Davidson's Beef Squad, 225.
Davila, Miguel, 24.
Davis, Dr. A. B., 230, 236.
Davis, Miss Ada, 356.
Davis, Gov. Edmond J., 265, 266, 267, 271, 281, 341.
Davis, Governor E. J., Regime, 266.
Davis, J. M. G., 284.
Davis, Jefferson, 198, 244.
Davis, Lee R., 41, 42, 44, 47, 49.
Davis, W. A., 287, 288, 297, 358.
Davis, Wm. A., 283.
Davis, Mrs. W. A., 356.
Daws, ..., 253.
Dawson, Britton, 28.
Dawson, David, 28.
Dean, Mrs. ...., 284.
Dean, John, 158.
Deaton, E. L., 177.
Deckerd, B. S., 310.
Democratic leaders, 196.
Denman, W. P., 110, 347.
Dennis, Joseph, 111, 112, 113, 117, 122, 124, 125, 127, 130, 227.
Dennis, Neal M., 124, 143.

Index

Denny, H. C., 141, 188, 257, 306, 310, 385, 386.
Denson, Dr. T. C., 349.
Depew, Joseph, 103.
Dial, Joseph, 242.
Dickinson, Rev. W. K., 284.
District Court, 155.
Disturbances in County, 250.
Diversions of settlers, 135.
Donaldson, M., 103.
Donley, ..., 193.
Dooley, Thos. P., 159.
Dougherty, George, 22, 24, 82.
Douglas, ..., 196.
Downs, F. F., 234,, 374.
Downs, P. L., 324.
Downs, P. L., Jr., 375.
Doyle, ..., 360.
Drake, James, 103.
Draper, James M., 187.
Drought, 166.
DuBose, Tom, 364.
Duffau, Francois T., 9.
Duggin, Alexander, 23, 24.
Duncan, Charles, 41.
Duncan, Green B., 41.
Duncan, Newton C., 42.
Duncan, Thomas, 61, 150, 160, 253.
Dunlap, John, 121, 122, 124, 130, 150.
Dunlap, E. L., 284.
Dunn, James, 28.
Dunn, Moses, 158.
Dusek, Joseph Adolph, 370.
Dyess, E. E., 360.

Eager, Prof. P. H., 363.
Early, John, 150, 192, 252.
Early settlers of Robertson County, 15.
Eastland, Cyrus, 158, 284.
Eastland, Mrs. Helen M., 139.
Eastland, Dr. Wm. D., 120, 129, 137, 138, 139, 141, 144, 163, 187, 227, 236, 350.
Eastland, Wm. M., 9.
Eaton, Alfred, 41.
Eaton, Stephen, 28.
Eaton, Thos. H., 41.
Economic situation following World War, 379.
Edrington, ..., 85.
Edrington, Mrs., ..., 159, 283.
Educational institutions, private, 349.

Edwards, Gustavus E., 19, 20.
Edwards, W. H., 310.
Elgin, Lewis, 261.
Elledge, Rev. W. A., 284.
Elliott, Henry B., 86, 114, 119, 126.
Elliott, Robert L., 103.
Ellis, Ben, 230.
Ellis, Cyrus, 158.
Ellis, P. L., 111, 138, 240.
Elms, David, 160, 180, 181.
Embree, Elisha, 150, 159, 167, 187, 227, 268.
Embree, Dr. John W., 143, 187, 188, 189, 190, 191, 196, 226, 236, 257, 306, 310, 381, 390.
Emmons, Bradley, 41.
English, Miss Kate, 365.
Enterprises, new, 309.
Epps, James, 192.
Epps, Thos. A., 238.
Erath, George B., 9, 33, 40, 42, 44, 45, 46, 47, 54, 76, 81, 185.
Ervin, Lieut. ...., 62.
Estes, Ed. T., 150, 159, 356.
Estis, Ed. J., 190.
Etheridge, Burrell, 274.
Etheridge, Dennis, 274.
Eubank, Jno. T., 258, 283.
Evans, Alfred, 117, 159, 229.
Evans, Lieut. Wm. G., 65, 71.
Evetts, Sam, 160.
Ewing, Dr. J. A., 141, 144, 283.

Fairs in county, 390.
Farley, Masilion, 9.
Farley, Moses, 9.
Farmer, David M., 41, 44, 52.
Farmer's Alliance, 301.
Farming, agitation for relief of, 327; efforts to improve methods of, 344; post war conditions of, 378; spread of, 294; tenant, 329.
Federal occupation in county, 248.
Felt, Judge G. M., 112.
Ferguson, C. D., 362.
Ferguson, Rev. James E., 86, 269, 288, 297.
Ferguson, Gov. James E., 366, 386, 387, 388, 396.
Ferguson, John, 70.
Ferguson, John F., 160, 191.
Ferguson, Joseph G., 6, 160, 191.
Ferguson, Mrs. Mary, 362.
Ferguson, Mrs. Nancy, 70.

Ferguson, Robert, 28, 41.
Ferguson, Wesley G., 159.
Ferry, license for, 126.
Feud, Early-Hasley, 250.
First Texas Cavalry, Roster of Company K, 206.
Fisher, King, 229.
Fitch, Benjamin F., 28, 41.
Fitzgerald, Prof. B. S., 363.
Fleming, Andrew J., 160, 189, 191.
Fleming, Berry, 274.
Fleming, Ira, 274.
Fletcher, James, 150.
Fleury, Robert, 9.
Flint, Ed. S., 158.
Flint, Col. Jno. T., 143, 167, 190, 227, 283, 287, 349, 384.
Flippen, Joseph, 72.
Fokes, John, 44, 47.
Folks, John, 41.
Fontaine, Col. W. W., 363.
Food available for settlers, 20, 43.
Ford, Col. John S., 204.
Foreman, Eli, 71.
Fort Bryant, 72.
Fort Gates, residents, 100; roster, 102; settlement of, 81.
Fort Griffin, 45.
Fort Milam, 10; establishment of, 10; mutiny at, 65.
Fort, T., 64.
Fort, Tilman C., 71.
Foster, Rev. Finis E., 142, 143, 161.
Foster, Robert B., 140, 144, 148, 167.
Fowler, Capt., ..., 284.
Fowler, Miss Cora, 356.
Fowler, Miss Laura, 356.
Franklin, James J., 226.
Franks, ..., 53.
Franks, David R., 152.
Franks, John, 156.
Frazier, Alex, 130.
Frazier, Miss Caroline (Mrs. G. W. Chapman), 128.
Frazier, Catherine, 19.
Frazier, Dr. J. M., 369.
Frazier, Margaret (Mrs. William H. Taylor), 19.
Frazier, Stephen, 9, 17, 19, 27, 41, 57.
Frazier, William, 17, 19, 27.
Frederick, Albert Willie, 370.
Freeman, ..., 165.

Freemasonry in county, 381.
Friley, Job, 87.
Frost, Abner, 72.
Fry, Geo. W., 191.
Fulcher, Emiline, 19.
Fulcher, John, 16, 19, 24, 28, 29, 112, 113, 122, 124, 130; and family, 82.
Fulcher, Martha, 19.
Fulcher, Mrs. Mary Josephine, 19.
Fulcher, Willis, 19.
"Fulcher's Colony," 82.
Fuller, J. F., 284, 299, 300.
Fullerton, Henry, 28.
Furman, H. M., 309.
Furniture, early, 133.

Garland, Peter, 184.
Garner, William, 191.
Garrett, Miss Ann, 356.
Garrett, Elmer V., 370.
Garrett, Miss Pinkie, 356.
Garrett, Judge Wm. H., 284, 287.
Garrison, Mrs. ...., 227.
Garrison, Dr. Geo. P., 394.
Garrison, Mitchell, 82.
Gatesville, settlement of, 81.
Gavin, Mrs. ...., 356.
Gavins, ..., 64.
Gay, Thomas, 64, 67, 71, 72.
George, Freeman, 274, 275.
George, James, 274.
George, William, 274.
Gevin, Charles M., 71.
Giddings, Calvary, 124.
Gilbert, John T., 143.
Giles, G. F., 160.
Gilmore, Thomas, 160.
Givens, Matthew, 119, 129.
Glenn, Alex, 103.
Glenn, H. C., 375.
Glenn, James M., 103, 129.
Gold hunters, 174.
Gold rush, 176.
Gomer, John, 323.
Goode, ..., 86.
Goode, E. N., 82, 85.
Goode, Dr. William, 236.
Goodman, Jno. B., 103.
Goodman, Stephen, 71, 119, 127.
Grange, 299, 324, 327.
Grant, Richard G., 87, 152.
Grant, Gen. U. S., 244, 260, 266.
Graves, Capt. G. Wat, 158, 167,

Index

203, 221, 239, 381; Graves' Company, 221.
Graves, Rev. H. L., 363.
Graves, James A., 9, 130, 158.
Graves, Lieut. John A. T., 28.
Graves, Mrs. Mary A., 130, 159.
Graves, Thomas A., 12, 28.
Gray, David, 159.
Gray, Miss Jennie, 322.
Green, George, 9, 154.
Gregory, Dr. J. J., 284, 306.
Gresham, O. P., 324.
Gresham, R. O., 324.
Griffin, D., 192.
Griffin, John H., 160.
Griffin, Moses, 9, 15, 16, 18, 24, 28, 29, 44, 45, 46, 93, 124, 252; and family, 77.
Griffith, L. A., 284, 299.
Grimes, G. W., 64.
Grimes, J. Alex, 158, 192.
Grimes, Louis P., 158.
Gross, Jacob, 9, 41, 44, 47.
Grumbles, William Henry, 303.
Gulf, Colorado, and Santa Fe Railroad, 313.
Guns, 133.
Guthrie, E., 258.
Guthrie, S., 284.

Haag, Walter G., 335
Haggard, ..., 161.
Hair, D. F., 288.
Haldeman, Horace, 87, 102, 196, 226, 242.
Haldeman, Col. Peter, 226.
Haley, Geo. W., 136.
Hall, ..., 64.
Hall, Ad, 53.
Hall, H. M. C., 64, 67, 69, 71, 72.
Hall, Mrs. Thos., C., 374, 375.
Halley, Miss Augusta, 356.
Halley, Miss Emma, 356.
Halley, Robert Bonner, 159, 196, 203, 204, 205, 220, 228, 283, 302; Halley's Company, 220.
Halley, Mrs. Velma Bailey, 383.
Halley, Dr. W. B., 383.
Halpain, Joseph, 191.
Hamblen, Miss Mary, 356.
Hamblen, Miss Sallie, 356.
Hamblen, Rev. Wm. K., 283, 306, 358.
Hamil, Robert C., 159, 227.

Hamilton, Gov. Andrew J., 246, 255.
Hamilton, John, 230.
Hamner, W. T., 323.
Hampton, Wade, 274.
Hancock, Wm. P., 284, 299, 300, 314.
Hanna, Maj. A. M., 142.
Hannan, M. J., 71.
Hannan, W. W., 71.
Hannon, Sam C., 159, 190.
Hannum, ..., 64.
Hansel, G. W., 64.
Hardeman, Constantine, 226, 257.
Hardeman, J. P., 192.
Hardeman, Peter, 150.
Hardeman, Capt. Wm. P., 192.
Hardy, Dr. John Crumpton, 363.
Hare, Col. Silas, 144, 192, 226.
Harkey, S. H., 284.
Harkey, W. H., 284.
Harrell, Jacob M., 9.
Harris, ..., 27.
Harris, Capt. A. J., 269, 283, 354.
Harris, A. V., 227, 310.
Harris, G. Berry, 103.
Harris, Henry, 103, 167.
Harrison, Miss Narnie, 365.
Hart, Josiah, 82, 111, 112, 113, 122, 123, 159.
Hartrick, William T. J., 253.
Harvey, Miss Pearl, 365.
Hasley, Andrew, 160.
Hasley, Drew, 251.
Hasley, Samuel L., 251, 252.
Hasley, Mrs. Sam, 45.
Hastings, M., 64
Hastings, Warren, 71.
Havens, David, 129.
Havens, John, 130.
Havens, Thomas, 124, 127, 129.
Hawkins, Joseph H., 160, 230.
Headley, Dr. Alexander M., 236.
Headrights, conflicts in, between American and Mexican settlers, 23.
Heise, August J., 190, 191.
Hellerman, Henry, 283.
Henderson, James Pinckney, 79.
Henderson, Miss Katherine, 8.
Henderson, Wm. F., 58.
Hendrickson, John, 160, 284, 287, 307.

413

Henry, Jno. C., 115, 116, 140, 143, 227, 257, 393.
Hensell, Geo. W., 68, 69, 71.
Hensley, James, 71.
Hensley, Wm., 71, 159.
Hickey, Rev., ..., 161.
Hickey, James, 72.
Hickson, W., 71.
Highways, 379; and roads, Bell County, 149.
Hill, Dred R., 82, 111, 126, 151, 167, 168, 196, 227.
Hill, Wm. F., 82, 110, 111, 119, 124.
Hill, Captain William W., 29.
Hirsh, David, 141, 191.
Hodge, Alex E., 159, 230.
Hodge, Jas. W., 159.
Hodge, Milton, 188, 190, 191.
Hodge, Wm. J., 71.
Holcomb, James C., 187, 190.
Holiday, Robert, 159.
Holman, W. S., 310.
Holsworth, Charles, 283.
Honey, Geo. W., 271.
Honey incident, 271.
Hood, Joseph L., 23.
Hoover, H. F., 103.
Hoover, Hon. Herbert, 373.
Hopson, Jack, 9, 41, 44, 47.
Hospitals, Temple, 331.
Hotels, 332.
Houser, J. C., 335.
Houses, early construction of, 132; of early settlers, 43; type of, used by early settlers, 20.
Houston, M. L., 160.
Houston, General Sam, 26, 27, 56, 74, 75, 91, 185, 190, 194, 197, 198, 200.
Howard, B. M., 322.
Howard, Rev. W. H., 374.
Howeth, Maj. William, 226.
Howlett, James, 9.
Hubbard, Gov. Richard B., 390.
Hubby, Caleb M., 9.
Hudson, James, 28.
Hudson, Dr. Taylor, 310.
Hughes, ..., 58.
Hughes, J. H., 64, 71.
Hughes, John, 158, 193.
Humm, Samuel, 23, 24.
Hundley, William, 117.
Hunt, Geo. W., 310.
Hunt, W. A., 103.

Hunter, Lewis L., 71.
Hunter, Sam H., 159.
Hunter, W. S., 369.
Hunton, Geo. P., 374.
Hunton, Rev. Jno. W., 284.
Hutchison, C. B., 375.
Hutton, ..., 238.

Ice machine, 309.
Ickleberger, Henry, 9.
Immigration, 296.
Improvements, Public and Private in 1890's, 330.
"Independent Blues," 187.
Indian attacks, on Colonel Sparks and the Rileys, 1836, 37; Kickapoo, 58; on Morgan and Marlin families, 60; on Taylor family, 33; better protection from, 79; fight, 89; at "Battle Creek," 59; Bird's Creek, 61; between Captain Ross and "Big Foot," 73; on Elm Creek, 46; at Fort Milam, 41; Fraziers' participation in, 57; at Morgan's Point, 60; Morrell's description of, 57; the Post oak Massacre, 52; on Walker's Creek, Milam County, 18; Walker Spring, 30; last, 273; Nolan Creek, 175; Nolan Valley, 175; at Tenoxitlan, 72; on Nashville, 58; in Little River and upper Milam County area, 56.
Indians, 88; 1850, 174; Anadarko, 56, 178; Caddo, 42, 56, 178; at Bird's Creek, 63; Cherokees, 56; Comanches, 56, 73, 90, 91, 174, 177, 184; encounter with, 91; incited to uprising by Mexicans, 28; Ioni, 56, 178; Keechi, 56, 178; Kickapoos, at Bird's Creek, 63; Kiowas, 56, 177; Lipan, 21, 56; Perryman fight with, 179; removal of, to Territory, 185; reservation for, 176; Riggs fight with, 180: Tonkawas, 33, 56, 89, 92; Wacos, 33, 56; White's council with, 177.
Institutions of County, 381.

Index

International and Great Northern Railroad, 313.
Interurban, 335.
Irby, Ben H., 160.
Irvin, James Dee, 370.
Irvin, Joe R., 323.
Irvin, Riley, 157, 175.
Irvine, Lieut. James, 65, 67, 68, 70, 71.
Isbell, Mrs. A., 143, 242.
Ivey, A. J., 64, 71.

...., Jack, negro belonging to Col. Wm. C. Sparks, 37.
Jail, Bell County, 145, 270, 307.
Jalonick, Isaac, 141, 143, 381, 384.
James, Thomas, 41.
James, Wm. W., 338, 386.
Jarrell, A. J., 374.
Jenkins, Mrs. ...., 284.
Jocelyn, Edward, 71.
Johnson, Miss ...., 364.
Johnson, President Andrew, 244, 245, 246, 255, 258.
Johnson, C. A., 130.
Johnson, Frank W., 9.
Johnson, Sam, 41.
Johnston, Gen. Albert Sidney, 62.
Joiner, Hezekiah, 72.
Joiner, J. M., 323.
Jones, ..., 193.
Jones, Anson, 78, 361.
Jones, Mrs. Charlotte Halloran, 365.
Jones, Enoch M., 28.
Jones, Isaac V., 297.
Jones, Miss Lillie, 356.
Jones, Dr. Samuel J., 360, 364, 365.
Jones, T. J., 297.
Jones, Col. Thos. H., 284, 286, 287, 358.
Jones, Col. W. Goodrich, 396.
Joplin, James J., 152.
Jordan, Henry, 187, 190.

Karnes, C. G., 103.
Karnes, Wm. K., 126, 130, 161.
Karr, Jacob, 103, 130.
Kattenhorn, Henry, 9.
Kay, William G., 311.
Keggans, John, 150, 159, 192.
Kegley, Sam, 144.
Kell, James, 119, 158.

Keller, A. M., 148.
Kelly, Wm. A., 370.
Kelton, Marcus A., 187, 188, 190, 256.
Kelton, Mrs. Sarah A., 144.
Kendall, Geo. Wilkins, 44.
Kendrick, Dr. Carroll, 159, 163, 283, 349, 350.
Kenzie, Thomas, 103.
Kerr, Gus, 84.
Keys, Hal, 159.
Keys, Henry, 227.
King, Jno. E., 284, 289.
King, Judge Rufus Y., 72, 325, 400.
King, William B., 9.
King, William H., 9.
King, Willis, J., 284.
Kingsbury, Chas. H., 190, 191.
Kingsbury, Silas A., 140, 227.
Kinnan, Edward W., 142, 143, 187, 190, 191, 195, 227.
Kinney, R. D., 144.
Kirk, John, 72.
Kirk, Silvester P., 158.
Kiser, John, 149.
Kitchen, ..., 283.
Kleberg, Louis, 64, 71.
Ku Klux Klan, 1867-70, 262.
Kuykendall, ..., 82, 85.
Kuykendall, Abner, 158, 161, 229, 230.
Kuykendall, Bob, 241.
Kuykendall, George, 187.
Kuykendall, Matthew J., 161, 187, 190, 397, 400.
Kuykendall, Minnie, 241.
Kuyzer, ..., 64.
Kyger, Benjamin P., 71.
Kyle, Ishmael, 192.

Lamar, Mirabeau B., 56, 77.
Lambert, James, 141, 212.
Land grants, additional granted in Robertson's colony, 22; conflicts in, 23; location of, 16; Mexican law pertaining to, 1.
Lane, Uncle Dee, 275.
Lane, Walter P., 58.
Lang, ..., 322.
Langford, Milton H., 103.
Lawler, Levi T., 113.
Lawler, Mrs. Sarah, 115, 116.
Leach, Mrs. Abigail, 283.
Leach, Miss Ellen D., 242.
Leach, James, 247.

415

Leach, John, 229.
Leath, Thomas, 189.
Leatherman, D. K., 374.
Leatherman, Samuel G., 229, 230.
Lee, Ambrose, 160, 181, 183.
Lee, Baldwin P., 179.
Lee, Ben D., 308, 331, 390, 391.
Lee, Edward, 151.
Lee, John H., 144.
Lee, Gen. Robert E., 244.
Leftwich, Robert, 2, 12.
Lemly, W. S., 369.
Lewis, Frank M., 103.
Lewis, J. F., 323.
Lewis, John, 130.
Lewis, Samuel, 103.
Library, first, in Bell County, 161.
Lightfoot, T. W., 71.
Lincoln, Abraham, 196, 197, 244.
Lishley, ..., 47.
Little River, first settlements along, 12; Fort, 42, 44; Fort, abandonment of, 52; pioneer settlers return to upper, 76; residents, 96.
Little, Robert M., 298.
Living conditions of settlers, 131.
Long, Ben, 41.
Long, W. J., 268, 310.
Longino, James T., 258.
Longley, Bill, 303.
Longley, Campbell, 284, 304.
Love, Joe W., 299.
Lowry, J. J., 330.
Lucken, Thomas, 164.
Ludlow, Henry, 190, 191.
Ludlow, Miss Kate, 209.
Ludlow, Wm. G., 307.
Lumpkin, (Wm. L.?), 159.
Luther, Dr. John Hill, 362, 363.
Lyles, J. T., 284.
Lyman, Warren, 23, 28.
Lynch, Mrs. ...., 356.
Lynch, Green E., 71.
Lynch, J. C., 349.
Lynch, M. L., 312.
Mabry, Carter, 160.
Mabry, J. E., 284.
McAllister, Robert, 284.
McAninch, John F., 160.
McCandless, ..., 6.
McCelvey, Dr. J. S., 331.
McConnell, Miss Jennie, 322.
McCorcle, A. T., 115, 116, 123; children of, 86.

McCorcle, Mack, 111.
McCoy, Green, 41, 44, 47.
McCrarey, Neil, 71.
McCray, Jim, 251, 252.
McCrea, James, 103.
McCulloch, Colonel Ben, 204, 205.
McDaniel, Bob, 252.
McDaniel, Granger, 124, 150; children of, 86.
McDonald, G. W., 230, 242.
McDonald, J. S., 303.
McDonald, Jeremiah, 28, 41.
McDonald, Marion, 303.
McDowell, Hamilton, 190.
McDowell, John, 159, 187.
McDowell, William, 187.
McFalls, Jack, 370.
McFarland, Judge Wilson Y., 144, 157, 165, 167, 196, 256.
McGrew, Hardin, 28.
McGuines, Joseph, 71.
Machu, Emil, 370.
McIlhenny, Marshall, 143, 165, 227.
McKay, Daniel, 9, 150, 227.
McKay, Henry, 87.
Mackensen, Otto, 310.
McKenzie, Dan H., 374.
McKenzie, Thos., 103.
Mackey, Columbus M., 242.
McKie, Dr. B. D., 283, 366.
McKinney, Dr. ...., 27.
McLaughlin, ..., 283.
McLaughlin, E., 167.
McLaughlin, James M., 122.
McLennan, John, 9, 28.
McLennan, Laughlin, 9.
McLennan, Neil, 9, 54.
McLochlan, James, 41, 42, 44, 46, 47, 49, 50, 51.
McMillan, Andrew, 61.
McMillan, Edward, 28.
McMillan, James, 28.
McMillin, Daniel, 167, 196, 234.
Macune, Dr. C. W., 324.
McWhirter, Geo. M., 159, 270, 297, 382, 391.
McWhirter, Mrs. Martha, 391.
McWhirter, Thos. G., 242.
Maedgen, Mrs. W. L., 374.
Magness, Thomas, 103.
Mahuron, Thomas, 152.
Mail, horseback, 138.
Manchaca, Antonio, 24.

Index

Manion, A. B., 256.
Marcy, Capt. R. B., 176.
Marlin, John, 28, 60, 61.
Marques, Sidney N., 268.
Marschalk, (editor), 171.
Marschalk, Andrew, Sr., 167, 195.
Marschalk, Frank, 187.
Marsh, Joseph S., 64, 71.
Marshall, Geo. P., 374.
Marshall, J. D., 71.
Marshall, John, 123, 124, 126, 155. 196.
Martin, James, 71.
Martin, W. L., 349.
Masonry, Indian story concerning, 60.
Masonic sign, Indian fight prevented by, 59.
Mather, Sam, 163.
Matthews, R. H., 41.
Matthews, Thomas, 41.
Matthews, William, 41.
Maugham, Arthur, 284.
Maule, C. E., 165.
Maxwell, Rev. W. R., 362.
May, Stephen D., 158.
Mayes, John D., 158.
Mayes, William, 158.
Mayo, Dr. S. L., 374.
Meek, J. J., 183.
Meek, Moses, 175.
Menefee, Jarrett, 72.
Menefee, Sabou, 72.
Menefee, Thomas S., 71.
Menefee, Thomas A., 72.
Menifee, ..., 64.
Mercer, J., 90.
Merrill, Capt. N., 90.
Merritt, Lewis, 46.
Methodist, organization, 160.
Methvin, L. T., 310.
Methvin, M. M., 273.
Mexico, war with, 78.
Milam county, boundary differences, 153, 154; county seat of, 9; frontier, advance of, 77.
Military Commissioners' Court, 247, 254.
Military rule, first period of, 245; return to, 258.
Mill, cottonseed oil, 311, 330.
Miller, E. D., 242.
Miller, Isaac, 117.
Miller, Joe, 60.

Miller, Col. J. Z., 257, 306, 310, 334, 385, 386, 387.
Miller, J. Z., Jr., 334, 386, 387.
Miller, Robt. C., 141, 234, 257, 384, 385.
Miller, Sam, 192.
Miller, Thomas J., 72.
Miller, Wm. A., 257, 268, 385.
Mills, ..., 64.
Mills, E., 141, 227, 234.
Mills, John, 103.
Mills, Robert, 72.
Mills, William, 103.
Mills, 168; cotton, 334; first, in Belton, 117; flour and grist, 297.
Mirear, Wm., 103.
Minute Men, Bell County, 188.
Minyard, Judge W. M., 322.
Missouri, Kansas and Texas railway, 313, 317.
Mitchell, ..., 334.
Mitchell, J. C., 371.
Moffett, Dr. C. W., 158.
Moffitt, Robert, 28.
Moffitt, William, 28.
Monroe, Daniel, 28, 30, 31, 52.
Moore, ..., 144, 283.
Moore, A. G., 103.
Moore, David, 84.
Moore, Jack, 153.
Moore, James, 150.
Moore, James W., 226, 227, 230, 261.
Moore, Jonathan E., 319.
Moore, Lewis, 41, 43, 44, 47, 49.
Moore, Lovick, 34.
Moore, Morris, 9, 41, 44, 47.
Moore, William, 9.
More, Lewis, 9.
Moreno, Maximo, 24.
Moreton, James M., 71.
Morgan, Andrew J., 28.
Morgan, G. W., 28.
Morgan, George, 60.
Morgan, John C., 28.
Morgan, Stephen, 28.
Morgan, William J., 28.
Morrell, Rev. Z. N., 17, 57.
Morrill, Frank, 32.
Morrill, Reese, 82; and children, 86.
Morris, Andrew, 242.
Morris, F. G., 158.
Morris, James, 158, 229.

Morris, John M., 158.
Morris, M. W., 158.
Morris, Oliver B., 187, 190.
Morris, Patton, 150.
Morris, Robert P., 158, 187, 190.
Morris, Sam, 158.
Morrison, Horatio M., 103, 152.
Morrison, M., 103.
Mumford, David, 22, 24, 82.
Mumford, Jesse, 22, 24, 29, 82.
Munroe, Daniel, 80.
Murphy, Jim, 303.
Murrah, Gov. Pendleton, 244.
Murrell, Joseph W., 183, 191.
Myers, John, 159.
Myers, Robert C., 205, 226.
Nash, Jesse E., 64, 68, 71, 72.
Nashville, 5, 7; colony, 1; county seat of Milam County, 9; early settlement of, 7; or Robertson Colony, 1.
Neal, ..., 58.
Neale, Claiborne, 41, 44, 52.
Needham, John, 16, 18, 24, 27, 29.
Neff, Noah, 152.
Neibling, Frederick, 130, 158.
Neighbors, Henry T., and child, 86.
Neighbors, Thomas J., 82, 89, 124, 150.
Neighbors, Robert S., 176.
Nelson, N. B., 230.
Nelson, Robert C., 159.
Newman, Paul, 191.
Newspapers, 236.
Nichols, Mrs. ...., 283.
Nichols, Isaac, 229.
Nichols, Col. Jacob, 158.
Nichols, John, 159.
Nichols, Ramon, 364.
Nichols, Robert, 187, 191.
Nigro, V., 140.
Nolanville (Belton), beginnings of, 115; changed to Belton, 139; county seat, 113, 114; movement to change name of, 138; postoffice at, 137; surveying of, 125.
Nolan Valley (Cowhouse) residents, 99.
Norris, Col. Jas. M., 59, 60.
Northcutt, J. I., 187.
Norton, Col. N. L., 299, 390.

Odd-Fellows in county, 383.
Odell, Simon, 103, 116.
Officers, Confederate, from Bell County, 225.
Official records, care of, 307.
Ogle, Dr. Louis A., 103, 150, 283.
O'Hair, J., 298.
O'Hair, Wm., 298.
O'Keefe, Hugh, 159.
"Old Corn Road," 87.
"Old Phantom Hill Road," 87.
Old Settlers' Association, 397; papers read at 1902-1904 reunion of, 399.
Old Trail, 291.
Oliver, ..., 334.
Orgain, John H., 284.
Orgain, Mrs. Kate Alma, 355, 356, 365.
Osterhout, J. P., 310.
Outlaw gang, break-up of, 301.
Outlaws, 303.

Pace, George, 370.
Pace, W. A., 159, 283.
Panic, 1907, 337.
Pappas, William, 370.
Parchin, Luther T., 42.
Parker, A. G., 71.
Parker, Cynthia Ann, capture of, 29.
Parker, Elder Daniel, 6, 7, 9.
Parker, Dr. H. H., 258, 284.
Parker, Hulsey, 188.
Parker, Isaac, 9.
Parker, J. J., 159.
Parker, James W., 6, 7.
Parker, Elder John, 6, 7.
Parker, Mitt, 276.
Parker family, massacre of, 29.
Parker's Fort, 7; tragedy of, 7.
Parsons, ..., 41.
Patrol districts, Bell County, 151.
Patten, William, 159.
Patterson, Wilson, 189.
Payne, John M., 85, 115, 116, 144.
Pearce, W. L., 282.
Pease, Gov. Elisha M., 146, 164, 260, 266.
Peña, José Antonio de, 24.
Pendarvis, Caleb, 117.
Pendleton, Frank, 143, 157.
Penington, Elisha, 160.
Pennington, John H., 83, 103, 130, 160.

Index

Pentecost, G. W., 71.
People's party, 328.
Pepper's Creek residents, 100.
Perkins, Wm., 191, 192.
Perryman, John M., 159, 179, 180, 183.
Peters, Jonathan, 71.
Peters, William, 64, 71.
Petty, J. Rough, 160.
Petty, Theophilus, 103, 130.
Peyton, C. W., 323.
Phillip, Walker, 28.
Phillips, J. M., 167.
Phillips, W. E., 374.
Pickett, Geo. E., 89, 90, 102, 103.
Pierce, Geo. F., 369.
Pierce, Wm. L., 159.
Pierce, Young, 180, 181.
Pierson, John, 188.
Pitts, Jesse, 160, 284.
"Playparties," 136.
Police Court, 304.
Politics, County, 324.
Polk, Thomas, 23.
Pollok, Dr. L. W., 369.
Pool, Frederick, 72.
Pool, John, 9.
Pope, John M., 144.
Pope, John T., 187.
Population trends in county, 1890-1910, 340.
Porter, J. M., 323.
Porter, R. H., 124.
Postoffice at Nolanville, 137.
Potter, Drury D., 159, 187, 189, 190.
Potter, John, 89, 103, 152, 160, 175.
Potter, Wm., 159.
Potts, A. D., 141.
Power company, 331.
Powers, ..., 64.
Powers, H. A., 71.
Powers, Jno. H., 141, 257.
Powers, Tazewell W., 141.
Presbyterian church, organization of, 161.
Presidential campaign, 1860, 196.
Price, Lou, 185.
Proctor, Joseph, 41.
Proctor, Newton M., Sr., 150, 159, 227, 282, 288, 349, 358.
Prohibition, 325.
Prosperity, 334.
Provisions brought by early settlers, 20; in early times, 133; provisions of settlers, 43.

Public Schools, improvements in, 341.
Puett, Elisha, 103, 159.
Puett, J. L., 152.
Puett, Warren, 103, 129, 150, 157, 192.
Pugh, James W., 152.
Punchard, Dr. William, 156.
Purdon, Henry, 23.
Pyle, Charles Weaver, 370, 377.

Quillian, M. C., 365.

Racing, horse and pony, 136.
Rackley, J. J., 310.
Railroads, 256, 311, 312; agitation for more, 338.
Railway, Santa Fe, depot, 331.
Ramsdell, C. H., 284.
Ramsey, Dr. A. K., 187, 190, 192, 196, 281.
Ramsey, Mr. and Mrs. Chalk, 227.
Rancier, Ed, 258.
Ranger Service, 275.
Rangers, at Bird's Creek, 61; at Fort Milam, 39; at Little River Fort, 44; organization of in Milam County, 28; Bell County Volunteers, 166; frontier, 174.
Rather, Sam, Jr., 273.
Rather, W. S., 141, 196, 203, 223, 257.
Rather's Company, Captain Wm. Samuel, 223.
Ratification of secession ordinance, 198.
Rawhide, importance of, 133.
Ray, Abe, 276, 277.
Ray, John W., 284.
Ray, S. M., 310.
Raymond, Nat C., 9.
Reconstruction, 244; in Bell County, 267; economic conditions during, 256; local self-government in, 255; loss of property during, 248; negro trouble during 248.
Rector, E., 71.
Rector, G. W., 192.
Redding, J. W., 284.
Reed, Ed. T., 160, 251.
Reed, Elijah, 29.

419

Reed, James P., 142, 192, 270, 297, 306, 310, 383, 384.
Reed, Jefferson, 15, 16, 19, 24, 27, 126.
Reed, John B., 150, 227, 230, 250, 251.
Reed, Joseph, 29.
Reed, Michael, 16, 19, 24, 37; and family, 78.
Reed, Thomas J., 29.
Reed, William, 15, 16, 19, 24, 27, 111, 119, 123, 129.
Reed Wm. M., 388.
Reed, Wilson, 61.
Reed, Dr. Vol, 388.
Reese, J. H., 240.
Reid, John C., 73, 115, 118, 121, 122, 123, 126, 128.
Renick, Bates, 183.
Renick, Robert Arch., 274.
Renick, R. B., 283.
Reorganization of County, 269.
Residents in Bell County, 1850, 90.
Revenues and expenditures, Bell County, 148.
Revolution and the "Runaway Scrape," March-April 1836, 26.
Rhodes, "Old Man," 6, 18.
Rhodes, ..., 30.
Rhodes, Washington, 72.
Rice, James Porter, 158, 381.
Rice, Wm. H., 159.
Rich, Mrs. Cornelia, 15, 46.
Richard, Abram W., 144, 164, 247.
Richard, Geo. D., 187.
Richards, James, 103, 130.
Ridgeway, Jarrett, 72.
Riggs, Jas. Leonidas, 187, 189.
Riggs, Jane (Mrs. John), 180.
Riggs, John, 160, 180, 181.
Riggs, Margaret, 180.
Riggs, Rhoda, 180, 184.
Riggs, Thomas, 180, 284.
Riggs, William C., 180, 184.
Riggs, William S., 137, 187, 189, 190.
Riley brothers, 38.
Roads, 86, 305; movements for good, 345.
Robbins, O. A., 334.
Roberts, Cornelius Bent, Sr., 82, 111, 112, 122, 124, 126, 183, 187, 227; and children, 86.
Roberts, C. Bent, Jr., 111, 190.

Roberts, James D., 117.
Roberts, John B., 111.
Roberts, John T., 144.
Roberts, N. T., 227.
Roberts, Redding, 19, 23.
Roberts, Thomas, 9.
Roberts, William, 9.
Roberts, William J., 113.
Robertson, A. J., 318.
Robertson, Baldwin, 23.
Robertson Colony, 1; archives of, 12; disputes concerning, 3; land grant obtained for, 3; scarcity of records concerning, 12; settlements in, 5.
Robertson, Mrs. E. S. C., 355, 356.
Robertson, Elijah Sterling C., 3, 9, 10, 12, 28, 29, 85, 148, 159, 162, 163, 167, 196, 197, 204, 226, 258, 281, 282, 283, 349, 350, 358, 359, 360, 381.
Robertson, Huling P., 318.
Robertson, Miss Luella, 356.
Robertson, Theophilus H., 152.
Robinett, ..., 64.
Robinett, James, 9.
Robinett, James W., 69, 71.
Robinett, Thomas, 71.
Robinson, Ezekiel, 6, 17, 30.
Rogers, John S., 299, 300.
Roman, John, 71.
Rosborough, D. D., 158, 192, 196, 226.
Rose, Andrew J., 284, 289, 298, 299, 308, 357, 362, 381, 399.
Rose, Miss Alice, 356.
Rose, Miss Helen, 356.
Ross, Capt. Shapleigh P., 54, 73.
Ross, Thomas, 29.
"Rovers, Bell County," 189.
Rowan, ..., 64.
Rowlands, Amos, 283.
Rowland, Joseph, 9, 72.
Royall, Jesse, 157.
Royall, Mrs. Sarah E., 157.
Royall, Dr. Wm. W., 363.
Rucker, Ed. T., 270.
Rucker, Mrs. J. R., 375.
Ruiz, Colonel Francisco, 7.
"Runaway," second, 29.
Runnels, Gov. ...., 185.
Runnels, Hardin R., 194.
Russell, D. L., 310.

Index

Saint Charles Hotel, 140.
Saint Clair, Duncan, 160.
Saint Clair, John, 72.
Salado, bid of, for state institutions, 289; early families of, 283; founding and early history of, 282; free public schools of, 289; mill-dam controversy of, 287.
Salado College, 283, 284, 288, 349; opening of, 300; first building, 350; stone construction of, 351; social conditions at, 352; list of teaching staff of, 353; clubs of, 355, 356; bell of, 356; efforts to found University of Texas at, 257; further addition to, 359; new organization of, 359; first trustees of, 163.
Salado Creek residents, 95.
"Salado Mounted Troops," 204.
Salem Baptist church, organization of, 161.
Sanches, José David, 23.
Sanctificationists, 391.
Sand, Noah, 284.
Sandlin, A. K., 187.
Santa Anna, General, 26.
Sarahville de Viesca, 10.
Saunders, Judge X. B., 144, 183, 187, 201, 203, 216, 226, 227, 228, 255, 272, 397; Saunders' Company, 216.
Sawyer, Caston, 306.
Saxton, ..., 103.
"Scalawag," 259.
Schools, 85, 162; early, 163; public system, 308.
Scoggin, Isaac, 160.
Scoggin, Jesse, 160, 181.
Scott, Dr. A. C., 331.
Scott, Jeremiah D., 158, 187, 190.
Scott, Jeremiah D., Jr., 190.
Scott, Jesse G., 187, 190.
Scott, John Wesley, 144, 148, 158, 227, 228, 231, 234, 247.
Scott, Miss Lucile (Mrs. Preston Childers), 375.
Scott, Robert M., 189.
Sebastian, Mrs. Ida, 322.
Seigmond, Joseph, 157.
Self-government, return to, 281.
Sermon, first preached in Bell County, 17.

Settlers, amusements of, 135; living conditions of new, 131; new, 1850, 158; provisons brought by early, 20; return to houses, 27; return to Little River, 32; social life of, 135; temperament of, 135.
Shackelford, ..., 30.
Shackelford, Lieutenant M. B. 28.
Shanklin, Miss Etta, 212.
Shanklin, Gordon W., 83, 84, 159, 163, 195, 227, 350.
Shanklin, M. H., 83, 397, 399.
Shanklin, N. L., 374.
Shanklin Mill, 83; residents, 95.
Shark, M. P., 64.
Sharp, William P., 71.
Shaw, Jack, 89.
Shaw, James, 9, 82.
Shaw, Stewart, 371.
"Shaw Crossing," 82.
Shelly, Abram, 126.
Shelton, Mrs. ...., 228.
Shelton, Horatio, 103, 129, 144, 283.
Shelton, John, 103, 242.
Sheppard, Morris, 397.
Sheridan, Gen. Phil, 258, 260.
Sherrod, Jas. T., 103, 129, 159.
Shields, Nathaniel, 82, 119, 128.
Shriver, Isaac, 159, 183, 187, 226.
Shields, Nicholas, 130.
"Shinplasters," 235.
Shipp, Ben E., 159.
Shipp, Geo. F., Sr., 103.
Shipp, Geo. F., Jr., 103.
Shipp, Thos. G., 159.
Sinclair, Daniel, 103.
Sinclair, E., 258.
Singletary, Evan, 103.
Slack, Sergeant J., 64.
Slack, John B., 183.
Slaughter, Owen 159, 227.
Smith, ..., 31.
Smith, Major .... 50, 51.
Smith, Abner, 23, 24.
Smith, Donald, 156.
Smith, Gen. E. Kirby, 203.
Smith, Capt. Geo. A., 284.
Smith, Henry, 320.
Smith, Hugh C., 371.
Smith, J. M., 185.
Smith, J. R., 159.
Smith, Prof. James L., 283, 354, 356.

421

Smith, John, 103.
Smith, John D., 29.
Smith, Jno. F., 141, 191, 203, 217, 218, 384, 385; Smith's Company, 217.
Smith, J. Morton, 85.
Smith, Rev. M. V., 362.
Smith, N. K., 335.
Smith, Niles F., 14.
Smith, Obadiah B., 122.
Smith, Sterrett, 41, 44, 52.
Smith, T. E., 258, 390.
Smith, William ("Camel-back") 30, 58.
Smith, William, 144.
Smith, Maj. William, 41.
Smith, William C., Jr., 89, 103.
Smith, William S., 303.
Snelling, Capt. James G., 87.
Soape, Thomas M., 314.
Social life of settlers, 135.
Sorghum, Chinese sugar cane, 166.
Southwestern Traction Company, 336.
Southern States, convention of, 197.
Spain, War with, 332.
Spanish American War Veterans, 332, 333.
Spanish rule in Bell County, 1.
Sparks, John, 227.
Sparks, William C., 22, 24, 29, 37.
"Spicewood Spring," 82.
Spiva, Andrew, 160.
Spiva, James A., 160.
Spoonts, Joseph, 160.
Spoonts, Wm. W., 193.
Stack, Joseph H., 71.
Stackpole, Ellis M., 140.
Stage lines, 137.
Standefer, Isaac, 80, 109, 112, 118, 119.
Standefer, Miss Sue, 356.
Starke, C. B., 374.
Steele, William H., 10, 12.
Steelman, James, 157, 164.
Steen, J. S., 192.
Steiner, J. M., 185.
Stephens, Alexander H., 198.
Stephens, William, 82, 124.
Stephenson, Jas., 64.
Stevens, William, 123.
Stewart, Benjamin L., 124, 129.
Stewart, E. E., 117.
Stewart, Irving, 103.

Stickney, Mrs. Catherine Childers, 15, 82.
Stickney, E. Lawrence, 9, 82, 86, 114, 115, 118, 119, 122, 125, 127, 164, 270.
Stinnett, Wm. H., 159, 287.
Stith, J. H., 284.
Stockard, R. S., 192.
Stoddard, J. M., 71.
Stokes, J. C., 160, 242.
Stone, Thornton, 23.
Stringfellow, Jas. A., 140, 187, 192, 227, 228.
Stroud, Ethan, 9, 61.
Stroud, Ira, 119.
Stuart, C. H., 283.
Stubblefield, Elisha D., 158, 381.
Stubblefield, Isaac N., 103, 158.
Stubblefield, R. Lock, 103, 158.
Sullivan, Augustus, 80.
Sullivan, Gus, 9.
Supple, John B. B., 242.
Supple, Theo. A., 85, 115, 116, 138, 227.
Sutton, Anderson, 159.
Sutton, James R., 150, 160, 185, 189.
Sutton, Jesse, 159, 183.
Sutton, Jesse Wilson, 370.
Swisher, Jas. G., 9.
Sypert, Wm. Carroll, 165.

Talbot, James, 284.
Tankersley, Don, 276.
Tanner, John J., 152.
Tatum, Howell, 159.
Tax, county, 269.
Tax levy, first in Bell county, 127.
Tax rates, 304.
Taylor, ..., 59.
Taylor, Chas. W., 371.
Taylor, "Cow House," 89.
Taylor, J. Wilson, 19, 128.
Taylor, John, 9, 119, 123, 124.
Taylor, Josiah, 17, 19, 27, 82.
Taylor, Levi, 29.
Taylor, Lewis, 160.
Taylor, Mrs. Margaret, 128; and children, 182.
Taylor, R. H., 227.
Taylor, Seymour Brown, 19, 128.
Taylor, William, 283.
Taylor, Wm. G., 307.
Taylor, William H., 16, 18, 32.
Taylor, Mrs. William H., 15, 33.

Index

Taylor family, 34.
Teague, Hiram, 276, 277.
Teal, Richard, 29.
Telegraph company, 309.
Telephone system, 331.
Temple, 315, 319; churches of, 323; newspapers of, 323; public school of, 322; rough element of, 321; Stag Party, 1893-1922, 396; water supply, 320.
Temple, B. M., 320.
"Tennessee Valley" community, 158.
Tenny, Levi, 142, 162, 242, 350.
Tenoxtitlan, settlement of, 7.
Terrell, A. W., 355.
Terrell, J. E., 312.
"Texas Association," 2.
Texas Cooperative Association, 300.
Texas Farmer, The, 300.
Texas and Pacific Railway, 313.
Texas Revolution and Indian troubles, 26.
Texas Volunteer Infantry, Company I, 218.
Thatcher, William, 330.
Thomas Arnold High School, 364.
Thomas, Frank, 151.
Thomas, John, 161.
Thompson, ..., 70.
Thompson, Empson, 6, 41, 44, 47, 49.
Thompson, Jasper N. M., 29.
Thompson, John, 159.
Thompson, John D., 71.
Thompson, John S., 227, 229, 323.
Thompson, Tyre, 303.
Thompson, Wm., 122.
Thompson, Wm. D., 80.
Thomson, A. Crom, 159.
Thomson, Alexander, 9.
Thomson, Thomas C., 9.
Thomson, William D., 9.
Throckmorton, Gov. James W., 255, 260, 273.
Tichenal, W. H., 116.
Tinnin, Jack, 258.
Tobler, Albert, 144.
Tobler, Julius, 258.
Tomlinson, Thos. G., 150, 160, 227.
Townsend, Dr. E. G. 363.
Townsend, Mrs. Eli Moore, 363.

Townsend, J. E., 190.
Townsend, J. M., 190.
Townsend, Joe, 115, 116, 175, 191.
Traynham, Joseph H., 14.
Trimmier, Thomas, 123, 124, 150, 157, 167, 183, 230.
Trotter, Wilson, 273.
Tucker, John, 41.
Tucker, Thos. C., 196.
Turnbo, ..., 276, 277.
Turner, Robert H., 143, 307.
Turnham, J., 80.
Twomey, William, 189.
Tyler, Miss Annie, 356.
Tyler, Mrs. Caroline (Childers), 6, 14.
Tyler, Geo. W., 309, 310, 312, 318, 334, 362, 370, 371, 373, 374, 382, 383, 397, 401.
Tyler, Louis H., 386.
Tyler, Orville T., 9, 14, 16, 19, 21, 27, 30, 31, 82, 87, 89, 121, 122, 152, 168, 283, 286, 287, 299, 306, 358, 390.
Tyler, Mrs. Orville T., 356.

Underwood, John H., 371.

Valdez, Manuel Maria, 14.
Vanclieve, Lorenzo, 103, 130.
Vanderhurst, M. M., 207.
Vanness, Theodore, 294.
Vaughan, G., 103.
Vehicles, traveling, 134.
Venable, Mrs. ...., 144.
Venable, Francis W., 159.
Venable, Wm. J. 188, 191.
Venney, Felix, 324.
Verm, Henry, 71.
Vick, Angus G., 369, 373.
Vickery, Bela, 71.
Vickery, J. W., 283.
Vickery, Miss Mollie, 356.
Vickery, Miss Sallie, 356.
Vickory, Sergeant B., 64.
Viesca, Sarahville de, 10; settlement of, 10.
Volunteer Companies of Bell County, 200.

Waco, founding of, 81.
Wade, Geo. W., 187, 196, 226.
Wade, William, 192.
Waggoner, J., 322.
Walden, Alvin A, 284.

Walden, Thomas W., 83, 84.
Waldrip, James R., 370.
Walker, ..., 31.
Walker, Judge Erasmus, 144, 157, 165, 242, 256, 314.
Walker, Henry, 30.
Walker, John, 29.
Walker, Martin L., 190.
Walker, Mrs. Sam S., 371, 372.
Walker, Maj. Walter H., 364.
Wallace, Miss Bettie, 165.
Wallace, Joseph L., 160.
Wallace, Warner, 160.
Wallace, Warren, 167.
Waller, Charles, 71.
Walters, Alex, 159, 189, 230.
Walters, Morgan, 284.
Walters, Tilman, 159, 189.
Walton, G. W., 160.
Walton, Nelson, 160, 227.
Ward, M., 103.
Warren, Col. E. B., 140, 143.
Warren, Geo. W., 188, 191.
Warren, Henry J., 140, 227.
Warrick, W. R., 283.
Washington, Lewis M. H., 9, 70, 71.
Waugh, John, 23, 128.
Weathersbee, Capt. Jas. H., 203, 222; Weathersbee's Company, 222.
Weaver, ..., 68.
Weaver, Sergeant Wm. H., 64, 71, 72.
Webb, Ezra, 29, 41.
Webb, I. B., 310.
Webb, John B., 29.
Webb, Thomas R., 29.
Wedermeyer, Prof. Chas. W., 364, 400.
Welch, John, 37.
Wells, A. C., 370.
Wells, Dr. E. H., 362, 363.
West, W. G., 306.
Weston, John, 72.
Whaley, W. S., 314.
Wheat, A. M., 170.
Wheat, Samuel, 82, 159; children of, 86.
White, A. M., 284.
White, Carey, 167.
White, Geo. B., 144, 165, 242.
White, James W., 195.
White, Miss Kate E., 365.
White, M. M., 370.
White, Dr. R. R., 331.

White, Robert M., 175, 189, 190, 196, 203, 207, 226, 228; Ranging Company, 190; White's Company, 207.
White, Robert W., 187.
White, Sterling B., 188.
White, W. Alex, 188, 190.
White, Wilson H., 188, 190.
Whitehead, Mack, 181.
Whitehead, Mrs. Mack, 181, 183.
Whiteley, C. B., 230.
Whiteley, Sam, 238.
Whitlow, H. M., 370.
Whitney, ..., 103.
Whitney, A. J., 103.
Whitson, N. M., 270, 297.
Whittington, Wm. B., 188.
Wilcox, Jack, 276, 277.
Wilkerson, Melville, 113, 122, 175, 229, 283.
Wilkerson Valley residents, 96.
Wilkins, Matthew, 103, 129.
Wilkinson, A., 29.
Wilkinson, John, 29.
Williams, ..., 90.
Williams, David, 103, 136, 144, 151, 175, 176, 187, 188, 189, 190 192.
Williams, Isaac W., Sr., 103, 111, 117, 175, 176, 187.
Williams, J., Jr., 103.
Williams, J. R. (Dock), 159.
Williams, James, 159.
Williams, Jas. E., 119, 126, 128.
Williams, Jas. M., 159.
Williams, John, 89, 103.
Williams, Loss C., 159, 294.
Williams, Sam H., 159.
Williams, William, 159.
Williamson, D. M., 160.
Williamson, Eli, 189.
Williamson, Dr. Thos. T., 210, 226.
Willingham, Archibald, 82, 126, 144, 150, 282.
Willingham, Jack, 282.
Willingham, R. S., 227, 228, 230.
Willingham, Thomas, 242.
Willingham, Wilson, 282.
Willis, John B., 82.
Wilson, Joe L., 310.
Wilson, Dr. Wm. A., 362, 363.
Wilson, Pres. Woodrow, 368.
Wilson, W. S., 9.
Wind-mills, 294.
Wingfield, ..., 303.

Index

Winkler, ..., 64.
Winkler, E. W., 94.
Winkler, William, 67, 71.
Wiseman, John S., 227.
Wiseman, Martin V., 227.
Witt, Thos J., 309, 364, 365.
Wood, Columbus, 188.
Woodford, William, 23.
Woodson, Dr. J. M., 332.
Woodward, John B., 103.
Woodward, F. G., 71.
Woolfork, Shapleigh, 73.
World War, 368; first of, 368; selective draft and local administration, 368; local civic organizations in support of war, 371; Red Cross in Bell County, 374; Armistice and return of soldiers, 376; material conditions during and after war, 377.

Wright, Mrs. ..., 118.
Wright, Jack, 118.
Wright, Miss Judith, 365.
Wright, Rev. Sam P., 355.
Wright, Thomas C., 118.
Wyatt, Jordan, 103,
Wyman, ..., 193.

Yarbrough, Absolem, 103.
Yarrell, Slade, 370.
Yarrell, Dr. Thomas, 366.
Yarrell, Thomas, Sr., 386.
Yarrell, Thos., Jr., 387.
Young, Miss Sallie R., 355, 356.
Young, Wm. A. 159.

www.ingramcontent.com/pod-product-compliance
Lightning Source LLC
Chambersburg PA
CBHW030314100526
44592CB00010B/430